IN THE REALM OF THE
DIAMOND QUEEN

IN THE REALM OF THE
DIAMOND QUEEN

Marginality in an

Out-of-the-Way

Place

Anna Lowenhaupt Tsing

PRINCETON UNIVERSITY PRESS

Princeton, New Jersey

Copyright © 1993 by Princeton University Press
Published by Princeton University Press,
41 William Street, Princeton, New Jersey 08540
In the United Kingdom: Princeton University Press,
Chichester, West Sussex
All Rights Reserved
Library of Congress Cataloging-in-Publication Data
Tsing, Anna Lowenhaupt.
In the realm of the diamond queen: marginality in an
out-of-the-way place / Anna Lowenhaupt Tsing.
p. cm.   Includes bibliographical references and index.
ISBN 0-691-03335-8 cl.   ISBN 0-691-00051-4 pa.
1. Dayaks (Indonesian people)—Government relations.
2. Dayaks (Indonesian people)—Social conditions. 3. Sex
role—Indonesia—Meratus Mountains Region. I. Title.
DS646.32.D9175 1993   323.1'18922—dc20   93-10521 CIP
This book has been composed in Adobe Sabon
Princeton University Press books are printed on acid-free paper
and meet the guidelines for permanence and durability of
the Committee on Production Guidelines for Book
Longevity of the Council on Library Resources
Printed in the United States of America

10 9 8

http://pup.princeton.edu

ISBN-13: 978-0-691-00051-0 (pbk.)

In memory of
Yang He Tsing and
Bessie Cronbach Lowenhaupt,
women of storied courage

CONTENTS

Preface   ix

OPENING IN THE REALM OF THE   3
DIAMOND QUEEN

PART ONE POLITICS OF THE PERIPHERY   39
1   Marginal Fictions   51
2   Government Headhunters   72
3   Family Planning   104

PART TWO A SCIENCE OF TRAVEL   121
4   Leadership Landscapes   127
5   Conditions of Living   154
6   On the Boundary of the Skin   178

PART THREE RIDING THE HORSE OF GAPS   207
7   Alien Romance   213
8   Riding, Writing   230
9   The History of the World   253

REPRISE   285

Notes   303
References Cited   321
Index   335

PREFACE

In 1971 media around the world picked up on the discovery of a Stone Age tribe in the southern Philippines. The Tasaday, it was said, were everything an urban audience wanted to hear about the good kind of primitives. They swung playfully around on vines, wore nothing but orchid leaves, and had no word for war. They were innocent and eager for protection from the international media and the Philippine state, in the person of Manuel Elizade, the director of the president's special commission on minorities. The Tasaday called Elizade a god. In 1974, Elizade closed their territory to visitors, to protect them from loggers and other exploiters from the modern world.

Perhaps it is not surprising that in the 1980s, after both Elizade and his patron President Marcos had fled the country in disgrace (Elizade was later to return), journalists arrived back in Tasaday country to expose the "hoax" of the Tasaday. The most radical claims argued that the Tasaday were paid actors who had been told to play at being primitives. Indeed, these claims forced a debate in which *either* the Tasaday were an archaic community that had been entirely isolated for thousands of years *or* they were cynical members of a rural proletariat forced to portray a contrived communal existence. Less remarked upon was the evidence that there might be a real Tasaday community but one not quite as pristine as Elizade and his media agents claimed; either the Tasaday were completely separate from the imagined "us" of modernity or else they weren't interesting enough to talk about.[1]

By 1990, media attention had turned to another rainforest people of Southeast Asia: the Penan hunter-gatherers of the forests of Sarawak, East Malaysia, the northern part of the island of Borneo. Media attention was sparked by Penan protests against logging; this time, the media fought state policy rather than being directed by it. From the start, local activists, from the village to the national level, were involved. The logging protests were at least loosely coordinated by the work of Sahabat Alam Malaysia, the Malaysian Friends of the Earth. Yet the news the media carried looked much like the original Tasaday story: The Penan were gentle innocents of the forest; until logging began, they lived encapsulated in their own timeless, archaic world. Ignoring the sophistication of Penan and other Sarawak activists, films and articles focused on the story of Bruno Mansur, a Swiss adventurer who had gone back to nature with the Penan. In two feature-length films, Mansur was depicted as the only conduit for outside knowledge about the isolated and shy Penan. Mansur, like Elizade, would be the champion of the tribes.[2]

The story of the Penan—like that of the Tasaday before them—was carefully orchestrated to offer urban audiences something they could understand. Media writers and ecology activists alike figured that only by invoking the abyss between the primitive and the modern would they have a story to tell. Since primitives, as a dying breed, are no longer thought to be dangerous, the story has provoked sympathy, curiosity, and romance. If the Penan were depicted as "modern" people living in an out-of-the-way place, urban audiences would suspect that Penan were merely shabbier, less educated and privileged versions of themselves. One could feel sympathetic, but there would be nothing interesting to learn from the Penan and thus no reason to single them out for special attention. Perhaps a few activists worry about the Tasaday parallel: If the Penan were "exposed" as more cosmopolitan than some of their portrayals imply, would they lose international support and thus all possibility of a Penan forest biosphere reserve? But no alternatives have emerged. Thus, those who, with all good intentions, represent the Penan to the world ignore the dangers of the Tasaday precedent and, with some awkwardness, construct a threatened Eden in the rainforest.

What these stories of the Tasaday and the Penan suggest to me is the poverty of an urban imagination which systematically has denied the possibilities of difference *within* the modern world and thus looked to relatively isolated people to represent its only adversary, its dying Other. The point of this book is to develop a different set of conceptual tools for thinking about out-of-the-way places—and, in particular, about Southeast Asian rainforest dwellers. Like the Tasaday and the Penan, the Meratus Dayaks of southeast Kalimantan (Indonesian Borneo) are neither my nor anybody's "contemporary ancestors." They share with anyone who might read this book a world of expanding capitalisms, ever-militarizing nation-states, and contested cultural politics. They also speak from perspectives that are distinctive from those of urban Indonesians, or non-Indonesians, but these are distinctions forged in dialogue, not in archaic isolation. I use the concept of *marginality* to begin discussion of such distinctive and unequal subject positions within common fields of power and knowledge.

To describe Meratus Dayaks as an embryo-like Other across an abyss of time and civilization would be to ignore their current political and cultural dilemmas. Yet it is difficult to speak harshly of the romance of the primitive, because it is a discourse of hope for many Europeans and North Americans, as well as a growing number of urban Indonesians concerned about deteriorating social and natural environments. Many people that I care about and respect know the primitive as the dream space of possibility against the numbing monotony of regulated life and the advancing terrors of ecological destruction, corporate insatiability, and military annihilation. Perhaps it seems hard-hearted on my part to work so hard to disturb these fragile dreams. I can only argue that there is also possibility and promise in the directions I suggest in this book. My sense of promise derives from attention to the cultural richness of the cosmopolitan world—and to the possibilities for play and parody as difference is continually constructed and deconstructed. This attention derives from an alertness I acquired in working with the Meratus Dayak woman I call Uma Adang; our encounters frame this book. Nor is this attention just another detached, ironic deconstruction of the play of categories. There is also curiosity here—a refusal to be numbed by terror in a terrifying world. The book is a self-conscious exploration of the possibilities of living with curiosity amidst ongoing violence.

I first travelled to the Meratus Mountains of South Kalimantan, Indonesia, in September 1979 and stayed through August 1981. I visited the same people and places again over several months in 1986. Much of the mountain area offers a densely forested and rough terrain occasionally dotted with fields and houses and crisscrossed with trails whose paths may change after a night of rain. This is a difficult, confusing terrain for administrators and tourists, and its maps continue to present conflicting detail concerning vegetation, settlement, and district borders. In this book I argue that the imagined constraints of travelling over this terrain, together with the necessity and pervasiveness of travel, form a technology of regional integration that holds in place a set of discussions constituting

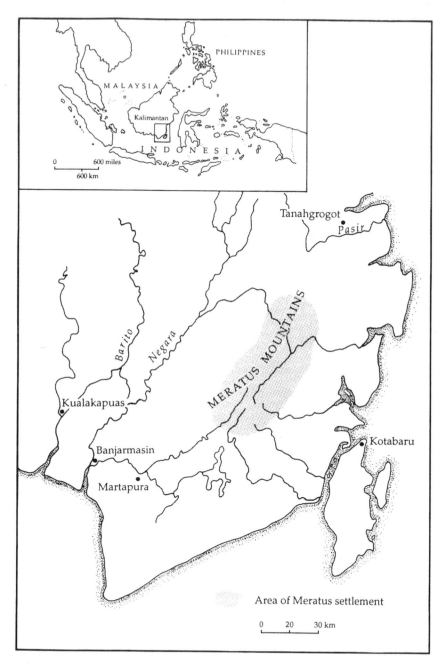

Southeast Kalimantan

Meratus "marginality." This is an area which, so far, has eluded the clarity and visibility required for model development schemes. I see no reason to intervene here. I have thus changed the names of all the places I mention in the Meratus Mountains.

I have also changed the names of all the people whose lives I discuss. Although I aim for accurate portraits, my hope is that the people not be so recognizable that the stories I tell in this book could be used to harass them. However, I have followed the Meratus Dayak system of naming through teknonyms. With a little attention to this system, readers can tell whether the person I name is a child, an adult, or an elderly person, and, in the last two cases, whether the person is a man or a woman.

Meratus Dayak children have names ("body names," *ngaran badan*) that are rarely used after adolescence. By the time they marry, at the very latest, both men and women are known by more complex names which, in principle, are teknonyms ("names by having children," *ngaran ba'anak*). Men are *Ma X* or *Pa'an X*, where X can be one of the man's children—or some other word; women are *Induan X* or *Dun X*. In this book, if I call a man "Ma Y" and a woman "Induan Y," I am indicating that they are a married couple, as indeed is most commonly the case with such a pair of names in the Meratus Mountains. More mature men and women may move up a generation in naming; *Awat X* and *Apih X* are "Grandfather of X" and "Grandmother of X," respectively. Again, X may be, but is not necessarily, the name of one of their grandchildren. In areas where Meratus Dayaks live in close proximity with Banjar, the regional majority population of South Kalimantan, Meratus may follow Banjar usage: *Pa X* and *Uma X* are the Banjar equivalents of *Ma X* and *Induan X*, respectively. I follow local usage in this case. However, in relation to another issue, I do not: Meratus are often known by different names by different networks of people; over the course of a few years their most common appellations change. Many of the people I knew in 1981, for example, were known by different names by the time I saw them again in 1986. So that the reader can follow my stories more easily through the book, I have given each person one and only one name.

In the area I describe, people sometimes mix vocabulary associated with the national language (Indonesian) with the Banjar regional majority and with various Meratus subgroups. Indonesian is used in administrative affairs in South Kalimantan; Banjar is the language of Banjar–Dayak trade; in Meratus houses and fields, local idioms prevail. All three are closely related linguistically, but the distinctions are politically significant. Generally, I indicate when the terms introduced were considered

Indonesian or Banjar by the people I knew. In spelling local terms, however, I try to signal local dialects while staying close to the spelling conventions that have been adopted for Hulu Sungai Banjar.[3]

The strength of my ethnography depends on being able to convince readers that I speak the local language well enough to understand what people tell me. This is ordinarily accomplished by providing the reader with long passages in the original language. In reading other ethnographies, sometimes I have found these passages helpful; sometimes they have seemed superfluous or even disingenuous proofs of authority or retranslations of things the author wanted people to have said. The question of how much Meratus, Banjar, and Indonesian to include in this book was not an easy one to answer.

Linguistically speaking, perhaps the most interesting materials that I discuss are shamanic chants; yet I translate only short sections taken from long chants. It seemed pointless to include Meratus versions of these excerpts without providing their larger context; however, there is no appropriate place in this ethnography for the whole chants. This will have to await another publication.

In Part Three, I discuss several shorter compositions: a song, a speech, a poem. In no case is the language of these compositions a good example of Meratus linguistic usage; each is idiosyncratic, even bizarre. Indeed, that is why I chose them for my analysis. It would be misleading to include original language for these pieces when I do not include it for more conventional Meratus compositions. However, I make an exception with the speech analyzed in chapter 9, because the use of Meratus–Banjar–Indonesian language is part of my interest there, and I include a transcription of the original version in the notes.

Another issue of language continues to trouble me: In what tense does one write an ethnographic account? This grammatical detail has considerable intellectual and political significance. The use of the "ethnographic present" is tied to a conceptualization of culture as a coherent and persistent whole. It creates a timeless scene of action in which cultural difference can be explored (cf. Strathern 1990; Hastrup 1990). This removal of ethnographic time from history has been criticized for turning ethnographic subjects into exotic creatures (Fabian 1983); their time is not the time of civilized history. Many ethnographers are thus turning to a historical time frame in which action happens in the past tense.

Yet, here too, there are problems in describing an out-of-the-way place.

Urban readers are only too ready to believe that those savages, with their strange ways, are passing out of the present into the past; "of course," I can imagine people saying, "those people aren't like that now." To many readers, using the past tense about an out-of-the-way place suggests not that the people "have" history but that they *are* history, in the colloquial sense. Indeed, these are some of the problems early twentieth-century ethnographers addressed in turning to the present tense (cf. Strathern 1990).

I cannot escape these dilemmas; I can only maneuver within them. In this book, I find uses for both the historical past and the ethnographic present. I am inconsistent. Sometimes I use tenses in a counter-intuitive style to disrupt problematic assumptions. For example, in chapter 3, I put my entire discussion of Meratus gender expectations in the historical framework of developments in the early 1980s. I am working against accounts of timeless and unmovable gender systems. In contrast, in chapter 9, my account of Uma Adang's social movement, which I also encountered in the early 1980s, is written in the present tense; since I do not know what has happened to her in the 1990s, my goal here is to keep open the possibilities and dreams that her movement stimulated.

This book has been long in the making. Many people and many institutions helped make it possible. I am grateful to the National Endowment for the Humanities, the Social Science Research Council, and the Wenner–Gren Foundation for helping support my writing. My research in 1979–81 was supported by the National Institute of Mental Health and the Social Science Research Council. In 1986, further research was supported by the National Science Foundation, the American Philosophical Society, and the Institute for Intercultural Studies. The Lembaga Ilmu Pengetahuan Indonesia sponsored my research, with the supervision of Professor Masri Singarimbun of Gadjah Mada University and Professor Gusti Mafudz of Lambung Mangkurat University. Dr. H. Noer'ied Radam provided me with much useful advice and information from his own research in the Meratus area. I am also thankful to Mr. S. Hasan and his family for their kind hospitality.

Throughout the writing process, I have benefited from the support and direction of many colleagues. My writing group at the University of California, Santa Cruz, deserves special mention: Shelly Errington, Diane Gifford–Gonzalez, and Carolyn Martin Shaw. I am deeply grateful to many who have read my work or discussed it with me, particularly the readings and comments of Jane Atkinson, Paulla Ebron, Faye Ginsburg, Susan

Harding, Rita Kipp, Sandra Morgen, Kirin Narayan, Mary Orgel, Ken Payton, Lisa Rofel, Renato Rosaldo, David Schneider, Mary Steedly, Toby Volkman, and Sylvia Yanagisako. Jane Sterzinger drew the maps. Kathryn Chetkovich and Scott Morgensen helped me through the final stages of revision. Many others, too, were essential to my research, thinking, and writing. Although I do not list their names here for reasons of privacy, my greatest debt is to the people with whom I have lived and worked in South Kalimantan.

IN THE REALM OF THE
DIAMOND QUEEN

OPENING IN THE REALM OF

THE DIAMOND QUEEN

. . . a disorienting caricature
of motherhood

This book is about the cultural and political construction of marginality. It is about the process in which people are marginalized as their perspectives are cast to the side or excluded. It is also about the ways in which people actively engage their marginality by protesting, reinterpreting, and embellishing their exclusion. Marginality has been an important concern in recent discussions of colonial discourse, race, class, and gender. I hope to contribute to these discussions; yet my account stresses the specificity of marginalizing discourses, institutions, and experiences. In this spirit, my book is an ethnographic account. It describes how, in the early 1980s, Dayak shifting cultivators of the rainforested Meratus Mountains of South Kalimantan, Indonesia, worked to define and redefine their situation on the periphery of state power. I explore the intersection of three processes within which Meratus marginality is shaped: state rule, the formation of regional and ethnic identities, and gender differentiation.

Hiking down from the forests and scattered swiddens of the Meratus Mountains toward the markets, offices, and mosques of the Banjar plains, I came to pass through the Meratus border settlement of Kalawan. Meratus friends in the mountains had told me of a Kalawan woman, Uma Adang, whom they thought I would enjoy meeting. But when I pressed for details, they had merely nodded knowingly. Alas, when I arrived late one afternoon in April 1980, no one was home in Uma Adang's neighborhood. Yet it was a convenient place to stop, a striking spot with sheer limestone cliffs jutting above neat bamboo houses, palms, and fruit trees. I was willing to wait. Leaving my backbasket, I wandered off for a lei-surely bath in the river. Imagine my surprise when I looked up from my bath to find a village official, crisply dressed in regulation khaki, bending low before me to shake my hand. Before I could gather all my clothing or half my wits, he had pulled me off, with all the punctiliousness of the White Rabbit, to a very important occasion.

As tea and sugar from the market, and deer and durian from the forest, appeared around me on the floor of Uma Adang's house, I observed that I was the guest of honor at an impromptu feast. Lines of women and men came through the door, each bending and extending a hand to me in an unfamiliar formal greeting. I had lived in the mountains long enough to know that this was no ordinary Meratus gathering. But what was it? Then Uma Adang herself, lovely and self-possessed, sat down by my side and began speaking to me in grave and unearthly tones—and I was mes-merized.

On Friday, June 21, 1974, at 5:00 in the evening, Uma Adang said, she began to hear voices from the ancient Indonesian kingdom of Majapahit. These voices had told her the true forms of history, ritual, and law, and for the past six years she had been teaching and leading her community in these rediscovered traditions. Her spiritual potency could be seen from the fact that during that time she had not eaten rice, the staple that forms the bulk of the Meratus—and, indeed, much of the Indonesian—diet. (Yet as a non-Muslim, she told me, it was important that she eat pork at least once a month.) She had also forsworn marriage. Her voices, she said, had begun to instruct her in all the languages of the world. Then she had dreamed of my coming; she had experienced the high winds, she said, of America, and she had known that I would retrace the steps of the Dia-mond Queen, who had come once before in ancient time to restore pros-perity to this isolated realm. My timely arrival fulfilled one stage of the prophecy of the past.

Seeing that I felt most comfortable with a pen and notebook in my hand, Uma Adang declared herself and her other guests completely open for my questions. Awash with confusion and awe, I hardly knew what to ask. But no matter; Uma Adang and her companions had their own agenda, and they patiently dictated ceremonial forms, destinations for shamanic spiritual travel, mythical eras of history, and classes of valuable, if generally invisible, heirlooms—all lessons faithfully restored from those of the original Diamond Queen—for my slow pen. When the ink finally ran out, Uma Adang was still talking; I grabbed a pencil. It was almost dawn when I risked rudeness to ask for a few hours of sleep.

As powerful demands for resources, land, and military control have guided state expansion to the most remote corners of the earth, the autonomy and mobility of the marginal cultural groups of once inaccessible places—rainforests, rugged mountains, deserts, tundra—have increasingly been threatened. The dominant frameworks for understanding recent encroachments, however, ignore long histories of marginality to posit conditions of "before" versus "after"—of pristine isolation, on the one hand, and rapid cultural destruction or modernization, on the other. In such frameworks, marginal people become archaic survivors who, for better or worse, are forced to "catch up with the twentieth century." These frameworks create "primitives" within a medley of interlinked narratives about progress and civilization. Whether as objects of romantic fascination or of missionizing zeal, these imagined primitives are a provocative reminder of all that civilized humanity has lost. In contrast, marginal "hillbillies" are disturbing to the urban consciousness in quite a different way: They confuse boundaries of "us" and "them," and they muddle universalizing standards of propriety, deference, and power.

In this book I explore the making of an Indonesian marginal culture. Meratus Dayaks could easily be described as primitives; they are probably as isolated as any Indonesian minority about whom I have read. They are subsistence cultivators and forest foragers of thick rainforests. They live in rough terrain, often a hike of several days from the nearest market. They hunt with dogs and spears and bring their sick to shamans for healing rites. These are ways of life that invite a conventional set of questions about strange and different forms of knowledge and society. My focus on marginality involves a choice to formulate a perspective on culture and community that stands in contrast to those perspectives most commonly found in both popular imagery and classic ethnography.

I begin with an awareness that "the Meratus" are not just a site of endogenous, localized knowledge but are also, and always, a *displace-*

ment within powerful discourses on civilization and progress. As untamed hill people, Meratus are formed in the imagination of the Indonesian state, the "civilized" regional majority, and the visiting anthropologists and travellers who learn to "know" them. Indeed, the name *Meratus* itself is my own awkward imposition, offered to avoid the derogatory ethnic term *Bukit*.

Yet these powerful names and discourses do not have an unquestioned hegemony: Meratus respond, reinterpret, and challenge even as they accept and are shaped by these forms of knowledge. My analysis locates itself primarily at a "Meratus" level, in order to emphasize local negotiations—and, in the process, to reformulate anthropological ideas of the local. I feature stories, narratives of people and events, because these stories show sites of discursive contestation.[1]

It is in this genre-stretching sense that this book is an ethnography. I am concerned particularly with the way in which the women and men I knew explained and commented upon local cultural politics in the context of regional dilemmas. For example, Meratus relations to state power were rarely absent from local discussions of culture and community. In contrast to the self-generating solidarity basic to most ethnographic accounts of community, I heard Meratus describe community formation as a state project that they could fulfill or frustrate. Local leaders constructed their authority not by reiterating community hierarchy but by emphasizing their ties to state rule. Yet this enthusiasm forms the crux of a contradiction: Rather than integrating Meratus into Indonesian politics as citizens, national political discourse has demarcated Meratus as savages outside its reaches. It is this kind of contradiction that I explore under the rubric of *marginality*.

I argue, too, that gender-differentiated responses to peripheral political status are central to understanding the distinctive debates of Meratus culture. Most Meratus leaders are men; in a number of ways, women are disadvantaged political actors. Many women I met considered themselves politically uninformed. Yet they were not silent; even the least ambitious offered complaints and sarcastic remarks, and a few challenged local standards to become leaders themselves and publicize their views. Their comments reminded me not to assume that "community" inspires a homogeneous form of consciousness; instead, I began to listen for shifting, multistranded conversations in which there never was full agreement. Precisely because of their unlikely authority, unusually ambitious women pointed me toward the creative possibilities as well as the constraints inherent in Meratus marginalities. The commentaries of exceptional women play an important role in my project because they guide my analysis to linked asymmetries of gender, ethnicity, and state rule—yet they destabilize these asymmetries.

My project involves the study of intersecting discursive fields in which social identities, such as those I call "Meratus," are created and maintained. Such an analysis departs from more conventional cultural anthropology to the extent that it does not focus on underlying principles and structures that unite contextually and historically changing commitments and actions. Critics of the latter approach have suggested that the depth and coherence of culture are artifacts of a particular gaze from abroad, a gaze that focuses on the differences between a Western-trained "us" and a non-Western "them." These critics point to the way in which this gaze obscures local debates and historicities (for example, Said 1978; Clifford and Marcus 1986; Wolf 1982). I argue that an alternative lies in situating local commentaries—such as those of the Meratus women and men I knew—within wider negotiations of meaning and power at the same time as recognizing local stakes and specificities.

By putting gender at the center of my analysis, I create a continually oppositional dialogue with more familiar ethnographic genres which segregate an endogenous cultural logic from regional-to-global influences. Generally, studies of gender and wider political relations hardly overlap. Histories of local-global interconnections still ignore gender; and gender tends to be studied as an "internal" cultural issue. "External" influences are portrayed as influencing gender—as in much of the literature on women, colonialism, and development—only as foreign impositions upon once stable and self-regulating traditions.[2] These conventions obscure the regionally ramifying debates and practices that produce both gender and politics. By transgressing conventions of segregated "internal" and "external" cultural analysis, this book shows the connections between intercommunity divisions, including gender difference, and Meratus regional and national marginality. Attention to gender, as both an imaginative construct and a point of divergent positionings, brings wider cultural negotiations to the center of local affairs.

In this project I join many other contemporary scholars who are interested in cultural heterogeneity and the trans-communal links through which "communities" are forged.[3] Unlike much of this work, however, this book describes the kind of out-of-the-way terrain familiar from classic ethnographies, rather than focusing on urban centers, mass media, and the latest technological developments. Too often, generalizations about modern and postmodern cultural processes rest on surprisingly unrefurbished stereotypes of primitive, traditional enclaves. (I think, for example, of Pierre Bourdieu's analysis of "archaic" Algerian culture as a foil to "modern" France [1990], or, in a rather different vein, of Frederic Jameson's attempt [1991] to show a unilinear evolution to postmodernism.) In my analysis I refuse divisions of dynamic core and culturally stagnant periphery by showing the importance of analyzing heterogeneity and transcultural dialogue in even the most out-of-the-way places. In such contexts, perhaps even more than in the urban centers where researchers expect contest and debate, cultural analysts are challenged to reexamine theory and create new forms of description.

A few months after my first visit, when I returned for a longer stay in Kalawan, Uma Adang seemed to have accepted my self-designation as a student of local culture and history. I was a little embarrassed that I had never thought of a more creative counter to her significant looks and whispered question, "What are you really here for?" But I need not have worried; even as a student of culture I was swept into Uma Adang's pageant. Because it sounded grand and official, Uma Adang told people to call me Mahasiswa—the locally unfamiliar Indonesian term for "university student" with which I had identified myself. (Siswa is just "pupil"; maha means "great.") She announced that she had known all along that 1980 and 1981 were the Years of the Mahasiswa, just as 1982 would be the Year of the Religious Teacher and 1983 would be the Year of the Revealed Secret. Finally, she cautiously unveiled her knowledge of the great project in which she and I were caught together: Presidents and generals from across the world and on high were competing to sit upon the Seven Golden Thrones of the Era of Kings. They had sent out fortyone University Students to learn the true History that established the proper seating that could open an era of peace. She and I, she said, were engaged in the same task of searching for this powerful History. Of course I had come.

By this time, my awe and confusion had subsided to a tolerable level, and I was able to appreciate the playful parody that Uma Adang created in even her most bizarre announcements. Now more socialized than Alice in Wonderland facing the Red Queen, I nevertheless felt like the soldier who blundered into a mental hospital in which the inmates enact a ridicu-

lous parody of the even more ridiculous society of the sane, in the film King of Hearts. *In a regional political climate of state symbolism, Muslim piety, and bureaucratic order, what could be more intriguing than Uma Adang's inspired fake-Koran readings, pompous "government" speeches full of unintelligible patriotic verbiage, and eerie pronouncements about the political intersections of the past and the future?*

I suggest reading the following fragment slowly. Let the syllables ring clearly, and for a moment worry less about the content:

> *The date the seventh,*
> *the year 1800.*
> *Peace be with you.*
> *Including,*
> *To the honorable:*
> *speaking in the History of the World.*
> *Which contains the adat*
> *of the Prophet Lahat*
> *beginning*
> *to be*
> *broadened*
> *by History*
> *that is the most famous,*
> *or the highest,*
> *each day*
> *or each*
> *of us to actualize*
> *Peace and Perfection.*[4]

Uma Adang was not alone; her neighbors and kin responded with their own inspired parodies. Pa Bundi, Uma Adang's right-hand man, carried an albino monkey as the sacred image of royalty as he solemnly pronounced his devotion for Uma Adang "greater than a diamond like a banana blossom." (Was I to laugh? Even I knew that a reference to the large, ruddy banana blossom usually meant the penis.) Uma Uman—a respected matron in her sixties—carried, fed, and soothed a large plastic baby doll in a disorienting caricature of motherhood. Pa Hati, the village head, maintained a sharp government-style appearance as he whispered Uma Adang's secrets of the coming millennium behind his hand. His wife

Uma Hati, also pushing sixty, challenged me to photograph her with her skirts above her waist—and with a big mocking grin on her face. Nor could I be a spectator without a role of my own.

> All of us ask for Peace,
> or Perfection,
> and surrender to
> and I quote: huas ter
> al ai se na el ha
> *number one* kun hes ai der hai
> ai kun sai
> *number one.*

Perhaps I was predisposed to approach my work as Mahasiswa with the same tongue-in-cheek seriousness with which Uma Adang led her flock; for, in that spirit, Uma Adang and I enjoyed each other immensely. In my own script, I luxuriated in the pleasure of my role as the ethnographer of so willing an informant. In the dark of the night, we whispered genealogies as if they were state secrets. My tape recorder offered the rationale for formal speeches on every occasion. Sometimes, when we were alone, Uma Adang had me tape speeches, which, when an audience had assembled, she could play back with even more grandeur than the original. My commentary seeped into her cosmology. Momentarily oblivious to the standards of the presidents and generals our knowledge unwittingly served, our joint project in culture and history prospered.

As Mahasiswa, I could not ignore the theatrical political agendas of my own documentary conventions. I was forced to smile at the strange rituals of even my simplest empirical exercises; how different were they from Uma Adang's "crazy" historical methods? Uma Adang spoke to me about this again and again. Once she met me on a trail, counting my paces to make a local map. Our conversation went something like this:

Uma Adang: *Counting paces is a true part of the search for History, but you and I have different methods. You count each step, while I immediately know how many paces I have come when I arrive at a place. For example, I know that I am 222 paces from the last house in the settlement.*

AT: *Actually, I've counted 947 paces from that house.*

Uma Adang *(with a satisfied smile): So you see, I have bigger strides.*

It was irrefutable logic, which could only remind me of the distinctive exoticism of my own training.

My interest in Meratus marginality began during my fieldwork as I found that it was difficult to have a discussion about almost any topic I might want to explore—gender, forest use, ritual, etc.—without paying attention to the context of ethnic asymmetry and political status vis-à-vis the state. It was this context that made local culture worth discussing for the Meratus I knew; it gave shape to what was imaginable as well as interesting to talk about. At first, I thought of marginality as an ethnographic *feature*, which made the Meratus different from other groups. However, theoretical developments in cultural studies and anthropology have opened new ways to think about marginality. Scholars have developed an active discussion of the political processes of cultural production—inside and outside academe—in which "cultures" are no longer separate worlds. Rather than characterizing any given culture, marginality becomes key to reformulating cultural theory.

The critique of anthropology as a form of Western colonial discourse has become well known within the field, and it has stimulated a number of important responses. Anthropologists have criticized unself-conscious caricatures of tribal peoples, initiated careful textual analyses of past and present ethnographic writing, and turned toward the long-neglected study of dominant culture in Europe and the United States.[5] Yet many of these admittedly rich responses retain one of the most problematic features of colonial discourse: the fantasized gulf between the West and its Other. The responses turn from the study of the Other to the study of the West, but they continue to ignore the complexity of cultural production within the interactions of colonizers and colonized. Thus, anthropological writing is most commonly studied in relation to Western formats of representation—but not in its engagement with local (Western and non-Western) struggles over power and meaning. And the cultures of white people are still studied in isolation from Third World and minority dialogues. This retreat to an imaginary segregation does not improve anthropology's analytic tools.

In contrast, a number of self-consciously "postcolonial" and "minority" scholars, working from and across a variety of academic disciplines, have opened a theoretical discussion about the cultural engagements of people in politically asymmetrical positions. The most vigorous wing of this discussion asks about these engagements from the position of the excluded and the insubordinate: those at the "margins" of cultural domination. It is, of course, possible to differentiate scholars here—this one a Derridean, that one a Marxist—but it is precisely against the grain of these European genealogies that I introduce their focus on the marginal. Literary critic Homi Bhabha articulates the challenge of this emerging field in a question he draws from Frantz Fanon: "How can a human being live Other-wise?" (Bhabha 1989:147). This is a field that considers the negotiation of cultural differences that have emerged both because of and despite Western imperial power, as well as the ensuing nationalisms and ethnicities this power has bred. It is a theoretical discussion that anthropologists, as well as anyone else interested in global cultural interactions, can no longer afford to neglect. The promise of a postcolonial anthropology that goes beyond the re-analysis of its own problematic past depends upon engagement with the questions and challenges raised by those concerned with cultural heterogeneity, power, and "marginality."

The "marginal" began as a point from which theoretical criticism in academe could be launched. Literary critics crafted the marginal as intervention into Western humanism; margins are the sites of exclusion from this tradition from which its categories and assumptions can be seen more clearly. A number of critics have shown how asymmetries of race, gender, and colonial status have been produced *within* rather than *in spite of* humanist standards (for example, Spivak 1987; Irigaray 1985; Spillers 1987). Similarly, the marginal has been a rejoinder to Marxist class-oriented approaches that do not adequately address colonialism and racism. Unlike class, the latter power relations cannot be understood within a homogeneous, taken-for-granted cultural regime; they construct and bind systems of cultural difference. Thus, attention to the marginal has opened discussion of linked cultural constructions of domination and difference (Hall 1990; hooks 1990; Taussig 1987). From this criticism, then, marginality began to signal a discussion that moves beyond rereading dominant theories to formulate new objects of study. Yet, in contrast to conventional anthropology, this trajectory refuses a theoretical separation of analysts and objects of study as two distinct classes; marginalities created both inside and outside the academy are interconnected. The knowledge of an author, like that of the people about whom he or she writes, is always partial, situated, and perspectivistic (Lewis 1973; Haraway 1988; Clifford 1986).

A caution seems in order: Although self-positioning can be an opening move for crafting new forms of cultural analysis (Rosaldo 1989), this is not a literature of authentic or representative "voices" of excluded minorities. It would be easy and unfortunate to deintellectualize this literature as the recording of the essential experiences of Others. ("Let's hear," they say, "from the X perspective.") Instead, the goal is to open new possibilities for thinking and writing; anyone can participate.

Yet, the way in which writers imagine their own marginality is perhaps one way to understand a central tension that divides current scholars analyzing the marginal. Because it raises key questions for all cultural analysis, including the present study, it is worth some attention here. I refer to a tension around the political implications of notions of cultural difference. Edward Said (1978) has led the way among those self-identified as diasporic postcolonials (Third World scholars working in Europe or the United States) in emphasizing how colonial discourse constructs "other cultures" to separate colonizer and colonized. He and others show how the notion of cultural difference has been used to debase and control Third World peoples (Trinh 1989; Mani 1987). As Gayatri Spivak puts it, the "pluralist aesthetes of the First World are, willy-nilly, participants in the production of an exploitative society" (1987a:179). This analysis self-consciously draws from the experience of having to struggle for an academic voice—against classifications as an alien—despite the best Western education and talent (for example, Spivak 1989).[6]

In contrast, minority scholars in the United States have had more to say about empowering aspects of self-involvement with cultural difference. The discourse of domination that seems most constraining is not that of encrusted difference, but that of white privilege falsely universalized to erase the struggles, accomplishments, and dilemmas of people of color. Thus, Cornel West writes of the "modern Black diaspora problematic of invisibility and namelessness" and the importance of building "subcultures and networks of people of color who cultivate critical sensibilities and personal accountability" (1990:27, 34). Breaking out of the cultural homogenizations of the United States involves the creativity of making difference matter (for example, hooks 1989; Lorde 1984).

Both groups thus locate their critiques as border skirmishes that open up the carefully patrolled closures of dominant modes of thought. Yet, the cultural construction of domination looks different from each perspective. Postcolonial critics worry about "essentialist" political moves (see, for example, Najmabadi 1991; Spivak 1989a), as U.S. minorities argue against the elitist assumptions and obfuscations of poststructuralist (sometimes postcolonial) writing (for example, Christian 1988).[7]

A closer look at the work of individual scholars reveals many whose approaches cut across this dichotomization and call its terms into question. I introduce the contrast not in order to predetermine scholarly positions but to open a discussion that is easily neglected in throwing together "Other" perspectives. The tension is an intellectually invigorating one for my project, and it needs to be seen in relation to varied political and intellectual challenges.

An example can illuminate both the contrast and the complexity of scholarly positions. A number of postcolonial scholars theorizing the marginal have revived the work of anticolonial psychoanalyst Frantz Fanon. Homi Bhabha, for example, turns to Fanon to help focus discussion on the subjectivity of the colonized, at the margins of colonial discourse. Bhabha uses Fanon to move beyond theorists who overemphasize the hegemony of colonial discourse, such as, in his view, Edward Said: "There is always, in Said, the suggestion that colonial power and discourse [are] possessed entirely by the colonizer" (1990:77). Bhabha, instead, emphasizes the limits of colonial authority in its ambivalences, incongruities, misreadings, and vulnerability to parodic mimicry on the part of the colonized. Bhabha thus comes much closer to a notion of oppositional cultural practices than I have stereotyped above as the "postcolonial" position.

Yet the limits of Bhabha's interest in cultural negotiation are nicely pointed out in "Critical Fanonism," an essay by African-American literary critic Henry Louis Gates, Jr. (1991). Gates criticizes Bhabha—and other postcolonial readers of Fanon—for making Fanon a "global theorist" with an "imperial agenda" that ignores the cultural and political specificity of its own interventions. In Bhabha's scheme, the colonized can parody but can never remake culture. All cultural negotiation thus reproduces the dichotomy between a globally homogeneous Colonizer and Colonized. Gates also criticizes Gayatri Spivak, who, he argues, can see "nothing outside (the discourse) of colonialism": "Spivak's argument, put in its strongest form, entails the corollary that all discourse is colonial discourse" (1991:466). In contrast, Gates suggests that Fanon be historicized as a West Indian in Algeria whose background and training helped shape a particular utopian vision of a race-free Third World. Yet, of course, Gates's move toward cultural and historical specificity embroils his analysis in the logics of "cultural difference" and "historical narrative" which postcolonial critics such as Spivak have worked hard to show as colonial discourses that divide and conquer the empire's subjects. It may be useful to think of Bhabha and Spivak as speaking from the space *between* asymmetrically ranked nations; this space depends on unsettling the cultural and historical logics that support (ranked) nations. In contrast, Gates argues from a disadvantaged space *within* a nation in which unmarked "universal" status establishes privilege; this space inspires challenges to minority-silencing global agendas.

The way in which I have organized my exposition of these issues should by now reveal a good deal about my own stake in this matter. By pointing to the divergence of strategies between groups of scholars, I, like Gates, argue for recognition and respect for a variety of different political and intellectual agendas. This is not the same as a naive endorsement of cultural diversity; instead, the point is to specify the political challenges at hand.

The question of the marginality of Meratus Dayaks of South Kalimantan, Indonesia, poses challenges that tap and criticize both sides of the intellectual tension I have described. This project brings the issue of minority status out of the metropolitan context in which it has most commonly been discussed, and in which the political conditions of domination and debate are too often taken for granted. In contrast to much writing about minorities in the United States, my study forces analysis of the national ideologies and institutions that create minority status and shape minorities' attempts to be heard. The project also refuses global dichotomies of colonizer and colonized, as it requires a finer, more contradictory specification of national and regional discourses of exclusion and struggle. Yet the history of colonialism is never entirely absent in informing transnational projects such as this one; Meratus marginality in the Indonesian nation cannot be divorced from Indonesian marginality in international rankings. Raising the question of Meratus marginality thus calls attention to the complexity and specificity of cultural intersections.

The analyses of the marginal that have had the most to say about specificity and different kinds of marginality are those which have emerged within feminist theory. Yet, ironically, feminist theory is also the source of perhaps the most "global" and unspecified of all theories of the marginal. Feminists using and criticizing Lacanian psychoanalytic frameworks have explored female marginality in relation to phallogocentric subject formation;[8] these theories formulate only one globally and historically homogeneous kind of "woman." The fact that she is disadvantaged in the ways best known to privileged white women goes unremarked. According to these theories, female marginalization is *parallel* in its form to the marginalization of the colonized, the nonwhite, or the poor.[9] This is a formulation in which the intersection of gender with class, race, or national status necessarily remains invisible. At best, these factors are added on as additional layers of exclusion.

In contrast, and in response, many feminists have taken on the project of specification in which particular forms of "female" marginality must be studied in relation to the conditions of women's lives—as immigrants, minorities, wealthy, poor, black, white, sex workers, maids, or academics (for example, Mohanty et al. 1991; Bookman and Morgen 1988). This work rejects the notion that gender asymmetries are parallel to those of race, class, and nationality, for race, class, and national hierarchies are themselves everywhere constructed in gendered ways, and gender divisions are established with "communal" materials. The work I find most promising does not set up exemplar marginal women but, rather, opens up the defensive boundaries of cultural nationalisms by attention to gender (for example, Moraga 1983; White 1990; Ebron 1991). Yet a tension remains as feminists argue for specificity and refuse dominant, constraining readings of "difference." As feminist theorist Trinh Minh-ha (1989) explains, attention to "difference" both traps and empowers marginalized women as artists and political actors.

The analytic space created by this tension—in which ethnic and national marginalities are gendered (rather than parallel to gender), and in which marginality is a source of both constraint and creativity—is that which is explored in this book.

The next time I returned to Kalawan for another long stay, I was struck by how the community could pass as an ordinary peasant village. In this quiet time, I joined daily tasks of fetching water and firewood. We discussed local marriages and ceremonies and the fluctuating price of peanuts (the local cash crop) at the nearest market. Uma Adang and I developed a gentler respect and affection for each other. As I saw how her rhetoric could pass almost inconspicuously in and out of more "acceptable" political and religious forms, I was grateful that somehow I had managed a privileged glimpse of her most colorful side.

*When a Javanese engineer came through Kalawan surveying the area
as a possible transmigration site, he was entertained so conventionally by
regional standards that I doubt if he saw anything other than a typical
rural settlement. Here, parody became hard to differentiate from the expected rhetoric of acquiescence as Uma Adang and other Kalawan leaders
told the engineer how pleased they were that the central government had
signed away their lands to 2,000 Javanese settler families. They always
benefited, they said, from the wisdom of the government. I believe the
engineer got no hint of the anger and fear that had seized the community
with the news of the transmigration agency's plans. But I was firmly reminded of the "ordinary" political context that made Uma Adang's
strangest pronouncements seem sensible and creative interventions.*

*The transmigration location, incidentally, was later cancelled, offering
Kalawan a miraculous, if temporary, reprieve. The survey engineer told
me bitterly that an important Javanese general had removed the area
from the transmigration agency's domain by claiming it as his logging
concession.*

*Meanwhile, disastrous floods rolled into Kalawan, and we were up
to our waists in water on the main trail. Uma Adang and her neighbors blamed the actions on a Japanese prospecting team representing a
mining company interested in the gold and minerals of the sacred mountain at the headwaters of Kalawan's rivers. The Japanese engineer, they
said, had used a special "file" to look under the earth, where he had
seen paired blocks of gold as big as rice mortars balanced on the horns
of a fabled water serpent. Local people who had seen the engineer called
him a "hard" man. When he hurt his back, he would not rest but made
carriers bear him on a litter. They predicted he would continue to ignore
the dream warnings of the supernatural woman who guarded the mountain's treasures; he might not stop before he pulled out the key that
closed off the mountain's internal winds and waters. The winds and
waters would emerge and drown everyone in a great flood, of which
this was just a foretaste. Uma Adang planned to bring offerings to the
mountain, hoping to receive in return a timely warning of the coming
disaster.*

As I hiked upstream through the water with my belongings balanced on my head, I had to agree with Uma Adang's assessment that the flood was a transnational political event caused by inattention to local priorities, although I identified the chain of causality differently. Once I reached the mountains, I could see how the season's rains had hit recently abandoned logging roads (the company was Korean, not Japanese), causing dirt slides that took down the stumps and remaining trees and turned entire hillsides into rolling swamps of mud. And yet, I thought, one must consider that Uma Adang's "history" concerned the paradigmatic structures that brought the future as well as the past into the present. So perhaps she wasn't wrong about the mining company as well . . .

As I resumed my project with Meratus friends and acquaintances in the mountains, my experience with Uma Adang continued to inform my understanding of the region. It turned out that Uma Adang had quite a number of followers in the mountains, and some wanted a closer acquaintance with me when they heard that Uma Adang had adopted me as a "sister." By showing their respect for Uma Adang, these mountain devotees confirmed my sense that Uma Adang's perspectives, as atypical as they sometimes seemed to me, were comprehensible—and, for some, welcome—additions and interventions within ongoing discussions held throughout the Meratus area.

Perhaps her most important influence on me was my new appreciation for her insightful angle of vision. Uma Adang self-consciously offered a perspective from within the intersections of a number of dangerous and creative boundary zones: the boundary between pagan Dayak and Muslim Banjar, the boundary between women's roles and men's, the boundaries of state rule at the edge of "the wild." Reflecting this placement, her perspective was syncretic and playful. She was ready to unite the old religions and fabricate new ones. Her fanciful speeches could be described, in postmodern terms, as antiessentialist and decentered. Yet she was no glittery entertainer, reiterating the ironic necessity of the divisions she mocked. Even her most playful moods showed her deep engagement with the dilemmas of power and survival on both sides, as well as on the boundary.

Writing of Chicana experience in the United States, feminist theorist Gloria Anzaldua (1987) discusses the imaginative and empathetic use of a dual perspective as a "consciousness of the Borderlands." Borders are a particular kind of margin; they have an imagined other side. The image of the border turns attention to the creative projects of self-definition of those at the margins. By shifting the perspective to that of actors who imagine multiple possibilities, the image raises issues of agency without neglecting the constraints of power and knowledge. Renato Rosaldo has extended the concept of borders to write of "border crossings" as "sites of creative cultural production" (1989:208). Border crossings guide us toward intersections of power and difference, both within and across the interests of nations, classes, and local communities. In the places within groups where anthropologists once saw only coherence and homogeneity, Rosaldo suggests one look for multiple, diverging perspectives; between groups—where anthropologists once saw only cultural gaps—he suggests that there may be connections and overlapping agendas.

Uma Adang and I built our own small border crossing in our joint culture and history project. Uma Adang's first interest in me was as an unusual woman with unknown powers, obscure cultural knowledge, and an insubordinate spirit; I viewed her the same way. This small mutual recognition laid out the terrain of our work together, the realm where each of us could sometimes be a student seeker and sometimes a diamond queen. Out of respect for my vulnerabilities as a single woman and a traveller, she protected me with the role of Mahasiswa, a role to be stressed when young men made dirty jokes about me or rumors flew that I was a missionary or a spy. At the same time, I knew that my presence generated her wildest speeches. She had a great sensitivity to the needs of her audience and a fine ability to mimic different styles; I remember her dispensing meaningless mystical syllables to one young man and thoughtful discussion to another.

From the first, I brought out her parody-like national and international talk. Although she was always disappointed when I couldn't understand her inspired "English," we learned, even through our mutual bad imitations. We forged a terrain in which to explore our cultural connections and differences. She tried new ideas in my direction to watch my reaction. I loved to hear her tinker with new cosmologies with the fragments of everything around her. An overlap of imagination shaped the understandings we each developed.

Although it was always significant that I was a U.S. American anthropologist and Uma Adang a Meratus Indonesian, neither of us "represented" our respective cultures in any simple sense. As strange, strong-minded women exploring our own as well as the other's ethnic borders, we chanced into a dialogue that was complexly and contingently positioned. Much of the literature on the dialogic nature of ethnography presents just two positions: the Western anthropologist and the Other. My experience with Uma Adang suggests that this neat dichotomy obscures the nuances of cross-cultural relationships and privileges the unself-consciously elite observer who comfortably represents the West. One goal of this ethnography is to show a variety of unexpected personal intersections through which I was able to learn about varied Meratus positionings. I hope to show how my understanding of gender, power, and culture in the Meratus Mountains draws from particularistically situated dialogues; indeed, all ethnography is so constructed. The "Diamond Queen" in the title of this book refers not to Uma Adang, nor to myself as identified by Uma Adang, but to the conceptual space we created in our ethnographic interaction.

The notion of *marginality* has a particular significance in Indonesia, where state rule has been seen as emanating from the concentrated potency of "exemplary centers" which extend toward more and more unruly peripheries. This set of meanings underscores the importance of discussing marginality in relation to particular political cultures.

In writing about Meratus marginality, I am fortunate to be able to draw from a rich literature on political culture in Indonesia. Scholars have long been fascinated by Indonesia's Indic (and Islamic)[10] heritage and by the self-consciously concentric models of power of the kingdoms of Java, Bali, Sumatra, Sulawesi, and Kalimantan which preceded and overlapped with Dutch control of these areas (for example, Moertono 1968; Geertz 1980; Errington 1989). Furthermore, a number of scholars have shown how the postcolonial Indonesian state has structured Javanese notions of stratification and potency into its program of rule (for example, Anderson

1972; Dove 1985a). Political formulas familiar to international analysts become transformed in the Indonesian context. For example, Shelly Errington (1992) has argued that European temporal notions of progress and development have, in current Indonesian state policy, been transformed into an Indic spatial framework of exemplary centers (as showcases of "development") and disorganized peripheries (as the not-yet-developed). In this framework, the once-and-future glory of "Java" is the center of a national potency that extends outward to rule what, since colonial times, have been called the "Outer Islands."

Much of the literature on political culture in Indonesia stresses the contrast between Indonesian notions of power and political models from the "West." Read in only a slightly against-the-grain way, this literature on cultural contrasts also shows the emergence of "Indonesia" at the margins of the postcolonial world system. Internationally mandated "national" standards are reinterpreted as Indonesia struggles for a national identity both within and against the neocolonial logics that have allowed Third World nations to exist.

This framework makes it possible to think about the ways in which the nation-state has simultaneously endorsed both colonial and precolonial models of government. For example, under President Suharto's New Order, the state has adopted the authoritarian style of the Dutch administration of the late colonial period (McVey 1982). In the 1920s and 30s, the Dutch colonial administration worked for "peace and order" as they quelled strikes and protests and silenced unions, communists, reformists, and nationalists. Since the 1965 military crackdown that brought President Suharto to power, the postcolonial state has used similar tactics to promote political stability and order. Indeed, the state has argued their necessity on the grounds of international sponsorship of economic growth. It makes sense that New Order officials would use familiar colonial logics to address what they see as a problem within transnational administrative standards. At the same time, however, the New Order is associated with a revival of Javanese culture that has helped shape the bureaucracy from village administration to the highest political levels.

The research of John Pemberton (1989) is especially illuminating in understanding this conjunction. Pemberton shows how New Order notions of Javanese culture also derive from the logics of colonial rule—but those of indirect, rather than direct, rule. He argues that New Order cultural models draw from the life-styles of the politically restricted but wealthy Javanese elites of the colonial era. Javanese rulers whose "rule" was paralyzed within colonial constraints turned their attention to ritualistic formality; this formality is the "culture" that has been revived and reinterpreted in the New Order. Indeed, New Order reenactments replay an earlier Dutch colonial revival: Although, in the first decade of the twentieth century, the Dutch discouraged the Javanese elite from "feudal" displays of status, in the late 1920s—following years of nationalist organizing, union strikes, and rural protest—they told officials to resume their old (but now outdated) signs of power, to create a nostalgically recalled stability. By the 1930s, Javanese began to speak of *upacara* "rituals" as stable, traditional ceremonies of power (1989:273–76). Drawing from this history, the New Order has promoted a nostalgic "Javanese culture," to promote stability and dispel the disarray of pre-1965 nationalist politics. "Culture" is endorsed as an alternative to "politics," as *order* is to *disorder*.

It is through cultural politics, then, that the New Order has established its focus on order itself as a ritualized stability in which, as Pemberton suggests, the greatest political success occurs when nothing happens. He describes how Indonesian elections have become a well-orchestrated "national ritual" (*upacara nasional*) in which the government party always wins by the same margin. Development programs are best expressed as floats in a parade; they present models for popular emulation. Although the New Order makes ethnic diversity an emblem of national unity, ethnic diversity is tamed within these Javanese cultural notions. Pemberton offers a striking example of state views of ethnicity: An exhibition at Mrs. Suharto's Indonesia Museum shows the nation as an elite Javanese wedding with ethnic minorities represented as differentially dressed guests. The image suggests that minority groups are "invited" into the nation as long as they bow to Javanese standards.

State programs conflate acceptance of this nostalgic and stabilizing cultural tradition with appropriate citizenship. Yet, this program has relied heavily on the pervasive presence of the army in rural and urban life to guarantee local quietude and cooperation with top-down development plans.

In turning to coercive but only partially successful government intervention in Javanese village ceremonies, Pemberton's work also draws attention to another challenge in studying Indonesian political culture: specifying the relationship between state and village. Study of the Indonesian state has long had the advantage over state-oriented scholarship in many other areas of the world. Moving beyond classic Marxist or Weberian frameworks, in which the state is an instrument of class interests or bureaucratic rationalization, Indonesianists have pointed to the symbolic fields in which power and politics are constituted. Such analyses take scholarly understanding of the state beyond the apparatus of government to show how the magic and power of the state are formed in everyday discursive practice. Continuities in political discourse between rulers and ruled become evident. Yet it is also important not to lose sight of disjunctions and discontinuities. Political discourse is not spread evenly across lines of class, region, ethnicity, gender, and urban-rural difference. Some scholars, such as Robert Hefner (1990), have usefully reintegrated political economy with symbolic analysis to show regional and class diversity in Indonesian national development. An alternative approach, which I pursue here, is to begin with the disjunctions created within national political discourse as they themselves shape—but never fully control—forms of unevenness.

In the Indonesian political system, a gap has been constructed between "the government" (*pemerintah*) and "the people" (*masyarakat*). In part, this gap is a heritage of colonial rule, which may account for some of its resemblance to European folk notions of the split between state and society. The Dutch, for example, instituted the codes that now differentiate "national" and "customary" law; those rural people associated with "custom" are conceptually segregated from national administrators. Even in this example of reformulated colonial policy, however, the split between rulers and ruled has its own contemporary specificity. In most areas of the country, governing officials are appointed from above at the provincial (*propinsi*), regency (*kabupaten*), and district (*kecamatan*) levels of government.[11] In contrast, village (*kampung*) and neighborhood (*runkun tetangga*) officials are expected to be community representatives. Villages look up to the governing apparatus, which looks down at them. The job of the village head (*kepala kampung*) is to mediate between "the government" and "the people." The split created by this bidirectional governing system is particularly evident under the current regime, as government policies stress that the village is the site of popular (i.e., nonstate) forms which must forcefully be brought into line with top-down development policy.

Other political dichotomies are overlaid on this split between "government" and "community." Center-periphery political distinctions distinguish Java from the other, "Outer" islands; people in Kalimantan tend to view government as a Jakarta project. Similarly, within status-ranked areas, low-status people may see government as a high-status project. Finally, groups which in official discourse are marginalized as tribal minorities, outside "civilization," are further peripheralized from the projects of governance. From the perspective of the people in the Meratus Mountains, the gap between government and local politics looks wide.

It is important to recognize that attention to this gap does not tell the whole story. Village politics contribute to making the state; the categories of state rule are actualized in local politics. Yet an analysis of the formation of local communities properly begins with the subjective experience of being both outside and subject to state power. In this book, I use the term *state* to refer to those aspects of the governing, administrative, and coercive apparatus that are experienced as external yet hegemonic.[12] In discussing perspectives from the periphery, I stress the coherent, imposed quality of state authority. I also work to expand analyses of the workings of the state to include the political negotiations of out-of-the-way people. My approach moves back and forth between these two perspectives on the state, to avoid two tempting but oversimplifying poles on a continuum of political analysis. First, I do not want to imply that official state categories have an "always already" quality wherever they are found. Second, I do not argue that the state is a recent, external intrusion into the domain of an independent "primitive society."

Can one be simultaneously inside and outside the state? This is the dilemma of marginality. Uma Adang introduced me to the paradox: Marginals stand outside the state by tying themselves to it; they constitute the state locally by fleeing from it. As culturally "different" subjects they can never be citizens; as culturally different "subjects," they can never escape citizenship.

One of my first reactions to Meratus social life was confusion about what I saw as unquestioning submission to state authority. The people I knew were quite aware that government programs endangered their resources and denounced their everyday lives as "savage." Why, then, were leaders so eager to endorse state rule? Uma Adang changed my perspective by carrying the rhetoric of all-encompassing state wisdom to unexpected extremes. She conflated ancient rajahs and modern presidents; she made offerings intended to regulate the transnational economy. Some of the Meratus male leaders I met could pass in my eyes as the state agents they claimed to be, but Uma Adang was clearly unrecognizable as a state agent. I saw in her leadership what officials see in all Meratus: the trans-

formation of state policy into exotic ritual. Only then could I begin to appreciate the link between submission and claims of autonomy. Her opposition occurred in the mimicry, hyperbole, and distortion of her attempts to get closer to power, rather than in defining herself against this power. In her obsession with ceremony, Uma Adang overfulfilled state requirements for attention to order.

Meratus leaders limit, as well as elaborate, the reach of state power as they make administration a ceremonial obligation; between ceremonies, their communities claim an unceremonious mobility and freedom. Yet this is not a clean escape. The prominence of the armed forces is always a reminder that state demands are deadly serious. The Meratus leaders I have known do not doubt official knowledge. They require state rhetoric to build their authority and gather communities. Their efforts incorporate state rule, but they also slip from its grasp. Uma Adang's parody is particularly illuminating of this mix of accommodation and resistance, because she makes a mockery of accommodation, yet incorporates it as a key element in all her local projects.

Regional officials appoint no women. Unlike male leaders, Uma Adang is unable to work toward a position as a local official. She is denied even the frail state contacts that sustain the enthusiasm of male leaders; this distance surely encourages her parodic style.

This book turns attention from political centers to political peripheries. Where most studies of the state situate themselves where state authority is strongest and examine the project of rule from the perspective of the center, I look for where state authority is most unreliable, where the gap between the state's goals and their local realization is largest, and where reinterpretation of state policies is most extreme. Just as viewing the Indonesian nation in the neocolonial periphery casts light on the unstable hegemony of European political models, so, too, does turning to state peripheries shed light on both the limitations and the strengths of state agendas. An out-of-the-way place is, by definition, a place where the instability of political meanings is easy to see. The authority of national policies is displaced through distance and the necessity of reenactment at the margins. The cultural difference of the margins is a sign of exclusion from the center; it is also a tool for destabilizing central authority.

Rainforest shifting cultivators such as the Meratus Dayaks who are, one might say, on the periphery of the periphery, were mainly invisible in the national discourse of the Sukarno era except as they defined national boundaries—for example, with Malaysia. Under Suharto's New Order, however, such groups have quietly become icons of the archaic disorder that represents the limit and test of state order and development. From the perspective of the elite, "primitives," unlike communists, are not regarded as seriously dangerous but rather as wildly untutored—somewhat like ordinary village farmers, but much more so. Disorderly yet vulnerable, primitives are relatively scarce, and their taming becomes an exemplarly lesson in marginality through which the more advanced rural poor can be expected to position themselves nearer the center.

Since 1974, the government has operated a program for the Management of Isolated Populations.[13] "Management" (*pembinaan*) implies both administrative regulation and cultural leadership.[14] Populations are to be moved into resettlement villages where they can be offered cultural, political, economic, and religious guidance. In the province of South Kalimantan, the Meratus are the only group selected for this guidance. The Meratus, officials say, are "not yet ordered" (*belum diatur*). Thus, state rule in the Meratus Mountains is envisioned by officials as having a civilizing mission.

There is another major national discourse that shapes how Meratus are integrated into the New Order nation: the discourse on ethnic and regional identity. All Indonesians are expected to have an ethnic affiliation. Ethnic groups (*suku*) are expected to compete for political status within the nation, although all must, if only reluctantly, accept the premise of a Javanese center. Furthermore, certain ethnic groups have established themselves as regional powers which claim the right to cultural hegemony emanating from regional centers, in the same way that Javanese claim the national center.

Regional dominance in southeast Kalimantan is held by the Banjar, descendants of those who, until the late nineteenth century, formed the kingdoms of the Barito River delta and areas beyond. Banjar portray themselves as Muslims who take their religion much more seriously than do the central Javanese who rule the nation. Their Muslim identity has been central to their construction of southeast Kalimantan—particularly South Kalimantan province—as a significantly autonomous region within the nation. Islam forms a basis for both claims of connection with and difference from "Jakarta" national policies. Banjar cite Islam as a way of asserting their patriotism and cosmopolitan knowledge, as these confirm national citizenship. Yet their Islam also forms part of an oppositional discourse that differentiates Banjar from the less pious ruling Javanese.

Meratus negotiations with state administration are mediated by their ethnic relations with Banjar. On the one hand, Meratus tend to know the national government through Banjar regional officials; from the Meratus perspective, differences between Javanese and Banjar officials are often unimportant. On the other hand, the importance of Islam in regional identity, as understood by Banjar, creates a distinctive category of Meratus marginalization. Just as officials conceive of the Meratus as disorderly primitives, Banjar construct the Meratus as immoral pagans. Many Meratus are aware that this ethnic-religious disparagement is not the only possibility within national policy; indeed, Meratus speak of supporting the national government as a hoped-for protector of ethnic and religious pluralism. Yet, because of their status as an "isolated minority," Meratus attempts to claim national protection in an ethnic model have been limited.

Meratus do not easily shrug off the negative characterizations of their Banjar neighbors or state officials. They have lived on the border of state rule and Banjar regionalism for centuries and have elaborated a marginality that has developed in dialogue with state policies and regional politics. Indeed, I argue, it is this elaboration of marginality that regional officials mistake for an isolated, primitive tradition.

In this world of long-distance power and travel, is it possible to separate local, indigenous Meratus culture from foreign impositions? This question turns attention to what Indonesians consider the essence of the local: adat. Like many other Indonesians, Meratus use the term adat (or hadat) to refer to customary law, ritual conventions, marriage rules, and other formally articulated norms and ideals. This usage appears at first to offer the framework for an easy assessment of what is locally distinctive. This was the Dutch perspective. Colonial rule was seen as coordinating independent adat communities across the archipelago. Dutch codification of customary law influenced the postcolonial understanding in which adat, as "local custom and tradition," continues to represent the "diversity" within Indonesian unity. The state coordinates diversity by national laws which supersede local adat.

Yet Uma Adang's claims about adat provide an unsettling counterpoint to the dominant understanding. Uma Adang says her adat is the adat of Majapahit—a fourteenth-century Javanese kingdom too far re-moved from the Meratus Mountains to be considered even vaguely "local." She reverses the relationship between local communities and the nation implied in national recognition of adat. Local adat, she says, was formed from the start in submission to state rule; its continuing impor-tance shows Meratus assimilation into, rather than independence from, national standards. This reversal makes it clear that the question of what is local is a matter of intense negotiation.

In Uma Adang's understanding of regional asymmetry, a locally de-rived adat is not a powerful adat. Her access to extra-local knowledge is important to her authority. Further, since her adat discloses structural continuities of past and present regimes, in claiming Majapahit adat she reaches for ongoing state support. Since national officials appeal to pre-colonial kingdoms (especially Majapahit) in legitimizing contemporary policy, Uma Adang seems on widely acceptable grounds in conflating past kingdoms and current nationalisms. Yet it is a subtle subversion for her to locate herself as an inside "national" interpreter of state policy rather than a passive "local" object of policy. The politics of such subver-sive positionings fuel debates about the local.

Uma Adang is not alone here. I met no other Meratus leaders with "Majapahit" adat, but others claimed the adat of the post-Majapahit Ban-jar kingdoms. Some leaders argued that adat is, by definition, an instance of contemporary national law. One man told me that Meratus marriage adat was the same as the recently passed national marriage law: The fact that he knew none of the details of the national law merely exemplified, for him, the difficulties of properly creating order in an out-of-the-way place. If adat and government standards are, in principle, identical, he is a state spokesman, not a subaltern. This common Meratus leadership strategy has contradictory results. It is a tactic for claiming cultural citi-zenship within a framework that makes local communities mute objects of administration; yet it also reaffirms state authority as a prerequisite for political speech while silencing those without claim to a state connection.

Administrators never seriously consider Meratus claims for the re-gional legitimacy of their adat. Indonesian social scientists describe Mera-

tus adat as a local "traditional culture" that state development policy must work to overcome. In insisting that their adat is an extension of state administration, Meratus leaders contest the stereotypes of administrators and anthropologists, creating cross talk and misunderstanding both between and within political discourses identified as international, national, regional, or local. This creative space of misunderstanding is the subject of much of this book. Here, Uma Adang is an excellent guide.

These kinds of specification are necessary to introduce Meratus perspectives on marginality. Yet Third World detail is often classified by metropolitan readers as "description" that can be skipped as one searches for the "theory." These reading practices need a few prods, just as familiar notions of theory are ready for a change.

The most exciting challenge for the rapidly emerging field of cultural studies, I think, is to move beyond its roots in Eurocentric literary criticism and philosophy and participate in a cultural dialogue that crosses professional, ethnic, and national boundaries between the West and the Third World. This challenge requires turning one's back on the analytic distinction between theory and ethnography, in which the former looks out confidently from the particularized and unself-conscious world of the latter. The European canon is inadequate as the sole source of analytic insight for cultural studies; cultural studies scholars take part, willingly or otherwise, in complex global conversations which take into account European desires, but which also exceed them. These conversations involve everyday axioms, popular movements, and political and commercial campaigns, as well as academic dialogue. A starting point for careful participation in these conversations is the recognition that theories cannot be abstracted from global positioning.

Theories stimulate critical awareness of the assumptions of research and writing. What makes this awareness *critical* is self-conscious engagement with local struggles for power and meaning. By "local," I do not mean to invoke tiny bounded communities, but rather acts of positioning within particular contexts. The scholar's local, critical awareness is stimulated in interaction with other local commentaries and understanding, with their own forms of critical awareness. Scholarly theory cannot be separated from local dilemmas and propositions which it engages in dialogue.

Locally engaged theory is eclectic, not exotic, theory. To discuss Meratus marginality it is not necessary to use some special, cordoned-off knowledge called "Meratus theory." Transcultural conversations sensibly make use of fragments of whatever theories are available; I see no reason not to make use of European theories. Yet there is also no reward here for pursuing the coherence of an approach to its logical end, a common goal of earlier theory building.[15] Locally engaged theory can take various pieces of classic approaches and apply them in addressing particular intellectual challenges. Theory is situated as it engages with locally specified puzzles.

Attention to theory requires attention to writing. As scholars have discussed the political construction of knowledge, ethnographic writing has become a focus of intellectual debate not only among anthropologists but among cultural critics more widely. My work joins that of many anthropologists who are reexamining the colonial heritage that shapes modes of cultural representation, and who have embarked on experimental projects to disrupt disciplinary conventions that link domination and description. The theoretical edge of this work lies as much in how the story is told as it does in its conclusion.

If the links between anthropological convention and modes of domination were singular and simple, the task of creating new, critical ethnographies would be as straightforward as criticism of the problems of any given orientalist text. However, ethnographies have been shaped by a host of problematic and contradictory influences, and the key political issues reflected in modes of representation vary by areas of the world, eras of history, and particular, conflicting genres and agendas.

Thus, in writing about South Kalimantan, I find myself confronting a variety of troublesome conventions. White male adventurers continue to write of their travels to dusky Bornean jungles to find themselves amidst the seductions of fast-growing vines and sloe-eyed women. In contrast, proper British-sounding ethnographers (mostly from Australia and the United States) carefully erase these images as they describe the neat structures of local propriety. Here, a colonial panopticism too well-seated to mention its force or philandering invokes the neutral eye/I of science. Ecological activists argue for the conservation of Bornean rainforests based on images of nature-loving primitive tribes. Such images of primitive conservatism are also used by developers to prove the necessity for progress in the form of forced resettlement and export-oriented resource expropriation. In this context, any singular representational theory confirms some power-laden conventions as much as it denies others. Instead, the guerilla tactics of multiple, uneasily jostling theories and stories can at least disrupt the smug assumptions of comfortably settled monologics. In this book, I attempt a writing strategy in which curiosity is not overwhelmed by coherence.

This book piles up stories that do not fit with each other easily. In my shifts of tone, personal involvement, and narrative style, I aim to present cultural frameworks without suggesting their homogeneity or unquestioned hegemony. I use and discard fragments of currently popular theories. These textual strategies are intended to counter the exoticizing techniques of earlier ethnographies while, at the same time, opening other possibilities for attending to cultural difference.

My project is guided especially by feminist critiques and revisions of ethnography. Contemporary feminist ethnographies are critical experiments to the extent that they both invoke and criticize dominant representations of culture. On the one hand, feminist anthropologists have used "local meanings" to expose and contest theories that universalize male and female standpoints; they have stressed the importance of situating women and men in the context of the particular ideas and practices that create "male" and "female" interests and identities (for example, Strathern 1988; M. Rosaldo 1980). On the other hand, feminists cannot be satisfied with the homogenizing perspectives of cultural authorities. Feminists have exposed the gender dynamics in which "official stories" of culture are told—whether by anthropologists or by their senior male informants. Recent feminist work in anthropology increasingly has attended to local critiques and dissatisfaction with prevalent gender arrangements—in "subordinate discourses" (Boddy 1989; Abu-Lughod 1986); emergent social movements (Ong 1987; Ginsburg 1989); and individual subversions (Martin 1987). By their complex self-positioning and uneasy authority, feminist authors have stimulated attention to gendered negotiations of meaning and power, illuminating and challenging the fixed alterities—West and Other—of classic ethnographic texts.

In attending to critical female perspectives, Marilyn Strathern's *The Gender of the Gift* (1988) is an important caution against easy assumptions: that women everywhere are the same; that women's speech reveals a "woman's point of view"; that women always speak from the gender identity of "woman." Strathern stresses the necessity of investigating the forms of power and discourse framed by the exclusions and oppositions of gender; these become the starting point for discussing both the "femaleness" and the "agency" of any woman's agency.

In working with Meratus, my opening has been the mutual embeddedness of gender, ethnicity, and political status. The three are mutually constituted. State politics shape ethnic and regional identity and are, in turn, informed by them. State and ethnic politics are gendered just as gender difference is created through state and ethnic discourse. Yet each of the three creates divided dispositions that destabilize the communities of interest formed by the other two. The state's concentric model of political status both orders and disturbs the dualism of gender and of ethnic differentiation. Gender difference breaks up ethnic unity and stimulates divergent attitudes toward the state. By treating women and men as individual commentators on their culture, I ask about disruptive as well as unifying features of their perspectives without assuming gender, ethnic, or political homogeneities.

What difference does it make that Uma Adang is a woman? What difference does it make that she is a community leader? Uma Adang's perspectives are not identical to those of Meratus male leaders nor to those of other Meratus women—and even less to those of women globally. Yet her insights draw attention to the specificity of gender and ethnic dilemmas. Uma Adang's creativity draws from her contradictions as a politically ambitious Meratus woman.

Uma Adang does not fit Western stereotypes of ambitious feminists crashing through traditional rules. Her practice—which, in fact, involves inventing "traditional rules"—has evolved within the specific subtleties of Meratus gender asymmetries. Meratus women are not formally excluded from political participation. I saw no all-male spaces; I heard no aphorisms of female limitation. In much daily discourse, women and men are called similar or complementary coworkers. Women and men work together in growing rice, the center of Meratus livelihood. Adat rules do not differentiate women and men—for example, as inheritors of trees. Or they contrast male and female as equal complements (for instance, as husband and wife with similar marital rights). Most of the Meratus I asked did not rule out the possibility that women could be political leaders; yet most leaders are men, in part because men are better able to present themselves as transcending local vulnerabilities. Men have an easier time than women showing themselves brave and articulate enough to confront, turn, and tap external spiritual and political powers, including those of the state. In the process they create the prowess that is local leadership (see Tsing 1990).

To show herself a leader, Uma Adang fiddles with Meratus concepts of gender as well as with visions of leadership. Her strategy has been to stress adat rules, carrying adat to a daily prominence far beyond what it has in other Meratus communities. (The bizarre formality of my welcome reflected this invigorated adat.) Part of this plan is a separate-but-equal gender segregation. Uma Adang imagines a tradition of "female shamanism" that complements men's efforts. In meetings, she has women sit on one side of the room and men on the other. In most Meratus settings, community politics informally shapes a different spatial patterning: Ambitious men form an engaged central circle, with women and disinterested men in short, peripheral lines. (Children scatter themselves all around.) In Uma Adang's ideal plan, she need not break into the men's circle; with formal gender lines, she sits sedately in the center, between the women and the men.

Uma Adang's ability to argue convincingly for these schemes draws from the regional legitimacy of Banjar standards. Banjar gender arrangements contrast sharply with Meratus arrangements: Women and men socialize separately; women are out of place in many political and religious settings; people generalize easily about male and female attributes. Uma Adang borrows the prestige of Banjar ideas about the relation between propriety and gender segregation; yet she must scramble around the derogatory implications of Banjar segregation for women. In Banjar settings, women sit at the back of the house as men entertain guests in the front; men and women are not separated side by side.

These are not easy discrepancies to resolve, and they draw Uma Adang into a flurry of contradictions around the gender consequences of her leadership. Her leadership requires continual revision as it argues for and against local expectations about gender, ethnicity, and state power.

This book is divided into three sections. In the first, "Politics of the Periphery," I explore the imaginative responses of community leaders in a dialogue with regional authorities on the terms of political subjectivity. I show how these regional responses stimulate divisions (particularly gender divisions) within Meratus communities. The second section, "A Science of Travel," examines the local practices and forms of knowledge that shape the terms of Meratus regional marginality. I argue that travel links local and regional concerns at the same time that it creates caesuras along lines of gender, ethnicity, and political status. In the third section, "Riding the Horse of Gaps," I turn to individual women's commentaries about their culture, especially about asymmetries of gender and ethnicity. I find these commentaries especially useful in thinking about how extraordinary viewpoints illuminate cultural dynamics.

This book is framed, here and at the end, by a discussion of the movement led by the charismatic Uma Adang. I found Uma Adang's eccentric, playful perspectives enormously clarifying. Yet one educated Indonesian, to whom I played a recording of one of her speeches, responded: "She's crazy." Even without knowing her local context—in which she is not considered crazy—he must have seen how she struck at powerful vulnerabilities in the structure of authority, for he added: "She should be arrested." Uma Adang's parodic skill helped me see the gaps in regionally dominant ideologies, at the same time that I learned to appreciate Meratus understandings of the unpredictabilities, absurdities, enormous power disparities, and creative openings in their regional political status. Thus, Uma Adang's movement is both an introduction and an exemplification of the themes of this book.

Uma Adang is not a deviant among the normal, nor a lone innovator among traditionalists. I do not intend a Durkheimian analysis in which strangeness reaffirms the norm. I introduce her because she taught me about cultural negotiations in which *every* Meratus participates. The more I turned away from a search for a unified "Meratus culture," the more creative and unusual were the intersections I learned from: women who intruded on men's domains, adult bachelors with many homes, Muslims "gone Dayak," respected leaders with no one to lead. Even a staid, respectable village head began to look like an impossible acrobat juggling civilization and savagery. My encounter with Uma Adang encourages me to begin from the marginal—not to head back to an imagined center, but to extend my account toward other marginalities.

Like the Diamond Queen, I first arrived in the Meratus Mountains from the west and hiked to the east. Unlike the Diamond Queen, I went back and forth across the mountains, and I eventually returned to the United States. I generally entered and left the area from the west side, where I lived with another of my Meratus mentors, the great shaman Awat Kilay, whose work I describe in chapters 5 and 6. I studied shamanship with Awat Kilay, who often told me that I would meet spiritual guides in my dreams who would continue my apprenticeship when we were far apart. One night before I left his place I dreamt that I met an old man who began to teach me hidden sciences and spiritually charged names. Awat Kilay's teachings had finally taken root. He was pleased the next day as he told me that his sponsorship would continue as I would learn in dreams or spirit encounters the words and names through which we accept, control, or position ourselves in relation to power and knowledge.

Awat Kilay himself had travelled everywhere around the region and survived several rounds of political terror. His sponsorship, like that of Uma Adang, opened my thinking about mobility and marginality. Even in the dreams he helped me toward, I would learn to glimpse that domination and discourse that shapes our lives, although we are barely able to trace its source or wider effects. In the long time it has taken me to compose this book, I hope I have maintained some tie to this guidance—and its perspective on survival as creative living on the edge.

PART ONE POLITICS OF

THE PERIPHERY

". . . dressed all in black, dressed all in green":
Spirits, like soldiers, militarize the everyday
landscape. Here, the spirits are rice-flour
offering cakes.

Central to the problem of this book is an unintended Meratus challenge: Everyday Meratus existence offends official ideals of order and development. Two aspects of official definitions are crucial to Meratus negotiations of their political status. First, national political culture encourages portrayals of the Meratus as stuck in a timeless, archaic condition outside modern history. Second, this same official framework shows Meratus mobility across the landscape—as well as the limited accessibility of the forested mountain landscape for administrative travellers—as cause and consequence of their disorderly, precivilized character.

On the whole, it seems fair to say that Meratus reject the notion that they are outside history, or that their relation to the state and its "civilization" is new. Instead, they invoke a long, continuous succession of rule in which contemporary state policies are a minor variant. Their responses to state initiatives draw on this history—arguing for its relevance even as their arguments go unrecognized by government officials. Similarly, Meratus imply that mobility, rather than isolating them, increases their access to external power and knowledge. Meratus interpretations refuse the state's implied contrast between administrators' rights to unhampered mobility and the necessity of an immobilized subject population.

This section introduces state rule in the Meratus Mountains. I describe "the state" and "the Meratus" as coherent, stable social elements because it is within such an imagined opposition that particular government officials and particular Meratus begin contemporary political negotiations.

Very different kinds of "states" have ruled in southeastern Kalimantan. Between the fourteenth and nineteenth centuries, various kingdoms claimed sovereignty. In the nineteenth and early twentieth centuries, the area came under Dutch colonial rule. Since 1949, the Meratus Mountains have been part of the Indonesian nation-state. Each of these "states" offered a different technology of rule.[1] Dutch colonialism, for example, invented "ethnic" differentiation as a feature of political administration; the earlier kingdoms seem to have sponsored a much more fluid traffic in cultural difference.[2] The Dutch codified adat law and stabilized communal boundaries.[3] They also built roads, established administrative boundaries, and introduced the conceptual grids for maps and censuses. These have continued to inform the Indonesian nation-state, even as it has sponsored new involvements with national political consciousness.[4]

Meratus Dayaks have been so peripheral to each of these designs of power that until recently they were barely noticed by regional centers. The classic Banjar chronicles fail to mention marginal populations.[5] Dutch accounts note the Meratus only as scattered and untroublesome survivors of many years of Banjar influence.[6] No longer authentic, their customs were hardly worth codifying. Ironically, under national rule, a number of reports have appeared in which the Meratus finally have become an authentic savage object.[7] Yet these reports only push Meratus farther to the margin of nation-building.

From a vantage point in the Meratus Mountains, continuities in state power over time become more apparent than the distinctions between eras. First, several centuries of state policies support a divide between Banjar and Meratus and an asymmetrical forest-products trade; Banjar funnel Meratus products to extra-regional sources. Second, Meratus leaders have long been assigned formal titles in state bureaucracies, to which they owe sporadic ritual submission. On occasion, states demand tribute in local products. Third, Meratus lands have been the ground of varied military operations, and the military has long been among the key contacts between Meratus and the state. These continuities are important within Meratus perspectives; I use them to introduce Meratus history in slightly fuller detail before returning to contemporary New Order policies.

Like Dayaks throughout southern Kalimantan, Meratus have long collected forest products for world markets. Before European control of the area, kingdoms in the Barito River delta and on the east coast attempted to regulate this trade. Court centers in the region first developed during the fourteenth century, perhaps under the sponsorship of the Javanese kingdom of Majapahit.[8] By the late sixteenth century, a harbor-oriented "Banjar" kingdom in the Barito River delta had grown to considerable regional power. This kingdom, in alliance with the Javanese state of Demak, sponsored conversions to Islam. This began the process in which Islam and court history became central to the identity of those who came to be called "Banjar."[9] "Dayaks" are those outside of Islam and its political sponsorship—but not outside regional political and economic relations.

As the Banjar kingdom expanded with the state-sponsored spread of pepper plantations in the seventeenth and eighteenth centuries, "Dayaks" were either incorporated or pushed back from Banjar centers.[10] The rough hills of the Meratus Mountains form an island surrounded by Banjar expansion. Even as pepper came to predominate the kingdom's trade revenues, however, Dayak-gathered forest products remained important; the state's harbor control created a Banjar-middleman role in this trade.[11] Some Meratus still have eighteenth-century European coins from this trade. Meratus oral histories variously mention ritual tributes to the Banjar kingdom or the smaller courts of the east coast. By the early nineteenth century, a few Meratus areas were paying tribute in gold; the clay excavations where people dug to gold-bearing gravel remain to remind current residents of these taxes.[12]

During the eighteenth and nineteenth centuries, the Dutch became increasingly interested in controlling southern Kalimantan.[13] European and Indonesian sources tend to disagree, however, on just when and how Dutch control was accomplished. European and North American sources note that a Banjar sultan ceded all Kalimantan territories except the central area of the kingdom to the Dutch East India Company in 1787, and that the Dutch colonial government abolished the Banjar sultanate entirely in 1860.[14] Many Kalimantan sources do not find the former treaty significant and point out that Dutch attempts at takeover in the nineteenth century stimulated a war in which the last Banjar patriots only surrendered in 1905.[15] The year 1905 also marked the Dutch abolition of the last small southeast coast kingdoms, rarely mentioned in European histories.[16] In either case, Meratus remained peripheral subjects.

Dutch colonial rule was accompanied by new export-production schemes. Rubber was first planted in South Kalimantan in 1904; by the 1920s, the area had become rich with rubber in every sense.[17] (Photographs from this period show Banjar markets jammed with shiny new cars.)[18] Banjar pressed into the western Meratus foothills with rubber plantings, pushing back Meratus settlement. The worldwide depression of the 1930s, however, hit rubber producers severely. In 1934, the Dutch joined a transnational rubber-regulation program to limit production.[19] Despite low prices, the succeeding few years were important in stimulat-

ing rubber-growing by Meratus in the foothills. Dutch officials slowed
the expansion of Banjar holdings in the foothills. Meratus gained a share
of planting and sales quotas. (Older foothill Meratus remember a "Mr.
Coupon" [*Tuan Kupun*] who handed out the quotas.) Meratus were also
hit by a colonial head tax, in the 1930s, which was paid in cash; this
encouraged them to engage in cash-crop production as well as wage
labor.[20] Some Meratus worked in Japanese pepper plantations on the
southeast coast to meet their taxes. As World War II approached, however, the plantation owners were recalled to Japan, and their Meratus
workers returned to the mountains.

The Japanese returned to invade Kalimantan in 1942, from the southeast coast, and maintained bases east of the Meratus Mountains throughout most of the war. Japanese troops marched back and forth across the
mountains to the populous west-side centers of regional administration.
(Meratus variously remember their alien discipline, their hiking sticks,
their condoms.) Yet this was neither the first nor the last military disruption in the Meratus Mountains. In the Dutch–Banjar war of the late nineteenth century, Banjar forces took refuge in the mountains.[21] Before this,
the soldiers of the Banjar courts, as well as Dayak raiders, sought mountain victims for head-taking or other sacrifices.[22] After World War II,
when the Allies returned Kalimantan to the Netherland Indies Civil Administration (NICA), the mountains remained an arena of military action
as anticolonial nationalist Banjar moved into the hills and were followed
by NICA forces.[23]

The Republic of Indonesia won full independence in 1949. By the mid-
1950s, another military interaction had permeated the mountains: Islam-
inspired anti-Jakarta rebels established guerilla bases in the eastern Meratus "jungle" and crisscrossed the mountains, running from government
troops and connecting with supportive Banjar villagers to both the west
and the east.[24] The rebellion was finally subdued in 1965. This was also
the year in which the army launched operations against the Indonesian
Communist Party and its supporters; a few Meratus in the western foothills were imprisoned (along with Banjar and other Dayaks) during this
campaign. By the late 1960s, outspoken dissidence and rebellion in the
region had been quelled. However, the armed forces remained promi-
nently visible throughout the 1970s and 80s. Every Banjar town large
enough to support a weekly market also has an armed forces post.

Postcolonial administrative intervention in the Meratus area was sporadic until the 1970s, when state expansion into the Meratus area became

more sustained. In the 1970s, the Suharto regime responded to international pressure by taking more direct military and economic control of the country's remote and resource-rich corners. Rainforest timbering has become an important development sector, with concessions falling under the control of army generals and their business partners.[25] Meanwhile, armed resistance to state expansion in East Timur and Irian Jaya has served as a continuing reminder of the possibility of rebellion in rural and even "tribal" areas.[26]

In this context, several state agendas for the Meratus Mountains have emerged. First, forested areas were divided into timber concessions. (By the late 1970s, the east side was being logged; much of the west side was, from colonial times, a watershed-protection area. Despite this, by the mid-1980s, logging was moving rapidly through west-side forests.) Second, new sites for Javanese transmigration were opened. (Several sites were located in South Kalimantan; I am unaware of any currently within the area of Meratus settlement.) Both programs assume the area as unpopulated; a third program, however, targeted local people. This is the government program for the Management of Isolated Populations, who are to be moved into resettlement villages, making forested land available for national priorities. "Disorderly" farming practices—that is, shifting cultivation—are to be controlled for reasons of both order and development.[27]

By the early 1980s, the western foothills of the Meratus Mountains were the site of about a dozen resettlement villages.[28] Meratus resettlement had a number of direct, immediate consequences. First, it opened the foothills to Banjar immigration, through state guarantees of services and "free" land. Second, it hastened degradation of foothill forests to brush and grassland by setting up densely contiguous farming plots and rapid cycling of swiddens and forest regrowth. Third, it formed pockets of dangerous health conditions, as Meratus were encouraged to eliminate, wash, and drink from the same crowded streams. Fourth, it laid the groundwork for dispossessing Meratus of land and forest resources by stressing the powerlessness of the Meratus in relation to state policy.

Other changes were perceived locally as benefits. Some children were attending school. New, closer periodic markets were set up. And resettlement residents had the political advantage of being described as models of state cooperation rather than as renegades. These political advantages sometimes sparked considerable enthusiasm about participation in "development."

In the 1980s, police and administrators only rarely ventured beyond the motor vehicle roads that ended at the borders of the Meratus area. Officials defined the Meratus area in relation to their own awkward, incomplete penetration; for most, hiking in the Meratus Mountains was uncomfortable, frightening, and confusing. Yet state officials assumed that Meratus ranged freely through the area. Thus, they constructed a gulf of inaccessibility between the "civilized" and the "nomadic"—albeit a gulf structured into zones of more or less reachable destinations. The possibilities for supervision, taxation, law and order, and development—as well as the very definition of the Meratus as a group of not-yet-citizens—were understood by state officials in relation to the difficulty of administrative travel.

Almost all the Meratus I knew travelled extensively. In contrast to the state stereotype of Meratus nomadism, however, Meratus travel did not assume an undifferentiated landscape. For each traveller, some places were more familiar and socially accessible than others. Meratus understandings of the social landscape begin with the notion of unevenness in the ease with which one travels to particular places. Great travellers—shamans and political leaders—are distinguished by their ability to forge links with less and less familiar places of power and knowledge as they overcome the dangers of travel.

Taken together, these various understandings and practices of travel (one could add those of Banjar pioneers, traders, and the occasional tourist or anthropologist) make up what one might call, following Foucault, a semio-technology of power and knowledge. The meanings and mechanics of difficult hiking anchor debates and discussions of Meratus marginality; they create this marginality as a contested domain. Travel shapes state interpretations of the Meratus and Meratus interpretations of the state.

The travel orientation of the administrative gaze can be seen, for example, in the construction of a "zoned" Meratus social geography. Resettlement policy and the extension of more direct government control has affected the entire Meratus area, though unevenly. Even in areas rarely visited by officials, Meratus have responded to the threats and promises of state expansion, but not in the same ways as those more regularly observed. Indeed, state expansion has re-inscribed the division of the Meratus area into three separate zones of administrative reach.

The western foothills are an area of nucleated settlements, many of them set up to copy or comply with the government's resettlement model. (In some river valleys, however, Meratus live in collective halls that house

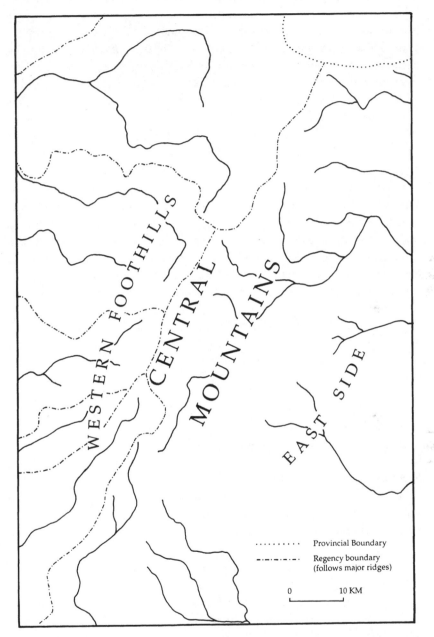

The Meratus Mountains

up to thirty families.) There are a few areas of scattered settlement, with houses on fields; given state demands, this has been hard to maintain. The western foothills are the most densely populated Meratus area. Tropical grass fields and young brush are common where rubber or bamboo— both cash crops—have not been planted. Government schools are found in or near some resettlement villages; a few children travel to Christian schools.[29] Police/army posts and weekly markets tend to be only a few hours' hike away; by the mid-1980s, new weekly markets were being started in the foothills. Anxiety about land claims had risen with Banjar immigration and more concentrated Meratus settlement. Legal cases, sorcery cases, and experiments with intensive agriculture were on the rise.

In contrast, the easier terrain but more remote location of the east side supported bigger, wilder, and more mature forests—until the logging companies arrived. In the early 1980s, there was still considerable forest, including valuable ironwood (*Eusideroxylon zwageri*) for Meratus to cut and sell. Meratus settlements in this area are strung along the trails—"so the government can see the people," as one local leader explained. Here, too, there are some government and Christian schools, and weekly markets and police/army posts are available to reach and return from in one day. In the 1980s, new administrative centers followed the logging roads inland, providing additional government outposts and attracting a wave of west-side Banjar. But here Banjar join Bugis and Dusun Dayaks in a somewhat more pluralistic ethnic climate.

Finally, in the central mountains, the steepest and least supervised area, settlement is almost always scattered. Dispersion has been, among other things, a way of staying out of the way of the state. The central mountains area is well forested, with a patchwork of secondary and mature rain-forest spotted with isolated swiddens and swidden clusters. In this area Meratus build their houses next to their fields, moving every two years or so as old fields are abandoned and new fields become too far from the house for convenience. Although there have been a few experiments with schoolteachers, none has lasted long. To attend school, a child must join relatives on the west or east side. Police and army officers come through a few times a year. A trip to market—or to vote in elections—takes several days of hiking.[30]

Travel across these zones is constant, although, as I have suggested, it is differentiated and irregular. Such travel is a central concern of this book. Yet I have also attempted to position the individuals and events described in terms of the distinctive dynamics of particular zones, for the imaginative shape of political engagement differs in each zone. I spent most of my fieldwork in the central mountains, and my generalizations most often refer to this area. However, what I learned on the west and east sides of the mountains is essential to the issues I raise. Indeed, Uma Adang's creative teachings from the east-side Meratus–Banjar border area drew my attention to the regional mappings of difference and power that commonly but variously engage all Meratus.

1 MARGINAL FICTIONS

Child of the soldiers,
Where are you gone to?
Buy me the cigarettes
called Dubiang Baru.

It is a love song, often sung as a lullaby. A woman's voice addresses a handsome young man, calling him a soldier to give him glamour, power, money, and knowledge of far places. No Meratus are soldiers, but in the love songs that romanticize them, all Meratus young men become soldiers or members of survey teams or coastal birds chancing into the mountains. Young men are most beautiful as travelling strangers, transient Others to whose grace familiar folk can only aspire.

Such love songs introduce an important Meratus insight into the paradoxical links between marginality and mobility: Men's travel both inscribes and erases the difference between powerful outsiders and vulnerable local people. The travelling Meratus bachelor is as glamorous as a soldier; yet, he is not a soldier. His free-spirited travel and romantic song is what makes the power and subservience of the soldier's more disciplined march forever beyond his reach.

As a traveller in the mountains, I too was sometimes offered the gender-crossed glamour of the powerful stranger. Just as I have learned to see this as one interpretation of my fieldwork, I have also been challenged to represent Meratus within these insights about marginality and mobility. The love song's frankly admiring gaze at the Other serves here as a reminder of the specificity and limitations of conventional anthropological claims about cultural description: The ethnographic gaze is said to be neutral and value-free, even as it situates itself in a European tradition in which to be Other is always to be excluded from full membership in humanity. Meratus love songs offer a radically different perspective on cultural differentiation. The Other is praised from below rather than exoticized from above. With other Meratus self-typifications, the love song refuses "objectivity" as it draws attention to passionate and relentless negotiations of difference and deference. In this chapter I explore issues of cultural identity as they require examination of Meratus discussions and "fictions" of ethnicity. I begin with ethnic terminology as a point of engagement between Meratus ethnic dialogues and my own writing practices. Then I turn to Meratus negotiations of marginality and the way in which these negotiations shaped my fieldwork and the analysis presented in this book.

Naming

Who are the Meratus Dayaks? This seems a straightforward question with which to begin an ethnography. Yet, every answer I have raises new questions as it leads to the interweaving of my representations with those of the Meratus men and women I met. I can begin, for example, with my responsibility for the term *Meratus*. I chose this ethnogeographic label together with Bingan Sabda, a Meratus man who, like myself, at the time was a graduate student.

Anthropologists are not expected to *choose* names for the groups they study; conventionally understood, our job is to pick the most authentic label of local identity. Yet none of the ethnic terms available for describing the Dayak people of the Meratus Mountains is particularly "authentic." The most prevalent terms used by those who write are considered derogatory and insulting by the Meratus I know. Colonial travellers followed the Meratus' Banjar neighbors and used *Bukit*, with its connotation of "hillbilly." Contemporary government bureaucrats label them *suku terasing*, "isolated tribe."[1] Bingan Sabda and I wanted to avoid these labels, yet be able to write about culture and social life in the Meratus Mountains. Mr. Sabda was, to my knowledge, the first Meratus to gain a postgraduate education. Tragically, he died in a plane accident soon after he finished his master's degree, as he was preparing to take up his first teaching position. I am left alone with our choice.

Originally, I liked the label *Meratus Dayaks* because it refers to Dayak inhabitants of the Meratus Mountains. Bingan Sabda liked the term for a different reason; to him, *Meratus*, with its root *ratus* ("hundreds"), evoked the diversity of the people. He explained it as a kind of anti-ethnic label, a label for a group of people who are all very different from each other. I have appreciated the term's disruptive edge of diversity more and more as I have tried to describe my fieldwork without false homogeneities. Yet I am also aware that my choice to use this ethnic label, or any ethnic label, exists within a political field. Many Meratus I knew did not want to be marked by an ethnic label, since their experiences of labelling had been negative. Others such as Uma Adang campaigned for ethnic pride in the face of Banjar devaluations. Choosing among these positions is not just a matter of factions; each individual's stance shifted eclectically in various contexts. In making my choice to speak of Meratus, I take a position with limitations as well as strengths; yet the term offers a beginning, not a boundary, for analysis.

The asymmetries that marginalize the Meratus in South Kalimantan involve not just ethnic discourses but also administrative practices and regional economic divisions. A history of regional asymmetries has decentralized Meratus politics; Meratus have become oriented outward toward the authority of surrounding Banjar centers of power. Meratus negotiations of cultural identity begin from this asymmetry but do not end in its passive acceptance. Meratus cultivate dispersal as a form of autonomy and form multiple, shifting alliances through which to negotiate marginality. In this process, the diversity and flexibility of cultural identities—Sabda's "hundreds" in the "Hundred-ing [Meratus] Mountains"—have flourished. The next sections elaborate each of these themes.

Regional asymmetry

The issue of ethnic contrasts that identify the Meratus as distinctive is viewed by both Meratus and Banjar in the context of political, economic, and cultural asymmetries. The "facts" of Meratus difference are contested political issues, and it is impossible to offer a neutral description. As I introduce the Meratus cultural situation, every scientific statement contains its own destabilizing critique.

Banjar and Meratus speak closely related Malayic dialects. While my language work and informal listening suggest this simple assessment, almost no one in South Kalimantan would agree with it; it ignores the negotiation of language differences. Banjar are convinced of profound racial and cultural differences which divide them from Meratus ("They're our American Indians," cosmopolitan Banjar said to me, situating themselves with white Americans). In contrast, many Meratus deny difference. Banjar claim that the Meratus language is unintelligible to them; Meratus are more likely to argue that they speak exactly the same language.

"All Kalimantan people speak the same language," argued a respected Meratus elder as we hiked out of the mountains. He urged
me away from the Banjar villagers with whom I was discussing kinship terms; they would be the same as the Meratus ones I already
knew, he assured me. Actually, I elicited different terms than those
used by my Meratus host.

Conversely, even border-area Banjar in everyday contact with Meratus
told me they could not understand a word of Meratus speech. I often
heard Banjar make fun of words they identified as distinctively Meratus;
then I heard them use these same words unself-consciously in their own
speech. Border-area Meratus, copying a Banjar stance, claimed they
could not understand those who lived further into the mountains despite
constant social interchange between these areas—as well as the denial by
mountain people of any speech variation. Mountain people, in turn,
make fun of those from other neighborhoods for their *really* hick forms
of speech. "Those people from X are truly Bukit!" someone might say,
slighting them with the term with which Banjar insult all Meratus.
Clearly, questions of language and dialect are politically charged issues in
this area.[2]

Banjar are Muslims; Meratus are not. This lopsided contrast is sustained in definition by the fact that a Meratus Dayak who converts to
Islam becomes a Banjar (*masuk Malayu*), at least for many purposes. A
small proportion of Meratus are Christians. What religion are the others?
Meratus practice shamanism, conduct elegant rice-field rituals, and construct elaborate cosmologies. But in the context of regional asymmetry,
the most direct answer is "not Islam."

Religion in Indonesia is as much a matter of state policy as individual
belief. Every citizen is expected to believe in a singular God (*Tuhan Yang
Maha Esa*) and to belong to one of six officially recognized religions:
Islam, Buddhism, Catholicism, Protestantism, Hindu-Bali, and Confucianism. Minorities that ignore this expectation can expect official harassment instead of state services.[3] For example, in South Kalimantan it is
difficult to attend school without choosing either Islam (for state schools)
or Christianity (for missionary schools).

Proud of their Islamic piety, Banjar see their religion as supporting
basic claims to citizenship and regional status, as well as a sometimes
critical perspective on national policy. In contrast, state discourse on religion encourages a view of the Meratus as primitives who "do not yet have
religion" (*belum beragama*). Meratus argue against this, claiming theo-

logical similarities between Islam and Meratus beliefs, or sometimes the priority or superiority of Meratus beliefs. But the conjunction of state policy and ethnic domination compels Meratus to judge their beliefs and practices in relation to Islam.

Many issues of daily life—food, etiquette, gender, sexuality, and curing practices—are implicated in this asymmetric interethnic dialogue. For example, Banjar do not accept food-oriented hospitality from Meratus, nor do they offer food to them, because Meratus eat pork, which is forbidden to Muslims. Meratus provide travelling Banjar with raw vegetables and rice for the latter to cook in their own pots; but they receive no reciprocal generosity in Banjar villages and towns. Yet Meratus sometimes laugh at Banjar prejudice, reversing its barbs. Here, for example, a Meratus boy mocks the Islamic declaration of faith (*La-illaha illa-Allah, wa Muhamada rasul-Allah*):

> *Illah-illah illallah*
> *Makan bayi buruk disabalah.*

> Illah-illah illallah
> Eating rotten pork on the other side.

Meratus and Banjar are both disadvantaged minorities in the national and international political economy. This is an important step back from regional tensions. Robison (1986) draws the contours of a Javanese, Chinese Indonesian, foreign transnational alliance of political and financial clout that had come to dominate Indonesian capitalism by the 1980s; here, both Banjar and Meratus are small fry. Leslie Potter's research on rural Banjar (1992) shows how Banjar, like Meratus, are pushed around, resettled, and "developed" according to the whims of national policy. Potter describes how Banjar are compared unfavorably with Javanese migrants in regional policy formulations.[4] Yet this is difficult to remember within the noisily subsuming conventions of the markets, police posts, and district offices that surround the Meratus Mountains. The state and the international economy most often appear in Meratus lives with a Banjar face.

Banjar are middlemen in the regional economy. Particularly since the 1970s, when Chinese Indonesians were banned from rural areas, Banjar have dominated buying and selling at the small weekly markets at the ends of the roads (and navigable rivers) that lead into the mountains. Meratus hike or raft down to these markets, where they sell rattan, rubber, peanuts, mung beans, ironwood, bamboo, incense woods, wax, and numerous other minor crops and forest products. They buy clothing, salt, metal tools, and a few luxuries. Meratus complain heartily about the asymmetric conditions of expensive buying and cheap, unpredictable selling; yet they have no alternatives. Young Meratus men sometimes buy a few extra blocks of salt or sarongs to peddle in the mountains. Meratus, however, are discouraged from expanding either trade in manufactured goods or wholesaling their own products by *ethnic* disadvantages: inability to get credit from Banjar dealers; estrangement from Banjar owners of trucks, motorboats, rubber smokehouses, and warehouses; lack of networks for getting capital, storage facilities, and places to stay in Banjar towns; limited access to Banjar expertise about marketing conditions; etc. Although Banjar eventually pass many Meratus products to extraregional entrepreneurs, Meratus learn their global economic vulnerability from Banjar traders.

Meratus also know the regional state bureaucracy through Banjar. Higher-level officials in South Kalimantan tend to be Javanese, but they rarely meet Meratus. District officers, police and army sector officers, and other rural officials who come in contact with Meratus are predominantly Banjar. This is the context in which Banjar proprieties (as Meratus understand them) take on a great deal of power, as they inform Meratus of the links among authority, administration, wealth, and culture.

Two brothers

One common idiom through which Meratus discuss ethnic difference with Banjar is the story of two ancestral brothers. The descendants of the older brother, Si Ayuh (or Sandayuhan), are the Meratus, whereas the Banjar are descendants of the younger brother, Bambang Basiwara. In this formulation, Meratus have the precedent of age; Banjar, however, have the advantage of a "big voice"—the younger brother's name. The Meratus I knew often told stories about the two brothers; yet the self-characterization is unexpectedly unflattering. It is Bambang Basiwara who is the clever, successful brother. Si Ayuh is neither stupid nor mean; but he has no sense of discipline, so he never achieves any kind of wealth or power. Both brothers, for example, had animals: Bambang Basiwara kept control over his—the domestic animals; Si Ayuh's animals all escaped into the forest and became wild game. Thus, Meratus hunt for their meat. God gave both brothers Holy Books, but Si Ayuh ate his. Thus Meratus look for spiritual inspiration within the body, without the guidance of the written word. One senses pride in the Meratus alternatives offered in these stories. Still, it is Bambang Basiwara who sets the standards of accomplishment.

The power of Bambang Basiwara's standards becomes even clearer in stories about the ability of the two brothers to bring home and share food. Si Ayuh brings home ghosts instead of game; Si Ayuh eats his family's entire meat distribution and has nothing but the pickings from his teeth to bring his wife. (As I heard it, this was considered funny, not shameful.) Si Ayuh's problem is one of self-control. His dilemmas are illustrated by the following story (presented here in synopsis) of the festival of the singing worms. (*Lingut*, which I translate as "singing worms," were described to me as large yellow worms that crawl around the branches of big forest trees at night. I never saw one, but I often heard their melodious notes coming from the trees after dark.)

Bambang Basiwara was castnet fishing. He went so far upstream that he didn't know the area; night fell. Suddenly, he heard the sound of drums. He followed the sound until, at last, he approached the noise of a big festival. It was the festival of the prince of the singing worms. [But the worms looked and acted like people.]

Bambang Basiwara was warmly greeted, invited inside the house, and offered cigarettes and betel. Putting his castnet and the fish he had caught in the rafters, he sat down to a delicious meal, then joined the all-night party. His hosts warned him not to fall sound asleep, because it was important that he leave for home well before dawn. "Our place is different by night and by day," they warned. Bambang Basiwara slept lightly and gathered his nets and fish before dawn. Before he left, he was given a generous distribution of the rice tubes and sweet rice cakes the hosts had made for their guests.

When he arrived home and distributed these treats, Si Ayuh wanted to know how he got them. Bambang Basiwara told him everything, and Si Ayuh set off immediately, castnet fishing to the head of the stream, waiting for night to fall, and following the sound of the drum to the festival. He, too, was invited into the house graciously, told to put his net and fish in the rafters, and served a delicious meal.

But Si Ayuh fell sound asleep. When his hosts tried to wake him before dawn, he groaned and went back to sleep. The gibbons called and the cocks crowed, but Si Ayuh did not stir. When he woke up well into the day, he was sleeping high above the ground in the branches of a tall forest tree. His castnet and fish were much higher still, entwined in the tree's crown. And his host had become a worm crawling in the tree's epiphytes. Frustrated, Si Ayuh smashed the worm. Never again did singing worms let humans come to their festivals.

Furthermore, it took three days for Bambang Basiwara to find Si Ayuh and build a scaffolding up the tree to help him down.

Among the Meratus I knew, Meratus self-characterizations as bumbling and unsuccessful did not inspire a uniform reaction. Ambitious Meratus leaders were presented with a contradiction: To rise above the disorder of Meratus life, they must be more like Bambang Basiwara than Si Ayuh. Yet their ties and loyalties remained with Si Ayuh to the extent that they loved the communities they would lead. In contrast, for those without this kind of ambition, the "Si Ayuh" characterization inspired a simpler and more lovingly self-deprecating humor.

The story reminds me of the contrasting styles of two brothers I knew in the central-mountain neighborhood of Rajang. The older brother, Ma Rani, is quiet and unpretentious to the point of awkwardness, while the younger brother, Ma Salam, is articulate and ambitious. Ma Salam is a neighborhood leader; Ma Rani is content to make comments from the sideline. Not surprisingly, perhaps, Ma Rani loves to tell folktales, including Si Ayuh stories. (The story above is Ma Rani's version.) I never heard Ma Salam tell a Si Ayuh story. The only folktales he loved were Banjar-style tales, less current among Meratus, telling of the poor boy who, despite obstacles, becomes king.

Yet it is Ma Salam, and not Ma Rani, who is consistently able to represent his community and its cultural identity to outsiders, whether non-Meratus or Meratus from other areas. Although I liked and admired Ma Rani, it was Ma Salam who became my close friend and consultant. While Ma Rani didn't always know what to say to me, Ma Salam sought me out as someone interesting to him, someone with foreign and fascinating knowledge from which he could learn. He was curious about everything I could impart to him, and he allowed me to bask in my own curiosity. He explored my equipment as I explored his house; we exchanged ideas on global geography and the reproduction of plants. When I spoke Indonesian, he tried to pick up new words to use in formal speech. And he begged me to teach him English.

What use was English, I wondered, where there were no English-speakers. But Ma Salam explained the power of language by telling me of an incident in his life. As a child, he had hiked to the market—three days away in a Banjar town. He was humiliated when he tried to buy a spool of thread by using the Meratus term for thread. The salesman looked at him as if he were crazy, although the thread was directly in front of him. Ma Salam never wanted to be caught again using hillbilly speech in town. As I came to understand the force of powerful knowledge, we began our English lessons.

Ma Salam worked hard to achieve a regional cultural literacy. He spent hours perfecting his signature—to make it appropriately unreadable—so he could sign letters without embarrassment. When local leaders were asked to produce census data, he lovingly tabulated population figures. But it would be a mistake to stereotype Ma Salam as an antitraditional bureaucrat with a traditional older brother; "traditional" is not an important category to either of them. Tradition implies a localized reference point for power and knowledge, whether the point is being abandoned or reclaimed. Instead, the brothers share a framework in which they and those around them are marginal to order and authority. They have situated themselves differently in relation to marginality; but both are equally decentered.

At this point, one might pause to wonder about the sisters in these families. The "two-brothers" formulation of ethnicity in the Si Ayuh/ Bambang Basiwara stories obscures women's participation in ethnic relations. Indeed, it is through such formulations as these that ambitious men like Ma Salam imply that their leadership has nothing to do with gender, since their knowledge and discipline transcends the weaknesses of Meratus men and women alike. Yet men and women have different kinds of interethnic relations, and men have clear advantages in becoming community leaders. Like Ma Salam, men can emulate Bambang Basiwara, but women, with less access to regionally valued knowledge and connections, are more likely to find themselves in the position of the Meratus "everyman," Si Ayuh. The three sisters of Ma Salam whom I knew best (another lived elsewhere) tolerated, supported, and teased their ambitious brother; but, like Ma Rani, they did not challenge his right to speak for them.

Ma Salam's sisters were shy and rarely told long stories; other women I knew, however, were accomplished storytellers. Women knew Si Ayuh tales, but they were particularly known for their telling of the song epics of the heroic Bungsukaling, who pursues his lovers and adventures in a world without ethnic differentiation or disadvantage. The *kaling* people of these epics (cf. Indonesian *keling*, "Hindu" or "Tamil") are magical people of long ago. Although, in many ways, they are as "Other" as Bambang Basiwara, the epics sidestep contemporary regional asymmetries by positing potency not as a matter of ethnic emulation but of remembering a distant past. In this task women are as capable as men. For some of the most articulate women I knew, including Uma Adang, Bungsukaling epics formed a resource for a vision of the authenticity of their knowledge, rather than its ethnic devaluation. Yet, in the houses of ambitious men like Ma Salam, epics were most often consigned to the periphery of attention. I remember one evening in which an elderly uncle of Ma Salam launched into a Bungsukaling epic. (Some men sing epics too.) Ma Salam turned on his radio and started a loud conversation, which kept everyone from listening. In this setting, it was clear that the dream of magical power of the Bungsukaling epics was a dream of those more profoundly displaced than Ma Salam or even Ma Rani.

Decentralization and Meratus political culture

Meratus people's understandings of their marginality have developed with a history of administrative decentralization. The current government follows colonial precedent in drawing administrative boundaries along the ridges of the Meratus Mountains, splitting the Meratus area into numerous regencies (*kabupaten*) and component districts (*kecamatan*), each of which includes a much larger population of Banjar than of Meratus. Indeed, the Meratus area includes tail-like segments of eight of the nine regencies into which the province of South Kalimantan is divided; as of 1980, Meratus were found in perhaps twenty-eight of the seventy-two districts into which these eight regencies were divided. Yet the Meratus population (13,000, according to some estimates) is a tiny fraction of the Banjar population of the province (more than 1.7 million). These administrative divisions separate Meratus from each other and encourage them to look toward regional political authorities in centrifugal directions. Trade routes also orient Meratus toward various downstream market towns in the plains surrounding the mountains.

Without a homogenizing structural orientation, microdifferentiations flourish. The landscape offers no bounded arenas of "local" knowledge as it signals continual divisions and relocations. A number of axes of difference stand out. Stylistic distinctions—of shamanic ritual, housing, craft work, and dialect—have become associated with the river valleys leading out of the mountains. Just as clear are cross-cutting differentiations by proximity to Banjar trade and administrative centers: The dense villages of the western foothills contrast with the scattered houses of the central mountains and the trail-side settlement pattern of the east side. Further, most Meratus have at some point lived in very different local areas. Individuals cultivate eclectic cultural resources as they form personal histories of mobility across the landscape. Shamans, for example, learn a variety of river-valley-based styles and from them form their personal variations. Mobility over a diversified landscape fosters a proliferating appreciation of differences; Meratus note minute distinctions of taste, language, and style between themselves and their neighbors, even between housemates.

Ma Salam's mother was explaining food taboos for nursing mothers, and I asked about chili peppers. "No one here eats chili peppers," she said.

What about the bush at her cousin's, the next house upstream?

"I don't know about *other people*," she said; "they're different from us."

The government calls Meratus mobility "semi-nomadism" and regards it as a sign that all Meratus are runaways from state discipline. From the Meratus perspective, mobility and microdifferentiation offer the pleasures of autonomy as well as the stigma of disorder.

The practical autonomy of Meratus political and economic relations owes much to the fact that, until the transnational timber extravaganzas of the 1980s, the area was insufficiently attractive to outsiders to warrant their continual attention. Until mammoth bulldozers cut timber roads in the last decade, the roads and rivers passable to motorized vehicles ended at the base of the mountains. Like Meratus, travellers, traders, and security patrols have had to hike over rough local trails. These rough trails have protected Meratus, particularly in the central mountains, from everyday state supervision and massive Banjar immigration. They have allowed the continued development of Meratus cultural alternatives that would not be tolerated in the "civilized" Banjar plains.

When I visited the western foothills in 1986, new timber roads had been opened everywhere. The Meratus I knew found these roads, intended for giant trucks, unbearably hot and muddy for any serious travelling by foot. At least at that point, we were able to follow the established forest trails that crossed back and forth across the timber roads but which avoided their reconstruction of the route. In the sense offered by this image, Meratus cultural strategies have sometimes sidestepped state control and Banjar dominance.

Mobility, diversity, and autonomy

The central mountain area is the Meratus landscape of dispersion par excellence. Here, both the pleasures of autonomy and the stigma of disorder are at their most intense. Both are maintained through practices which involve mobility over a finely differentiated landscape.

When I first arrived in the western foothills, my Meratus host, Induan Kilay, discouraged me from travelling into the mountains. There was nothing there to see, she said, except "a house, a swidden . . . a house, a swidden." Besides, she argued (repeating the Banjar stereotype of all Meratus), the mountain people would steal me blind and slit my throat. No one attacked me, but she was right about the landscape. Houses in the central mountains are built on shifting swidden fields; between the houses lie tracts of regrowing and mature forest. But mountain Meratus do not find this landscape boring; they appreciate its dynamic diversity and specificity.

Induan Kilay lives in a resettlement village in which Meratus are encouraged to recognize a primary distinction between the settled, human space of the village (*banua*) and the wildness of the forest (*hutan*, which can include even swiddens). In the central mountains, however, this formula would seem strange. One descends the house stair-log not to a village but to the ground (*tanah*), which becomes rice fields (*huma*), secondary forest (*jurungan*), mature rainforest (*katuan*), and other more specialized vegetational niches. The landscape is known as a patchwork not only of these vegetation types but also of specific places. Large, emergent trees often have *individual* names—not just species names—which can be used to identify particular groves and hillsides. Through foraging, travelling, and memories of old fields regrown into forest, central-mountain Meratus become familiar with a number of forest sites. As the sites themselves take on overlapping and varied social connotations, each user gains a loose sense of connection with other users, past and present. Social identities in the mountains are not forged in "domesticated" villages; they take on the complexity of associations with the forest landscape as a fabric of diverse social and natural resources.

Land in the central mountains is not regulated by jural decree. People claim not land but the trees and crops they and their forebears planted. Meratus in this area choose where to forage, clear their fields, and build their houses with a great degree of latitude, although past and concurrent uses of each site delimit the social context in which choices are made. Some individuals range widely, while others circle closely around their well-known places. In each case, people value the autonomy to travel and farm where they please and to form diverse, shifting identities and affiliations in conjunction with this mobility.

Meratus farms, like forests, are heterogeneous vegetational niches that support farmers' efforts to diversify their social ties and landscape identifications. Central-mountain Meratus are shifting cultivators whose agroforestry involves long cycles (five to fifty years between clearings) of farm-forest rotation. They usually grow rice for two years on a cleared plot before letting the forest return; thus there are both first- and second-year rice fields, each supporting numerous distinct varieties of rice interplanted with dozens of other crops: banana, papaya, eggplant, maize, sugar cane, cucumber, squash, tobacco, taro, cocoyam, sweet potato, millet, Job's tears, stringbean, wingbean, sesame, ginger, basil, cockscomb, and more. The diversity of crops in the field is valued, in part, as an index of the breadth of the farmers' social ties; farmers collect seeds or cuttings from a variety of relatives and acquaintances. Diverse plantings and wide social ties signal the farmers' self-sufficiency and freedom of action. Furthermore, the field remains a site for developing the social identities of the farmers even after the final rice crop has been harvested. Farmers' familiarity with the many useful weeds and long-term crops that remain in the regrowing forest helps maintain their interests in their old swiddens. Old swiddens provide new forested sites from which people reposition themselves physically and socially.

Autonomy and sociality in the central mountains

The creation of autonomy amid diverse and flexible affiliations can also be seen in the formation of social groups.[5] Meratus call the group that makes a swidden farm together an *umbun*. While recognizing that individuals within umbun form their own divergent courses, Meratus identify umbun as principal units through which autonomy is enacted. Thus, attention to the internal and external alliances of umbun is important to understanding the relation of mobility and independence in the central mountains.

Farming involves both male and female responsibilities; umbun are nearly always founded by a man and a woman. Most founders are married couples, but they may also be brother and sister, grandmother and grandson, or other combinations. Umbun embrace a variety of dependents who have not founded their own umbun, including children as well as single, recently married, disabled, or widowed adults. Dependents (especially adults and children whose parents are divorced or deceased) often circulate among umbun rather than opting for the limitations of a single umbun affiliation.

When a couple marry, they usually remain dependents in either the bride's or the groom's umbun, or they circulate between the two, for a number of years, until they have had several children. Slowly they separate (*bahining*) to form their own umbun, with its own swiddens and rice stores. Once adults have formed their own umbun, they are hesitant to return to the status of umbun dependent. Yet, with the making of new rice fields, umbun must be reconstituted every year, and vicissitudes of disability and widowhood may put this project in jeopardy. Widowers remarry quickly in order to maintain themselves as umbun founders. Widows often create umbun with bachelor sons, nephews, or grandsons, at least until they remarry or lose their health. Elderly couples maintain their umbun independence as long as they can walk.

Umbun are proud of their autonomy; part of this autonomy is their ability to affiliate freely with other umbun. Many umbun choose to form a common household with one to five other umbun; they may also choose (with or without a common household) to farm contiguous swiddens in a small "swidden cluster." In these households and clusters, sharing and cooperation across umbun boundaries is daily and informal. As new farms and houses are contructed, however, umbun may join or form an entirely different group.

Umbun also affiliate more widely, forming propinquitous groups of scattered households (I call them "neighborhoods") in which neighbors often share game, fruit, and honey, attend each other's work parties, and sponsor festivals together in a *balai*, a neighborhood-maintained ritual hall. There are no unambiguous Meratus terms with which to designate "neighborhood" or "swidden cluster" or "household" units; in each case, locational labels are used to refer to the people living and farming in such-and-such place. These terms can be broadly or loosely interpreted; similarly, the boundaries of cluster and neighborhood units are always under negotiation. Umbun can choose among festivals forming in different directions; they can attend work parties with neighborhood groups of their own choosing. However, despite the fuzziness and flexibility of their boundaries and composition, neighborhoods do have reasonably well accepted names through which residents contrast their local affiliation with that of others.

One part of the definitional stability of these neighborhood groups, at least during my 1979–81 fieldwork, derived from the groups' identification with administrative "neighborhoods" called *RT* (for *rukun tetangga*). These neighborhoods are subunits of "villages" (*kampung*), the highest unit of locally headed administration and directly below the district. Until the mid-1980s, most Meratus "villages" were very large territories. Administrative reorganization then broke up these territories, transforming many neighborhoods (or small groups of neighborhoods) into "villages."

Meratus village heads (*pambakal*), assistants (*wakil*), and neighborhood heads (*pangerak* or *RT*) have generally been appointed by distant district officers. Yet these officials exercise their duties within Meratus social conditions. They have few tools with which to convince their neighbors of their authority except the prestige of their connection to unpredictable state support. Like local shamans with equally unpredictable spirit connections, some local officials are more successful than others in creating communities that acknowledge their leadership. (I reserve the word *community* for the continually renegotiated and re-imagined constituencies of local leaders.) In this context, former officials and men with even less palpable government ties may be as successful in becoming neighborhood leaders as are current titleholders. Furthermore, even as local leaders copy state rhetoric and rail against dispersion, their practice depends on the mobility and flexible alliances through which Meratus activate and confirm social ties.

Walking fieldwork

When I first arrived in the Meratus Mountains, I expected to do a village study, as is still the predominant practice in the cultural anthropology of the rural Third World. Yet when I reached the central mountains, I found no villages to study. Lacking a stable group with which to "settle in," it seemed best for me to move around. That is how I came to travel across a wide swathe of Meratus country, staying primarily with five loosely connected umbun in different neighborhoods.

In the process of moving around, I acquired various names, dialects, kinship statuses, and friendships. Certainly this kept me juggling competing definitions of appropriate behavior. At every festival, for example, I had to choose (or waffle) between identifying with the hosts or the guests. If I had friends in both groups who were less than cordial with each other, it was a wrenching choice. Yet most Meratus also experience diverse affiliations. They are called different names in different places, know various ritual and linguistic styles, and juggle multiple demands for loyalty. My experience with multiple affiliations—as it both overlapped and diverged from the experience of those around me—helped me appreciate both strategies of networking and dilemmas of community identification.

Ethnographic practice influenced theory. Village ethnography begins with the premise of a local group that is stable enough for study; it then moves easily to the search for a cultural tradition capable of maintaining that stability. As I involved myself with a network that stretched across the mountains, I moved increasingly further from structural models of local stability and came to recognize the open-ended dialogues that formed and reformed Meratus culture and history. My own shifting positioning made me especially alert to continual negotiations of local "community," to the importance of far-flung as well as local ties, and to the array of local responses to regional challenges and dilemmas. Moreover, a culture that cannot be tied to a place cannot be analytically stopped in time. As I observed communities in flux, it became difficult to avoid the fact that local agreements about custom, ritual, language, and livelihood were also open for renegotiation.

Instead of a single arrival on the scene of ethnographic difference, I negotiated multiple arrivals and departures. In writing of these experiences, no introductory fieldwork sketch can provide a point of insight from which my ethnography follows as a piece. To tell of cultural disjunctions and ongoing negotiations requires discrepant stories of varied "arrivals," as well as stories of the subtler insights of everyday journeying. In the opening chapter, I narrate my encounter with Uma Adang's genius. Here, contextualized in warnings about overgeneralizing, I offer a little more about my guidance into everyday travels.

With Ma Salam

It was with Ma Salam that I first learned how to walk through Meratus social space. Where I at first saw only the forest's natural beauty, he showed me how to read the forest socially. He taught me to differentiate the light green (*kuning*, also "yellow") leaves of secondary forest regrowing from old swiddens from the dark green (*hijau*, "green/blue") of the mature forest that begins slowly to show its presence after forty to fifty years of regrowth. He pointed to the remains of old cultivation and inhabitancy that I might otherwise never have noticed. Red coleus leaves that once decorated the ritual "eye" (*pamataan*) of someone's rice field still flourished in five-year regrowth amid trees as thick as one's arm. Fruit pits once tossed out of someone's window had grown into productive trees before the forest was ten years old.

The pace and mood of our hikes shifted dramatically with the landscape's social associations. In forest that Ma Salam associated with those he didn't like much or know well, we marched through at a businesslike pace. On socially familiar ground, Ma Salam would relax, and suddenly we could laugh and meander along. Ma Salam told me the names of plants and looked around for special ones. We sweetened our mouths with the tiny bulbs of *ma'undingan*. He scaled a towering wild *tarap* tree and brought down a mess of sticky fruit; we ate the ripe fruits, spitting out the seeds as we walked along, and Ma Salam tied the young fruits to his waist to take home for dinner. We reached under rocks in the stream to gather minnows. It seemed unimportant how soon we might reach our destination.

Approaching the houses and swiddens of those with whom Ma Salam did not wish to socialize, we hushed our talk and tried to slip by quietly, although calling out politely, *Hayut* ("We're passing") if people spotted us. At other houses, we walked right up to the porch to call, *Pamali, kah?* ("Is it off limits for us to come in?") And if our hosts urged us inside, we would climb up the stair-log—spears left by the porch, bush-knives unstrapped at the door—to sit inside and socialize.

Inside the house a different set of social spaces beckoned. There are no rooms; bamboo-slat floors are divided into sections of slightly different heights in a single open space. On the lowest section is the hearth; on the higher sections, people sit during the day and unroll their mats to sleep at night. Near one wall are the great bark bins in which each umbun's unhusked rice is stored separately.

As guests, we sat near the doorway, and our hosts brought us betel, tobacco, and, with luck, fragrant palm syrup to quench our thirst. New arrivals, we exchanged stories of the forest or the market: sightings of migrating bees, wild-boar tracks, or forest flowerings; the latest price of rattan. If hours passed and our hosts brought forward nothing to eat, Ma Salam would find a way to excuse us, saying, *Bajalanan* ("We're off"). Hungry now, we might hurry off to his house. Only at one's own house can one eat any time one pleases.

I remember with special fondness one summer at Ma Salam's house. I had relaxed into the dailiness of my relationship with the four umbun with whom I shared the house. Ma Salam had planned his house as a festival site, so the house was big and, like other Meratus houses, airy and filled with light. My language skills, and my knowledge of local gossip, were good enough then that I could learn a great deal merely by listening in on other people's conversations.

Ma Salam and I talked endlessly that summer and came to call each other siblings. He took me around with him as he visited neighbors, discussed crises, and arranged dispute settlements. (He had been appointed neighborhood head the year before.) As a visiting stranger, I probably gave him a little more authority; I certainly learned about neighborhood affairs in leaps and bounds. At the same time, I gained a less clearly articulated closeness with his mother and sisters as we worked together, sang each other songs, and affectionately picked through each other's hair.

The rice was good that year, and so was the hunting. Sometimes I would go out to harvest with the other women. We covered our heads from the sun with old cloths and put sharpened bamboo tubes over our thumbs to cut each rice stalk individually between thumb and finger. (Some women made thumb knives from the metal casings of batteries; alas, my initially thrilling American batteries had no metal casings.) When we grew hot and tired, we rested in the field, slicing open the huge, sweet cucumbers that ripened in the midst of the rice. And when we went back to the house, there was wild boar to add to our cucumber feasts.

My harvesting in the field was sporadic, reminding the women of my privileged difference. Once Ma Salam's mother tried to flatter me by saying that I didn't "work" (*bagawi*) but only "travelled" (*bajalan*). My first thought was to take offense and argue for my industriousness; in the United States, to do no work is to be worthless. But I soon realized my mistake: For Meratus to "work" is to do repetitive caretaking activity, while to "travel" is a process of personal and material enrichment.

Ma Salam's mother explained the work I did not do with the hand motions of weeding, her left hand grabbing each imagined plant and her right hand slashing at its base with an imagined work knife. Weeding is perhaps the best example of work. When one works, one is "busy" (*aur*), preoccupied with details that fill up one's attention and sap one's energy without directly creating a product. Although both men and women work, women do the most painstaking, intensive kinds of work.

In contrast, travelling through the forest to hunt, gather, visit, or go to market allows a person to find his or her livelihood and also build personal experience. Even in discussing rice farming, Meratus foreground travelling: Site selection and omen-reading involve travelling through the forest; ritual involves the spiritual travels of an expert, as well as the rice. The harvest is not an automatic return to labor but a successful finding of livelihood through travel. Both men and women travel; but men, and particularly young men, do the most. In stressing my travel, Ma Salam's mother was classing me with her son as an ambitious young person.

After the harvest, the women had more time for talk and craft work. Sometimes one or two men went out at night with a flashlight and brought home frogs or sweet river eels for breakfast. In the evenings, neighbors visited to sing love songs into my tape recorder and play lonely tunes on the bamboo flute as they wove baskets and we lay in the dark, gossiping.

> The feeling of desire
> in this child of a soldier
> In the mountain lands, seeing *ke'e*.
> In the city lands, oh this *ke'e* now.

Love songs came into and out of style as young men spread them across the mountains; one of the most popular songs that season was "Ke'e." *Ke'e* is a small palm found in forest undergrowth; the elegant parallel leaflets are particularly admired when young and light green. In the song, ke'e refers to a woman whose beautiful form is that of the plant. In contrast, the man who courts her is a traveller, a soldier, a cutter of plants. But to fell the plant—that is, win the woman—he must have money, in order to court her with presents and to offer a marriage payment. This version was improvised by Ma Salam's sister's husband, Ma Buluh:

> It's not throwing away money,
> says this soldier,
> Seeing ke'e, you know it's the real thing.
> The leaves seem to quiver on this ke'e palm.

The song brings my discussion back to the strains with which I began the chapter. The handsome young man is a soldier, a powerful traveller from afar. As in the tales of Si Ayuh and Bambang Basiwara, the outsider becomes an object of emulation. Unlike the stories, however, the songs do not pose a contrast between Meratus and Banjar, self and other. Instead, they erase lines of difference to glamourize Meratus experience.

> The feeling of love,
> the feeling of sadness,
> Looking at ke'e, you know it's richly thriving
> In the delta lands.

It's true this militia guard
has his orders.
He can't fell this ke'e now
Without throwing out lots of money.

But he would lose indeed,
He would lose not to tend this ke'e.
The one they call a militia guard,
In the rows of ke'e.

Both men and women gain the glamour of identification with outsiders. If men are soldiers, women as ke'e are situated "in the city" and "in the delta" as well as "in the mountains." (The fact that ke'e is a forest palm not found in the towns or well-populated Banjar deltas, however, is a reminder of the ambivalence of these foreign localizations.) Yet love songs offer an asymmetrical portrait of gender. "Soldiers" have the violence, wealth, and power of faraway places. They "fell," "tend," and buy female intimacy. "Palms" are passive, dependent on their suitors. Even for their clothing and personal decoration, women must depend on their boyfriends or husbands; women's identification with beautiful outsiders unreciprocally requires male gifts and attentions. Women use such imagery to tease handsome travellers into giving them more gifts: "Go ahead and tend for me," the women sing. Or women can recognize their marginality in emulating "delta" beauty. Ma Buluh's wife, Induan Buluh, answered her husband with self-deprecation which can be interpreted as either coy or resigned; she does not have enough beautiful things to deserve admiration.

What's the use of this ke'e?
This ke'e must withdraw.
With no money, no finery saved away.
I'll just withdraw.

What's the use of this ke'e?
She's at the side,
Withdrawing to the edge of things,
This ke'e.

You must throw out lots of money
in travelling around.
This ke'e is too plain,
With no finery.

Such female versions reproduce gender asymmetries. The gender dichotomies of love songs appear to offer no platform for women's ambitions, even as they give women both a sense of beauty and a chance to express themselves. Only a subversive reading of the genre (see chapter 8) can draw gender complementarity from this asymmetry. Yet this complementarity is one that can challenge the gender omissions of other Meratus expressive forms.

Love songs are one arena in which men and women negotiate identity. Understandings of identity develop within particular practices, and the discrepancies between these practices create contradictions and alternate possibilities. Love songs and Si Ayuh stories offer contrasting prescriptions for defining masculinity: The gallant bachelor basks in a glow Si Ayuh can never achieve. As statements about what it means to be a Meratus man, they are no more similar than the glamour of Westerns and the self-deprecating humor of situation comedies as each of these speaks to what it means to be a U.S. American. Meratus genres also offer contrasting disadvantages for women: The female is immobilized in love songs and omitted in Si Ayuh stories. The challenge for an ethnographer—a traveller with a limited, if rich, interactive experience—is to show enough of the coherence of these "fictions," yet enough of their discrepancies. I tackle the first of these tasks without neglecting the second by locating negotiations of identity in relation to predicaments of regional marginality.

The next chapter elaborates another aspect of regional asymmetry by taking up concerns with the state and the cultural shape of both accommodation and resistance. I raise questions about the Meratus imagination of the state and the state imagination of the Meratus. In their reciprocal visions of violence, the ironies of a Meratus masculinity caught between identifying with soldiers and with savages become even more apparent. I postpone a clearer discussion of female positionings until the following chapter.

2 GOVERNMENT HEADHUNTERS

At the border between state rule and the wild stand those who dare to define, defy, and demand administration. These are the men (indeed, they are mainly men) whom I call "leaders" because they are ambitious enough to tell the government that they represent the community and their neighbors that they represent the state. These leaders are the accomplished visitors and hosts who travel widely in the mountains and beyond. When they visit the markets at the edge of the mountains, they stop in to greet the police; occasionally, they may meet the district officer. When visitors arrive in the neighborhood—whether army officers, traders, anthropologists, or Meratus guests—leaders are generous and eager in their hospitality. Between visits, they talk politics bravely with their neighbors and make official noises at sporadic ceremonies.

Leaders must respond to state policies that require Meratus submission. Those whom I knew best faced this threat as shamans who pleased and pacified the state, who recognized its ferocious beauty, and who drew on its power for their own leadership. Such leaders cannot lay timeless plans but must maintain a flexible vigilance attuned to changing events. Particular forms of knowledge flourished in their hands: a wary attention to rumors and subtle clues; a relentless search for travelling messages and higher truths. In the unpredictable shifting clashes of spirits and soldiers, these leaders found a sporadic, contradictory authority which considered itself both local protection and regional deference.

This chapter is concerned with understandings of state rule cultivated by central-mountain Meratus leaders within the context of regional violence and administration. My subject is the imagination of power. The term *imagination* highlights magical and meaningful aspects of concrete political practices. The term signals my refusal to view the state as a set of institutions and procedures whose political significance is obvious without reference to cultural categories. At the same time, my focus is on political practices of creating magic and meaning. State rule is known through its technologies and activities (including talk). In this chapter I use positioned storytelling—one kind of discursive practice—to tap and energize the analytic tension between appreciating the imagination and investigating its mechanisms.

Storytelling is a key skill for Meratus shamans and leaders. Personal stories create "experience"; for the shaman/leader, stories forge an identity as a witness and survivor at the borders of state authority and violence. Through crafted memories, a leader builds his preeminence within current social relations; he conjures up the past to reconstruct the political contours of the present. The storyteller builds the beautiful and terrifying aspects of power on which his own political agency depends. He recalls the state as the exemplar of power and reconstitutes political subjection and subjectivity in his listeners. Thus, stories give shape to politics, political communities, and political actors.[1]

In my discussion I lean heavily on insights gained from one of my most generous shaman teachers, a man everyone called "The Bear." When The Bear heard I was in the area, he invited me to attend one of his ceremonies. I was charmed by The Bear's hospitality and impressed by the beauty of his shamanship; I made it a practice to stay at his place whenever I had the chance. Nor was I alone as an alien guest; The Bear befriended traders, officials—even stray Banjar wandering alone in the mountains (one of whom ended up staying and marrying The Bear's former wife). The Bear was a marvelous host and an enthusiastic teacher. His attention to strangers was not a sign of eccentricity but of skill; leaders move beyond local terrain. Thus, too, our conversations were part of his leadership craft, not a secondary reflection about leadership. The Bear died in 1985, and I offer this selection of reminiscences in his memory.

In 1980–81, The Bear and his wife lived in a rickety ritual hall with a motley group of kin and other associates, including the former Banjar. At the time, The Bear was a renowned leader with not much community to lead; yet his social network was wide. His hall was placed at a convenient crossroads, and many travellers—kin, former neighbors, old allies, and others attracted by his brave and big-hearted reputation—would stop off there. It was in this context that The Bear was known as a masterful storyteller.

Sometimes The Bear wanted to tell most of the stories; sometimes the storytelling—ranging through folklore, cosmology, gossip, and reminiscence—passed from one person to another as stories sparked others and "answered back and forth" (*balas mambalas*). In the spirit of those evenings, I present this chapter as a series of reverberating short stories. I begin with a section that outlines major themes.

In a world of nation-states, several narratives of power are easy to take for granted. One might begin with the great timeline of political history: One administration succeeds another. This story spills into others: the convergence of bureaucracy and self-discipline, in which citizens expect the state's rules to frame their daily needs with ever greater precision; the differentiation between legitimate force and dangerous violence, in which police action, by definition, is never terrorism. Stories of central-mountain Meratus leaders disturb these assumptions about history, administration, and violence, challenging their taken-for-granted status.

These leaders do not draw their models of power from a cultural space outside state rule; they locate themselves within that space. Through their skills as mediators of state power, they draw together and form political communities; thus, in their eyes, Meratus communities always emerge in the shadow of the state. Yet these leaders do not reiterate the understanding of state rule that regional and national bureaucrats hold to be self-evident. In particular, they tinker with official notions of time, stealing a timeframe of leadership and community survival from the jaws of administrative discipline. The official model portrays Meratus as caught in an archaic prehistory, before national historical time. Mountain Meratus leaders turn this around to show the state as timeless. And within state timelessness, these leaders imply, Meratus subjects can sustain an improvised time of social networking and provisional community-building. The narrative of an always advancing history of successive administrations is pushed aside. All administrations are structurally the same.[2]

This disfigurement of official history is not, as civil servants might have it, a resurgence of primal myth, but, rather, is a reasoned, creative assessment of the corners of state practice that Meratus leaders in the central mountains know best. It is important to remember here that the rational development rhetoric of the state is not a representation of truth obscured by hillbilly ignorance; it has its own bizarre, tenuous association with local events. The tentative successes of shamans in promoting Meratus survival depend on shamanic entrée into the instabilities in the relationship of state logic and local practice.

Violence is a key element in both official and shamanic narratives, and it marks the difference between them. In the official narrative, legitimate force defines "government"; legitimate force separates order from chaos and divides bureaucrats from terrorists. Yet, central-mountain Meratus leaders insist that there is no difference between legitimate and illegitimate force; violence is a prerogative and necessary aspect of power, and power is not an issue of morality. The police are terrorists because terror is the appropriate job of the police.

"Administration," too, is contested; in the hands of Meratus shamans, bureaucratic discipline is re-presented as spectacle. Ceremonies create government authority. Indeed, government is a matter of beautiful and proper ritual presentation. Thus, there is no difference between local custom and state command.

This view is neither delusion nor rebellion. Besides, even distorted or oppositional forms of consciousness can reproduce the contours of power. The reach of the state forms through the unstable negotiations of which Meratus shamans, like national politicians, form a part.[3]

WAR STORIES

Regional officials who deal with the Meratus make fun of them for being out of touch with political realities. "They never heard of the president; they think Kalimantan is still ruled by kings," a Banjar census taker told me. Indeed, Meratus in the central mountains sometimes conflate the terms for past rulers and present officials. For those who, like census takers and anthropologists, are surrounded by the historical narrative of important men, it is easy to believe that central-mountain Meratus know no political history at all.

National and international political history tells of wars and political succession. Because I knew this kind of history best, I assumed at first that such war stories could form a framework within which to chronicle "Meratus history." Thus, I gathered stories of soldiers and officials who had passed through the Meratus Mountains. I did not expect Meratus stories to shake the ground of familiar histories, dislocating their narrative frameworks and conventions of objectivity. Yet, what I heard was much more than a local version of a master narrative.

Stories of soldiers struck me particularly strongly. Most were about events with which I am familiar: World War II, the nationalist revolution, the Islamic Banjar rebellion of the late 1950s. Yet the Meratus stories I heard were not moral narratives of struggle, that is, histories. The stories ignored issues of partisan conflict and highlighted the possibilities for survival: dispersing, hiding out, appeasing soldiers on every side of the conflict. Although I thought I recognized the events, the art with which they were reconstituted was unfamiliar and disorienting. For me, this art had the force of magical realism; it disrupted my assumptions about the nexus of agency and power in which presidents and generals contribute to history because they command armies for a *reason*, whether lofty or base. In the Meratus stories, the only explanation for these armies is the existence of power itself. Wars are just an ordinary form of terrorism.

Bearings

Many of the central-mountain Meratus I knew cared little about the identity or goals of passing soldiers. They knew the soldiers were powerful; they offered the men rice and chickens and tried to stay out of their way. The Bear was different. He loved stories of blood and guns. He told stories of kings, colonizers, nationalists, and rebels; he knew them all. I trust the accuracy of The Bear's recollections, for his memory was keen; but the truth of his stories is situated in a shamanic objectivity. They seem best told via a detour through the grounds of The Bear's self-positioning. Here, one must remember the significance of *telling* stories about soldiers. Telling taps the power of soldiers. Like spells, stories create the teller's invulnerability; and like shamans' chants, they offer the teller a personal and extraordinary potency.

The Bear told war stories about moments of power and danger. He prided himself on his adventurous spirit and ability to learn from men of power.

I followed Tuan Maskapi [a Dutch-era surveyor] up to the top of Windy Day Rock. We were so high that we had to look down to see the sun rise.[4] I saw that it must be true that the sun is lower than the plane of the sky.

The Bear gained force from witnessing these men of power. He was a man who aimed to transcend the vulnerabilities of Meratus fear. Fluent in the masculine language of spells and magic that connect Muslim Banjar and pagan Dayak, he cemented our relationship by giving me ("Your brother could use it") a spell for stopping bullets, by melting them. The spell addresses bullets as follows:

You are semen. White divinity. A clotted drop. Closed with a key. Fluid iron. Fluid semen.

The Bear had been shot three times by the rebels of the late 1950s, he said, but his spells protected him. The power of the spell, of course, is not available in this translation but in the mystic terms of the original, which, as in other spells, draw Banjar and Meratus together in mutual awe through their Islam-inspired authority and their disruptive pagan charm. These secret words bring men together in masculine trust.

As a fighting man, The Bear was a powerful mediator, ready to settle Meratus disputes because he was not afraid of other authorities. He told of past and present conflicts with the assurance of a warrior.

These are the peoples who were cannibals in the past: Lastar, Pari, Mudang, Kahayan, and Karinei.[5] **They came here to find people to kill. The shamans danced with rows of animal fangs and a human head on the porch. They tied someone to a post and together killed the victim. They came here in groups with all their warriors, all their bravest men. The people here opposed them. Everyone ran away when they came, but if these warriors stole anything they would be hit with a blowpipe dart.**

These events occurred before The Bear's time; yet he told of them as if he had been there. He told of them as a man of experience.

In shamanic chants, The Bear travelled to past and present places of power in order to "borrow" their potency. His favorite shamanic style was one that addresses *dewa* spirits. Dewa are often described as Banjar spirits; they display the beauty and authority of Banjar power. Dewa shamanism features beautiful ceremonies of elegant food, music, and dancing. The shaman speaks with ancient kings and sublime as well as dangerous spirits and invites them all to enjoy his hospitality. This is a shamanic style filled with stories of South Kalimantan's past, particularly the war stories The Bear savored. I don't know whether they are "true"; but some are telling parables of political relations in the region.

The Banjar king at Kayu Tangi built his palace in a grove of thorned bamboo, where it could not be seen by invaders. But the Dutch shelled the grove with pieces of silver. When people saw the silver, they cut down the bamboo to gather the money. Then the Dutch captured the palace, and the king was forced to disappear at the headwaters of the Barito River.[6]

Sometimes I wondered whether The Bear's eyewitness recollections also drew on his shamanic talents. Somehow The Bear always seemed to be on the spot for important events. He was on the east coast, he said, where the Japanese invaded Kalimantan in World War II. The Japanese dropped three bombs, he said. They gang-raped the two wives of the Dutch controller until their stomachs were swollen with semen and they had to be pumped out. The soldiers ate human flesh. The Bear was in the western valleys, he said, when the Allies recaptured the province. Leaflets were dropped from airplanes to warn people before the bombs fell. A deaf man picked up an unexploded bomb and brought it to the hospital.[7] I was never sure whether physical or spiritual encounters informed these accounts. The Bear had somehow also met every regional VIP who had ever come near the mountains. Certainly, he was a local leader; but he was no greater than many other Meratus men with influence over a small cluster of kin and neighbors. Perhaps he exaggerated the status of his guests and his personal role in dealing with them.

I kept these considerations in mind as I listened, fascinated, to The Bear's true stories of his experiences in the nationalist uprising and the regional rebellions after World War II. These were stories which, like dewa chants, allowed The Bear to "borrow" regional power. As with the chants, they tell of power that passes through but has no local interests except deference and hospitality. The stories tell of multiple, competing powers unpredictably emerging from different directions. Each power is more ruthless than the last. This is not a situation, then, in which one can afford to have partisan attachments. For The Bear, the trick—with soldiers as well as spirits—was to host all competing authorities with equally passionate loyalty.

Hostilities

I had asked The Bear to tell me about the death of Ma Jawa, a west-side Meratus assistant village head who had married a relative of The Bear's. (Ma Jawa's name had come up in a local dispute, discussed in chapter 4.) Ma Jawa was killed in the late 1940s by Banjar nationalists who considered village-level officials to be "dogs of the Dutch." Although I had heard related versions of the killing from others, I was struck by The Bear's version, which told of a time of wariness, fear, and senseless violence. The story both reproduced and evaded this terror, as it established links among witness to violence (The Bear was there), survival (he lived through it), narration (he told the tale), and potency (the telling of his

witness empowered him as a brave man). In the nostalgic telling of violence, fear becomes ferocity and witness becomes "experience."

The nationalist struggle was an empowering political transformation
in much of South Kalimantan, but nationalists never made political connections to central-mountain Meratus. Instead, Meratus in this area
mainly encountered the struggle as Banjar revolutionaries ran into the
hills to stay away from the colonial forces. Meratus, together with other
rural people in South Kalimantan, call the Banjar nationalists of this period *Astrimis* or *Satrimis*, from the Dutch word for "extremist."

Ma Jawa came to the Tidung festival. A lot of people were there, including two Banjar men, Amat and Ibas, who were carrying a hand grenade. They were Astrimis. A letter came from the government to arrest
these two men because they were troublemakers. So all the men who held
government titles agreed they should do this. The women were afraid and
left the festival hall.

In this climate of fear, Ma Jawa faltered.

Ma Jawa wasn't brave enough to say anything. I was sitting at the food
stall holding my bush knife. Finally, another Banjar guest asked the Astrimis to show him the hand grenade. Ibas said, "It will get ten times
darker than this before it rains." Everyone thought the fighting was about
to begin, and they all ran out of the hall.

Under the spell of the grenade—ready to unleash ten times the darkness of a storm—confusion reigned. People ran.

Amat asked where everyone was going. Grandfather Ma Sa'at said,
"This is a mess." Amat said, "Well, we're leaving." Amat and Ibas went
out and came up to Ma Jawa. "Who are you?," they asked, and he told
them. Then they left.

The dispersal of violence is as unpredictable as its return.

Two weeks later, they appeared again. Ma Jawa was visiting his wife's
relatives in Tidung. I was in the house when Ibas came in and tried to
grab Ma Jawa. Ma Jawa jumped out. Half the people were running away.
Amat caught Ma Jawa by cornering him in a swamp. They tied him up
and called him a dog of the Dutch. Grandfather Ma Sa'at tried to oppose
them, but they threatened him, and he ran away, telling everyone else to
run too.

They brought Ma Jawa to a deep pool in the Tidung River and held him under water. When he was almost dead, they hung him on a tree and slit his throat. Everyone from Tidung had run away.

The gruesome, terrifying nature of Ma Jawa's death was stressed in every version I heard. Yet there was no moral to this story; the death was neither necessary nor unnecessary. Violence demonstrates only its own nature. And going past what might have been its end, The Bear's story repeats and layers the randomness of violence.

Ibas and Amat came one other time, bringing a Meratus woman they had taken from another area. They came with Isan Basri [Hassan Basry, the nationalist leader in South Kalimantan]. Isan Basri told me to stop people from following the Dutch. He asked for rice and chickens. Then he went across the east side of the mountains. There Isan Basri criticized Ibas for taking the woman. He told Ibas to go on, and he shot Ibas as he crossed the river. Another Banjar man wanted the woman, and this man took her to a different area, where they were both killed by village officials. Amat still lives in the district seat on a pension.

Some are shot; others, inexplicably, are rewarded. This is power. And it is a power that can pursue people even into the mountains.

The government heard that something had happened in the mountains, and they came and arrested many people. Assistant Village Head Awat Tunggal was held in prison for three months in Barabai. The village head was brought to Kota Baru and held for three months and nine days. Awat Bagai was held for fifteen days, and Pa'an Mabar and Ma Pamal were each in prison for more than one month. I was one of the few titleholders left in the local area.

The government proved to be even more terrifying than the rebels.

The Lahung hall was surrounded by the Dutch military. The commander came in and told me not to run away. I told him I had never heard of Isan Basri. The commander picked up one of the children and threatened the boy. I told him that some men had come, but I had thought that they were government men because they were wearing green uniforms and carrying guns. The commander told me to report it if they came again.

The army had closed off all the doors and the windows because they were afraid of the Satrimis. They had captured two Meratus men from a different area. They let them outside on a rope to relieve themselves, and they got away. The soldiers stood around and shot in every direction.

They asked me to go find the men who escaped. I tried to get them to stop shooting so I wouldn't be hit. When my uncle came that night with a torch, I told them not to shoot him.

The soldiers were afraid, and so they shot wildly. Only a brave man, it would seem, can engineer escapes.

Later, however, government troops became even more coercive, forcing Meratus to congregate without subsistence or protection from the weather. Although The Bear did not mention this, some I spoke to remembered how the elderly and sick died from exertion, on the way to the army camp, or from neglect, abandoned at home.

The Dutch authorities made everyone come together at Minanga Adu. Three groups of colonial soldiers were there. They took some of the Meratus men and put them into a corral with no roof. Everyone had to come live in Minanga Adu. We had to ask permission to get supplies of rice and other things. We had fifteen days for everyone in the area to be there.

Even strategies of appeasement were difficult in this situation.

They said government officers were coming to Minanga Adu and we should have rice and chickens for them. But the soldiers wouldn't let people go anywhere. I went to get rice from my house at Lahung Falls [a half-day's hike away]. I found the Lahung hall full of Banjar Astrimis. There were twenty-seven men, all with new rifles. They told me to stay away from Minanga Adu, but I went back because I heard the government was almost there. But by the time I got back, the Dutch had already lost.

As opportunities for leadership opened up again, it became possible to return to a sly rhetoric of submission. The Bear's story shows Meratus afraid to admit even to compliance with the other side's coercions.

A Javanese officer who was "two-headed" [a double agent] had arrived. I went to meet him. He told me to gather all the people to talk with him. All the men, women, and children were arranged by villages.

He asked why the people were gathered at Minanga Adu. No one was brave enough to say anything to him. Finally, someone said they had chosen to get together to stay away from the confusion. He said we must go kill the Dutch officer who had escaped into the woods. He ordered the colonial troops to throw away their guns, and the people carried the soldiers' belongings to the east side of the mountains.

Independence from colonial rule freed Indonesians to build a new nation. A renaissance of political sensibility spread across the country. In the central Meratus Mountains, however, independence did not usher in a new political era. At first, state authority retreated to more populous areas; but by the late 1950s, another regional conflict had brought soldiers into the mountains. A rebellion pitted Banjar nationalists against the authority of the central government in Java. The rebels established a base in the thinly populated area on the east side of the Meratus Mountains. They used mountain routes to reach their targets in the Banjar plains to the west. Meratus on the east side fled into the forest; mountain Meratus hosted rebel and government soldiers alike. The rebellion was not considered fully suppressed until 1965. Most rural people in the area (both Banjar and Meratus) remember the rebels in their version of government jargon as *Gurumbulan* (*gerombolan*, Indonesian, "bandits").

Meratus I knew who had experienced Gurumbulan visits spoke mainly of staying out of the way. Some east-side Meratus spent several years trying to farm inconspicuously in tiny plots surrounded by difficult-to-penetrate forest. In contrast, The Bear told of his connections—ambivalent but palpable. Again, his personal witness to violence spoke both to the terror of the times and to his courage in making it through. Here are a few of his recollections. Interestingly, the Bear began with the violence of the state.

People were allowed to buy only one small block of salt at the markets. Otherwise, they were suspected of helping the Gurumbulan.

The rebels, too, were fierce. Their power involved the ability to almost simultaneously assault him, imprison him, and make him their agent.

The Gurumbulan killed people if they stole, gambled, committed adultery, or did not tithe. If you stole, they cut off the tips of your fingers. If you got pregnant, they split your stomach. They wanted an Islamic state.

They came and hit me on the head once because they heard I had seen a theft but hadn't reported it. They arrested me for three nights and then sent me home and made me the local Head of Order.

The Bear, knowing the dangers, was ambitious enough to befriend all the leaders.

Once, Ibnu Hajnar [Ibnu Hajar, the leader of the rebellion] and thirty men stayed at the Tidung hall. They told us to bring thirty kerosene cans of cleaned rice. I went to meet them. The second wife of Ibnu Hajnar was

there, and I was told to carry her across the river while Ibnu Hajnar hung on to my arm. He had his automatic pistol in my back as we crossed.

The closer one gets, the more dangerous the situation becomes: "He had his automatic pistol in my back as we crossed." But there could be gains.

That evening, Ibnu Hajnar wanted to know why we had been gambling. I brought him a chicken and some eggs. I told him that gambling here was a custom that began with our ancestors; it was different than gambling in the market towns. Ibnu Hajnar said it was all right for us to gamble, but we shouldn't let outsiders join.

"It was all right for us to gamble": The Bear has evaded the threat. And so he ended with a flourish:

All these movements—the Japanese, the Astrimis, the Gurumbulan, the Headscarf Militia [the central government's response to "Gurumbulan" rebel organizing]—none of these ever bothered this village.

Indeed, this last statement cut off the conversation. But I heard in it The Bear's pride at his ability to repulse the forces that might destroy his local sphere. Without his hospitality, he suggested, the community might have been harmed. In this conclusion, all the terrible uses of force he had so far recounted become points of personal prestige. He had experienced their ferocity, entertained it, and turned it away.

Powerful Tellings

The Bear was an old man when I knew him, but his stories were not the memories of a youthful initiate in a distant battlefield. His were local stories told in a context in which state power continues to be experienced as armed and unpredictable. The Bear's contemporary reputation as a leader depended on such stories as these, in which he proved his abilities as a fierce and generous host who could turn the ravages of power.

As The Bear established his abilities, stories of the past blended easily into stories of more recent disputes. One night, after telling a story about the Gurumbulan, The Bear launched into an explanation of a dispute over a case of alleged adultery that had happened two years before we spoke. An uncle of the alleged adulterer had countered the accusation with threats against the husband's relatives, saying the police would arrest them. The uncle accused the relatives of having been involved in the disappearance of two Banjar men twenty-odd years earlier (during the Gurumbulan events), and he found a Banjar ally willing to carry the matter to the authorities. Regional security forces rarely follow up on Meratus complaints; but the threat, with its terrible possibilities, seemed real enough to be frightening. Only mediators unafraid of the police could be effective, and The Bear had offered his services.

The Bear said that he had arranged the final settlement of the case. My sense, however, is that there were a number of not-so-final mediations. Uma Adang also claimed to have mediated the decisive settlement of this case, in which, she said, she exposed as a fake the threatening letter from the police brought by the adulterer's side. Moreover, repercussions of this quarrel had not died away. A recent dispute over rights to a durian tree had stirred emotions, as several participants in the earlier dispute again became opponents. This time, a kinsman of one of the men who had earlier been threatened with police action decided to report to the security forces. Among other things, he hoped to convince the security forces that police authority in the earlier case had been falsely used. Meanwhile, an alarming story was spreading about the police sector chief, whom the kinsman hoped to bring in. The sector chief had suspected a Banjar villager of stealing, and had almost drowned the man by holding him under water in an attempt to make him confess. Here was an authority one had better obey.

One afternoon, as The Bear and I were talking, a young man marched in clad in army green and wearing enormous rubber boots. Like most Meratus men, Pa'an Tini usually wore shorts and perhaps a singlet; but now he was in official garb, as head of the village militia. Attempting a military bark, Pa'an Tini announced that he had been ordered to arrest everyone involved in the durian dispute and to take them to the district seat. It was a ridiculous plan, with no guns to enforce it. The disputants were scattered over a wide area; besides, they would never agree to a hike of several days just to turn themselves in to a maniacal sector chief for an undefined crime. I wanted to laugh at Pa'an Tini for his military pretensions, but The Bear was wiser. He calmed Pa'an Tini by pointing out that no one was likely to be around at that time. Then he talked about strategies. If they didn't arrange a local settlement, he argued, the matter might indeed be turned over to the police or the army, both of which were dangerous and unpredictable.

Like The Bear, Pa'an Tini was self-confident, ambitious, and brave. He was also a dewa shaman, and his performance was filled with high drama. He had not, however, developed The Bear's grace, humor, or ease in awkward situations. Perhaps his almost parodic military bearing offered a glimpse of what The Bear might have been like as a young man reaching out for connections with powerful and dangerous authorities. Of course, times had changed. But each of the two men drew from a heritage of war stories of fierce eyewitnessing and fearful survival.

Rural people all over the world have been caught in the crossfires of irrelevant armies. Meratus, however, are not the vulnerable "little people" of familiar antiwar imagery. Perhaps they are more isolated, more self-sufficient, and more egalitarian than the conventional imagery allows. Meratus do not suffer the insults of elites who make wealth, rank, and power necessary for a decent life. In Meratus stories, wealth appears as a luxury of force, not as the mover of force. Soldiers are like spirits, in part because they do not include local sons and nephews. The most pressing dilemmas are not the crush of daily patronage but the management of extraordinary and unpredictable interventions. This is the context in which shamanism forms a model for political leadership: The shaman is a man who can manage regional terrorism.

The next set of stories brings the theme of terrorism up to date. Meratus tellings of contemporary state terrorism open a surprising space from which to reconsider scholarly theory about modernity and the state.

TALL TALES OF DEVELOPMENT

Urban Indonesians think of Dayaks, such as the Meratus, in the imagery of headhunting. Banjar have their own images of savagery. The Meratus, they say, are bandits who pounce on unsuspecting travellers. They even kill their own grandparents as old age sets in. It is the responsibility of the state, Banjar reason, to control and civilize the Meratus. Because these kinds of stereotypes are familiar to English-speaking readers, it may seem surprising that the Meratus view the situation in reverse: The headhunters are employees of the state, commissioned to take Meratus heads.

In the spring of 1981, the rumor spread in the western Meratus Mountains that government headhunters were on the loose. People connected the raids with malfunctioning drills in the oil fields operated by Pertamina, the government oil company, about seventy kilometers to the north. The government, people said, had ordered the Javanese oil workers to obtain heads to ritually restabilize the machinery. According to my Meratus friends in the western foothills, the police and the army had been instructed to let the raiders do as they pleased.

Everyone was terrified. Hiking from one community to another, even from one house to another, became treacherous and frightening. Several times my hiking companions smelled cigarette smoke on the trail and heard suspicious rustling noises in the bushes. Once we found a half-eaten lunch, perhaps hastily abandoned. My housemates reported meeting strangers hiking at night without apparent destination; others we knew had glimpsed unknown men huddled under the trees. One man said he had seen a stranger wearing a "chain mail shirt" (*baju rantai*).

People were afraid to work in their fields. My friends dragged me to isolated swidden sites, asking me to transcribe festival or dispute tapes loudly to simulate the sounds of a crowd. Finally (or so report had it), the body of a headless child was found on a trail to a Meratus community to the south of where I was living.

This wasn't the first such headhunting scare. People told me that a few years earlier, a French engineer had begun construction of a hydroelectric dam to the south, and raiders had been sent to find heads to ensure the dam's stability. On several occasions before that, the great bridge at Martapura had needed repairs; on each occasion, a head was needed to sanctify the bridge. Meratus trace their vulnerability as victims of state-sponsored headhunting back to precolonial kingdoms, when kings used heads to consecrate public monuments. Now "development" required new sacrifices for its bridges, dams, and oil wells. Meratus conflate the Indonesian words *pembangunan* ("development") and *bangunan* ("buildings"), and they use them interchangeably; to Meratus, development *is* public construction work. In terms of ritual requirements, contemporary development projects logically appear to parallel precolonial royal construction.

I didn't believe the rumors of headhunting, and as a result, I was quite brave throughout the scare. I assumed these rumors were distortions of the modern world I thought I knew. (I didn't even think of the reports I had read that said the Indonesian army had sponsored Dayaks in taking Chinese heads in West Kalimantan in the late 1960s, since I classified that as modern ethnic violence rather than archaic human sacrifice.)[8] I felt a little more unsettled, however, when I talked to educated, cosmopolitan Banjar acquaintances about the headhunting scare. I remember particularly two similar conversations—one with a teacher in the regency seat and one with a journalist in the provincial capital. Each confirmed the historical precedents of the rumor. Precolonial kingdoms, they said, had organized raids to obtain human heads for the sanctification of public buildings. Both equivocated over the possibility that such a practice might still continue. "Of course, that happened in the old days," one said; "nowadays, they probably use the head of a water buffalo."

I began to lose my sureness that I knew the world of oil drills and hydroelectric dams. Why had I dismissed the headhunting rumor out of hand, with no evidence against it? I never gathered more decisive evidence; nor would it be fair to say that it doesn't matter whether the rumor was true. What I learned was the danger of hasty skepticism—a skepticism bred in my own heritage of stories about the state and modernity. It is these stories for which Meratus knowledge of government headhunters, whatever its epistemological status, offers a new hearing. In the remainder of this section, I present some of these stories as appraised in the light of headhunter tales. To maintain the frame in which serious social analysis can be seen as storytelling, I have interspersed theoretical discussion and headhunting anecdotes.

> The first film I saw in Java featured primitive Dayak villains. Banjar men told me they could use this stereotype when travelling in Java. All they had to do was say they came from Kalimantan, and everyone acted afraid.
> The myth of the savage, they implied, is always a strategic myth.

The Meratus story of government headhunters refuses to become a chapter in the narrative of modernization in which diverse traditional societies are transformed into familiar modern ones by advances in education, technology, and health care. The narrative of modernization has been criticized so often that I wish it were unnecessary to bring it up here.[9] Yet, although perhaps discredited for talking about the neocolonial relationship between Third World and Western countries, this story still seems to organize discussions of the relationship between states and tribal minorities. States are seen as the agents that "integrate" their tribal minorities into internationally approved development agendas, rescuing the tribes from isolation. Even critical voices endorse these same assumptions about both modernity and tradition to the extent that they describe how modernity threatens the traditional vitality of once autonomous cultures. Anthropologists' efforts to show the coherence and effectiveness of local cultures rebound in implications that new developments must be familiar modernizations since they move beyond the cultural systems we describe. In the anthropology of Borneo, for example, the classic studies focus insights about difference at the level of analytically synchronic and autonomous Dayak social systems.[10] "Change" appears as a category which, by default, brings us toward what we know. The story of traditional people at the doorway of the state-sponsored modern world (with which we are already familiar) readily emerges here.[11]

Lately, interest in modernity has been revived by recent readings of the work of Michel Foucault. Foucault alerts us to the disciplinary aspects of "modern" power and the forms of knowledge with which it develops.[12] This "modern" power is particularly well developed in the technologies of twentieth-century nation-states. Yet, despite its fascinating possibilities for an anthropology of differences between and within state-sponsored institutions and discourses, all too often, the inspiration has been to offer chic new clothes to a familiar history of increasing "modern" homogeneity. In this view, disciplinary politics and destabilized ironic consciousness advance unchanged across the globe.[13]

Just as the discourse on traditional cultures creates the familiar dynamic "modern" as its reflex, the homogenizing discourse on modernity implies a varied but passive, static, and unreflective "traditional."

> I returned to a Banjar town after the period of the headhunting scare to find that a rumor of dangerous men had been circulating there, too. Banjar women told me that an outlaw motorcycle gang was on the loose. The gang had entered a house, the women told me, and found a woman and her infant child; they raped the woman and threw her baby out the window. The men in the gang were so well protected by invulnerability magic that the police had been unable to capture them.
>
> Was this a Banjar version of the headhunting story? A separate set of fantasies is engaged. These are law-and-order fantasies of closed, moral households and bad men on the streets. I know of similar fantasies in the United States. Yet, it makes no sense to let familiarity disguise the imaginativeness of such stories.

To get around pervasive expectations of a fully known, advancing modernity requires careful attention to particular cultural agendas. Scholars of the Indonesian state have tried to do just this in their analyses of the cultural construction of state power. A discussion of state power began in studies of precolonial kingdoms as scholars argued that architecture, regalia, ceremonies, and processions were important elements in creating the power and potency that allowed kings to rule. Clifford Geertz (1980), for example, has explored how the nineteenth-century Balinese *negara* created its rule through theatrical display. This discussion also touches on the contemporary state. Benedict Anderson (1972) has shown continuities between the political symbolism of Javanese kingdoms and Sukarno's nationalist regime of the 1950s and 60s. Niels Mulder (1978: 90–98) has explored how Javanese mysticism enters government development plans. Although this literature offers an important antidote to assumptions about culturally transparent modern politics, much of the work draws on models of culture that stress coherence over internal political dynamics. These models make it difficult to talk about diversity, opposition, and change. They offer no way of understanding the divergent cultural commitments of subordinate and peripheral groups, except to see such groups as independent cultural units.

A police and army post is found at the end of each vehicular road approaching the Meratus Mountains from the west. I was expected to report to the post whenever I went into or out of the mountains. On one occasion, I found the walls of the army office covered with maps of the area. Most surprising to me was a security map showing several areas in the Meratus foothills as *daerah rawan*, "zones of disturbance," while Banjar villages nearer the market town were marked *daerah pengunduran*, "fall-back zones." I was puzzled because Meratus neighborhoods, both there and elsewhere, were extremely peaceful. The Meratus I met had been quick to speak of their respect for the government, whatever its policies—much quicker than were people in town, where many voiced worry about inefficiency and corruption. What was being pacified?

In response to models of power that posit an internal cultural homogeneity, some scholars have become interested in the concept of resistance. In this direction, James Scott's *Weapons of the Weak* (1985) explores "everyday" resistance in a Malaysian rice-farming village. Scott shows that poor farmers do not accept increasing economic inequalities with resignation; they rail against the greed of the rich and boycott the fields of those who use harvesting combines (which take away jobs). This analysis is useful in breaking up false expectations of an unquestioned hegemony. It keys scholarly attention to cross talk and back talk, as well as to political contests in which dominant meanings are established. Yet there are no surprises—no government headhunters—in the articulate economic analyses of each class, although the poor hold on to an archaic vocabulary of moral decency that the rich have abandoned for capitalism. To avoid the implication that farmers are universal class exemplars whose resistance is carried as an essential attribute, perhaps Scott could have turned more to the other intersections of power and difference—gender, ethnicity, regionalism, state control—within which the poor and the rich find their oppositional identities.[14]

Aihwa Ong (1987) does explore these complex intersections in her research on Malaysian factory women. Instead of beginning with a framework of class-based resistance, she maps the intersecting, discursive fields that shape the identities of the factory women: rural Malay values, Japanese management concepts, Islamic movements, state campaigns. Within these fields, the women create their own strategies, which mix and manipulate contradictory discursive streams: They see spirits under their microscopes; they claim no contradiction between religious piety and personal freedom. This is a useful approach for my project, for government headhunters reveal power-laden cultural negotiations in some of the same ways as spirits in microscopes do.

But what if, for a moment, we allowed ourselves to think that government headhunters might exist? Ong assumes that spirits in microscopes do not exist; thus, she can dismiss women's possession as a "safety valve" that does "not confront the real cause of their distress" (1987:201). As a confused strategy, seeing spirits seems disconnected from more rational attempts to gain respect or independence. In this vein, Richard A. Drake (1989) analyzes Dayak rumors of government kidnappings for public-construction sacrifice as a confused expression of real anxieties about the tribal-state relationship.[15] In my analysis, I want to give the rumors a little more room. By suspending disbelief, even for a moment, it becomes possible to find structural elements that are useful in describing the Meratus situation.

The story of government headhunters offers a number of clues about Meratus-state relations. The story reiterates that Meratus marginality is an ongoing relationship with power, not a recent feature of "contact" and "acculturation." The story also emphasizes the importance of force in state power. Certainly, the military historically has been key in bringing state rule to Meratus communities.

Then, too, the story suggests the maintenance of a peripheral vulnerability rather than an attempt to integrate the populace into the core population. Raiders don't subdue a population as much as scare it. Army patrols and police border posts are, in many ways, similar to raiders. Development schemes promote "national integration" only as they reproduce and intensify relations of terror.

The story of government headhunters also recalls the importance of ceremonial projects of "building" as a state activity—and of "building" understood locally as "development." I found it sobering to read that about half of Indonesia's development budget during this period was spent on building and civil construction (Robison 1986:181). The popular understanding of "development" as having something to do with promoting human well-being is not the issue. "Development" consists of the promotion of state construction projects, and state construction projects—planted with water buffalo or whatever other heads—are an issue of state ceremony.[16]

Finally, the necessity of human heads for state building projects suggests Meratus appreciation of a relationship between core and periphery, city and frontier, such that the ostentation of the first requires the vulnerability of the latter. These are indeed the conditions of uneven development.

By necessity, rumors play an important part in unpredictable and vulnerable situations. Rumors offer a clue to knowledge not yet generally established by suggesting where powerful centers may shift. Like changing market prices, rumors cannot be ignored where quick evasions are necessary for survival. Even as unfounded rumor, the story of government headhunters offers much information about the terrors of regional asymmetry.

In appreciating local wisdom, however, it remains obvious that this wisdom does not replicate national standards. Government headhunters are a striking reminder of globally interconnected but locally incongruent imaginings of power.

At the height of the headhunting scare, I attended a festival at which an assistant village head gave a speech in which he asked everyone to carry government identity cards at all times, as specified by government policy. The main reason he gave was that if someone died on a forest trail, people could identify the body. At the time, this seemed odd to me, because most Meratus are illiterate (and so could not read the cards). Besides, the chances of dying where no one could identify the body seemed slim. In hindsight, the speech makes sense as a response to government headhunters (who can read I.D. cards, as well as take away other means of identification—i.e., one's head). Perhaps it was a fragment of discipline thrown back at the source of both chaos and order.

In my next story, I turn to order and its relationship to force. Whereas the state labels order the antithesis of violence, the Meratus know order as the prerogative of the most violent. The imposition of state-endorsed order can be one of the state's most terrifying threats.

COSMIC CUISINE

The table below is taken from a government publication on a Meratus resettlement village, in a section entitled "Advances that have been achieved" (Soetanto et al. 1978:12, my translation).

> They are already aware of bodily cleanliness, as can be seen from the manner in which they wash their bodies (bathe) on the average:

Bathing once a day	19%
Bathing twice a day	78%
Bathing three times a day	3%

> Similarly, [progress] can be seen from their eating and drinking:

Three meals a day	3%
Two meals a day	97%
One meal a day	—

The resettlement program makes it clear that the goal of state policy is not just military control, but new forms of order in daily life.[17] Since the 1970s, regional models for the transformation of Meratus life have been derived through the national project for the Management of Isolated Populations.

> In Indonesia there are 1,484,748 or 1.5 million members of isolated populations. The manner of life and livelihood of these people is very simple. They live in small groups isolated and scattered in mountain areas. Their beliefs still have an animist or dynamist character; they still believe in invisible powers and spirits. Their social life is influenced by a tribal way of life, and they are always suspicious of what comes from outside. Their thought patterns are very simple, static, and traditional. Thus, too, their social system, economy, and culture are backward. *They lack everything: nutrients, knowledge, skills, etc.* In the effort to raise their standard of living, the program to care for isolated populations is operated with the goal of *guiding the direction of their social, economic, cultural, and religious arrangements in accord with the norms that operate for the Indonesian people.* (Hamda 1979:2, my translation, my emphasis)

In the 1970s and 80s, the most visible activity of the Isolated Populations project in South Kalimantan involved gathering Meratus in resettlement villages in the western foothills. Resettlement facilitated administration and, as one program description explained, it allowed government guidance "until [the people] are capable of growing and participating in accord with the demands of development" (Suhud 1979:38)—confirming the idea that rural people must work to please Development, rather than the other way around. Officials hoped that resettlement village standards would also influence those Meratus not yet resettled. Indeed, Meratus quickly ascertained the importance to government aesthetics of clustered rows of houses. In the western foothills, they built new clustered settlements; even in the central mountains, model clusters were built—so the houses would "look good if the government comes to visit," as one local leader put it. Residents of the central mountains hoped that signs of deference to resettlement standards locally would prevent relocation to the eastern or western side of the mountains, far from their farms, forest resources, and familiar places. "I wouldn't know where to find fallen durian; I wouldn't even know the trail to the river," explained Induan Hiling, one of The Bear's neighbors, in concrete imagery that evoked much larger anxieties.

Resettlement, was only a beginning, however. Government publications stressed that guidance must target mental as well as physical characteristics of the group and that new values must be introduced. The table at the beginning of this section suggests the importance of disciplined habits in officials' plans for this metamorphosis.

Meratus take these government demands seriously. One Meratus village head used a mealtime metaphor of order that could be taken directly from the publication quoted above. He was explaining why Meratus were considered "not yet ordered" (*belum diatur*): "Banjar drink in the morning," he said, referring to coffee or tea and a pastry, "and then have two meals during the day. We [Meratus] sometimes eat five times a day and sometimes once a day. It's not ordered." I thought he was speaking apocryphally until I heard numerous references to eating habits in government rhetoric. Reorganizing eating habits allows officials to bring together the ideals of science (nutrition) and administration (personal discipline). Furthermore, government models of food preparation can provide a spectacle that officials hope will impress the populace into acknowledging state authority. I saw one such event at the opening of a resettlement village. It featured a "nutrition demonstration" arranged by the Bureau of Family Welfare (*Pembinaan Kesejahteraan Keluarga*): elegantly prepared curry dishes and spicy sautés of locally unavailable meat, vegetables, and tofu exposed the local people to the sophisticated styles and smells of urban cooking.

Meratus stage spectacles of beautiful cooking, too—for spirits. In these events, correct cooking demonstrates an appreciation for order as well; yet the state's agenda is subtly transformed. The state's disciplinary order, with its daily monotony, becomes a sporadic celebratory order which enlivens without imprisoning its participants.

In a number of shamanic ceremonies, sweet rice desserts decorated with flowers and fragrant herbs are prepared for hosting the spirits. In dewa ceremonies, there are offerings of cakes made in the shape of the pleasing and powerful possessions of dewa spirits, such as boats, airplanes, scissors, combs, jewelry, flowers, and lines of uniformed soldiers sometimes sculpted with their rifles. It is understood that dewa can be dangerous; but this is not merely an appeasement of dewa ferocity. The beauty and order of ritual hospitality empower the community. Meratus communities put on their finest celebrations at shamanic festivals.

The spirits are invited to savor the smell of the food. In return, the spirits are asked to look benevolently upon their hosts. Shamanic metaphors sometimes explicitly invoke the state; the spirits are asked to restrain their "armies" or restrict "taxation." Dewa, in particular, include kings, administrators, and soldiers. In acknowledging the official-like power of dewa, shamans point to the dewa-like power of state officials. Like dewa, the state is a source of standards of beauty, order, and final knowledge, as these transcend ordinary experience. Like dewa, the state orders and beautifies, in part, by requiring standards of fine hospitality which local people must train themselves to offer.

Of course, sporadic hospitality is not actually the ultimate goal of state officials. There has been a crossing of alien tongues: Officials malign traditional ritual for holding people back from state penetration, while Meratus shamans offer more deference to state authority through ritual. State officials scheme to replace "static, traditional" thinking with "rational, dynamic" thought. Meratus shamans assume that the state's demands are formal and ritualistic. In the context of the central mountains in the early 1980s, the shamans had a point.

The shamanic interpretation that hospitality is central to state demands for order is the necessary background for the the story Induan Hiling told me about the visit of an east-side police sector chief to the central mountains in the spring of 1981. This was the same sector chief who may have nearly drowned a villager from a Meratus–Banjar border area a few months before. I missed the sector chief's visit (I was on the west side amidst rumors of government headhunters); but many Meratus I knew told me stories of how the sector chief managed a local dispute about a durian tree, to the dissatisfaction of both sides, and then later stripped a young man wearing army-style pants. (I mention these stories in chapter 4.) Induan Hiling's account differed in focusing on his message of order rather than his ferocity; but the authority of force and order are, of course, connected. Her story opens a discussion of the contradictory local consequences of ritual accommodation to the state.

In 1981, Induan Hiling was a neighbor, but not an admirer, of The Bear. Instead of following his ritual leadership, she had begun to develop her own shamanic skills (an unusual path for a woman; see chapter 8). In this, she had the encouragement of Uma Adang, of whom Induan Hiling was a devoted fan. Emphasis on proper order was a leadership style cultivated by those central-mountain Meratus, both male and female, who called upon Uma Adang's authority.

When the sector chief was staying at the Ukut hall, I went there to meet him, and I talked to him about the possibility of developing the villages. He said he was inspecting development, but he hadn't seen anything good.

Ukut, he said, was really not yet ordered. He told me about the problems he had with the food. They had butchered a chicken, but they had cooked it without any sour spices or chili peppers. Sour spices and chili peppers are the first two requirements of the government! The chicken was tasteless, without even enough salt. He was only able to eat two mouthfuls of rice. The rice was even served on banana leaves.

He also had a problem with the sleeping arrangements. He slept on a mat on the floor, and no one even gave him a pillow. He was stepped on by dogs, and he woke up to find a python crawling on his knees. Truly! Other people screamed, but he was forced to lie quietly.[18]

He asked me to take over the cooking. I went with him to the Tidung hall, and I cooked a chicken. I added coconut milk, sour spices, chili peppers. I also cooked young cassava leaves, which he praised as being full of nutrients. He ate two platefuls of rice and told me I was an intelligent person. This time, he slept on the raised bed that a young man had made; and he wasn't bothered at all by dogs. So he said Tidung was really a much better place than Ukut.

After the sector chief made a speech, he asked if anyone had any suggestions for the government. No one said anything, so finally I spoke up. I said what we needed from the government was plates, glasses, pots, and kettles—not for our own use, but so as to serve important guests properly.

"Sour spices and chili peppers are the first two requirements of the government."[19] Central-mountain Meratus rarely use such spices in cooking; but Induan Hiling understood their importance in the dominant regional aesthetic. Actually, the sacrifice of a chicken for dinner in Ukut was an honor by Meratus standards, but, according to Induan Hiling, the sector chief could not recognize it because the chicken was not cooked properly. Similarly, Meratus ordinarily sleep on mats and serve rice on banana leaves; but, she argued, this was not appropriate for a government man. No wonder, then, that he chose Tidung over Ukut as the more orderly, better developed neighborhood. Finally, given that hospitality appeared to be what the government wanted, what could be more appropriate than to ask the police to provide the dishes for future receptions?

Induan Hiling's story is based on the premise that, despite the opportunity for atrocities, when the security forces can be appeased with a few nicely cooked chickens, central-mountain communities are in a good position for survival. Of course, this kind of appeasement is not possible without a rhetoric of total deference to state authority. Yet, as long as the officers go back to their posts, the ritual trays are put away, and shamans become ordinary farmers and foragers for a while, then, perhaps, the flexible, mobile "disorder" of everyday life and social relations can be provided another growing season. The continuing existence of Meratus settlement suggests that this logic of compliance has indeed had its moments of success.

My final section turns from powerful offerings to powerful words as I explore the political strategies of shamanic chants. In responding to state demands for an obedience defined by styles and forms, shamans see ritual and talk as important political arenas. In this context, shamanic chants renegotiate the state's terms for political subjectivity. Chants are the travel passes through which shamans try to outmaneuver the state's protection racket. The text I question here is one in which I was tutored by The Bear.

THE VILLAGE FENCE

> Angkalilililililih
> Burning incense
> Smell of resins
> Rising to wrap around the hall
> Rising to slip around the temple
> Curling around the hall's house posts

Sending up a waft of fragrance
Piercing the ridgetop of the roof
Separating the low tree branches
Piercing through the high tree branches
Forming eight links
Becoming eight bridges.

Words such as these open the chant in a dewa ceremony by transforming the smoke of incense resin into a bridge for spiritual travel. These particular words are translated from a somewhat simplified chant that The Bear dictated to me one day to ease my frustration in trying to follow intricate all-night performances. A dewa performance—whether for curing, celebrating the harvest, or "fencing the village" in the rite called *basanggar banua*—lasts hours or days. If I tried to take the reader all the way through just one performance—or even through my twenty-six-page learner's text—we, too, would be here all night. Instead, a few lines from this text should give a sense of the poetry of shamanic politics.[20]

As every Meratus shaman can explain, the first principle of shamanic travel—whether on dewa or on other spiritual routes—is the ability of words to build a framework of perception. The chants allow the shaman to move in an empowered cognitive space.

What looked far appears close
What looked close appears far

In this empowered space, the body is a landscape and the landscape is the body. Travel over the landscape is accomplished as the chant re-frames one's knowledge of the landscape of one's own body. The contours of the body are where The Bear's dewa travel begins:

Falling to the twin mountain peaks [the shoulders]
The mountains old as existence
The mountains old as birth
The mountain peaks that face each other
The mountain peaks that sit in a line
Then taking off again
Swinging to another place
The place where the golden wells [the eyes] are found
The two wells to which one climbs
The wells that are walled with standing swords [eyelashes]
The wells that are walled by hanging knives

> The golden wells that throw off light
> The diamond wells that reflect a shine
> That cleans the shamans' dancing floor.

Identification between body and landscape facilitates wider travels to places that become part of the shaman's expanding self. As the shaman incorporates new locations through the chant, he is able to "borrow" their power.

Each visit replicates the shaman's own circumstances. A spiritual shaman is "surprised" at his or her ceremony. There are no clear distinctions between powerful people, places, and shamanic leaders. Mountains become court centers, and rulers become mountains; all are shamanic leaders in the sense of "those who hold together [a ceremony and a community]" (*panggalung*, from the root word "coil"). On the summit of Mount Kalawan, for example, the shaman finds a great city of dewa which roars and gurgles with the mountain's springs:

> Mount Kalawan City comes into view,
> And the two siblings are surprised
> In the city of Mount Kalawan.
> The ones who guard the key to the waters,
> One hears the sound of water rushing,
> A festival full of sounds of laughter,
> A festival full of sounds of merrymaking,
> In the city of Mount Kalawan.

Are the dewa crowds the same as, or more than, the laughing waters of Mount Kalawan? Is this a way of seeing Mount Kalawan—a story of its ritual history, a visit to its spirit rulers, or perhaps just a detour to some part of the shaman's body? All are true; the ambiguities that blur distinctions of body, landscape, ruler, rite, spirit, spell, and shaman are the vehicles for empowering shamanic travel. In the process, the contrast between city and countryside—a contrast of which Meratus are very much aware as an element of their vulnerability—is erased. Similarly, wilderness and court are both center and periphery; the shaman can "borrow" and blend the authority of each.

The dewa chant allows the shaman to absorb the potency of many an old-time hero and ruler whose history reverberates in the shamanic landscape.

> Following the line of vision quests
> To remnants of past sacred kingdoms,

> Ghosts of original sacred kingdoms,
> The ones that are called ancient auras.
> Queen Majapahit the original:
> The shaman who holds together the ceremony.
> I borrow your heroes, your fighting magic,
> The heroes of ancient sacred kingdoms,
> The magic of original sacred auras,
> The ones called the seven heroes,
> Who sit at the mouth of Broken Banjar Stream,
> Who guard twin cannons, male and female,
> The sound of their firing shakes the earth.[21]

Many stories are condensed in these lines. According to The Bear, Queen Majapahit was the first ruler of Kalimantan, and she was foremother of all succeeding rulers. Such royalty do not die, but disappear in the mountains, where, occasionally, they offer vision-quest encounters. The Meratus Mountains are full of meditating Banjar nobles who fought Dutch colonial takeover and eventually disappeared into the wilderness. Moving at lightning speed, the chant recalls these stories without a long telling; there are other places to visit before the night is over:

> Falling to the Mountain in the Center of the World,
> Going to the Mountain in the Center of the Earth,
> The Bearded King is surprised
> Out on Halao-halao Mountain.
> His hair is like strings of palajau flowers,
> Leaning bamboos are his moustache,
> His beard is a palm inflorescence.
> The king shaman of the Center of the World,
> His skin black as resin smoke,
> He stands reaching up to the sky.
> His skin is dark as a dying sugar palm,
> The king protector at the Center of the Earth.
> His warriors frighten fiends,
> His warriors frighten ghouls,
> He closes off the Center of the World,
> And he is called King Shaman [*Panggalung*].
> The shaman whose head is wrapped in clouds,
> The shaman whose head is wrapped in mist.

The highest peak in the Meratus Range, Halao-halao Mountain[22] rises dramatically and can be seen at a great distance. The mountain is aptly described through the image of the dark king wrapped in clouds. As the "Center of the World," it is a place of power—but it is not the only center. In its own way, every stop on the shaman's path is a center. When I tried to draw the places of the dewa chant on a piece of paper, I merely annoyed The Bear; he rejected every draft because there were too many central places that were not in the middle of the drawing. His dewa chant maps a non-Euclidean topology of multiple centers.

This political vocabulary applies equally to the spirits and to the state. The Meratus Mountains are divided into numerous districts, which extend toward separate regency hierarchies. From the mountain perspective, each district official's authority seems autonomous. Boundaries within the mountains are vague and contested; administrators claim overlapping spheres. Police officers from each Meratus border post tour the mountains as independent commanders; their integration at the provincial level is so distant as to have little local relevance. The advantage of good relations with one sector chief may be cancelled by the actions of another. Similarly, each dewa center must be appeased independently, and a shaman must travel to be politically effective.

> Can one stop here at this level?
> Can one rest here at this post?
> Not every invitation is issued,
> The full count is not yet made.
> The invitations must be issued higher,
> The count must be extended further.

The shaman's travel is a political act intended to defend a community. Dewa spirits, like the state, extend sporadic threats by means of their uniformed security forces:

> Dressed all in black,
> Dressed all in yellow,
> Dressed all in white,
> Dressed all in green.

Like the state, the spirits offer their protection in exchange for well-ordered ceremony and gracious, deferential hospitality.

> Pity us, pity us, offer your umbrella.
> Have compassion, offer us help.

You are the only one we revere,
Every year we come to you.

Through ceremony, the shaman builds a *pagar banua*, a protective
"village fence." This is a fence of words and rites, a fence of ritual performance. It is a fence that needs to be understood in relation to the total
absence of fences on the Meratus landscape. The chant promises to transform a motley group of neighbors into a recognizable (fenced) "community" for the authorities; in return, the authorities are expected to keep
their armies out.

If there are no runaways,
If we are corralled, enclosed;
In this country, in this village,
If you want to make our fence,
If you make our boundary space,
Don't overrun us with ogres,
Don't overrun us with demons,
Won't we party, won't we gather,
A hundred or two thousand years.

The party, and its chant, are the fence that holds back demons. *Banua*,
the word used here for "village," is a term ordinarily used by Meratus to
characterize Banjar ("village people") in contrast to Meratus. (The word
"country," *nagari*, is not used in ordinary speech.) The chant converts
disorderly mountain communities into administratively acceptable villages. It domesticates the Meratus in exchange for protection.

The chant suggests that Meratus communities are in danger because
dewa mistakenly see people as wild animals. According to the chant,
dewa see "fish in [people's] hearts and wild boar in [their] livers"; they
don't recognize the people as human. The chant aims to intervene:

Don't come hunting [for us] at the source of the rivers,
Don't come fishing [for us] at the source of the streams . . .
Don't come and see us wrongly,
Don't come and recognize us falsely.

The chant claims a human community that deserves autonomy and respect. This is the political message of the chant among both humans and
spirits. The state may consider the Meratus wild animals or savages, but
the chant contests these categories, declaring that Meratus form civilized

communities. The shaman, empowered in the chant as a peer of any ruler in the capital or the wilderness, is the leader who can tell the state that his neighbors are truly citizens.

> Turning around and going back,
> Back from the world of hospitality,
> Back from the world of invitations.
> Who comes back first?
> First the protected community,
> Followed by the youthful drummer,
> Only then the accompanist singer,
> Then the shaman at the last,
> Drags his apprentice at the end of his belt.

Holding on to The Bear's belt, I return to summarize my arguments about local leadership and the state. Meratus leaders counter the threat of a fierce, unpredictable state authority through respectful ritual. Through ritual, they offer submission intended to evade a more costly disciplinary regime. One of the most important parts of this kind of ceremony is *talk*, talk that redefines the terms of political subjectivity and local leadership. This talk is found in both shamans' chants and more secular and less stylized forms of political speaking.[23]

Shamans' chants contest state understandings of the Meratus. The chants show shamans as respectful subjects as well as free agents who finesse their relationships with numerous independent authorities. Bureaucratic titles such as "assistant neighborhood head" do not capture them in a hierarchy but instead empower them to "corral" a community. From such a position, these leaders claim the full citizenship of their imagined constituencies. Their communities, they say, are not outside state control, as the state claims, but are nicely organized *within* it. These people are not wild. As The Bear put it, they are "chickens of the government."

The occasion for this metaphor was a discussion of the plight of the Ukut neighborhood (which had failed miserably to please the section officer who had such a bad evening there). The Bear was heatedly criticizing the neighborhood head of Ukut (who was not present) for not creating a centralized village settlement. I was taken aback at his criticism—first, because no one had made me aware of any advantages of this kind of settlement; and, second, because The Bear himself did not live in such a settlement. I asked him why he thought creating a centralized settlement was such a good idea.

The Bear looked at me in surprise and asked: Doesn't everyone in America live in crowded groups? Perhaps I was overreacting against dominant Indonesian standards that make a subway station at rush hour seem the pinnacle of civilization when I told him that it varies. I described my father's place in northwest Pennsylvania where farms and houses are well separated. That is when he replied, kindly and philosophically, "In America, everyone may be clever; but here, we are chickens of the government."

For a long time I saw his comment as merely a statement of submission. Chickens are easy sacrifices. A chicken demands little attention and no equality with its keepers. I have come to think, however, that the chicken metaphor also involves pride. In the Meratus context, chickens are uncooped and quite independent. They forage all day by themselves; except as chicks, they are not fed—although they steal a good bit of rice if no one drives them off. At night they come home to roost on the rooftop; at daybreak they scatter.

Chickens are also fighters, and Meratus respect them as such. "Which of my chickens are squabbling today?" asks a high supernatural in one Meratus tale as the hero duels with death beneath her house in the sky. To the supernatural, the hero is a dependent chicken. Yet, is there not courage in the fact that he has taken as his opponent Death himself—whom he challenged first to a cockfight, and when he lost that, to a sword fight that took them from the underworld up to the sky?

The Bear, too, was a cockfighter and a proud fighting man. Even in submission, he was ready to stand up to the forces of death.

3 FAMILY PLANNING

The neat lines of contraceptive pills in their plastic-and-foil bubble pack were among the first things to greet me when I came to the government resettlement village of Niwan in the western Meratus foothills. "Syntex, Palo Alto, California," read the label, reminding me that I was not the first California product to make it to these hills. The pills belonged to Induan Kilay, the first Meratus woman to befriend me, who proudly showed them to me as a sign of civilization. She explained that she took them to improve her health and sense of vigor.

The lines of pills could have been a miniature display of the lines of government-issued houses, each carefully numbered and registered in replicating bureaucratic charts and files. Daily pills and houses in alignment each advanced the discipline of time and space so central to the state's standards of propriety and progress. Yet the orderly displays I saw allowed alternative interpretations. The pills I knew in the United States as artifacts of medical science had been transformed by Indonesian state discourse into an icon of bureaucratic order, and transformed again, within South Kalimantan Banjar acquiescence, into the daily health-promoting herbal tonics of folk medicine, and again into nodes for Meratus acceptance of Banjar and state models of civilization. These interpretations coexisted uneasily, each threatening but never fully displacing the others. The houses properly assigned to single families often seethed with the life of extended kin groups or, like temporary habitations on shifting swidden sites, were abandoned.

Perhaps this kind of instability of meaning and practice in a resettlement village does not seem startling. Instability might be interpreted, for example, as the inevitable product of "assimilation" and "change" as "tradition" is threatened. This view presupposes a site of intact tradition somewhere up in the hills or, at least, somewhere in the recent past. But, what if tradition itself is always negotiated in relation to state demands and local concerns about regional and ethnic status? As I trace gender and fertility practices and debates into the central Meratus Mountains in this chapter, I find no locus of premodern social reproduction but, instead, more variations of the cross talk of Meratus regional marginality.

Theorizing gender and reproduction

Conventional accounts of marginal groups such as the Meratus have not ignored state and regional politics; however, these accounts tend to portray wider political influences as imposed on a solid core of traditional social and cultural organization. In such models, gender and fertility lie at the core of internal affairs. Here is a territory rich with puns on the various meanings of *reproduction*—begetting and bearing babies, on the one hand, and social and cultural continuity, on the other. The blends and matches have been various: Marxist household relations reproduce gendered labor power; structuralist connubial exchanges reproduce "difference"; psychoanalytic families reproduce gendered psyches; structural-functionalist lineages reproduce (gender-divided) societies. Each model locates the cultural construction of gendered parenting together with the very mechanisms seen as producing cultural integrity and autonomy. Although external influences may have an impact on gender, gender is not—in the first instance—historically constituted.

These models draw on European and North American cultural assumptions about gendered reproduction in both senses. In recent years, however, it has become more difficult for European and North American cultural analysts to take reproduction in either sense for granted. Public controversies about abortion, sterilization, surrogacy, and other issues concerning birth control, pregnancy, birth, and childcare make it clear that gender and childbearing are contested cultural domains rather than "natural facts." At the same time, those models of culture and society in which reproduction is envisioned as an unchanging continuity have been widely criticized as colonial fantasies. New approaches show culture as internally heterogeneous, as emerging from events as much as underlying them. Furthermore, these two challenges have not been independent. Among the more important theorists criticizing mechanical models of cultural reproduction are ethnographers of those gender debates that have problematized ideas about biological reproduction.[1]

This conjunction is as important for the ethnographer of out-of-the-way places as it is for the ethnographer of U.S. cities. The instability of discourses on gender and childbearing is not just a feature of the contemporary West. Only as ethnographers abandon a priori links among gender, childbearing, and cultural reproduction can the study of gender and parenting reveal heterogeneity and debate.

To describe discourses on gender and fertility in the central Meratus Mountains, I begin, then, with regional political developments. During the 1970s and 80s, nonresettled Meratus came under extraordinary pressure to show their conformity to state standards of development—or else risk resettlement. Ambitious Meratus men attempted to impress both government officials and Meratus neighbors by embracing regional authority. In this process, they endorsed the state's model of order in which their own communities, by definition, represented disorder. Although this understanding of regional asymmetries was not new, it became exceptionally important. And it brought to the fore its own contradictions and dilemmas, including dilemmas of gender and contraception.

To be qualified to lead, leaders needed to present themselves as transcending organic connection to the community. This model of leadership downplayed status divisions among Meratus, since no internally derived rank, gender, or generational position could itself support a leadership that depended on external sources of power and knowledge. At the same time, the model created its own divisions by setting the conditions of acquiescence and dissension.

Gender was implicated in a number of ways. Regional authorities had little interest in communicating directly with Meratus women; and Meratus women had less opportunity than men to do the kind of travelling that might have allowed them to make claims to regionally legitimate knowledge despite the wishes of the authorities. Women were not singled out in Meratus political discourse as a disadvantaged or protected category. Leaders presented themselves as extraordinary individuals who could transcend community vulnerabilities; few women managed such self-presentation. Women and less ambitious men were stuck being seen as ordinary Meratus—the peripheral, the disorganized. As reproductive practices became a node of state intervention, male leaders and ordinary women grew even more polarized. Subtle disagreements between men and women about the division of labor in parenting became issues of leadership and the right to speak. In this context, gender negotiations took place not so much in the substance of public speech but in the interplay of public speech, inarticulate practices, and quiet back talk.

This rather dense reading of the situation can be unravelled by telling a story. During my fieldwork, I thought the story funny, but inconsequential. My notes are brief jottings; perhaps details of the version presented here have been distorted by the chain of informal oral tellings through which the incident remains so clear in my memory. Yet, as I have turned my fieldwork goals inside out—from learning about the Meratus despite their marginality to writing about marginality itself—such stories become my ethnographic subject.

Pa'an Tini's list

In the 1970s and 80s, the government-sponsored Family Planning Program expanded rapidly as it was tied to local bureaucratic duties across the nation.[2] In Java, the program recruited women directly. In the early 1980s, officials organized mass "safaris" that gathered thousands of peasant women to have IUDs inserted (Hartmann 1987:77–83).[3] In Bali, family planning was integrated into household and community organization. "Household heads [met] once a month to discuss community matters, as well as the [family planning] status of eligible women in their households. A [hamlet] map identifie[d] each household according to the method of contraceptive use" (Chernichovsky and Meesook 1981:17).

In South Kalimantan, however, Islamic opposition to contraception (and to Jakarta policies more generally) among Banjar made birth control an affair of community spokesmen. Government pamphlets, for example, targeted local Banjar leaders and addressed religious issues. In peripheral areas of the province, regional officers delegated program goals entirely to local male officeholders. This is the context in which, in September 1980, Pa'an Tini was told (or so he claimed) by the district officer that village elections would be held if, and only if, he could enroll forty women in the national Family Planning Program.

Pa'an Tini lived in the central-mountain village of Ayuh, a huge administrative unit containing many scattered neighborhoods. In 1980, Ayuh had no village head. The previous village head had resigned in embarrassment after being intimidated by regional authorities from a different district. In the past, Ayuh (and other Meratus) officeholders had always been appointed by distant district officers. Banjar villagers, however, held elections for these offices. Ayuh men were excited that they might be allowed a mark of citizenship—an election.

In the last chapter I introduced Pa'an Tini briefly as a youthful militiaman, a neighbor of The Bear gearing up for his own shamanic and political leadership. Like The Bear, Pa'an Tini prided himself on his ability to deal with regional officials and, more abstractly, with "the government" they represented. Though young for the post, he was hoping to be selected as the new village head; and he was doing everything he could to show off his leadership skills. Once, for example, I heard him recite the names of cabinet ministers (or names that could have been cabinet ministers), to exhibit his abilities among the local people, who, like myself, knew nothing of these great names. When, at one of the season's biggest harvest festivals, Pa'an Tini spoke of having discussed village elections with the district officer, he was showing off his prowess in dealing with regional authorities. Yet his announcement might only have stimulated casual conversation had he not added, dramatically, that they had but five days in which to turn in the completed list of forty Family Planning acceptors, or the elections were off.

The announcement attracted a group of men eager to discuss the possibility of village elections. Despite the fact that the men intended to enlist women acceptors, no women other than myself joined the tight clump that formed for the discussion. After all, no woman had ever been appointed to village office, nor were women likely to be approved as candidates in an election. Some women, however, listened and made fun of the men from the sidelines. When one man suggested that they hold an election every six months to a year to encourage the elected official to work quickly, a woman called out, laughing, that they should vote every ten days. Another woman joked that the only village "developing" (*bangun*, or "getting up") that she had seen locally was "getting up from sleeping" every morning. The men tried to ignore this talk from the margins. At first I took notes, but soon I was too involved to write.

The national Family Planning Program is known as KB, which, for those in the know, is short for *keluarga berencana* ("family planning"). As the men spoke of the necessity of getting women to "enter KB," I became increasingly aware that most had no idea of the program's purpose. Confused by the direction of the talk, I interjected an explanation of contraception. The men around me were shocked; how could the government possibly want them to *limit* the size of their families? After all, weren't communities already too small and weak? Such a program, they said, was ridiculous. There had been a misunderstanding.

Pa'an Tini, however, was ready to explain the project from another angle. The district officer had specified nothing about limiting reproduction; all he said he wanted was a *list* of women. Compiling this *list*,

Pa'an Tini argued, was their task at the meeting; everything else was ir-relevant.

The men quickly understood and agreed. They set to work and before long had compiled a list of the names of married women. Pa'an Tini hiked down to the district office with the list. A few months later, he was pre-sented with a large supply of oral contraceptives. He brought these back to his house and hung them under his rafters. And there, for the most part, they stayed.

A few women relatives begged for a pill or two because, they said, they wanted to try them out. Pa'an Tini said they stopped asking when they found that the pills had no particular effect on their feeling of health. Asking repeatedly would not have been easy for those who valued their independence. Besides, as I had learned in administering antibiotics, instructions for daily use struck most women—and nonbureaucratically inclined men—as merely another form of government discipline to be po-litely ignored whenever possible.

Meanwhile, the district officer had his quota. (How many such inci-dents do national statistics bury?)[4] And, although the elections never materialized, Pa'an Tini was on his way to a reputation as a man with powerful government connections.

Planning families

Working the edge of state authority, Pa'an Tini mediated cross talk on family, consanguinity, generation, and gender. His story begins to illumi-nate the layers of crossed messages between regional officials and male Meratus leaders—and between leaders and ordinary women. But he was no neutral translator; his own ambitions shaped the kind of politics he could articulate.

Pa'an Tini's ingenuity offers the trickster's entry into the more general predicaments of Meratus leaders facing state demands. Yet, at least in 1980, Pa'an Tini was not a playful man; he was full of enthusiasm for law and order and the wisdom of the government. Longing for the legitimacy of village elections, he had invited state intervention and welcomed Fam-ily Planning. But he was caught in the contradictions of his own leader-ship. He could not really fulfill the district officer's order, because he could neither imagine nor invent plannable families.

In asking community leaders to meet Family Planning goals, the state envisions particular kinds of families and communities. These conjugal "families" (*keluarga*) have male "heads" (*kepala keluarga*) who represent, and are responsible for, their wives and children. Bounded groups of family heads are led by a neighborhood or village "head," who represents them for the regional government. These are families and communities that can be counted, taxed, mapped, administered—and whose fertility can be planned.

Pa'an Tini, however, had no such conceptions with which to work among his constituency. When they reported to regional officials, the Meratus leaders I knew slipped local umbun, swidden-making groups, into categories that required government "families" whenever possible. Umbun resemble government "families" in several ways. They form around a responsible man and woman, usually a conjugal couple; and they generally include the couple's children as dependents. Yet umbun are not government "families." Founding couples can be brother and sister, aunt and nephew, or other nonconjugal combinations; dependents are even more varied. Even when a male founder is husband and father to other umbun members, he is not a "head." Responsibility for umbun affairs rests with the founding couple, not with the man. Furthermore, the umbun is not a political cell of a stable community. Umbun founders form tentative, shifting alliances with other umbun; but they claim the prerogatives of choice and autonomy. Umbun founders consider themselves the potential focal point of their own political community, rather than as a brick in a predesignated communal plan.

Ambitious men like Pa'an Tini used not umbun but a cross-cutting rhetoric of consanguineal kinship to bring together political constituencies. Unlike the status-delimiting kinship rhetorics familiar in anthropology, this one invoked an inclusive vision of consanguinity that collapsed collateral difference, absorbed affines, embraced adoptions, obscured gender differentiation, and brought in just about anyone who was willing. (Thus, even where I wasn't explicitly adopted as a cousin-sibling, I could be considered one by common descent from the generation of Adam and Eve.) Two basic principles were disseminated by this kinship rhetoric. First, consanguines should share resources and cooperate on common projects. Second, members of a younger generation should respect their elders, who, in turn, should care for their juniors. Invoking these principles, men like Pa'an Tini exhorted their neighbors to join together in festivals, work parties, dispute settlements—and meetings about family planning. Perhaps it is obvious how conceptually important having babies might be in this framework of respect and cooperation. The parent-child intergenerational relationship is the model of the respectful attention on which this political rhetoric depends. It made no sense for Pa'an Tini to limit anybody's descendants when they were his own potential constituents.

Yet Pa'an Tini and the men with whom he gathered would be the last to emphasize discrepancies between their stance and state agendas. They needed state support to maintain their local prominence. The leaders I knew argued, at least indirectly, that the consanguineal idioms with which they forged communities had been endorsed by the state. Far from staging confrontations of "kinship versus the state" (as described elsewhere in the literature on state expansion[5]), they identified their kinship idioms, like their adat, as an extension of national policy.

Indonesian national standards do not disallow the importance of kinship in politics. Kinship idioms abound, although they are often abstracted from genealogical connections. Politicians, for example, may be *bapak* ("father") patrons who protect their *anak buah* "followers" (*anak* means "child"). Meratus bring these idioms slightly closer to genealogy when men call their children, nephews, and nieces *anak buah*, children-followers. Banjar politicians also build constituencies through kinship ties. Kinship is not part of the discourse on Meratus-Banjar ethnic division; nor does kinship enter into the discourse on progress and civilization through which Meratus are criticized. Meratus leaders made use of these fragments and silences to develop their rhetoric of regional legitimacy.

Even as leaders pointed to the importance of kinship in building community unity and order, it was clear that this was not a language that supported administration and planning. Pa'an Tini could not imagine planning families because he did not supervise collections of family heads. As he attempted to influence an expandable network of kin, he could not instruct the men as "heads of families" nor could he expect the women to obey their husbands. He could only exhort them as cooperative cousins and respectful nephews and nieces. So he offered a superficial acquiescence to state policy that he hoped would leave a margin for local autonomy as long as the state did not supervise too closely. Indeed, he became a community protector, contradicting his own stance of state submission.

Yet Pa'an Tini protected only the community envisioned in his leadership. His leadership effectively barred women from access to state-provided contraception. Just as Pa'an Tini created a margin of autonomy for his community, he also helped shape the conditions of local dissatisfaction and dissent.

Women against the community

Ironically, Meratus women everywhere I lived and visited were interested in limiting the number of children they bore. Some women claimed to know quite a lot about fertility control. Pa'an Tini's aunt, for example, said she knew how to turn a uterus after childbirth so that further conception was impossible until remanipulation.[6] Others knew herbal potions thought to induce temporary or permanent sterility. Still, most women were hungry for more knowledge; they asked each other and pressed me for contraceptive advice and technology.

Clearly, their wishes went unheard in Pa'an Tini's arrangement with the district officer. This was not because the women were being silenced as women. Indeed, the men had disavowed the state's vision of gender-differentiated families with male heads, in favor of an imagined community of consanguines with no conceptual gender distinctions. In the process, however, a different kind of gender differentiation was created, one which polarized those (mainly men) who spoke in the central circle of a public meeting and those (mainly women) who sat on the sides, throwing out sarcastic remarks.

This is not the kind of gender segregation commonly described in cross-cultural literature. Meratus do not describe women and men as entirely different categories of social beings. Women's talk is not "complementary" to that of men (March 1983; Weiner 1976). Nor is women's talk a "subordinate discourse" that confirms male dominance as it defines female difference (Messick 1987; Boddy 1989). The Meratus I knew saw women and men as equally essential to a political community. Yet women and men—in uneven, sporadic, and contextually shifting ways—became differentially positioned in relation to both regional and local discourses. In the context of local leadership concerns with community unity and expansion, positive discussion of birth control became a form of back talk against community authority.

Neither women nor men formed a homogeneous group in relation to ideas about birth control. Teenage girls joined bachelors in an interest in herbs that might prevent the pregnancies through which love affairs became public problems. Postmenopausal elders alluded to experience as midwives and herbalists to attract the respectful attention of younger relatives. Married women with young children were the most openly eager for any kind of contraceptive advice.

Claims to knowledge about contraceptives were also geographically uneven. Contraceptive expertise was concentrated in Meratus–Banjar border areas. Interest in contraception was high in the central mountains, but fewer women claimed to be experts. Expertise was stimulated by ethnic interchanges in the areas visited by Banjar seeking magic and herbs. Banjar stereotype the Meratus as those who know about traditional contraception. Among Banjar, I heard more public concern about encouraging rather than impeding conception; however, those Banjar who did want contraceptives—particularly men pursuing nonmarital affairs—found border-area Meratus women an appropriate source. To Banjar, Meratus women are disorderly pagans. Yet, by invoking the power of their trade connections, Meratus herbsellers were able to claim some of the potency of external ties more commonly associated with men.[7] And this, in turn, created a certain local legitimacy for their own concerns.

Despite disrespectful Banjar stereotypes, the interethnic trade in herbal contraception gave women throughout the Meratus area some claim to regional authority with which to maintain talk about birth control. In the places where I lived, this talk was never a public cause. It survived within a network of gossip and complaints on the margin of the community framework that would tame or stifle it.

As women spoke with a redoubled marginality in relation to both regional and local authority, they assumed oppositional positions not just on contraception but on a variety of related issues about parenting. From the perspective of Meratus leaders, having and raising children was an enterprise that benefited the political community as well as parents. Women who complained about having too many children, it was implied, spoke against the community. Yet complain women did. Bearing children, they said, brought them through a frightening near-death experience. Caring for young children kept them from visiting relatives, going to market, attending festivals, or having love affairs. The women I knew enjoyed their children; at the same time, they expressed themselves about the pain and work of raising children.

In contrast, leadership discourse downplayed women's bodily engagement during pregnancy and their asymmetrical burden of childcare responsibilities. Like growing rice, raising children was always described as a joint project of husbands and wives. Further, men's contributions to the project were given particular recognition: Men's initiative stimulated the project's conception; men's spiritual insight guided its key transitions.

Although women did not reject these dogmas, they sometimes talked back. When a respected male shaman explained to me that women were the "empty buckets" in which semen developed into babies, women surrounded him to argue that women provided half the baby-making "water."

In contrast to assertions that only men could deliver babies (because only they knew the proper spells to welcome the baby into the world), some women claimed skills as midwives. In some neighborhoods, women had attended enough births to establish their role as "custom." In others, however, "custom" deferred to the husbands of pregnant women. The disagreement was not just about roles; men were more likely to emphasize the spiritual status of the newborn, whereas women relatives (officially assisting or otherwise) worried about the health of the mother. Such gendered dissension destabilized the discourse of leadership and created openings for transformations. Dissension also created areas of inarticulateness for women. When I asked women about the kinship and community issues central to leadership discourse, they often became shy or professed ignorance, telling me to ask the men.

In the central mountains, the positions of young married men and women in relation to issues of leadership and parenting were particularly polarized. In the early 1980s, the booming price of rattan made luxuries and prestige available to the young able-bodied men who sold rattan in Banjar weekly markets. (Until the mid-1980s, rattan was plentiful and easily available throughout the central mountains; but only the men who carried it to market reaped the rewards of the trade.) These young men were in an especially advantageous position to enter the arena of local politics. When young men married, however, they were expected to show respect and deference to their parents-in-law. Only after having children and starting independent rice farming could they attain the pose of autonomy needed to vie for respect and leadership. Young married men were thus quite interested in having children.

In contrast, their female counterparts had few resources with which to gain the prestige that comes with external connections. They had little to say at community gatherings that would be listened to. The newly married women I talked with were reluctant to begin having children, because they would only gain the burden of childcare and, then, independent rice farming. They expected no benefits of community leadership from parenting and independence. Only later would children be a source of help and power.

The force of the situation becomes clear only when more unusual events are told. The following story is not easily analyzed. It continues to challenge and puzzle me.

This is a story about an ambiguous neonatal death. It is not a story about the practice of infanticide; infanticide is not a locally relevant category. Instead, it is about practices at the edge between silence and speech, the area of inchoate understandings without fully developed, public articulations.

The incident involved an unusual conjunction of events. Certainly, it was not typical of anything. Why, for example, were no men around? Meratus women and men socialize together; it is unusual to find oneself with only women or men. This time, however, so many wild pigs were running through the forest that even men who had never hunted before couldn't bear to stay home. Why did I get involved? I could say that I was writing letters that morning, and that half my mind had flown home to another way of life. Would the women have responded differently if the men had been there or if I had continued to interfere? Possibly—but it might have made no difference for the life of the infant.

The event has alternative interpretations. I know that a premature infant died and that the women did not engage with it as a social person. Did they refuse to nurture and grieve *because* the baby was unwanted or because, sensibly, they recognized the infant's poor chances? I cannot resolve this issue. Either way, the incident requires an understanding of half-articulated choices at the margin of acceptable attitudes and categories.

This story is about a different kind of marginality than that of Meratus leaders who speak the language of order and violence in imagining a community. This marginality exists beyond what is possible to clearly say.

Induan Amar's baby

In 1981, Induan Amar was probably about eighteen years old. She was married, but her marriage had little stability. Not long after their wedding, her husband (Ma Amar) had wandered off to a Banjar town for several years, returning only when Induan Amar's brother and brother-in-law went to find out if he was coming back. Even after this, they seemed rather tentative as a couple. Much of the time he slept at his parent's house, while she slept at her mother's. Induan Amar participated in her mother's rice farming; he worked mainly with his parents. As her mother told me, Induan Amar "wasn't ready to have a husband."

When Induan Amar suddenly went into labor one morning, Ma Amar was off with Induan Amar's older brother on a hunting trip. They had gone to a distant well-forested watershed where Ma Amar used to live and were not expected back for several days. For various reasons, the men of the household were gone; but the women were all nearby. It was rice-harvesting season. In addition to the women of the four umbun who shared a common household, two other women were there to help out with the harvest. Induan Amar's labor raised a problem; in this neighborhood, men—usually the woman's husband—delivered babies. Women claimed they knew no birth magic with which to welcome the newborn.

The birth was unexpected and very fast. The infant boy was small, premature but well developed and not unhealthy-looking. Induan Amar's older sister ran off to fetch her husband as the nearest available midwife. Until he arrived, the baby lay where it had emerged between the new mother's muddy feet. When the sister's husband came, he recited the spells to welcome the newborn appropriately into the world. He washed the baby, tied and cut the cord, and laid the baby gently on some cloth. He helped Induan Amar set up her own ritual and health needs, including a hot bamboo node to roll on her stomach. Then he went back to work in his field hut, bringing the placenta in a basket, as is appropriate, to hang in a fruit tree. Meanwhile, Induan Amar avoided looking at the baby and didn't touch it.

At this point, it becomes difficult to continue the story without mentioning my participation. My first intervention was as "ethnographer"—yet, there were no appropriate cultural categories for me to learn. I stumbled awkwardly and inappropriately through a situation I found disorienting. For example, I admit with embarrassment to taking photographs of the birth procedures. Afterward, Induan Amar's sister said, "How could you?" As a responsible ethnographer, I was recording custom. Nor was Induan Amar's sister hostile to this aim. If custom is public performance, however, this event, tinged as it was with "anti-custom," was not the stuff to record.

After I was finished being ethnographer, I somehow became missionary doctor. As I've said, I had been thinking in English, writing letters. As I watched the brother-in-law work, I mumbled something about the fact that, in the United States, a premature baby like this would certainly live. I was thinking of incubators. But, when the brother-in-law begged me to do my best to help this baby, I couldn't resist; I didn't want this baby to die for lack of technology. In a burst of nurturing, I urged Induan Amar to hold the baby. When she remained reluctant, and the baby started to get too cold, I warmed it by holding it to myself. Caught up in caring for the child, I did not notice until sometime later that, with the exception of one flaky old woman who had come to help with harvest, the other women in the house were paying no attention to the baby.

The women suspected that the infant might not survive its early birth. Yet it seems important that the one man who had been in the house—the one considered the expert on births—had followed the procedure for a full-term, healthy infant and had urged me to do the same. He thought the infant was worth nurturing, and I felt similarly until several hours later when, sitting around the fire with the baby, Induan Amar's mother gave me a new set of clues. "She wasn't ready," Induan Amar's mother gently told me. The phrase was ambiguous: she wasn't full-term; she wasn't ready to bear a child. But as we talked I guessed for the first time that the baby might have been unwanted. I noticed that Induan Amar's sisters limited their comments about the baby to clinical remarks about its small size and its newborn's cheesy skin. Induan Amar was surrounded by attention and support; but until I intervened, the baby lay unattended.

At this point I was thoroughly disoriented. Shocked, first, that no one had touched the baby, I was even more shocked that I might have been helping an unwanted baby live that I wasn't planning to raise. Painfully, I tried to judge what was going on. The women remained solicitous about Induan Amar's health and comfort. Sometimes Induan Amar's sister and mother also picked up the baby, but never with enthusiasm; I thought perhaps they were trying to please me. Finally, I resolved to keep my hands off this baby. I was relieved when I had a chance to go outside to join the harvest.

The baby lived through that day and the night and through most of the next day. All the other women of the household were harvesting when Induan Amar came out to the field with a sheepish grin to tell us that the baby had died. When we returned to the house, the younger girls fooled around with exaggerated terror, daring each other to touch the corpse. There was little mourning as we once again waited for a man, this time to bury the body. The women said they could not bury the corpse because they were afraid to touch or carry it. They joked and complained about its creepy presence. I began to be spooked by the idea of spending the night with this icon of confusion. Was this a dead person or a piece of flesh? Abandoning any shred of my cultural-recorder persona, I offered to carry the corpse if someone else would dig the hole. My hosts seemed relieved. Two of us were halfway out the door when an old uncle appeared. He grabbed the body away from me and gave it a simple burial, a person's burial, but with only myself and one curious teenage girl in attendance.

Late the next day, Ma Amar came home. The news stunned and depressed him, and he sat silently for hours, refusing to talk or eat, as the women tried to convince him that the baby was too small to have lived. His mood did not dissipate. Induan Amar looked increasingly guilty and sad, and after several days of trying to cajole her husband from his stupor, she herself broke down crying. I remember thinking at the time that he might just have pushed her into a new attitude. Next time, I thought, she would really want her baby.

For whatever it is worth, when I visited Induan Amar in 1986, she was still married to Ma Amar and the doting mother of a cute and very spoiled two-year-old boy. By that time, too, Induan Amar's male relatives recalled the story of her first birth as a late miscarriage, frustrated for just a moment by the actions of a naive anthropologist. And, of course, that was true.

Motherhood, marginality, and the state

This story has continued to haunt me. When I returned to the United States, it was impossible for me to see American ideas about mothering and childbirth with the same eyes. Stories I might not have noticed earlier jumped out at me. In the mid-1980s, a series of prosecutions emerged against young American women who delivered babies in toilets, or motel rooms, parking lots, or other inappropriate places. Reading about these cases, I could no longer produce the baby-saving sentiments I had brought to Induan Amar's childbirth. This time I found myself as astounded by American assumptions as I had been by the Meratus scene I have sketched.[8]

The divergences are sharp. In the United States, debates over reproduction have pressed the personhood of the infant-fetus farther and farther toward conception; women are increasingly expected to mourn the death of fetuses, wanted or unwanted. In the abstract, it seems unthinkable to treat a newborn baby, however premature, as a nonperson. Prosecutions follow this cultural logic in criminalizing inappropriate or unsuccessful births. Further, the inappropriate disposal of newborn and fetal corpses, whether in clinics or ghettos, has become a symbol of the disintegration of civilization. Most important, perhaps, U.S. American culture makes reproduction a female domain to which men are peripheral. Women charged with endangering newborns in U.S. prosecutions are presented as offending standards of female responsibility and morality.

In contrast, Induan Amar's baby was conceived, first and foremost, as the product of her husband's responsibility and desire. His semen formed a fetus in her womb; his hand should have welcomed the newborn. Customary law would have made him responsible if she had died in childbirth; after all, he made her pregnant. Her lack of interest in the baby did not show rejection of womanhood or motherhood but, instead, frustrated her husband's interests. I am not claiming neglect of neonates as a regular feature of Meratus culture, but the incident makes sense within the framework of 1980s Meratus understandings of gender and parenting.

In recent years in the United States, the state has intervened more and more directly to enforce standards of parenting. Increasingly, women are penalized for what is seen as inappropriate behavior during pregnancy and childbirth. In the central Meratus Mountains, the state does not reach so close to women's lives. The marginalization of women is not enforced by the state but is instead, indirectly, a result of women's distance from state-endorsed authority. As long as Meratus leaders ritualize their acquiescence to state rule within a consanguineal, "parental" framework of leadership that privileges male political action, they banish women's work in childbearing and rearing to the periphery of community discourse. In this context, women's illegitimate agendas have no clearly articulated public voice. They reside, instead, in disorganized support for fleeting refusals of men's desires.

Such marginalization is difficult to describe in part because it finds little precedence in anthropological accounts. Generally, studies of the cultural construction of gender focus on the coherence of local knowledge rather than on regional dialogue and cross talk.[9] Furthermore, in assessing local knowledge, anthropologists emphasize the *said* rather than the *unsaid* of dominant community discourses. Yet a central challenge for feminist anthropologists is to position the cultural statements of their informants politically. This involves paying attention to competing gender formulations variously situated in relation to local groups and hierarchies.

In conversely related inattention, studies of state power and regional inequalities rarely analyze internal community differentiation. Most research on indigenous minorities is content to show the marginalization (or assimilation) of entire ethnic groups from the perspective of community leaders.[10] In my analysis, I have attempted to show the connection between the internal heterogeneity of Meratus communities and their relation to the state. Pa'an Tini's marginality differs from that of Induan Amar.

Here, of course, I am describing only one area and one moment in time. Even during my fieldwork, women in other Meratus areas were in substantially different positions. I began this chapter with Induan Kilay's state-dispensed oral contraceptives: The politics of resettlement villages made birth control pills de rigueur for the wives of neighborhood leaders. Further, Induan Kilay had become a rather powerful neighborhood leader herself. The commentaries of articulate and ambitious women are the subject of the last third of this book. Here, however, I have traced less directly expressible forms of marginality. These forms make it especially clear that politics is more than a simple matter of accepting the rules of authority or "standing up for one's rights." Instead, I have shown a more complex, messy, and culturally rich process of negotiation.

PART TWO A SCIENCE
OF TRAVEL

*Travelling: a man, a chicken,
and a dog.*

The title of Part Two is a pun on the Indonesian word *ilmu*, "science," which refers to both European-influenced scientific disciplines and esoteric, magical knowledge. In South Kalimantan, esoteric knowledge is particularly important as it facilitates travel. Like anthropology, this knowledge is a "science of travel." Part Two brings anthropological "science" into dialogue with a diverse array of regionally relevant "sciences of travel."

In defining itself as a science that can travel anywhere, anthropology has classically constituted its objects—"cultures"—as essentially immobile or as possessing a mobility that is cyclical and repetitive. The contrast between a travelling science and its fixed objects is displayed in the expected practices of fieldwork: The anthropologist travels; the culture is found in a set place. This distinction has arisen in anthropological writing, together with a stylistic opposition between well-travelled "theories" with general applicability and the data for these theories—local "cases," which, themselves, are interesting only at home.

As developed within this framework, *culture* emerges from stably localized communities. A number of anthropologists have shown how this notion of culture has been placed in opposition to *history*. The more culture is attributed to a place, the less has its history been recognized, and vice versa (Wolf 1982; R. Rosaldo 1989:198). Similarly, those with culture are expected to have a regular, delimited occupation of territory. If they move, they must do so cyclically, like transhumant pastoralists or kula-ring sailors. One anthropologist suggests that culture has been understood as a map (Bourdieu 1977:2); thus, culture creates a regular territoriality.

Recently this framework has been the target of considerable criticism. Critics have argued that, in the contemporary world, those called "natives" have been travelling at least as much as those called "anthropologists." Thus, both "native" and "anthropological" forms of knowledge should be offered equally generalizable status; each is produced as travellers exchange stories (Clifford 1992). Collaborative projects and polyvocal texts have been suggested as an alternative to mobile theories and fixed cases (Clifford 1988). This position has produced its own critics, however. These critics (for example, Strathern 1987) argue that Western scholars only obscure the specificity of their own agendas (and their power to promote them) when they claim collaboration with disadvantaged rural people called "natives."

Between the poles of this debate lies a shared insight into the importance of self-consciousness about the practices in which knowledge is produced. By breaking down the categorical distinction between mobile theories and fixed cases, it becomes possible to reexamine specific knowledge-producing practices. Much of the work generated from these insights has focused on the cultural practices of anthropologists. However, as the culture of anthropology comes into view, culture is freed from assumptions of stable community, and it becomes possible to attend to other forms of mobility.

Taking diverse forms of knowledge and community seriously means paying attention to the travel practices with which they are associated. I think of Benedict Anderson's discussion of the formation of the idea of the postcolonial nation within the travel practices of colonial civil servants. The nation, he argues, took shape from the travel pattern that took them back and forth between a colony's capital and its hinterlands (Anderson 1983:57–59). But what of backwoods farmers who have, for the most part, never been to the provincial capital, much less the nation's capital? Are they not an exemplar of localized stability? In the following three chapters I argue that travel practices and travel-related forms of knowledge are essential to understanding the cultural and political shape of Meratus marginality.

First, I show that the nature of Meratus "communities" can be understood only within the context of Meratus mobility—from daily visits to annual field movements to long-term trajectories across the landscape. In chapter 4 I am especially interested in the organization of leadership, male political privilege, and Meratus integration into the region, since these are linked to the travel routes and routines of ambitious men. Second, I argue that Meratus travel is best examined in the context of the travel of state officials and of Banjar traders and adventurers, as well as the forms of knowledge about the Meratus that these travels have produced. The political charge of Meratus mobility draws from the confrontations between overlapping and contrasting regional travel patterns.

Each chapter begins from the perspective of a different travel agenda. Chapter 4 develops its vantage point within Meratus community dynamics. It shows communities and their leadership in constant flux as ambitious men work to maintain or expand the boundaries of their authority. From the perspective of these men, ethnic and administrative boundaries are irrelevant to travel in the pursuit of power. In contrast, both state and Banjar perspectives delimit and exoticize the Meratus by banishing their travel agendas across a conceptual gap. Chapter 5 begins with the perspectives of state bureaucrats, travellers from administrative centers who consider stable villages units of local administration. For them, Meratus mobility is, by its nature, a transgression of authority. Chapter 6 begins, instead, with the perspectives of Banjar travellers who, from the state's perspective, are at least as transgressively mobile as Meratus. Yet Banjar travel in the universal space of Islam, and this opposes itself to the pagan lawlessness of Meratus mobility.

In describing the "travel sciences" of Indonesian officials, Banjar traders, and Meratus shamans, I find myself deploying a familiar anthropological style: a generalizing, homogenizing style that seeks out cultural principles underlying particular instances and events. Yet, rather than using this style to develop the classic anthropological contrast between the West and its Other, I highlight those perspectives that are most obscured by the classic contrast—the perspectives of the locally relevant nation state and a cosmopolitan regional majority. These hybrid, historically shifting perspectives—not those of some homogeneous, analytically distanced West—are most directly involved in shaping the negotiation of Meratus-ness. I argue that each "theory" of Meratus travel jostles against others, creating misreadings, reinterpretations, and odd alliances. It is these which best illuminate the exclusions and creativity of Meratus marginality.

In contrast, chapter 4 raises a different challenge. In offering a "travel perspective" on Meratus community dynamics, I want to tell a long story. Why a story? A story disrupts the possibilities of reading for homogeneity and repetition (Trinh 1989); it shows process from the perspective of idiosyncratic alignments and unpredictable changes. As a form of analysis, a story opposes itself to a "case study" surrounded by generalizing explanations. Stories are neither data nor laws; they can be swapped and disputed by differently situated observers. Yet, readers of social science are not used to being asked to immerse themselves in the fate of particular individuals and the outcome of events. Will Parma marry the man of her choice? Will Ma Salam get revenge for his murdered uncle? Can The Bear mediate between Ma Salam and Awat Lumuh? Only if the reader is willing to get involved in these kinds of questions will the following chapter make sense. I believe the payoff comes in an appreciation of both specificity and possibility.

4 LEADERSHIP LANDSCAPES

The asymmetries I described in the last two chapters make little sense from the reference point of stable, unified communities. Why should Meratus be so impressed with the power of the state and the Banjar, given that they have their own spheres of autonomy? How can I speak of "leaders" at all if leaders have no coercive powers—and, furthermore, if their constituents are dedicated to (and capable of) extraordinary personal independence? Where do men obtain their advantage over women, when both are equally founders of gender-complementary umbun, the most clearly defined local social and economic units? These questions would stop my analysis short if the only possible responses referred to the self-generating internal structure of meaning or economy within analytically autonomous communities.

Yet, Meratus politics are a politics of travelling. Political discussions range widely across the mountains, foray into and out of Banjar villages, offices, and markets, and tap even broader spheres of thought and action. Particularly in the central mountains, going from one household to another involves travelling; there are no clear boundaries between local and foreign spaces. Neighborhood-based communities are shifting and flexible. Those who would be neighborhood leaders continually renegotiate their constituencies as they visit past and potential constituents. Effective travelling and visiting become central practices of leadership and community-building. The politics of travelling bring regional authority and male privilege into the heart of local concerns.

The "science" of travelling on the decentralized Meratus landscape is a science of external power. I refer to the magical "sciences" (*alimu /ilemu / irmu / ilmu*) that Meratus use to protect and strengthen their bodies for travelling. This is a science which, like these Meratus versions of the Banjar/Indonesian term *ilmu* (here, "esoteric science"), has evolved in interethnic dialogue. I also invoke the imaginative locus in which travelling becomes possible. Only the "borrowed" power of extra-Meratus and extra-ordinary (spiritual) authority encourages travellers to brave the dangers of unfamiliar diversity. To *borrow* in this sense, as I explored for The Bear's stories, is to turn external submission into local authority. Like a colonial passport, mention of external connections is used to override local hostilities at the same time that it brings its own hierarchical and divisive understandings.

Travelling is a practice in which women, because of their greater responsibilities in caring for children and crops, are disadvantaged in comparison to men. Women complained that their everyday responsibilities kept them from visiting and travelling as often as they wished. With limited opportunities to travel, women have less access to markets and less ability to forge political connections. They have more difficulty claiming experience and bravery. They cannot attend the social events which might provide them a public voice. Women point to these limitations as their gendered political disadvantages.

In order to describe the politics of travelling, it seems best to present a narrative that exemplifies the dynamics in which claims of leadership and community are made and challenged. In this chapter, I tell a long story, one that draws from the regional spread of my own Meratus travelling. Everywhere I went between November 1980 and June 1981, people were talking about these events.

This is the story of a rather unremarkable, quiet young woman named Parma and the two men who courted her. Although the story swirls around these young people, they hardly figure as the story's major dramatis personae. Instead, my telling calls out their *asbah*, senior kin who arrange marriages, and the government titleholders and *pangulu* ("marriage officials") who assert their right to legitimate the proceedings.[1] The story follows the competitive posturing of leaders, the unstable alignments of intercommunity relations and cross-cutting kin networks, the sudden reemergence of grudges long buried, and the unexpected consequences of government intervention. As such, it is a story of marriage adat and its negotiation.

This is not, however, the story adat experts might want told about their authority. Assumed in adat talk is the compelling nature of adat's authority for all those under its command. Instead, this story shows the

---

The Two Weddings

Wedding I in Ukut

	Head *asbah*[a]	Other *asbah* in story
Bride: Parma	Ma Ulin	Induan Bilai
Groom: Ma Kapal	Ma Linggu	

Marriage Officials: Ma Pasta of Ukut; Ma Tupai of Rajang

Wedding II outside Tidung

	Head *asbah*	Other *asbah* in story
Bride: Parma		Three uncles living outside Tidung
Groom: Gasai	Awat Lumuh	

Marriage Official: The Bear

[a]*asbah:* senior kin of the bride and groom who take part in the marriage.

---

practice of adat formation, in which no authority is ever certain. In showing negotiation, the story introduces the ambiguities of travelling politics.

First, the story shows both the importance and the weakness of local leaders. Even as they succeed in bullying, enticing, or impressing a group of constituents, they must struggle to keep their "communities" from slipping from their grasp. Would-be leaders compete with each other and redefine local spheres. In this process, the line between leader and non-leader dissolves; even the least aggressive can shift the possibilities of community by moving or joining another group.

Second, the story shows regional authority as simultaneously unassailable and empty. Leaders are respected because they threaten to call the police to force their opponents to comply. Both sides, however, know that the police are unlikely to come in answer to a Meratus call. Leaders set arbitrary fines that are far above anyone's ability to pay. They claim that regional authorities will back them up, but everyone knows they probably will never see the money. Nevertheless, their opponents may capitulate or, at least, move away to avoid trouble. Issues are further complicated by the fact that when regional authorities do arrive, no one knows what they will do. A leader's predictions may be fulfilled; then again, all those fabled connections he claims may fall away in disarray.

Finally, although the story gives a sense of the political disadvantages of women, it does not show them as powerless. In the story, women do not become leaders; yet outspoken women talk back, while shy women stay away, each refusing leadership's claims.[2] The quiet bride does end up with the love of her choice, despite her aggressively posturing male relatives and in-laws—not because she is given a public voice, but because she and her husband go off to farm in an isolated place where no one who opposes their marriage cares to go find her.

This travelling politics depends on the dynamics of landscape differentiation introduced in chapter 1. Over time, social locations shift. Centers of activity become forests as their old adherents move in various directions; uninhabited groves of trees—and their social associations—are recalled and revived as community foci. Current unities suppress, but do not erase, multiple cross-cutting processes of division. Thus, the story begins with the shifting terrain of community alliances.

The setting

This story includes an exceptionally large and diverse number of aspiring and recognized adat experts, in part because it concerns an out-of-the-way area which many considered politically up for grabs. In the late 1970s and early 1980s, the Ukut River valley, in the heart of the Meratus Mountains, was an isolated, fragmented backwoods—the kind of place where, as people noted in half-shocked gossip, some women lived with two husbands and where ne'er-do-wells from the Banjar plains "went Dayak" to escape from their misdeeds. Although houses and swiddens were scattered up and down the valley, no leader had emerged who was able to draw them into a single neighborhood community. Many umbun developed social affiliations with more unified neighborhoods, even though doing so tended to involve long hours of hiking.

Twenty years earlier, the same valley had been a Meratus political center. In the late 1950s, as government troops and Muslim Gurumbulan rebels battled it out on both sides of the mountains, Meratus retreated from well-travelled routes and border areas. Ukut was a stronghold of "runaway" Meratus culture. By the late 1970s, excitement pointed elsewhere. A brisk rattan trade, along with the possibility of government subsidies, created thriving neighborhoods along the main trails and closer to markets in the foothills. The powerful village head who had "ruled" from Ukut had died; those who tried to revive his charisma had come up with little except a deteriorating, rarely filled ritual hall. Neighborhood leaders

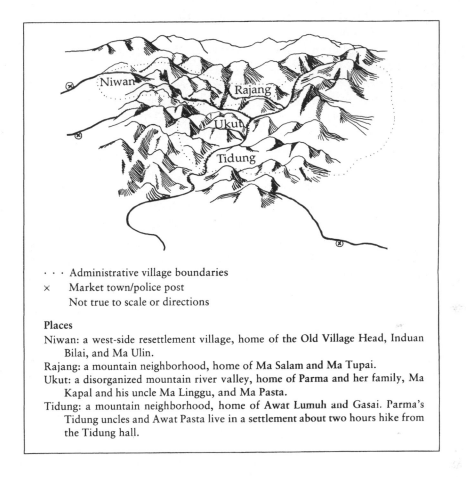

· · · Administrative village boundaries
×   Market town/police post
Not true to scale or directions

Places
Niwan: a west-side resettlement village, home of the Old Village Head, Induan
    Bilai, and Ma Ulin.
Rajang: a mountain neighborhood, home of Ma Salam and Ma Tupai.
Ukut: a disorganized mountain river valley, home of Parma and her family, Ma
    Kapal and his uncle Ma Linggu, and Ma Pasta.
Tidung: a mountain neighborhood, home of Awat Lumuh and Gasai. Parma's
    Tidung uncles and Awat Pasta live in a settlement about two hours hike from
    the Tidung hall.

from outside the Ukut valley lured Ukut allies and kin to affiliate with
them, and Ukut, though well settled, became a ghost neighborhood.

One neighborhood leader with an eye on Ukut was my close friend Ma
Salam, neighborhood head of Rajang. He lived a half day's brisk hike
away from a cluster of umbun (including cousins of his) who were farming near an Ukut tributary. In an expansionist frame of mind, he declared
their settlement part of Rajang. It was a bold move, and one not guaranteed to last, since the cluster was not closely affiliated with other Rajang
people. Ma Salam's leadership was on the rise, however; he was a good
diplomat with budding connections to regional authorities and the prestige of an anthropologist-in-residence. When Ma Salam declared neigh-

borhood jurisdiction over the marriage of Parma, a young woman who lived in this Ukut cluster, he received the cooperation of Rajang's wedding sponsor (*pangulu*), who, because he offered to marry the couple, found himself committed to the expansion. Yet, an Ukut wedding sponsor also thought it his right to marry Parma. At her first wedding, the two sponsors sanctified the wedding in independent counterpoint.

Parma's kin were spread in several directions. Uncles and aunts in two separate areas disagreed about whom Parma should marry, as each of Parma's two suitors promised a different direction of alliance. Furthermore, several neighborhood officials hoped to use the marriage to build their leadership; the dispute would not have been as fierce and prolonged had it not been supported by these ambitious men. These leaders were especially quarrelsome because each drew legitimacy from regional connections in different directions: Ukut was equally accessible (or inaccessible) from three different district seats. Threats to "call the police" might refer to three separate police forces. At the same time, Ukut's isolation in rugged countryside meant that no district government had much idea what happened there. Meratus leaders were free to issue threats on their own.

As the story begins, Ukut was torn by a number of ongoing quarrels. Two men were quarreling over rights to a durian tree; rumor had it that one of the men was watching the house of the other, waiting for a chance to kill him. The man who lived in the house held the title of assistant village head, but he had proved incapable of assembling a dispute settlement. People also still talked about a fierce dispute over adultery that Uma Adang (and, separately, The Bear) had mediated.[3] At this time, Ukut was without effective leadership. As Ma Salam put it later, supporting his own claims: "They're all afraid. The police want to arrest them all."

TWO WEDDINGS

Parma did not want to be married. She had retreated into silence as her parents coaxed her and as her uncle from Niwan came to tease and bully her, and even as her relatives began to assemble for the wedding. Her future groom had gathered his kin, who, in preparation for the wedding feast, had slaughtered chickens and cooked rice. But Parma refused to join them. By then, even her parents weren't sure this was a good match.

As the wedding day wore on, more guests arrived. Tensions rose as it looked doubtful whether the marriage would take place. But the groom had already invested so much. The food was prepared; the marriage offi-

The Characters

The bride and the grooms:

Parma: a young woman
Ma Kapal: the first groom, from Ukut
Gasai: the second groom, from Tidung

Relatives of the bride and the grooms:

Induan Bilai: the sympathetic aunt in Niwan, sister of Parma's mother
Ma Ulin: Parma's uncle in Niwan, and her head kin representative for her
  first marriage
Parma's Tidung uncles: two brothers and one brother-in-law of Parma's
  father, all of whom supported and helped carry out Parma's marriage
  to Gasai
Ma Linggu: Ma Kapal's uncle and head kin representative for his marriage
  to Parma
Awat Lumuh: Gasai's head kin representative for his marriage to Parma,
  and a respected elder spokesperson for Tidung

Local Leaders:

Ma Tupai: the Rajang pangulu who, with Ma Pasta, married Parma and
  Ma Kapal; head shaman of Rajang
Ma Pasta: the Ukut pangulu who, with Ma Tupai, married Parma and Ma
  Kapal; a man with ideas about adat but little ability to draw a con-
  stituency
The Old Village Head: once village head in Niwan, he was consulted about
  breaking up the Parma–Ma Kapal marriage
Awat Pasta: the pangulu who conducted the faulty divorce of Parma and
  Ma Kapal; a Rajang man living with his wife outside Tidung, he was
  blamed by both sides
Ma Salam: the young neighborhood head of Rajang who opposed a mar-
  riage relationship between Parma and Tidung people because of the
  murder of his uncle Ma Jawa there, years before
The Bear: the charismatic shaman who married Parma and Gasai and
  tried, unsuccessfully, to mediate between the kin of Gasai and Ma
  Kapal

Others:

Haji Biguli: a Banjar travelling salesman who supported Ma Salam's interest in calling the police
Ma Jawa: a Rajang man who was killed while visiting Tidung by Banjar
  nationalist guerillas around 1949
The section officer: a policeman who toured the mountains and confiscated
  a young man's pants

cials had been convened. The bridewealth was ready. Kin and neighbors were assembled. As night fell, Parma and her parents yielded to the force of public presence. Senior kin of the bride and the groom made their final agreements about marriage payments. Parma and the young groom had their faces beautified with delicate lime and charcoal dots before they were led to stand under a white chicken and then to sit back to back through shamanic plainsong lasting far into the night.

When the guests went home the next day, their cohabitation could have begun; but Parma was still uncompliant. Like many unwilling Meratus brides, she held proudly to her detachment and chastity. Within a few weeks, her young husband, Ma Kapal, grew tired of hanging around her parents' house, where his bride ignored him. He spent more and more time at his own parents' place, and his visits to Parma became infrequent.

I did not attend Parma's wedding. This version derives from Induan Bilai, a sister of Parma's mother who lived in the west-side resettlement village of Niwan. At the time she told me the story, Parma and Ma Kapal were already living separately, and Induan Bilai was concerned about the appropriate conditions under which they could be divorced. The main problem, as she saw it, was how to return the marriage payments to Ma Kapal. A large portion of the payment, some Rp 30,000, had been taken by Ma Ulin, an uncle of Parma's who had represented her senior kin in negotiating this wedding. Ma Ulin had lent the money to a nephew, who had used it for his own marriage payment. How, Induan Bilai complained, would Parma's kin be able to return it?

Induan Bilai was critical as she told Parma's story. No one had consulted her about the advisability of this marriage, even though she was a closer relative of Parma's than her cousin, Ma Ulin. She would never have pushed Parma to marry against her will. Despite this, Induan Bilai had hiked for two days to attend the wedding. Yet Ma Ulin had not even offered her a share of the bridewealth. In addition, Ma Ulin had mismanaged the sum he kept for himself.

Induan Bilai was not annoyed at Parma for wanting a divorce. Many young Meratus women are married against their will, and such marriages often last a few weeks or months. I knew several middle-aged women, each of whom had been through more than half a dozen short, early marriages. Many women told stories of how they had resisted the advances of unwanted grooms. Parma and Ma Kapal, said Induan Bilai, just had no *juduh*, no "compatibility"; there was no real match.

Not everyone shared this view. As it turned out, a number of ambitious men were willing to stake their reputations on the continuing appropriateness of Parma's marriage to Ma Kapal. As these men rallied to the cause, I found myself increasingly appreciative of Induan Bilai's back talk. Those men, she said, had no right to interfere with what Parma wanted. Yet, back talk of this sort does not create authority. Induan Bilai was always on the verge of hiking to Ukut to give them a piece of her mind. But she never went.

A meeting in Rajang

Ma Salam prided himself on his charm, politeness, and appropriate comportment. He addressed his elders with respect and his peers with warmth. He never let a guest leave without having eaten. But sometimes, circumstances tried his patience. That's how it seemed one evening in January.

Ma Salam had been excited as he hiked home full of talk about that evening's planned honey hunt. This tree had eleven combs, each as large as a winnowing tray. The honey hunt would be an all-night party, with the dangerous thrill of climbing a hundred feet in total darkness and the sweet reward of the honey. In this mood, he was not prepared to find a crowd of guests sitting silently waiting for his return.

It was clear from the expression on their faces that their business was serious. Ma Salam, however, began with the calm chatter of the season—honeycombs seen along the trail, new government policies. He knew the distinguished older man—Awat Lumuh, an important leader from Tidung, more than a day's hike to the southeast. The two hard-faced young men at Awat Lumuh's side were brothers of Parma's father who had married into the Tidung area. Ma Salam also knew two of the other Tidung men, one of whom was a brother-in-law of Parma's father. But he had never seen the handsome, moody-looking boy.

Everyone was impatient, and, with little urging, the guests moved directly to the purpose of their trip. Awat Lumuh explained: According to adat, Parma's marriage to Ma Kapal was invalid. She had already been promised to another suitor, Awat Lumuh's nephew, Gasai—and here he acknowledged the handsome boy. Awat Lumuh demanded that the Parma–Ma Kapal marriage be annulled immediately. He imposed a Rp 30,000 fine for breaking the engagement. Only then could Parma and Gasai be properly married.

Ma Salam did not look flustered. If they could talk adat, so could he. How could Gasai be engaged to Parma if his relatives hadn't taken his suit to all her relatives? Proper adat, he advised, required the groom's kin to "go up and down a lot of house steps." Some of Parma's father's relatives in the Tidung area supported Gasai's suit. But what about the others?

Awat Lumuh had his reply ready. They had consulted another of Parma's uncles, a relative of Parma's mother, who, incidentally, had strong ties to Rajang. This man had told them to go "straight to the base of the tree"—to Parma's parents. Parma's parents had given their permission for the suit. What else was there to say?

Ma Salam was annoyed. These Tidung men were not taking his authority seriously. As neighborhood head of Rajang, Ma Salam had approved the Ma Kapal marriage. He was offended that they might marry Parma to Gasai instead. He summarily told them to go ask Parma's uncle, Ma Ulin, in Niwan, more than a day's hike away. It was Ma Ulin who had represented Parma's kin in the Ma Kapal wedding. Perhaps, Ma Salam said, mixing anger and humility, he did not know enough adat for their purposes. Abruptly, he got his work knife and left for the honey hunt, leaving his guests in the darkening house without a host.

I had been following Ma Salam around all day. Because he was nearly always polite, I was surprised at his rudeness. Yet I had missed a crucial line in the conversation, as Ma Salam explained to me at the base of the honey tree. One of the Tidung men had threatened him, saying: "One of your area's leaders has already died on Tidung ground." Ma Salam assumed he was referring to Ma Salam's uncle, Ma Jawa, who had been killed by Banjar guerrillas more than thirty years earlier, during the Indonesian revolutionary period. This is the man whose story The Bear narrated. As an assistant village head, the man was considered by the guerrillas an agent of the Dutch colonial government; and they had ambushed him while he was visiting his wife's relatives in the Tidung area.

Ma Salam's version of the story was more gruesome than The Bear's. According to Ma Salam, Ma Jawa was a spiritually powerful man who was hard to kill. The assassins tried several methods, including drowning and slicing, without success. Finally, they drove a stake from his anus through his mouth and left him to die. Ma Salam's and Ma Jawa's other west-side relatives assumed that the killing could not have happened without the cooperation of Tidung people. In Ma Salam's view, they were complicitous guides rather than potential victims, even if they had not participated directly in the murder.

As the first climber made his way up the honey tree, Ma Salam had me write a letter to be sent secretly to Ma Ulin, Parma's uncle in Niwan. "For the future good of relations with both Ukut and Tidung, you must break off Parma's ties with both Ma Kapal and Gasai," he warned, and he mentioned the threat. Perhaps Parma's marriage with Ma Kapal could not be saved; but at least he could thwart Gasai's plans.

Meetings added, meetings omitted

It is a long hike from Tidung through Ukut, Rajang, Niwan, and back. Given that each of these names refers to a large unbounded area of scattered households, the task of visiting more than a few key figures becomes immense. The Tidung delegation did not stop at some houses, and the occupants were more than a little miffed at the omission. Despite being bypassed, they deserve a moment of recognition.

First, there were the two shamans who had served as marriage officials in the Parma–Ma Kapal wedding. This was unusual, since one sponsor (often representing the bride's community if the bride's and groom's are different) is normally sufficient. In this wedding, no one could decide where, in terms of "community," the bride lived. Thus, one pangulu from Ukut and one from Rajang had married the couple.

One pangulu was Ma Pasta, a quiet married man who farmed near the large ritual hall which still offered possibilities as the community center of Ukut. Ma Pasta was a great admirer of Uma Adang, and he wanted everything to be done properly according to the timeless adat of old. No one paid much attention to his adat determinations, however. What could he do?

The other pangulu was a more seasoned leader: the restless, wiry Ma Tupai of Rajang. Ma Tupai was ambitious and respected; but, at the same time, he prized his eccentricity. He was unwilling to wait around for visitors, being content to live on his own hilltop far from the main trail. To juggle these contradictions, yet claim a position of senior leadership in Rajang, required allies, and Ma Tupai leaned on young Ma Salam, who, while too young to pull a community together alone, was adept at smooth government-style manners. Through his interest in this marriage, Ma Tupai expressed support for Ma Salam's claims for the reach of Rajang.

In the abstract, many might have agreed that these were the men to consult about Parma's divorce and remarriage. Yet the Tidung delegation bypassed them, as well as other Ukut neighborhood officials, the groom, Ma Kapal, and Ma Kapal's senior kin. Awat Lumuh had told Ma Salam, in Rajang, not to worry about Ma Kapal, since he, Awat Lumuh, counted himself among Ma Kapal's senior kin. "The issue of Ma Kapal is easy," he had said.

Adat experts are created only as they succeed in being acknowledged or forcing their way into public recognition. If Ma Pasta, Ma Tupai, or Ma Kapal's asbah had been known as the key figure in a strong community, Awat Lumuh might have stopped by. At this time, none of these men was able to answer Awat Lumuh's neglect except by spreading rumors about their anger at him. Similarly, Gasai's broken engagement would itself have gone unrecognized had not Awat Lumuh or some other assertive leader been ready to mount a campaign in his behalf. Without activation, there is no adat.

Without activation, too, there are no kinship ties. Meratus couples are supposed to be married by their respective senior kin, reckoned bilaterally and with no clearly defined collateral limits. Most adults are related, if distantly, to dozens of young people scattered across the mountains, whom they may barely know. In any particular instance, only a few choose to assume the rights and responsibilities of senior kin. As their relationship became notorious, Parma and her two suitors, Ma Kapal and Gasai, acquired more interested kin. They also lost a few, as some decided not to get involved.

Awat Lumuh and his delegation made it to Niwan, where they met with the Old Village Head and with Parma's uncle, Ma Ulin. Many years earlier, the Old Village Head had been head of a west-side administrative village. As with many respected leaders, people still knew him by his title. Indeed, his words were still widely influential. I was not there to witness their meeting, but everyone I heard speak about it agreed on certain essentials. The Old Village Head had told Awat Lumuh that he was free to marry Parma and Gasai as long as Parma was properly divorced from Ma Kapal and peace was made between Ma Kapal's and Gasai's people.

This simple story, however, changed subtly but significantly from telling to telling. Had the Old Village Head emphasized the proper divorce, or the peace-making, or the possibility of a new marriage? Rumors and accusations flew. Some criticized the Old Village Head for acting in a case that was none of his business, some for betraying his kin and neighbors. Awat Lumuh, however, praised him as among the fairest of mediators.

Others claimed that Awat Lumuh, in spreading the news of what happened at the meeting, had simply lied.

The discussion of Parma's conjugal future began to create its own loyalties and antagonisms. Versions of the adat negotiations both cohered and conflicted—not as they were formed within a community, nor between two communities, but in all the links and gaps between individuals, umbun, households, clusters—the links and gaps through which communities were formed and reformed. The fortunes of Parma and her suitors were reviewed in chance meetings on a trail, in the opening chatter of visitors, or on breaks at work parties. Contradictory, idiosyncratic, marginal, such talk might be ignored by an anthropology that begins and ends in the hegemonic stability of cultural locations. Yet these interstitial tellings and retellings formed the uneven network of talk from which the legitimacy of community-based authority could be both constituted and questioned.

Another wedding

Ten days after the trip to Rajang and Niwan, another wedding party gathered. Parma remained quiet; but this time, as she was once again beautified for the ceremony, she seemed content. Gasai, too, looked pleased. Yet, as the bride and groom exchanged shy glances, their guests, among whom I was included, were more than a little on edge.

Rumor had it that Tidung people were afraid to let the wedding take place in their ritual hall; Ukut could not have hosted this wedding. Therefore, for the occasion, an uncle of Parma's, who lived about two hours from the Tidung stream, built a festive extension on to his porch. The anxious, excited wedding party crowded around his house.

Everyone expected Ma Kapal and his relatives to show up in force to stop the wedding. Of course, he was offended; he had never agreed to a divorce. A token divorce fee had been sent to him by messenger. But this wasn't much of a divorce. Ordinarily, divorce requires the face-to-face exchange of divorce fees between spouses in the presence of the wedding sponsor. Once again, the rice was cooked and the chickens slaughtered; but no one was sure that the wedding would occur.

But neither Ma Kapal nor anyone who spoke for him showed up. Neither did Parma's parents arrive. Some said the parents were ill, yet no relatives of Parma's from outside the Tidung area had come. Could the wedding proceed without them?

At this point, Gasai's father began to speak about the negotiations leading up to this wedding: Gasai's engagement to Parma, Ma Kapal's insult to the engagement, and, finally, the trip to Rajang and Niwan, with its successful outcome in which the Old Village Head had sanctioned the marriage. As the father spoke, people relaxed in the belief that Ma Kapal's supporters would cede the case. The wedding would proceed.

When the Tidung marriage official seemed hesitant to do the wedding ritual, The Bear, a distant relative of the groom, offered himself. The Bear was head shaman and thus marriage official in his own small neighborhood, several hours distant. The Bear considered himself a man of action who was hard to scare. He knew the divorce was not entirely in order; but, at the same time, he noted that it was of little importance compared to the greater fault of marrying Parma against her will. Adat does not allow forced marriages, he stated, to general agreement. "It's government law," he added. With this authority, he pronounced his first benediction as the groom sacrificed a white chick:

> Informing the old ones who guard the rules,
> Here is the white bird of binding.
> To tell them to be of one heart, one desire,
> To tell them to be of one sleeping mat, one bed.
> Let it not ruin the fruits of the harvest,
> Let it not turn to floods and rain.
> Don't marry them to a shortened lifespan,
> Don't marry them to death and illness.
> Marry them to luck and fortune,
> Marry them to a long future. . .

CONFRONTATIONS AND EVASIONS

The Bear was renowned as a first-class shaman. He was respected as an articulate, brave, funny, and generous leader. Great crowds flocked to his festivals. Yet in the everyday affairs of his closest neighbors, he found it difficult to create community consensus. People did not show up for work-exchange groups; nor did they bother to fix the ritual hall, which had a leaky roof and rotten floors. Most shared their wild boar only, he complained, with those nearest them. And his neighbors were forever threatening to take their rice to festivals elsewhere.

Perhaps this lack of unity contributed to the diversity of opinions I heard when I spent a month in The Bear's neighborhood after the Parma–Gasai wedding. I heard mainly criticism, though from many different angles. The Bear's support for the union silenced no one. Ma Kapal's supporters claimed that the Old Village Head of Niwan had been bribed to sanction the wedding. The wedding sponsor from Ukut visited a neighbor (not The Bear) to say that he was ready to fight for the Ma Kapal marriage. Visitors from Rajang reported that the wedding sponsor there was so mad that he had denounced the Old Village Head ("Since when does he think he's still a government official!") and demanded a fine for not being consulted.

According to critics of the wedding, even Parma's father had deserted Gasai. He had not attended the wedding, he said, because he was out hunting honey; he was not sick. Declaring, *Biar juduh sadapa*, "Even if their compatibility is an arm's length long!" (that is, "I don't care how much they love each other"), Parma's father demanded that a fine be imposed and that a divorce be granted, on the grounds that the wedding was held without him.

The Bear himself had begun to back down. He had been fooled, he said, about the conditions of the divorce and tricked into marrying Parma and Gasai. Mediation between Ma Kapal's and Gasai's people was in order. But he could not understand why the Rajang officials were so upset, especially since they had given the case to the Old Village Head. I didn't understand either until I was summarily called back to Ma Salam's place in Rajang. As soon as I arrived, Ma Salam, with great vehemence, explained his view of what had happened.

Ma Kapal and his group hadn't come to Parma's second wedding. It was far out of their familiar territory, and it would have been a tough fight. But they had not dropped the case. Their next step was to pursue an alliance with Rajang and Niwan leaders, as representatives of Parma's relatives who had supported the first wedding. An Ukut man affiliated with Rajang visited Ma Salam and "asked about the adat" for the case, thus giving Ma Salam the authority to negotiate for them. And Ma Salam was more than ready to get involved. Not only was it an opportunity to expand his leadership, it was also a chance to revenge the death of his ambushed uncle. Besides, he had the support of Ma Tupai, the Rajang wedding sponsor, who had been neglected in the Tidung wedding arrangement.

For the past few years in Rajang, the *basambu* ritual, in which the half-grown rice is protected from danger, had been held by individual farmers or by small groups. In 1981, however, there was to be a neighborhood-wide basambu, held at Ma Salam's house, with Ma Tupai as head shaman. News spread to adjacent neighborhoods that the ritual would be a big affair. On the afternoon before the ceremony, a large contingent arrived from the Ukut valley, including Ma Kapal and his uncle, Ma Linggu, who had represented Ma Kapal in his marriage to Parma.

By chance, an old man named Awat Pasta also arrived. Originally from Rajang, Awat Pasta still had a brother and several nephews in Rajang, although none were politically active. However, Awat Pasta had married into the Tidung area, near the place where Parma's uncles lived; he was the man who had handled the faulty divorce between Ma Kapal and Parma. Awat Pasta was a mild-mannered, socially awkward, somewhat retiring old man. In attending the Rajang basambu, he was visiting relatives, not looking for a fight. But Ma Salam could not ignore Awat Pasta's presence among Ma Kapal's people.

Ma Salam told me the story later. "Who gave you permission to divorce and remarry Parma?" he challenged Awat Pasta. "The Old Village Head of Niwan," was the reply. "Lies and slander," responded Ma Salam, with the support of other Rajang voices. Even if the Old Village Head had given his agreement, to do so was a mistake, for it did not imply the consent of other Niwan or Rajang leaders. Besides, the Old Village Head had given the condition that affairs be patched up with Ma Kapal, and that condition had not been met.

Ma Tupai, sponsor of the Rajang wedding, was angry. "If you don't give us Rp 120,000, we'll have the lot of you arrested by the police," he told Awat Pasta. The fine would be split in half: half for Ma Kapal's kin and Ukut officials, to answer charges of wife-stealing; and half to Rajang leaders for charges of "lies and slander" and for holding a wedding that many of the bride's kin did not attend. Yet the fine was too large to expect payment; it was a challenge, not a bill.

Always mindful of proper administrative form, Ma Salam gave Awat Pasta half an hour to think it over. Awat Pasta was quiet. In representing Tidung folks in the midst of their opponents, he was in a bad position. "All right," he finally said, "I'll go to Tidung and discuss it with people there. Within five days, I'll come back to Ukut with an answer." His reply was accepted.

As might be expected, five days came and went without the appearance of Awat Pasta in Ukut.

The closeness of Awat Pasta's ties to all the parties in the dispute suggests how complex are alliances formed in this context. A brother of Awat Pasta's had lived in Ma Salam's household until his death a few months earlier. The Ukut wedding sponsor who had continued to support the Ma Kapal marriage was Awat Pasta's son-in-law. Parma's kin were also connected. One of Parma's uncles had been married to Awat Pasta's daughter, now deceased. This former son-in-law had married a former daughter-in-law (once married to Awat Pasta's now deceased son) and moved to her place near Tidung. Awat Pasta had followed them to this place as he made a match with the woman's widowed aunt. His residence there had made it easy for Awat Lumuh to press him to arrange the Ma Kapal divorce. Yet he lived and farmed in a swidden cluster which only occasionally considered itself part of Tidung and which generally sought ties with the Ukut River valley. Although Ma Salam and Awat Lumuh had a stake in delineating "Rajang" (with some of Ukut) versus "Tidung" (with some of Ukut), community boundaries were far less clear to the neighbors they included among both their allies and their enemies.

If Awat Pasta, with kin in Rajang but his residence near Tidung, had been more assertive, he might have been able to mediate between Rajang and Tidung claims. Instead, caught as he was in a difficult middle position, he became a scapegoat for all sides. Ma Kapal's supporters blamed him for arranging a divorce; Gasai's supporters blamed him for not handling it properly. At The Bear's place, I heard him maligned from all directions. Yet The Bear, a much stronger leader, had been able to do no better.

The Bear tries to mediate

Unwilling to submit, Awat Lumuh was nevertheless willing to negotiate. As the story of the Rajang–Ukut challenge circulated, it was suggested that the dispute be brought to The Bear. The Bear wanted to mediate because he enjoyed being the host and leading a meeting. By this time, he had little stake in who won. His place lay halfway between Ma Kapal's and Gasai's. Then, too, The Bear claimed kinship ties with both grooms and had good relations with Ukut and Tidung people. Unfortunately, he had done the honors at the wedding of Parma and Gasai, which made it hard for him to appear unbiased.

The two sides were to meet at The Bear's *basambu* ritual. As expected, a large crowd appeared, with groups from both Ukut and Tidung. The Bear's rituals were always popular because he enthusiastically (and illegally) sponsored gambling and cockfighting at the same time that he put on a beautiful shamanic performance. Awat Lumuh came with Gasai's father and Parma's uncles from Tidung. The Ukut wedding sponsor arrived. A sister and a brother-in-law of Ma Kapal showed up. Neither Ma

Kapal nor any of his senior kin representatives appeared, however. Thus, there could be no mediation.

Nevertheless, the dispute was discussed, and the Tidung group had the floor. Ma Pasta, the Ukut wedding sponsor, and Ma Kapal's sister and brother-in-law never joined the conversation. Awat Lumuh was quietly self-righteous. An angry uncle of Parma's took center stage, however, ridiculing Ma Kapal and the Rajang leaders, laughing, and saying that they ate nothing but feces.

Ma Linggu, Ma Kapal's head kin representative for his wedding, had not gone to The Bear's ritual because he was busy cementing an alliance with Ma Salam in Rajang. Although they were not habitual travelling companions, they hiked to market together. Passing through Niwan, they confronted the Old Village Head and urged him to withdraw from the case. They had lobbied for more support from Parma's uncle, Ma Ulin. At the market, Ma Salam paid his respects to the police and military officers, thinking he might request their help later.

A little more than a week later, The Bear held a *basanggar banua*. (This is the ritual that creates a protective "village fence.") This time, Ma Linggu came with Ma Kapal and a large number of his Ukut relatives. No one from Tidung appeared. The Bear tried to set another mediation date, but Ma Linggu put him off. The Bear apologized for his role in marrying Parma and Gasai, saying that he had been tricked by Awat Pasta into believing there had been a proper divorce. He had remained silent, he said, when the Tidung crowd visited the week before; his only interest was arriving at the truth. Eloquent as The Bear was, though, he could make no headway.

Ma Linggu would only repeat the Rajang charge: If Tidung people did not come up with Rp 120,000, the police would be summoned. His words carried special weight because he was backed by a Banjar trader who had arrived with a Rajang man. The trader, Haji Biguli, was travelling in the mountains, offering costume jewelry for heirloom ceramics. His manner made it clear that he knew he was a civilized person among savages and that he offered a powerful connection to the non-Meratus world. For some reason The Bear could not make out, Haji Biguli supported Ma Salam's seemingly irrational anger at Tidung—and, perhaps, at The Bear himself. Why was Ma Salam destroying the prospects for local mediation?

What The Bear did not appreciate was the role of the long-dead Ma Jawa in fueling Ma Salam's intense involvement in the dispute. As far as Ma

Salam was concerned, The Bear might have been one of the murderers. Ma Linggu, Ma Kapal's uncle, would have lost his Rajang support if he had let The Bear mediate, and he needed support in order to be taken seriously as a disputant. Besides, Ma Salam's success with the Banjar trader had already shown this young leader's abilities in influencing powerful outsiders to support him.

Another outsider whose loyalty was on the line was myself. The Rajang man who came to The Bear's festival brought me a note from Ma Salam, ordering me back to Rajang immediately. Otherwise, Ma Salam said, he could no longer guarantee the safety of the belongings I had at his house. Disturbed and distressed, I set off for Rajang the next day to make amends. Once it was clear that I was back in his sphere, Ma Salam was quick to reestablish our friendship and happy to tell me everything from his side.[4]

Ma Salam develops his case

Ma Ulin, Parma's Niwan uncle, had promised Ma Salam that he would hike to Rajang to support him in the dispute. As several weeks passed and there was no sign of Ma Ulin in Rajang, Ma Salam became increasingly annoyed. He needed Ma Ulin, Parma's representative in her marriage to Ma Kapal, to make his case against Tidung.

At last, Ma Ulin appeared, and Ma Salam was all smiles. Ma Ulin himself was ready for a fight with Tidung. He now claimed never to have received Ma Salam's letter asking him to break off the Parma–Gasai engagement, and he agreed that the Old Village Head had no right to interfere in this case. As for Parma's mother, his "sister of one father and one mother's womb," she had better support them, or else!

Together, Ma Salam and Ma Ulin wrote a letter to Awat Lumuh, calling him and Parma's Tidung uncles to Ukut for a meeting, "like it or not." If they did not come, Ma Salam and Ma Ulin agreed, it would prove they did not want an adat settlement, and Ma Salam would be justified in summoning the police. Fetching the Rajang wedding sponsor, Ma Tupai, and rousing each other's ferocity, the men hiked to Parma's parents' house in Ukut, where they sent a messenger to Tidung. For the sake of good form, the Ukut wedding sponsor and the neighborhood head were called, as well as Ma Kapal, the jilted groom, and his uncle, Ma Linggu.

Predictably, Awat Lumuh sent back a reply stating that he was ill and could not come to Ukut. If they wanted a dispute settlement, they should come to Tidung. Ma Salam, Ma Ulin, and Ma Tupai had already agreed not to go to Tidung under any circumstances; thus it was the expected stalemate. Then one of Parma's tough-talking Tidung uncles showed up.

Both sides, the Rajang men told me, were tense, ready to fight. Startled that *anyone* had come, they were not planning to negotiate. After some shouting, they picked up their things and left for Rajang, their demands unchanged.

Before Parma's uncle came, however, another problem was aired: just where Parma's parents stood. Parma's father said he had never approved of the wedding to Gasai, that his Tidung brothers had planned things without his knowledge. After all, he had not even attended!

Ma Ulin did not believe him. The house was filled with signs of the new son-in-law's attentions: kerosene, salt, oil, wild boar meat, and store-bought biscuits. Anyway, Ma Ulin told Parma's father, if he had approved earlier, he had better not approve now. If the Tidung crowd did not come up with Rp 120,000, Parma's father would have to pay it himself, or pull his daughter away from Gasai and force a divorce. Under the circumstances, Parma's father agreed to cooperate.

Ma Ulin gave him ten days in which to get his daughter or the Rp 120,000. If he had done nothing in ten days, Ma Ulin would *sumpah pagat badangsanak*, "make an oath to break off their tie of siblingship." He would take back the rice pot he had lent the couple, and never again would they offer each other food. Then he would give his approval to Ma Kapal's kin to call in the police. If they arrested Parma's father or beat him up, it would mean nothing to Ma Ulin or Ma Salam or Ma Tupai. For Rp 30,000, it was suggested, the police would be glad to take on the case.

As these men became more aggressive, I found myself missing Induan Bilai and her down-to-earth disrespect for the big ideas of the leaders. The next time I was in Niwan, we sat down for a warm talk. The ambushed Ma Jawa, she affirmed, was surely irrelevant to Parma's love life. Perhaps, I suggested, all the threats did not add up to much. No, she reminded me, there was one person with some power who had become involved: the Banjar trader, Haji Biguli. He might really be able to get the police involved in the case. If someone offered the police money, who could tell what they would do? Induan Bilai had no interest in pretending to support her cousin, Ma Ulin. How dare Ma Ulin claim that he shared one father and one mother with Parma's mother—her sister—when he was actually just a first cousin! If he wanted to break off his kinship tie with her, too, what did she care?

Induan Bilai's dissent reminded me that Ma Ulin and Ma Salam, despite their aggressiveness and authority, were never successful at putting together a consensus of kin and neighbors. Even in the case of Parma's parents, Ma Ulin's worst possible threat was to break off relations. He could try to make life without his protection seem scary and dangerous, but, in terms of economic and social sanctions, he had little to work with. He could ask other Rajang and Niwan people to avoid Parma's family, but he could not prevent them from patching things up with their Ukut neighbors or, perhaps, from moving to Tidung. Parma's parents could live perfectly well without Ma Ulin's rice pot.

A MILITARY SOLUTION

In April, Rajang threw its biggest *bawanang* festival in years. Bawanang is the annual ceremony that makes the new rice "free" to eat. This festival would involve a week of dancing, eating, curing, courting, and talking, with guests coming from miles around. Ma Tupai was to lead the shamans; Ma Salam's house was the ritual hall. Young women arrived in gauzy blouses and brightly colored sarongs. Young men wore the velvet caps that signalled their Indonesian citizenship; their shoulders were draped with Chinese dish towels as elegant as scarves, and their wicker satchels held store-bought cigarettes. Old men extended their betel cases, while matrons offered home-grown tobacco sweetened with palm sugar.

Parma's parents came early the first evening. Soon Parma's father, with enthusiastic denunciations of Gasai and his kin, had renewed his membership in Rajang. He declared himself ready at last to divorce Parma from Gasai and to demand the Rp 120,000 immediately. In the clot of men discussing the case, the Banjar trader Haji Biguli was making himself prominent. As usual, he was prepared to extend himself to bring the police anytime. Why, he prodded, were they hesitating?

On the second evening, a new crowd arrived from Ukut; and attention turned to their story. The police section officer stationed at an east-side district seat had hiked into the mountains and stayed the night in the old, rambling Ukut ritual hall. Despite the importance of threats to call them in, police and army officers were rarely seen in the mountains. This visit (the same one Induan Hiling describes in chapter 2) had made quite an impression on everyone. First, a bachelor from Ukut headwaters had his pants confiscated. He was wearing market-bought green "army" pants; he must have thought he looked smart when he joined the party that gathered to see the officer. Instead, the section officer had accused him of wearing "government property" and forced him to strip on the spot. This was humiliating, indeed. The Rajang men tried to shrug it off by boasting that, if it had happened to one of them, they would have fought back; but their bravado was unconvincing.

Second, the section officer had commented on a local dispute, the case of the durian tree that two men were fighting over in Ukut. The officer said that, since no Meratus paid taxes, no one owned that durian tree or any others; those trees were government property. He fined both contestants for asking his opinion in the first place; this did not qualify as government business. The officer's purpose on this trip was to survey development. So far he had concluded that the Meratus occupied an "empty" location with no signs of development. If they did not shape up quickly, he declared, they would all be relocated to the eastern plains. Of all the settlements he had passed through on this hike, he continued, there was only one that showed any potential: Tidung.

There, indeed, several houses were clustered around a shingle-roofed ritual hall, the tight clustering a self-conscious attempt to meet government standards. Now, several days after the section officer's departure, rumor had it that the next village head of the east-side mountain administrative village would be none other than the respected Tidung leader, Awat Lumuh!

The section officer's hike from the eastern district seat had occurred just as anxieties about the government's intentions from western administrative centers were rising. The rumor had already spread to the Rajang bawanang that government headhunters were coming from the west side. With mathematical precision, one man announced that the government had released 1,000 bandits in the Meratus Mountains—500 thieves and 500 headhunters—to do as they wished. Niwan guests, as well as others hiking from the west, had arrived giddy with fear. All along the trail, there were signs of men in hiding: the smell of cigarettes, the sound of a cough in the forest . . .

Clearly, this was not the time to call in the police. It was particularly not a good time to use such threats against Tidung. Despite assurances from the trader Haji Biguli, even the bravest hesitated. A west-side neighborhood head attending the festival gave Ma Salam his opinion that he had better cool down. Before the bawanang was over, Ukut leaders had sent word that, as far as they were concerned, the Ma Kapal wife-stealing case was dead.

The section officer's visit set the conditions for the dampening of Rajang anger; but neither Ma Salam nor the wedding sponsor, Ma Tupai, was ready to give up. Parma's father did send back Gasai's marriage payment, refusing a Tidung offer of reconciliation. Although Awat Lumuh was willing to negotiate, he only made matters worse when (as Ma Salam told it) he sent a letter asking Ma Tupai to meet him in Ukut, then didn't show up. Ma Tupai, Ma Salam said, burned the letter and dragged Parma back with him to Rajang for three days. Ma Salam lectured her, telling her she had better not be seen near Gasai or any other man until Ma Salam himself gave the word. Rajang anger was not spent. Yet, shorn of rhetoric of regional power connections, the anger had nowhere to develop.

Denouement

By May, a fine wild-boar season had begun in the central mountains; and no one cared to spend time discussing Parma's marriages. Gasai and Awat Lumuh, however, still needed to at least reconcile with Parma's parents to allow Parma's marriage to Gasai to resume. Once again, Awat Lumuh set out for Rajang; but, this time, he brought no tough-talking young men. Instead, he brought two mature, respected men with no close ties to Tidung and with good relationships in Rajang. This time, too, Awat Lumuh bypassed Ma Salam's house and went straight to the isolated hilltop residence of the wedding sponsor, Ma Tupai. Ma Tupai's interest in the dispute, which had followed Ma Salam's, had never been so personal nor intense. Even if his case seemed hopeless, Ma Salam might not let his anger cool—but Ma Tupai would. Thus, Ma Salam was informed late of the meeting, and he arrived only when talk was well underway. When he saw how matters stood, Ma Salam remained silent and gloomy throughout the discussion.

A settlement was quickly reached. Awat Lumuh handed over Rp 30,000. The money could be interpreted as Gasai's marriage payment (now officially replaced), as a fine for unspecified wrongdoings, or as a payment for pushing out the first groom, Ma Kapal. Ma Tupai was left to oversee any distributions; thus, as Ma Salam later grumbled, he kept the entire sum himself.

Eventually Ma Kapal's relatives in Ukut heard about the settlement and sent a man to Ma Salam, asking why the matter had been settled and why they had not received a portion. Ma Salam, excited that the dispute might still be revived, went with the man to Ma Tupai, from whom he demanded an explanation. Ma Tupai was firm, however; the settlement and the money concerned only Parma's new marriage to Gasai. If Ma Kapal wished to pursue the case against Tidung, he should go ahead; but Ma

Tupai was no longer concerned. Ma Kapal's Ukut kin had never had the strength to make their case alone; they had reached a dead end. Ma Salam was forced to live with his anger and let it quietly dissipate. Parma and Gasai were already living together again, and there was no one able or willing to go find them and stop them.

♦

Stories on the move

The amount of hiking in this story testifies to the importance of mobility in Meratus politics. Men who lose the ability to hike lose the ability both to "borrow" power and to round up an audience to hear about it. My own fieldwork travel was modest compared to that of many of my hosts.

Hiking through forests and across mountains may seem more like primitive wandering than the transnational mobility associated with modern travel. Yet the travelling politics I describe is not nomadic. The *nomad* is defined as one who has no home. Meratus travel both expands social spaces and shapes political communities; it is not a practice of homelessness. Moreover, in anthropology, *nomadism* is understood as a repetitive, tradition-bound mobility. It cordons off a space of cultural purity and simplicity more "settled" even than the space of the seden-tary.[5] Meratus travel opens transcultural conversations that bring extra-local concerns into local negotiations of leadership, gender, and commu-nity. Travel creates heterogeneous Meratus histories situated unevenly within wider historical movements. The local character of Meratus travel does not isolate Meratus culture. Rather, Meratus travel stimulates criti-cal reflection on the cultural specificity of metropolitan travel agendas.

Negotiating community and culture

The events surrounding Parma's marriages show local politics con-structed within a recognition of regional authority. Leaders threaten to call the police and invoke the authority of the state by using administra-tive titles, by stressing ties between adat and national law, and by offering dramatic displays of state-endorsed order, whether clustered houses or proper marriages. Through a rhetoric of connection to regional author-ity, local leaders attract political constituencies that believe in their capac-ity to lead.

Local leaders, however, do not govern in the way the regional adminis-tration intends. Leaders' proclamations of law and their brave threats are misunderstood and go unrecognized by the regional administration. As the outcome of the dispute over the durian tree suggests, when regional officials *are* brought into local cases, their intervention often backfires against those who hoped for involvement the most. Meratus leaders strategize and compete within a context in which the consequences of regional power are known to be quirky and unexpected.

For this reason, the story told above has no local resolution. No local sense of cultural logic or justice was served. Instead, one leader—Awat Lumuh—became unassailable because he was endorsed by a police officer who knew nothing of this dispute and little about Awat Lumuh. Perhaps, as Induan Hiling told it, the officer had dined and slept well in Tidung, so he endorsed the senior man on the spot. Even this endorsement—coming, as it did, from an east-side authority—would only have raised the stakes for bringing in west-side intervention had not the west-side armed forces suddenly become, in local eyes, bandits and headhunters to whom no appeal was possible.

There is ample evidence here of the distinctiveness and creativity of Meratus political understandings. My account recalls cultural descriptions of other Southeast Asian "hill peoples"; yet I diverge from most other accounts in my approach to cultural analysis. In showing Meratus projects in their relation to government titleholders, police patrols, and threats of "development," my story opens an alternate view beside analyses that find the cultural in independent solutions to human existential problems. Such analyses can isolate the people represented from the world of readers in a dichotomy that overhomogenizes both sides. In showing cultural creativity in Meratus uses of regional materials, I invoke a common world, full of police officers and development schemes, but with diverse interpretive practices.

An unexpected feature of Meratus locations in this common world involves the degree to which debate and disagreement are ordinary occurrences. Internationally dominant representations of Asians show the West as the stimulus for local contestation. The further from centers of Western influence, the more harmony and consensus one expects. Yet, I argue that it is the extreme marginality of the Meratus—their political-cultural distance from national centers of postcolonial contention—that destabilizes regional and local authority alike, shaping local possibilities for political disagreement, competition, or realignment. The possibility of appeal to multiple regional authorities in different directions, and the unpredictability of appeals to and threats from these authorities, creates a context in which many Meratus men, and some women, can pose as leaders with regional connections. Community formation involves mobile, rather economically independent umbun. In this context, leaders compete to build and rebuild constituencies which, yet, are constantly dissenting.

The importance of this argument can be seen as it redirects anthropological attention to adat. In Kalimantan studies, scholars have represented adat as inspiring a stable, autonomous, and homogeneous local consensus. For example, J. D. Freeman, the best-known ethnographer of northern Borneo, approvingly quotes M. Hepell on Iban adat: "The *adat* itself is treated as if hallowed, and is regarded as a body of correct behavior essential to the continued existence of the society. . . . Each Iban, therefore, belongs to an *adat* community, the harmony and continued existence of which is dependent on the members behaving as the *adat* requires" (Hepell 1975:303; quoted in Freeman 1981:32). Freeman argues that the hegemony of adat creates a politically autonomous, egalitarian Iban society: "The absence of institutionalized authority in the traditional society of the Iban was directly conjunctive with their highly developed and comprehensive system of *adat* law" (1981:32). In contrast, I found that the "egalitarian" nature of Meratus social life is best seen in the *in*stability of adat authority.

As the story of Parma's marriages suggests, adat discussion is central to the process in which ambitious Meratus renegotiate political communities. Adat invokes order and tradition, but adat is discussed competitively. Because willingness to follow a leader's adat signals membership in his or her political community, adat adheres to particular, shifting constituencies. Although there is some agreement about what kinds of rules and customs can really be adat, adat must continually be reinvented; perhaps no one ever complies with a given adat suggestion.

Because Meratus adat lacks the power of daily disciplinary surveillance, back talk of the sort I attribute to Induan Bilai flourishes. Leaders and their adat are constantly being criticized, flouted, or ignored, even when adat in the abstract is praised. Criticism offers multiple strategic possibilities. It can marginalize a critic; it can facilitate transfer of loyalty to another leader; or it can signal an attempt to build one's own political constituency. Even the most successful leaders must threaten, bicker, and cajole in order to establish the framework of adat that offers them authority and knowledge. The most successful adat creates only a contextually specific moment of consensus.

The image of the harmonious adat community is entrenched in Indonesian studies. It is an image that has been preserved by both colonial and national policies even as other policies seek to break the imagined consensus for progress and development. The image of local harmony facilitates exploitation in the name of tradition and obscures innovation and resistance at the local level. It also provides a source of hope and an international platform for local groups struggling for their rights.[6] It has fostered scholarly explorations of cultural structure and coherence. Yet, an ethnographic style has been created which banishes plot, characters, and authors in exchange for the timeless voice of culture.

The story of Parma's marriages is intended both to disrupt the centers and to open up the boundaries of this image of culture and community. Regional authority makes local resolution impossible. Local disagreement fosters new adat formulations. A man dead for more than thirty years stimulates reformulation of social boundaries. And although no one in authority asked Parma with whom she wanted to live, it turns out that it was difficult to keep her away from the young man she preferred.

The tone of my discussion must change, however, as I shift from Meratus interpretations of the official to official interpretations of the Meratus.

5 CONDITIONS OF LIVING

Often they are unaware of their own estrangement.
*Seringkali mereka tidak mengetahui akan
keterasingannya.*

How do people become aware that they are strangers in their own lands? Someone must make them so. Sometimes they are forcibly removed. Sometimes they are just reclassified.

My epigraph is a caption for a photograph (of members of a minority group picking up welfare boxes) from an article on "isolated populations" which appeared in the Social Department's internal journal (Suhud 1975:41). (I have translated *keterasingan* as "estrangement," but the word implies foreignness as well as isolation.) The quotation forms an apt introduction to the contradictions between Meratus views and the views of the national and regional administration about Meratus conditions of living. Neither "Meratus views" nor "government views" exist as a unified vision. The Social Department's resettlement geometries and the Forestry Department's timber computations are not the same. Yet there are administrative convergences: Development goals draw together a relatively coherent official critique of local movement—movement as shifting cultivation, as shifting habitations, as unregulated resource use and travel. From the perspective of national politics, these practices are impediments to national security, as well as being a sign of backwardness and exotic isolation. To Meratus, in contrast, these are part of the ordinary way of making a living; they are necessary, perhaps, to the human condition.

This contrast is deepened in a contradiction that almost reverses its terms, exposing their context-specific values: Shifting cultivation and travel create Meratus attachments to place, such that individual and community identities are formulated in relation to the histories of particular patches of forest. Yet government agencies refuse to acknowledge a Meratus investment in forest places; the premise of resettlement is that docile subjects are disengaged from places and are willing to live wherever the government sets them down.

As state programs oppose people's livelihood strategies, making a living becomes a source of alternative political insights. The situation shapes and deepens the cleft between official ideologies and development programs, on the one hand, and ordinary Meratus lives, on the other. Contrasts proliferate. To illuminate these contrasts, in this chapter I go back and forth between perspectives of "the Meratus" and "the state" as these are oppositionally constructed with regard to conditions of living.

Movement

State programs identify the fundamental problem with "isolated populations" as movement, that is, as unregulated (perhaps impossible to regulate) movement. The category "Isolated Populations" is *defined* through forbidden mobility:

> Almost all of the groups of isolated populations live by shifting cultivation, that is slash and burn farming. After a maximum of three years, they move to slash and burn again and, continuing thus, almost never return to their original place. . . .
>
> The groups of isolated populations, according to the Social Department, are categorized into three types, as follows:
>
> 1) Nomads . . . populations whose livelihoods and living places continually shift and whose living conditions and means of subsistence are *still extremely simple*. They still live by hunting, fishing, and gathering forest products; their communications with the outside world are almost nonexistent.
>
> 2) Semi-nomads . . . populations whose living places have already become settled for a certain period and whose livelihood as well as living conditions and means of subsistence are *still very simple*. They already have communication with the outside world.
>
> 3) Provisionally settled . . . populations whose livelihood and living places are already settled in a provisional way but whose living conditions are still simple. They already have frequent communications with the outside world.

In working with the three groupings of isolated populations above, the Social Department's Directorate for Management for the Isolated Populations has suggested that the first priority is the *Semi-Nomadic* population groups. This strategy is chosen with the motive and goal that those who are guided can spread into the "nomad" population groups such that a doubly high effect will be obtained. (Suhud 1975:37–39, my translation, emphasis in original)

Like most of the government officials with whom I spoke, the author lumps together all forms of shifting cultivation (called, in some government reports, "disorderly farming" [*pertanian yang tidak teratur*]). The author argues that this method of farming inevitably causes erosion on slopes and thus permanent forest destruction. He also suggests that the shifting of fields is often motivated by irrational tradition: "One Dayak group in East Kalimantan even moves its fields if someone finds a centipede in the boat on the way to the field" (Suhud 1975:38). The wisdom of local forest farmers is given very short shrift. So, too, is an extensive scholarly literature on shifting cultivation that differentiates the ecological effects of various farming practices and population densities.[1] State stereotypes do not allow officials to notice the sophistication of Meratus farming. In the lightly populated central Meratus Mountains, for example, shifting cultivation takes place within long cycles of forest-field rotation. Long cycles allow forest regeneration and forest management: Cultivators come back to farm old fields, but often only after fifteen years or so of forest growth, when the site begins to be *jurungan tuha*, "mature secondary forest." Phased planting, multiple cropping, and selective encouragement of "weed" species retard erosion and integrate field and forest management.[2] One might think that ecological watchdogs would be more concerned about the serious erosion and forest destruction in the Meratus area that have developed with mechanized multinational logging in the last two decades. Yet, for officials, the key issue is movement.

For government officials, the rice field offers a site of hope for settling "for a certain period"—if only its shifting can be restrained. Yet, for many Meratus, even a single year's rice field is a landscape of journeying. The harvest is a product of travel: travel of the rice as well as of the farmers. Even if, for some reason, farmers used the same site over and over, they would not neglect the rice's "travel."

In many western Meratus areas, rice farming is described as sending the rice seed on a long journey to find companions and return home with them as the harvest. Movement is understood as opposing stagnation, not security; it represents the possibility of increase. Thus, the ritual expert's explanation of journeying and increase—offered in a rhythmic chant as

the rice is planted—introduces Meratus interpretations at a point of refusal of state discipline. This is a point not blessed by explicit dialogue; it
can be appreciated only across a gap of meaning and intention. In the
following excerpts, Awat Kilay speaks to his early rice in 1980.

> Girl, don't casually take off,
> If today has no luck in it, look for a day with luck.
> Look for a day with fortune, a day with profits,
> a day with power.

He flatters and coddles the rice, addressing it as a precious young girl
(*diang*, Banjar, "girl"), she who is "told to become young again" (*disuruh
ba'anum diri*). She must make herself attractive as she seeks comrades on
her journey: "Comb your hair. Oil your hair. Get ready to go."

He/r gender identification is not exclusive, however. (*Diang* is not used
in ordinary Meratus speech; the term flatters the rice as "Banjar" as much
as "female.") She slips in and out of male and female markers, the better
to prepare for diverse encounters.

> Girl, get ready like a warrior.
> Don't casually leave, don't casually stand up,
> For, girl, you have your trip's preparations.
> Don't put on black clothes [the color of rice mold],
> Don't put on green clothes [the color of rice mold]
> Put on white clothes
> White pants, a white shirt [men's attire],
> a head wrap decorated in white [men's attire]
> Clothes all white, all young, all new,
> Girl, don't casually leave.

S/he is prepared to meet he/r own needs and to face the dangers of
travel. The offerings of the planting party are her food, tobacco, and
betel; a work knife, an axe, and a sharpening stone are left in the field to
accompany he/r.

> Girl, don't get close to robbers and thieves.
> You have your own supplies; don't ask for things,
> You have your own costs; don't beg from others,
> Girl, don't pass the time with robbers and thieves.

In discussing The Bear's dewa shamanism, I introduced the system of
metaphors by which Meratus shamans travel. The rice travels the same

way, using images that blend the distant and the familiar and bring together the abstract and the concrete. Thus, the rice travels over the cool abundance of water. It rides in a boat over the "sea" (*laut*) of the field, where vegetables intermingle with the grain.

> If your boat doesn't have a rope,
> Your rope is cassava roots,
> Your rope is the roots of beans,
> Your rope is the roots of squash.
> As a pole, use a cassava stalk,
> As a pole, use a Job's tears' stem,
> As a pole, use a stalk of corn.
> As a paddle, use a banana leaf,
> It's not as if your boat has no rope.

In this way, the rice passes many places of power and wonder—places that can be interpreted as being in the field, in the farmers' or the ritual expert's bodies, or in the world beyond.

> Then going toward the original waterfall . . .

The rice visits a waterfall in Mecca—the land of wealth and plenty. It is also the waterfall of rice shoots in a single clump.

> Heading upstream on the harvest river,
> The river of the season's plenty . . .

"Heading upstream" is here *mananiti*, the term for hiking along a ridge. The river is a ridge; the land is the sea. The "harvest" (*tahun*) is also the "year," and its "season" (*musin*) is "plenty." Their cyclical, repetitive times create the transformative space for abundance-bringing travel.

> Falling to the tree of great abundance,
> Whose companion is Putir Bungsu Kuasa,
> The one who guards the tree circling the harvest,
> The tree circling the season's plenty.

The tree circling the harvest—and the one who guards the tree—is the farmer walking around the field. It is also a tree in Mecca and/or at the center of the sea. Through the rice's journeying, the magic of distant centers is brought to one's own rice field.

The goal of the journey is to find friends and companions and to return with them and all the wealth they represent. This requires that the rice present herself well among the rich and famous. The rice must tap the power of prestige and wealth not just in Mecca and the center of the sea, but in royal courts and bustling marketplaces.

> Don't act lower than others,
> Don't act higher than others,
> Girl, don't go to the margins,
> Girl, don't stay at the sides.
> Go to the middle.
> Don't you pass the time with the lazy,
> Don't get close to the poor,
> Don't get close to cripples,
> Don't get close to the disfigured.
> Get close to beautiful people,
> Get close to good-looking people,
> Get close to wealthy people,
> Get close to nobles, get close to kings,
> Get close to favored concubines.

By the time the rice returns home, the sea itself should have turned to the riches of the harvest, deserving of every praise.

> The sea with sands of gold,
> The sea with sands of silver money,
> The sea with sands of becoming.
> After the sea with sands of gold,
> Heading up the sea of clusters,
> The sea of becoming,
> The sea that surges,
> The sea that rises.

This journey leads to increase. It leads to an abundance no stationary vision has offered. It is in this context that one can see how all Meratus livelihood involves journeying.

Rajaki is "livelihood." It can also mean "luck," "rice," or "health." Rajaki is the "fortune" one has, for better or worse, and the "good fortune" that makes life worth living. But rajaki must be "sought" (*dika-yao*); it must be "followed" (*diumpati*) wherever it leads. Rajaki requires movement.

Hunting for game and selling forest products at market are two of the most obvious "travelling" aspects of "looking for rajaki." The man embarking on a hunting trip can never be certain what rajaki he will find; he must ramble around until he comes upon something. Similarly, marketing involves walking through the forest, facing unknown challenges. But, as the travels of the rice suggest, the journey need not be so obvious. Rice farmers search for rajaki in their fields; lovers and spouses follow rajaki in their relationships. Everyone seeks to increase the rajaki that maintains health and prolongs one's lifespan. Movement is life. When we find no more rajaki, our lives are over.

Places

From the distance of Jakarta—not to mention company headquarters in Seoul, Manila, or Tokyo—the Meratus Mountains appear covered with unbroken, uninhabited forest. Indeed, that is how this area appears on many national and provincial maps (see Map 5.1), in which just about the entire Meratus area is marked *hutan lebat*, "primary forest."

Even the most detailed official maps overestimate the amount of primary forest, showing only thin stretches of Meratus agroforestry. Map 5.2, for example, shows broad expanses of "primary forest" across the central mountains. "Secondary forest" (hutan belukar) created by Meratus shifting cultivation is shown only as narrow ribbons along the sides of major streams. Map 5.2 does not show nearly enough secondary forest given the population implied by even the few small spots of active cultivation shown. How could all the secondary forest created by those farmers have grown to "primary forest" so quickly?

Part of what is at issue is the definition of "mature forest." Only the youngest secondary regrowth is recognized in this map as hutan belukar, which, indeed, also refers to "brush." The rest of the forest is hutan lebat, a "dense forest" of more maturity. Yet the term hutan lebat also enters a national and international discourse, in which it refers to untouched climax forest without human settlement. By drawing the boundaries of primary forest so widely, the map restricts Meratus resource use in the central mountains to thin, stream-side ribbons, denying people's occupation of the entire territory.[3]

Ma Salam was fascinated by my maps of the area, and he quickly learned their conventions. Soon he was helping me make maps of his neighborhood. Carefully drawn to the conventions of the maps I brought with me, his maps offer little information about divergent local ways to represent space. Nevertheless, given the contours of our agreed-upon topography, his maps are useful for understanding local resource use and forest history.

Map 5.3 is adapted from Ma Salam's drawing of *katuan*, "mature

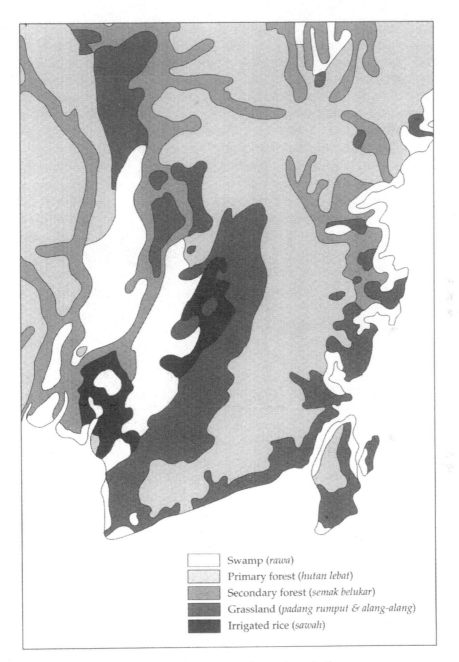

5.1   *Land use in southeast Kalimantan (redrawn from Soil
Research Institute, Land Use Map Indonesia, 1972)*

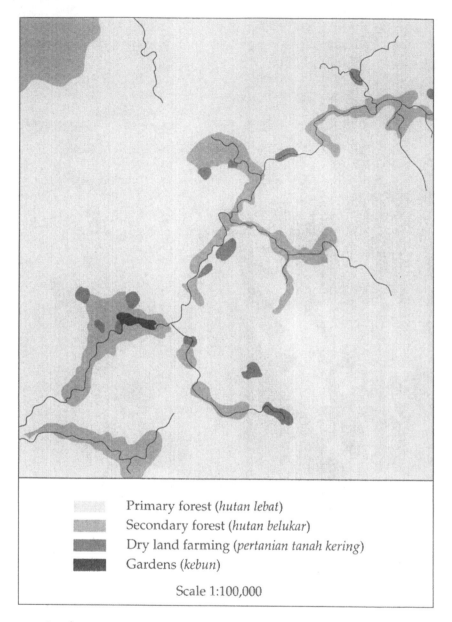

Primary forest (*hutan lebat*)
Secondary forest (*hutan belukar*)
Dry land farming (*pertanian tanah kering*)
Gardens (*kebun*)

Scale 1:100,000

5.2   *Land use in one area of the Meratus Mountains (redrawn from Direktorat Landuse, Departemen Dalam Negeri, 1970)*

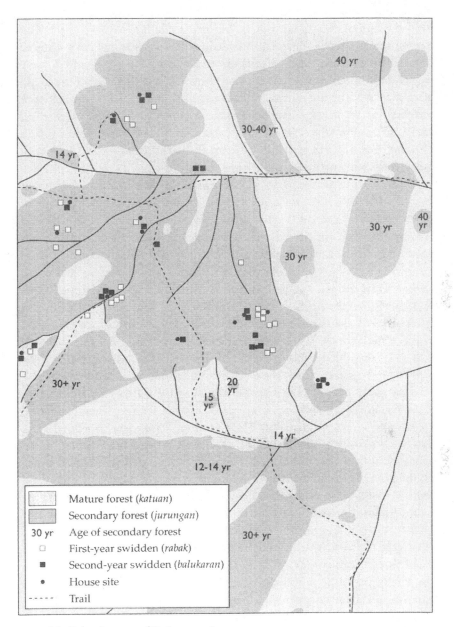

	Mature forest (*katuan*)
	Secondary forest (*jurungan*)
30 yr	Age of secondary forest
□	First-year swidden (*rabak*)
■	Second-year swidden (*balukaran*)
•	House site
- - - - -	Trail

5.3   Ma Salam's map of Rajang, 1981

forest," and *jurungan*, "secondary forest," in the area nearest the place he lived at the time. Ma Salam's map enlarges a small area of Map 5.2. His map is not just more detailed, however; it offers different information. Most of the area shown as "secondary forest" on Map 5.3—indeed, most of this map in general—falls into an area marked "primary forest" on Map 5.2.[4] In contrast to the official map, Ma Salam's drawing offers a complex history of the forest. Ma Salam drew not only young, regrowing brush only a few years old, but also older secondary forest felled before his time but still recognizable to him from the trees—and the stories through which trees enter conversation.

Meratus speak of the forest as being imbued with a history of human uses. As Ma Salam's map suggests, one of the most important ways in which the forest gains a history is through the cutting and regrowth that accompanies shifting cultivation. As people clear new fields, they do not forget the old ones. These old fields are rich sites for resources, as well as for stories. In the central mountains, a common way to recall a past event is to speak of the place where one's fields were located at the time. People also remember the fields of their neighbors and kin; much of the forest landscape around them assumes the aspect of a patchwork of old fields. Walking through the forest with Meratus companions, I became aware of how each section recalled a particular history of plant succession. The history of the forest is also the story of farms and farmers over time.

In the early 1980s, there were between twenty and twenty-five umbun in the Rajang neighborhood. Map 5.3 shows the scatter of neighborhood houses and swiddens in 1981. Most umbun in this neighborhood raise two rice crops simultaneously: one in a newly cleared field (*rabak*) and a second in a field that has already been farmed for one year (*balukaran*). To imagine the social history of the forest shown in Map 5.3, one could begin by connecting each rabak field with the balukaran cultivated by the same umbun. (In many cases, an umbun's rabak and balukaran are near each other; sometimes, however, an umbun clears its new field on the other side of the neighborhood, or even in another neighborhood.) One could then imagine backwards to connect these two fields with the site cleared by the same umbun two years before and now growing slowly into forest. As one continued to imagine backwards, one could construct a trail of an umbun's remembered, and still useful, field sites.

Map 5.4 shows the pattern of one Rajang umbun's swidden locations between 1958 and 1986. The black squares are swidden sites; the arrows indicate the direction of movement from year to year. This trail of remembered fields marks the landscape for the founders of this umbun. The

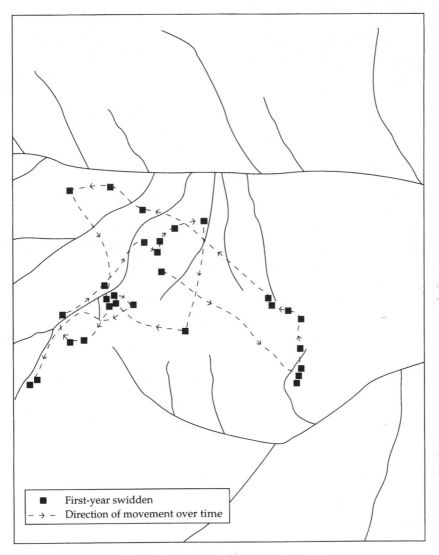

5.4   One Rajang umbun's first-year swiddens, 1958–1986

neighborhood becomes not just a forest with scattered current fields, but also a landscape of umbun movement over time, a life history remembered in regrowing forest.

When I tried to create a map that would show the crisscrossing trails of the past swiddens of a number of the umbun shown on Map 5.3, the map quickly became a confusing mess of lines, impossible to decipher. One can visualize such a map by imagining the 1981 fields on Map 5.3 in motion over time, across (and beyond) the terrain of Rajang. This is the process that creates the linked history of Rajang as forests and Rajang as community.

Forests

Large-scale timbering in Kalimantan is relatively new. A product of the New Order, it has proceeded quickly as the government divided forests into logging concessions and encouraged exports, first in whole logs, then, particularly since 1980, in plywood. In South Kalimantan, 1.19 million hectares have been classified as "production forests," that is, open for commercial logging (Moehji 1983:3). (Another 0.36 million hectares of forest are classified as "protected" or "conservation forest." Most of the remaining 3.7 million hectares in the province are classified as swamp, grassland, secondary forest, or farmland.) Although production increases have been more modest than those of some other provinces, South Kalimantan's forests—viewed from the perspective of the national economy—have been a growth sector. The optimism of national economists in the 1980s can be surmised from the figures in Table 5.1.

Table 5.1   South Kalimantan production and export of whole logs

Year	Production of whole logs (m³)	Export of whole logs (m³)	Whole logs domestically processed (m³)
1969	77,521.16	59,700.00	17,821.16
1973	659,980.69	536,851.14	123,129.55
1976	960,487.33	839,916.67	120,570.66
1980	1,474,184.15	633,659.07	840,525.08

Source: Moeji 1983, Table 1.

From the perspective of the logging industry and the state officials who arrange and encourage forest exploitation, a forest is a collection of commercial trees interspersed with "troublesome plants" (*tumbuh-tumbuhan pengganggu*). Kalimantan's forests are relatively valuable commercially because they contain many dipterocarps—forest giants that can be sawed up for the world plywood market. Forests in the Meratus Mountains, however, contain quite a mix of other trees. One forestry report offers the table shown here as Table 5.2 to describe the forest mix in one Meratus area, with its discouraging prospects for timbering (Sunardi 1975:127). The table is a graphic example of what a forest looks like to a forestry official.

Table 5.2   Forest composition in a 65,000-hectare plot in the Meratus Mountains

	Number of trees per hectare				Volume of wood per hectare (m³)			
	35–49 cm diameter	50+ cm diameter	Total	%	35–49 cm diameter	50+ cm diameter	Total	%
Commercial trees								
Dipterocarps	.27	.27	.54	1.49	.30	.80	1.10	2.03
Nondipterocarps	18.00	4.64	22.64	62.58	16.84	15.91	32.75	60.31
Total	18.27	4.91	23.18	64.07	17.14	16.71	33.85	62.34
Other species	9.82	3.18	13.00	35.93	10.61	9.84	20.45	37.66
Grand Total	28.09	8.09	36.18	100.00	27.75	26.55	54.30	100.00

Source: Adapted from Sunardi 1975.

The report's author notes that these data show that there are only twenty-three commercially valuable trees per hectare in this forest, and fewer than five of these have a diameter of more than fifty centimeters. (All other vegetation, by definition, consists of "troublesome plants.") This is certainly too few, he argues, to offer inviting profits if timber companies made use of the required Indonesian Selective Felling system, under which only a certain percentage of trees are logged. Even the average for the province's forests—which he calculates at thirty-four commercially valuable trees per hectare—offers no profit under the Selective Felling system. Instead, the author suggests, natural regeneration of the forests in the area is good enough to justify waiving the rules and allowing the logging companies free rein to cut whatever they want. He concludes that the Forestry Department should not place too heavy a burden of responsibility on the logging companies, since they are unlikely to accept it.

It is hard to imagine any hectare of forest—from the youngest regrowing brush to the oldest stands—in which Meratus would find only twenty-three useful plants. (The obvious exception might be areas left by the timber companies: steep hillsides choked with sliding stumps amidst thick mud; rolling red earth bedecked only with unanchored *balaran hirang* vines.) Meratus use forest resources in every aspect of daily life. They appreciate the diversity of the forest and learn its variations. Their resource use leads to forms of ecological knowledge that are much more locally detailed than those of the state or the logging companies.[5]

In contrast to the forest official's assumption that all regeneration outside of tree plantations can be lumped into an uncontrolled category glossed as "natural," Meratus create a variety of relationships to forest plants. Indeed, it is difficult to draw a line between "wild" and "domestic" in Meratus forests, because of the variety of ways in which people interact with plants and plant communities. When swiddens are cleared, some useful trees are spared and protected. These trees remain as forest dominants as the field regrows into forest. Some trees are planted in swiddens or grow from seeds casually deposited in household garbage. Some sprout from the stumps left in swiddens. Others take advantage of the light-gap created by swiddens, flourishing in old swiddens without human assistance. Further, even without clearing fields, Meratus influence the composition of the forest: Some trees are cleared of vines or surrounding brush to encourage their growth; some plants are harvested in ways that allow regrowth. As people walk through the forest, they continually check on the status of the plants they have planted, encouraged, or merely encountered before. It is through these varied interactions with plants that Meratus come to appreciate the diversity of the forest.

Consider fruit, for example. Meratus enjoy dozens of varieties of seasonal forest fruits. Some, like sweet-sour wild mangos (*hambawang*), are thought of as trail-side snacks rarely worth carrying home; others, like the strong-smelling, custard-like durian and the sweet, sticky *tarap* (*Artocarpus elastica*), can be major food sources. Each of these examples has a contrasting niche in Meratus agroforestry. Durian trees are among the most valuable of claimed trees. They are planted in old swiddens; they would certainly be saved in swidden-making; they also sprout in garbage drops and in the forest without human assistance. Ripe, fallen fruit belongs to the finder; in durian season, teenagers set out excitedly before dawn to collect the fruit that fell the night before. Only claimants, however, may climb the trees to harvest and distribute unripe fruits. In contrast, tarap trees are common, and anyone may harvest them; but sometimes a tarap tree will be saved in a swidden—and thus claimed. Hambawang trees are merely remembered in relation to their location; they become a goal for hikers anticipating refreshment.

Even closely related species can merit quite different treatment. Included among the mangos, for example, are the odiferous *binjai* (*Magnifera caesia*) and the tiny *rawa-rawa* (*M. microphilla?*), both of which can be planted, encouraged, or merely encountered in the forest, as well as the stringy, juicy *kwini*, which grows only as a cultivate. Durian relatives include the spiky red *lahung*, which can be planted or, if encountered, encouraged; the orange-fleshed *pampakin*, a cultivate; and the miniature *lahung burung*, never planted but appreciated as a trail-side snack. Other *Artocarpus* species (i.e., like tarap) include the large-fruited cultivate (or sometimes spontaneous) *tawadak* (*A. integer*), as well as the self-seeding forest trees *kulidang* and *binturung*. The latter two trees are plentiful enough in the forest to make their fruits one option for a temporary staple when rice supplies run out. In contrast, *nangka*, the jackfruit commonly planted in Banjar houseyards, is quite rare in the Meratus area, because the giant fruits require continual attention and protection. Except in some foothill areas, Meratus rarely create "domesticated" orchards; Meratus fruit trees must thrive—or, at least, survive—as part of the forest. But, in a sense, the forest *is* an orchard.

Some forest fruits are valued in ways that do not involve human consumption. Young men bird-lime the branches of *kariwaya* strangling figs to catch the birds attracted to the fruit. Hunters haunt fruiting *luak* trees, whose figs hang in clusters from the tree trunks, waiting for the deer that enjoy this fruit. Fish swim into traps baited with *kasai* (*Pometia pinnata*) fruit. Migrating wild pigs follow the fruitings of *sinsilin* oaks and *damar* dipterocarps; and men, with their dogs and spears, follow the pigs.

These trees provide more than fruit. Damar, for example, is a source of bark for construction and resin for lighting. Damar trees can also serve as supports for the nests of migrating wild honeybees, *indu wanyi*. The bees fix their combs under the branches, choosing sites exposed to light. This does not hurt the tree. In fact, Meratus encourage the tree's growth by encouraging the bees' comb-building: They clean off vines and clear underbrush. They say the bees come back year after year to their favored sites. From these combs, Meratus harvest honey, larvae, and wax. Only claimants can harvest and distribute the honey. Honey trees are claimed by finding and tending them. They are saved in swidden-making; sometimes appropriate trees are also planted. Some men claim as many as fifty productive honey trees.

Honey trees include many of the forest's big trees. Besides damar, people consider *mangaris*, *binuang*, *salang'ai*, *mampiring*, *alaran*, *tampuruyung*, *pulayi*, *luak*, *jalamu*, *hara wilas*, *kupang*, *mijuluang*, *kasai tikus*, *jalanut*, *simuan*, and *anglai* potentially good honey trees. Even without introducing Latin names, this list suggests Meratus appreciation of forest diversity. It seems worth noting that included in this list are species cut for plywood export (for example, *Shorea acuminatissima* [*damar hirang*] and *Octomeles sumatrana* [*binuang*]), species cut for construction wood, and species of no commercial value which may or may not survive the logging process. The contrast between the local detail of Meratus practice and the revenue-focused mathematics of national forestry interests should be clear.

In staging this contrast, it would be a mistake to remain in the loggers' discourse by considering only trees; there are many other useful plants in the forest. Meratus use bamboo, palm, tubers, herbs, and fungi, among many other plants. Most Meratus know where to find numerous kinds. For example, more than half a dozen species of bamboo are used variously for cooking utensils, firewood, food, basketry, house construction, musical instruments, ritual decorations, and carrying water. Finding the appropriate species is facilitated by the fact that many bamboos remain a rather stable element of the forest. Generally, bamboos are not killed even by swidden construction; they grow back even more densely as the forest returns. (In one western foothill area, Meratus plant bamboo in old swiddens to prevent the spread of *Imperata* grasslands and to hold claims on future swidden plots. This type of bamboo is also a cash crop.) As people traverse the forests grown from old forest clearings, old forest harvestings, and old forest tendings, they become increasingly familiar with the species composition of particular forest areas. Conversely, their knowledge allows them to use an area's resources more intensively.

Everyday traversings, along with the intimate knowledge they create, help establish and reestablish claims on a place and its resources. A person invokes a claim to fruit trees by checking to see when they are producing fruit; if the fruit ripens without being visited, someone else is free to take it. Only a few forest resources (for example, rattan, honey trees) provoke competition; for most forest products, there is scope for the overlapping, nonexclusive claims of neighbors and kin whose forest paths cross each other. In claims of familiarity, knowledge and use of the forest are mutually implicated. When a person moves away from an area with no intention to return, she might say that she has "forgotten" her trees there.

In 1986, a west-side timber company began offering a small compensation to certain Meratus who argued that their planted trees had been destroyed by timber company operations. In practice, the program offered local people little cause for excitement. For one thing, it was difficult to prove ownership; besides, the amount of compensation for each tree was small. In theory, however, the program could have blown apart the logging company's neat plans. Considering the complexity of Meratus connections with the forest, a claim could be made for nearly every forest plant. What if the timber company were asked to pay compensation for every tended, encouraged, watched, or cultivated forest plant that logging and logging roads had destroyed?

Tradition

The forest is a disorienting, frightening place for many urban Indonesians who imagine it as the home of wild animals and savages. This is one context in which to think about the defensively neat outlines of social science reports on the Meratus, in which all wildness disappears. In these reports, the forest is rarely mentioned; Meratus livelihood is described as farming. Meratus conditions of living are summed up in an orderly array of customs, rituals, and beliefs.

Stimulated by the government resettlement program, reports on the Meratus flourished in the late 1970s and early 80s.[6] Some were written as part of national projects, for example, for the Department of Education and Culture. Others were sponsored by the regional social bureaucracy or by various Islamic schools. The reports vary in quality and content, yet there are striking similarities. Almost all are written as outlines, giving the impression of answers on a form. Almost all are based on interviews with shamans or government-titled community leaders. Most focus on ritual procedure; in explaining ritual, they also list beliefs and the edicts of custom. And most describe Meratus culture holistically, including the categories of cosmology, economy, and custom.

Reading their lists and prescriptions, I think of recipes—for "cooking up" tradition. Following is an example from a resettlement official's report:

> *The equipment for bamula* [rice-planting ritual]:
> 1) two heads of shallots
> 2) two candlenuts
> 3) two areca nuts
> 4) a clump of lemongrass   } to be planted in the ground
> 5) a small piece of ginger
> 6) a pinch of salt
> 7) laos
> 8) galangal
> 9) a tube of sticky rice — to be eaten
> 10) a mirror
> 11) coconut oil   } to be brought home after
> 12) money   the ceremony
> 13) cotton
> 14) false cane [*tabu salah*, a plant]

15) cordyline
16) *kayu tulak* [a plant]
17) *bandang* (made of young sugar palm leaves) [a decoration]
18) *galung* pillar (made from wood)
19) *dundangan* (made from *pulantan* trees)

The method of the ceremony:
Two galung pillars are erected. The bandang decorations (made from sugar palm leaves) are placed on the galung pillars and the dundangan (made from pulantan wood) is hung on the bandang. The ritual equipment from numbers 1 through 8 is buried around the bandang; thus, too, the false cane and the cordyline are stuck in the earth. After all is ready, the ceremony is carried out by the expert (*balian*), who recites spells. (Saif 1978:9–10, my translation)

Such reports provide important, useful information. Clearly, they are no more biased or partial than my own reporting. (The quotation above describes a version of the same rice-planting rite I discussed earlier in this chapter in relation to the "travels of the rice.") Yet it seems fair to ask about the particular shape of their biases. I am especially interested in the contradictions in their attention to ritual structure and procedure. On the one hand, this focus makes it possible to condemn the Meratus as caught in a static culture that stands in contrast to dynamic, modern lifestyles. On the other hand, ritual forms a point of connection between Javanese and Banjar social scientists and their Meratus informants: All agree that ritual is central to order, and order to government.

These two frameworks overlap and compete in the structuring of the reports. All reports include an invocation of the narrative of progress and development in which the Meratus are portrayed as backward, illiterate, unhealthy, and disorderly. In some reports, this story is so dominant that Meratus culture appears only as a confrontation with the dark side through which the researcher confirms his own modern identity; he tells us what we should love to hate. In other reports, the story of progress seems pro forma, and the researcher's attention seems to be with Meratus ceremonies. These reports offer painstaking detail about ritual preparations and procedures. Here one can glimpse an allied effort by Meratus leaders and social scientists (mainly Banjar) to present Meratus ways of life as safe, stable, and utterly removed from the chaos of the jungle.

Thus, too, in these reports, Meratus ritual experts appear as guardians of tradition and representatives of known categories of leadership. In the following excerpt from a government-sponsored report, the status of Meratus shamans is assessed (Aziddin et al. 1980–81:111, my translation).

3. THE SYSTEM OF SOCIAL STRATIFICATION
  a. Social strata from the past
   1) Official social strata
    a) The basis of stratification
    For the Bukit [Meratus] tribe, indigenousness and seniority
  are the bases of stratification.
    b) The form of stratification
    The Bukit tribe knows several social strata, as follows:
     1. Shamans (religious leaders) who are composed of:
      a. Elder shamans
      b. Younger shamans
     2. "Door children" (ordinary inhabitants)

Banjar administrators, along with their Javanese overseers, may be comforted to find that Meratus have a stable structure of authority that mirrors Banjar and Javanese respect for traditional stratification. Further, the *exact* phrases and categories are reproduced in the next section of the outline, "b. Contemporary social strata." Repetition produces a timelessness in which rural villages can be imagined as safe repositories of stabilizing tradition.

The tradition produced in the collaboration between Meratus community leaders and sympathetic Banjar social scientists is filled with illuminating and accurate detail; yet the narrow scope of its vision requires contextualization to avoid misleading assumptions. For example, the Meratus social stratification created by giving Meratus answers to Javanese questions obscures the tentative, context-specific, and competitive nature of the authority of Meratus shamans. A successful Meratus shaman can achieve the power necessary to gather and perform for an enthusiastic audience. While an important kind of power, this is not one ordinarily imagined as "stratification." The authority of a shaman's knowledge depends on the conditions of performance as much as it does on the stipulation of "tradition."

One good place to begin to contextualize ritual authority might be the rice-planting rite described earlier. Both the ritual preparations and the expert's chant offer inviting detail for an anthropological account. However, it is important to note that throughout most of the rite, the expert sits alone in the middle of the field; no one is listening to his chant or watching him manipulate the ritual equipment. I should not exaggerate his isolation; his contribution is considered essential by those planting the rice. Most people in attendance know the intent of the rite and its general outlines. The expert is treated with respect and may, for example, be offered an especially inviting portion of the meal served in the field. But it is also true that most everyone at the planting party is preoccupied with planting the rice and socializing with each other; the ritual expert cannot command awestruck attention.

The knowledge expressed in the expert's performance is only one component of the knowledge elaborated and disseminated at the rice-planting party. Consider, for example, the expert's position on time and motion. I argue earlier in this chapter that the metaphorical travels of the rice depend on the expert's attempts to portray time as cyclical and repetitive. Each rice-cultivation year repeats other years, and the rice is "told to become young again" and to voyage again and again through space and time in order to prosper. In the chant, the rice is sometimes spoken to as a great-grandparent and sometimes as a baby; it passes back and forth between all ages. Just as this ritually construed rice confounds gender identification, it overlays generations and refuses unidirectional aging.

Although most of those planting the rice would be familiar with these strategies of increase, the rice planters have other concerns with time and travel as well. Rice is planted by a neighborhood-wide work party. For the hosts of the work party, the planting launches their rice rajaki at a particular site—a hillside or valley they have chosen from among other possible sites. This site takes its place within the story of the umbun's travels from one field to another, from one year to another. It is not equivalent to other fields from other years, as it is in the presentation of the ritual expert. While the progression of swidden-making tasks may be repetitive (felling, clearing, burning, planting, weeding, and so forth), the tasks each year are differentiated by their occurrence in a different location. This "placing" creates a progressive history of movement rather than a repetitive cycle.

Those attending the rice-planting as representatives of other umbun are aware that the rice rajaki being launched is not their own. Whereas the ritual expert constitutes his leadership by merging his own search for rajaki with those of all the rice fields at which he performs, to the rice planters, each umbun's rice rajaki takes a separate course. To them, the travel of the rice on this field does not represent their own movement toward prosperity, but rather one track in the complexly crossing paths that create the social dynamics of the neighborhood. Their own umbun travels veer toward or away from the host umbun as they choose their own sites for rice rajaki. Thus the understandings of travel as rajaki are developed differently in the ritual expert's performance and in the umbun-oriented conversations of those who surround the expert.

The importance of an umbun-focused "travel knowledge" itself needs to be viewed within the broader context of Meratus agroforestry. The rice-planting party is an exceptional moment for creating umbun agricultural units. Unlike other aspects of swidden-making—such as felling and weeding, during which labor groups that cross umbun lines may form quite casually—umbun exchange labor reciprocally at rice-planting parties (that is, an umbun expects to see the same number of representatives from umbun A at its own planting party as it sent to umbun A's party). Consciousness of umbun form and separation is especially well developed at these parties; in other contexts, cross-cutting ties of kinship and neighborhood may be more relevant. Even the growing of swidden vegetables erodes neatly drawn umbun boundaries, for household and swidden cluster members often share vegetables in a relaxed way across umbun lines. Furthermore, umbun are not the key units of forest use. Rights to trees, for example, are shared by common descendants of the planter; anyone who attends a group fruit or honey harvest gets a share.

Forest use involves constant inspecting and exploring that are not tied to a predictable seasonality. Individuals connect their fortunes with short-term changes and long-term developments in claimed trees and familiar territories rather than with an annual cycle in a bounded plot. Notions of time and travel developed in relation to forest use contrast with both the ritual expert's structural condensations and the umbun's narrative of yearly fields. These different kinds of travel knowledge compete, combine, and coexist within negotiations of individual networks, umbun confederacies, and leader-focused communities.

My main point here is that Meratus social relations and cultural conventions are formed with the interaction of various kinds of activities, including ritual, shifting cultivation, and forest use. I have mentioned several forms of knowledge in this chapter, including ritual knowledge and tradition, umbun narratives of swidden-making, and natural-social histories of the forest. I began the chapter by letting each stand alone as a form of "Meratus perspective" in contrast to the official views associated with resettlement and forestry policies. Now, however, I call attention to the internal relationship of these divergent forms of Meratus knowledge. I use this sense of internal differentiation in returning to issues of mobility and state rule.

Going home

Livelihood practices encourage Meratus appreciation of movement and forge personal attachments to the places that movement makes accessible. In contrast, government resettlement policies aim to suppress both movement and attachment. Resettlement removes people from their familiar places and demands their stability in imposed locations. Meratus leaders rarely articulate objections to resettlement, however. Instead, they collaborate with sympathetic state officials in portraying a static, stable ritual, one removed from the specificity of places. To prove that they are leaders, they present themselves as being in charge of a traditional order that works with state administration, not against it. Indeed, many tend to see resettlement as a form of ritual. Like a good festival, resettlement gathers together a community in the name of order.

Yet, as with a good festival, people cannot be prevented from going home again to resume their ordinary livelihood practices in their familiar places. Unlike regional officials, Meratus leaders know this just as well as do the least ambitious of their constituents. Leaders do not expect permanent gatherings. Moreover, they participate in dispersal as much as anyone else. Even the greatest shamans are also farmers and foragers following their own rajaki in umbun swiddens and familiar forests. Following one's rajaki can separate people just as it can bring them together.

In the central mountains in the early 1980s, state pressures inspired a leadership rhetoric of centralized settlement but did little to hold such settlement in place. I remember a spot called, appropriately, "Planning Flats," which The Bear and some other local leaders had built. It was to be a centralized settlement uniting three neighborhoods then current. People cleared the area and set out a few posts to mark the sites of some houses. But then the momentum was lost. No one moved there, and the clearing began to grow back into forest. The leaders had inspired a group effort in planning and clearing the flats; then everyone—including the leaders—went home.

In the western foothills, the state's presence has been much more immediate. Resettlement villages are built on instructions from above, and

Meratus merely move in. Officials are assigned to each project, thus making state guidance an everyday affair.

Yet, at least in the early 1980s, resettlement officials found it difficult to make people stay. Officials were puzzled, since they believed they had given Meratus much better houses—as well as access to new ways of thinking. Still, it appeared as though mainly those who already lived in the area before a resettlement village was built stayed in the new housing. Those brought in from further away returned to the areas from which they originated.

In the official explanation, Meratus nomadism was blamed. As one analyst stated, "Generally Bukit [Meratus] cannot endure staying for a relatively long time in one place" (Radam 1982:26). Indeed, people had moved on. But in moving, they did not act like the nomads of the government model, who can be moved at random since, to them, one place is just like another. Instead, they went home.

6 ON THE BOUNDARY OF THE SKIN

In his curing chant, the shaman Awat Kilay has taken on the perspective of a louse. The louse travels across the scalp, crossing the boundary of the skin with its seven-notched tongue. It is an intrusion that causes no pain or awareness of alterity. It is the kind of boundary crossing facilitated by the spirit agent Putir Galuh. "Where is Galuh?" Awat Kilay sings, letting his voice carry him.

> Where is Galuh?
> Galuh whose hall is in the even-spaced bamboo [the hair],
> Whose hall is in the even-sized bamboo,
> Whose hall is charcoal like a mountain [hair],
> Whose hall is bamboo that bends over,
> Who walks scratching back and forth over the earth,
> Who walks scratching back and forth over the world,
> Whose tongue has seven notches,
> In the form of the great teacher.

Not satisfied only with the perspective of a louse, Awat Kilay moves on to the perspective of a fly. The jingling noise of his rattle bracelets becomes the fly's buzzing as they travel as one. A fly can even cross to the place of corpses; it enters the fine bamboo tube stuck into the earth of a new grave. A fly also sits on the umbilical cord of a new birth. Flies pass into both our exits and our entrances.

> Where is the Galuh who can enter
> Enter the pipes of the earth [at the grave],
> Enter the pipes of the world,

The earth of seven numbers?
Where is another Galuh
Who rides the flying cobra [the umbilical cord],
Who travels with a buzzing/jingling noise,
Whose hall is dripping [with blood; the placenta] . . .

Flies? Lice? Classic imagery of dirt and pollution, a scenery of crawling scalps, rotting corpses, and dripping placentas. The (psycho)analyst is easily drawn to ponder what French feminist Julia Kristeva, in *Powers of Horror* (1982) has termed "abjection"—the horror and disgust of neat body boundaries undone. For Kristeva, clean and proper body boundaries are necessary in constituting a human subject who can participate in the symbolic order of language. Boundary transgressions—corpses, menstrual blood, and so forth—are sites of power and danger for the symbolic, the paternal law.

High language aside, Banjar villagers and townsfolk on the western boundary of the Meratus Mountains might agree. Meratus shamans like Awat Kilay are sorcerers whose dangerous power disturbs the integrity of corporeality and reason. Yet, Awat Kilay's shamanism has developed within a rather different "science," one in which speaking subjects are those who can expand, not defend, their physical and social boundaries. Awat Kilay's flies and lice are not dirty. To speak of them within their appropriate discursive context requires wariness of false universalizations of the body—from Banjar ethnic stereotypes to French feminist psychoanalysis.

In South Kalimantan's regional culture, state disapproval of Meratus nomadism jostles and blends with nonofficial Banjar fears about Meratus primitivism. For those Banjar who live close to the Meratus Mountains, the key issues are not stability and obedience, but religion and health. Meratus are ignorant pagans and dangerous sorcerers. As one Banjar medic explained to me, government clinics are not extended to Meratus areas because Meratus cause most of their own illnesses through sorcery.

These Banjar interpretations of Meratus shamanism create a gap between "Banjar" and "Meratus" systems of understanding. As I argued in the last chapter, the evocation of difference forces contrast but not always on the terms set forth by the dominant discourse. Yet, too, the contrast itself creates zones of mutual intelligibility as well as of incomprehension. The interaction between Banjar and Meratus has given rise to a dialogue in which healthy and ailing bodies emerge as sites of contestation. Assumptions about gender, ethnic identity, and the nature of power are at stake here, as the body's boundaries are interrogated according to contrasting, intersecting logics. This chapter explores both difference and dialogue generated by reading ethnicity and gender on the boundary of the skin.

Kristeva's work is useful in focusing attention on the embodiedness of the distinctions created here. Most analysis of the construction of Otherness points to linguistic category distinctions; bodies here are ciphers disciplined by the bureaucracy of language. Kristeva instead highlights the visceral nature of boundary formation. Disgust, violence, terror, awe, nostalgic longing, and erotic attraction accompany self-making acts of exclusion and expulsion. ("During that course in which 'I' become, I give birth to myself amid the violence of sobs, of vomit" [p. 3].)[1] In South Kalimantan, the emotional complexity of ethnic relations seeps into even the driest official reports in the squeamishness or vehemence of the language. The disturbing physicality of Othering is all the more evident in everyday interethnic interactions in markets and homes, and particularly in sorcery and curing.[2]

Kristeva's work reminds analysts of the gendered nature of these embodied reactions. Kristeva is not interested in differences among men and women as subjects; instead, she asks about the construction of masculinity and femininity as these shape subject formation for both men and women. She guides analysts toward the "strategy of identity" through which the subject within language comes into being: "the struggle each subject must wage during the entire length of his personal history in order to become separate, that is to say, to become a speaking subject and/or subject to Law" (p. 94). Questions about subject-making are a useful guide in understanding the intensity of Banjar involvement with the Meratus-Banjar boundary.

Most feminist readers of Kristeva generously ignore her use of anthropology; but this is somewhat more difficult in an ethnographic text. Kristeva's *Powers of Horror* rests on a problematic anthropology, in which she assumes that those people called "primitive" have a good deal in common with European children, poets, and psychotics. Kristeva reads anthropology in order to understand the primitive mind. *Powers of Horror* follows an insulting evolutionary track from Africans and Indians to Judaism, Christianity, and, at last, to French poets. In addition, she assumes an epistemological dichotomy between European "theory" and global "empirical" variation in which, by definition, the Third World can never be a source of theoretical insight (p. 68). These assumptions have no place in my project.

Up to a certain point, I can introduce the insightful angle of Kristeva's thought without bringing along her framework. Nevertheless, I run up against the problem of her assumptions. Her notions of theory (and her biologized scheme of pan-human development) prevent her from moving beyond the most familiar French processes of subject formation. In the second part of this chapter, I argue that the subject-making process endorsed by Meratus *putir* shamans runs counter to most of Kristeva's ideas about embodiment.[3] I argue that theorists must pay much more attention to cultural specificities—by asking classic ethnographic questions about local understandings. Particular arenas of discursive practice (in France as well as in Kalimantan) create notions about bodies, subjects, and consciousness that cannot be reduced to versions of a master text.

I begin, however, with Banjar perspectives from the plains to the west of the Meratus foothills in the early 1980s, a terrain in which Kristeva's concerns are very useful.

Religion, reason, and the wilderness

Most of the Banjar men I knew would agree with what I have characterized as a "Meratus perspective": Travel is essential to making a living. Many Banjar men are entrepreneurs who mix several trades (for example, farmer, peddler, rubber tapper) and who travel widely. Indeed, like Meratus, Banjar often run up against state rules that limit and regulate movement. Transportation and trade in the region involve a daily Banjar struggle to evade police posts along the roads, truck-weight regulations, import and export duties. Yet, Banjar do not identify these travel dilemmas with those of the Meratus. Instead, Banjar tend to think of Meratus as part of a Dayak "Other." This view of the Meratus involves not a critique of mobility, but rather a differentiation between lawlike and lawless forms of travel-knowledge.

To the west of the Meratus Mountains are the fertile rice-producing plains and swamps called Hulu Sungai, long a Banjar stronghold; to many Banjar in this area, Hulu Sungai is a peninsula of cosmopolitan civilization surrounded by a wild sea of "Dayaks"—Meratus to the east; Dusun, Lawangan, and Pasir to the north; Ma'anyan, and Ngaju Dayaks to the west. To Hulu Sungai Banjar, the contrast between civilization and the wild begins with what one might call religion—Banjar are Muslims,

Dayaks are not.[4] This is not "religion" as a distinctive set of beliefs and rituals; rather, it involves one's basic relationship to reason, knowledge, language, and subjectivity. From a Banjar perspective, Banjar knowledge is rational, cosmopolitan, and civilized, because it is universally illuminating. In contrast, Banjar see "Dayaks" as holding a dangerously indigenous knowledge so unbending to universalist standards—that is, so *localized*—that it has been pressed back to the untamed margins of civilization. Dayak knowledge is not considered useless; in fact, its irrationality is seen as the source of its power. Those Banjar in provincial towns who know a smattering of English often spoke to me of this knowledge as "black magic," and when I said I was studying Dayak culture, magic is what most everyone in these towns assumed I meant. For Banjar, "Dayak" is not a site of alternative logic, but the boundary of the very possibility of reason. It is, as Kristeva writes, "the place where meaning collapses" (p. 2).

Islam forms a basis on which Banjar men from different areas recognize each other as fellow humans (*umat*, that is, *umat Muhamad*, literally, "followers of Muhammad"). With "Dayaks," there is no such bridge for mutual acknowledgment. Thus, for many Banjar men—both educated townsmen and illiterate peasants—"Dayak" has become a name for fears of travelling in unknown villages where one's name, religion, and status are unknown and unrecognized. Banjar spoke to me of Dayak sorcery (for example, *ilmu hirang*, "black sciences") that strikes randomly at those without extraordinary protection, causing fever and jaundice. They spoke of supernatural poisonings and kindly loaded me down with food and drink when I left for Dayak areas. They spoke of "techniques" (*parbuatan*) that would prevent a traveller from returning home. Men who thought to take and abandon Dayak sweethearts might find their penises shrivelling and falling off when they tried to leave. Literacy, piety, hygiene, bureaucracy—all lost their power in these backwoods places. Dayak "science" formed a black hole that sucked up civilized subjectivity, leaving unwary citizens defenseless.

One man told me a detailed story of a Dayak ritual expert he had met on his travels. The expert knew many strange and wonderful techniques. He could move objects without touching them; he could cut faraway things with his work knife. He offered to give my Banjar friend this knowledge for the token sum of five rupiah. My friend thought carefully about the offer as he went back to his Banjar home, planning to return to the Dayak area. He consulted an Islamic religious leader who warned him of the terrible dangers of this kind of knowledge, saying that my friend would lose himself outside religion. My friend struggled desperately, weighing the promise and threat of power; the rationality of selfhood and religion finally won. Although he still looked back on this opportunity with awe, he knew he could never have escaped the devilish draw of Dayak knowledge.

Reason and the body

In distancing themselves from the wilderness, Banjar reaffirm particular understandings of the body, rationality, and consciousness. Like many other Muslim Indonesians and Malaysians, particularly those (including Banjar) classed together as "Malays" (*urang Malayu*), Banjar frame discussions of the body by making a distinction between *akal* ("reason") and *hawa napsu* ("bodily desire").[5] This distinction does not segregate the "mind"; instead, it shows the necessity of a body regulated by reason. Religion trains the body in the control of hawa napsu by religiously motivated akal.

Suppressing desire through the exercise of reason prevents illness and vulnerability. The Banjar men I knew sometimes boasted of how little they ate and slept, particularly when travelling or in other stressful situations. This, they argued, kept them from getting sick. Of special concern in this male project is the careful control of body boundaries. Boundary-protection spells, amulets, and bodily regimens seemed an almost obsessive male concern. The most popular men's magic (*pakaian lalaki*) produced invulnerability by making the skin impenetrable to metal or fire. Body boundaries were also discussed as being particularly vulnerable while eating and drinking, especially in the roadside food stalls (*warung*) at which men eat food that has been prepared by a stranger. Food poisoning causes the victim to cough, hemorrhage, and die, as weak boundaries are broached by the force of the poison.

Banjar also speak of an extremely dangerous condition of weakened body boundaries called *lamah bulu* (literally, "weak body hair"). It is described as a relaxation and opening of the pores of the skin, which permits illness to enter. Poisons (*wisah*) floating around in the air may penetrate the weakened skin of someone with lamah bulu. Such poisons are released by the owners of Dayak-produced magic oils, who revitalize an oil's potency by setting some free at least once a year to seek out a random victim. In addition, lamah bulu makes a person vulnerable to all forms of sorcery.

Protecting the body from weakness and making it invulnerable to sorcery depend upon using language to create rationality and differentiate one's "self" from the wild. Protective spells shield the body through religiously powerful words by articulating the true names of irrational dangers. Here is a spell that keeps off blood-sucking *kuyang* monsters:

> Jalmamarah run to the seven layers of the sky,
> Jalmamarah run to the seven layers of the earth.
> I know your origin from "Latup Kuhul Kumaratis"
>   [the true name of kuyang monsters]
> If you don't run you'll be hit by the blessed law:
> There is no God but Allah and Muhammad is His Prophet.

The speaking subject articulates the names of monsters in order to reconstitute the law and himself within it.

One method for gaining impenetrable skin involves a special bath during which passages from the Koran are scratched on one's back. To make the bath effective, the bather must recite daily a series of spells in which the body is renamed in mystic correspondences. Thus, the man with reason develops a body trained and tamed by language. He must keep careful watch against both internal and external excesses.

Gendered bodies

These understandings of the body depend upon important distinctions between women and men. Women are those who can never do a good job of controlling bodily desire or protecting the boundaries of the body. As a result, women are much more susceptible to illness. They are seen as more involved with food and sleep than are men; they are more likely to be lamah bulu. Moreover, the ability of women to use religious restraint on their bodies is weakened by the pollution of menstruation (*kuturan*, literally "dirt"). Menstruating women neither fast nor pray; thus, women can never achieve the same degree of religious control as men. Not surprisingly, menstrual blood is a potent sorcery substance, used against men by women gone bad. (Women operators of food stalls are particularly suspect; how easy it would be for them to add menstrual blood to the food.) Women, therefore, must be both protected and constrained by men. Indeed, the male control that allows men to shield and guide women is defined through opposition to female vulnerability and temptation.

Although superficially gender-symmetric, sexuality, interpreted within this discourse, further affirms gender distinction. Heterosexuality increases women's vulnerability, yet decreases men's. Women's sexuality signals boundary weakness; men's displays aggression that overcomes the weakness of others. In Banjar mysticism, the erect penis is not a sign of bodily weakness but an element of the controlling realm of language and religion. For example, it is equated with *alip*, the first letter of the Arabic alphabet. Through such mystical names as "God's water" (*air zamani-yullah*), semen, rather than a source of pollution, is made as sacred as holy speech. Men's sexuality, in direct contrast to women's, empowers their independence and embodies their religious rationality.

Male sexuality places men in a special relationship to language. It is men, not women, who seek protective spells and mystic writings. Women need men's protection, whereas men need to protect *themselves* in their sexually assertive encounters with the world. Unlike women, who already are female, men must brace themselves to avoid becoming female. Although transvestites in other parts of Indonesia have been described as figures of religious power, the Banjar men I knew spoke of male transvestites (*bancir*) with amused disgust as those who allow other men to have anal intercourse with them. Bancir are men who have lost their privileged access to the language of religion, power, and boundary control.

The gender-reversed equivalent of bancir are perhaps the blood-sucking kuyang mentioned above. If bancir are men without spells, kuyang are women with too many. Instead of guarding the integrity of their bodies, kuyang tear apart and invert their bodies to attack others. Kuyang are women who, with the help of spells and magic oils, remove their heads from their bodies and fly around at night, looking for blood. Their organs and entrails come out with the head, leaving the body a dumb, empty cavity. The head, dragging entrails, shines and sings or moans as it soars over rooftops. For all her spells, the kuyang head cannot speak; she can only return, parasitically, to the inarticulate, lawless maternal body. Kuyang are attracted to the blood of childbirth. Knowledgeable men are called in to protect women giving birth by chanting protective spells and Koran verses. Bloody women are both victim and aggressor; if childbirth creates women at their most vulnerable, it also creates them at their most dangerous.

Banjar friends described a former neighbor as a typical kuyang. She was a schoolteacher, large and assertive, and her husband could not control her. My friends claimed that they drove the woman out of the neighborhood because of her kuyang activities. Dayak women may also be kuyang, they said. They spoke of Dayak kuyang working as hospital nurses who take advantage of vulnerable patients to drink their blood.

This was one reason, they said, why Banjar women prefer not to give birth in government hospitals. My friends told me about a man who, a few years earlier, went to see his wife and newborn baby at the provincial hospital and found them dead, sucked dry of blood. The man had seen a nurse passing him on his way in, and she had had blood trickling from the side of her mouth. According to my friends, the nurse was arrested and tried for vampirism.

Talk of the threat of Dayak kuyang shows the interconnected construction of ethnicity, gender, reason, and identity in Hulu Sungai Banjar discussion of bodies. I have deliberately brought out features that offer a parallel with Kristeva's discussion of abjection. Following her clues, I call attention to the importance of language in constructing subjectivity and sexuality, and to the importance of gender asymmetry in this construction. I also move beyond her analysis to draw from related French feminisms that ask about female subjectivity, such as the work of Luce Irigaray (1985).[6] Where the phallus is equated with the word, to be "female" is to be outside the possibilities of speech and self-identification. The female is that which cannot articulate herself; "female subjectivity" is an oxymoron with which women must constantly struggle. Although, in addition, I would argue for the relevance of differences between the French and Banjar situations, concepts of phallic signification and paternal law seem powerful in analyzing Banjar cultural production. Through them, one can see how Banjar men are privileged as articulate subjects of culture through an association of male sexuality, reason, and culturally powerful language.

One goal of this chapter, however, is to explore how this psychoanalytic discourse applies to a restricted domain even in the situations where it is most powerful. Banjar subject formation does not take place in an isolated universe. Banjar discussions of gender interrupt, overlay, and misinterpret other voices. The challenge for gender analysis is to shed light on the interplay of these conceptual fields. Kristeva's analytic framework is inadequate for this challenge. Her understanding of gender is singular and universalized: The subject differentiates from the maternal body to enter paternal law. Gender difference is analytically prior to culture in this framework; the maternal is the ground from which phallic culture emerges. This precultural maternal terrain can never be explained within culture or history, nor can it generate transformation. Thus, Kristeva's theories cannot address heterogeneous and changing forms of gender and power. More useful here is an approach in which gendered notions of subjectivity are developed within particular cultural histories.

These histories shape and order the dialogue among ethnic groups, classes, and genders. I turn to the issue of interethnic "subversion" to ask both how this ordering is achieved and how it falters.

Exotic cures

As kuyang, Dayak women appear on Banjar landscapes in monstrous form. Dayak men, as sorceror-shamans, have a more ambivalent role: Banjar identify Dayak shamans as a source of both bodily dissolution and its cure. This assumption has sparked a series of social interactions between Meratus and Banjar. Throughout the mountains, Hulu Sungai adventurers wander in search of both sorcery and protection against sorcery. They demand techniques and charms that cause or protect against illness, that gain the user love or punish a resistant would-be lover, or that can be used in fighting. Each technique works at the body's boundaries. Love magic melts the boundaries of the loved one's resistance; love-revenge magic dissolves the sense of self of the once-desired lover. (The woman attacked by sorcery for refusing a suitor's advances becomes unable to recognize her own clean and proper reflection in a mirror; all she sees is a monster or a monkey.) Fighting magic protects one's boundaries or breaks through the enemy's defenses. Meratus—both shamans and nonshamans, both men and women—respond to this demand by providing magic oils, herbs, amulets, spells, and sorcery techniques.

Meratus shamans of the western foothills are invited into a more specialized niche: They are summoned into Hulu Sungai villages and towns to cure Banjar patients. Banjar assume that Meratus shamans are experts at sorcery; thus, shamans are also expected to to cure victims of sorcery. Meratus shamans perform various Meratus curing ceremonies for Banjar patients. In addition, they employ Banjar folk-healing techniques of body fortification and cleansing, such as smoke or steam baths. Banjar imagine Meratus cures which descend so deeply into bodily dissolution that they take on and challenge the body's vulnerability and restore a healthy selfhood.

In Kristeva's terms, Banjar suffering from sorcery, and their healers, are the fascinated victims of abjection. One might see the role of the Meratus shaman in much the same way that Kristeva describes the European literary artists she admires. Their writing "implies an ability to imagine the abject, that is, to see oneself in its place and to thrust it aside only by means of the displacements of verbal play" (p. 16). This kind of writing is a source of subversion; it re-creates dangerous and powerful maternal connections in the cracks of patriarchal law. " 'Subject' and 'object' push each other away, confront each other, collapse, and start again—inseparable, contaminated, condemned, at the boundary of what is assimilable, thinkable: abject" (p. 18). Similarly, the Meratus shaman's cure constitutes a subversive, feminine element within Banjar proprieties.

Yet Meratus shamans do not understand their own practice within Banjar notions of subversion. Banjar fears are only one corner of the play of power and subversion. Banjar technologies of Othering are never fully successful in shaping their objects; Meratus shamans do not see themselves as heroes of the abject. To learn more about interethnic subversion, one must turn to its surprises. Banjar misunderstand Meratus intentions. Banjar schemes are situated awkwardly, if powerfully, on the regional terrain; thus, the effects of Banjar initiatives are always complex and unpredictable. Kristeva's framework is inadequate for studying these multiple, conflicting, and unstable negotiations of difference.

The Banjar discourse constrains what counts as a "Meratus" response; it outlines a domain for Meratus accommodation and resistance. Yet, because Meratus are involved in activities and interpretations outside the scope of this Banjar discourse, they bring more to their responses than this discourse can predict. My next section jumps to the separate assumptions of one Meratus curing style to show rather different terms than Banjar categories allow. For this task, I must put Kristeva aside. Rather than either endorsing Banjar notions of boundary-protection-as-health or—as Banjar expect—gaining power by inverting reason and championing the dark side, Meratus shamanism offers its own terms for understanding health. Meratus consider curing effective when it overcomes the limitations of localizing boundaries rather than reinforcing them. From the shaman's perspective, the spiritually empowered skin does not guard against disease, but instead opens up to admit the fullness of the whole world. This perspective provides the context from which I can return to the challenges and compromises of Banjar–Meratus dialogue.

Curing with putir

The style of Meratus shamanism commonly called *putir*, after its key supernaturals, comes into closest contact with Banjar discussions of sorcery. First, its home location causes it to rub against Hulu Sungai Banjar fears and fancies. Although versions of putir style are practiced all over the Meratus Mountains, the style is most at home in several west-side watersheds where Meratus cannot ignore an expanding population of sorcery-obsessed Hulu Sungai Banjar. Second, putir is the style most elaborately concerned with bodies. Whereas all styles of Meratus shamanism are used for curing, putir is the most devoted to curing by creating new perceptions of the body itself. Thus, for example, where dewa shamans use metaphors of the body as a springboard from which to travel to far places, putir shamans use metaphorical travel to far places as a way to understand and empower the body.

Shamanic curing involves an all-night ceremony in which a shaman chants and dances to the accompaniment of a drum. The ceremony is identified as putir by the decorations, the drumbeats, the chant, and, to a certain extent, by the shaman's interaction with the patient. Putir curing minimally requires a circular hanging of young sugar-palm leaves, a basket of husked rice with a stalk of basil, a bottle of oil, and a white cloth. Putir is considered by its practitioners to be a "strong" (*gagah*) performing style and thus a particularly masculine endeavor. Indeed, it is a style that includes no specialized roles normally played by women: Not only is the shaman (*balian*) ordinarily a man, but so also is the assistant (*patati*), who holds dialogue with the shaman and the drummer (*pagandang*). (Dewa uses women assistants; *riwah* uses women drummers.) Putir is considered most appropriate for illness conditions with distinct loci of pain; these illnesses are most likely to be caused by a "disease splinter" (*suligih*) that the shaman can suck out or dissolve.

An illness-causing "splinter" is commonly acquired through the condition called *kapuhun*. The term refers to isolating oneself from others or from one's environment. One can *mangapuhun* another person by withholding something he or she requests, and one can be *kapuhunan* oneself by refusing offered food. By refusing food—and, by extension, social connection—one becomes vulnerable to accidents, such as bites by poisonous snakes or centipedes, as well as to illness.

The result of kapuhun can be a suligih splinter that causes pain and illness. The offending agent may be something in the forest, or it may be something much closer to home—domestic animals, children, even hearth stones can mangapuhun a family member, perhaps in response to an unintended slight. Except in the case of domestic animals, which are killed if determined responsible for a person's kapuhun condition, the curing focus turns from the agent to the removal or dissolution of the splinter itself. The shaman's job is to open up the boundary of the patient's flesh to suck out (*ma'alin*) the suligih splinter or allow a healing breath to dissolve it. The patient's skin is described as a barrier that must be broken, a dam of stones keeping the water from flowing. "Spread out the locked flesh," the shaman asks, "open up the dams of the skin." He calls on his spirit familiars, who, the shaman suggests, can enter like blood soaking into the ground or like mist blown through the air. The shaman must make the body wall permeable so that the splinter can be withdrawn. Alternatively, as his healing breath enters, the shaman asks the disease splinter to melt, dissolve, seep out like sweat.

Travelling in the body

The shaman's job is to increase rajaki, in the form of health. Like the rice-ritual expert described in the previous chapter (and most such experts are shamans), the healer uses metaphorical travel to create increase. Like the rice-ritual expert, the healer expands the definition of his own rajaki to encompass that of those for whom he chants.

The first body transformed in the healing practice of the shaman is therefore his own. He calls upon the putir spirits, which are also "titles" (*galar*) for his body: "The five siblings Putir" are his fingers; "Putir who stands up" and "Putir who hangs down" are his lower and upper teeth. Even terms that refer to distant destinations are body parts. "Putir of the rising sun" invokes both the rising sun and the eyes. The term supernatural is thus misleading in suggesting something outside the natural world. Although the shaman can speak with them or visit them and ask their help, Putir are not autonomous beings; they are spiritual empowerments of the body.

Through his metaphorical travels, the shaman constructs the healthiest body conceivable, one with the spiritual power of the entire cosmos. Further, the glorified body of the chant is not just the shaman's own body, but a model of the empowered body for all who listen. The shaman's metaphors create the healthy body for all his potential patients. Health proceeds from his body to encompass theirs.

The healthy body of the shaman's vision is the body without boundary restrictions. Unlike the patient's skin, which blocks the shaman's healing breath and splinter extractions, the shaman's skin is a spiritually charged familiar. It fits him exactly, yet does not constrain him; it can expand to broaden his horizons, yet be with him. In the chants, the shaman's skin is compared to clothes worn in layers. As the shaman exchanges "shirts" on his spiritual self, there is no single line between his body and the world. Putir shamans also call upon "shadows" (*bayang-bayang*) that blur the boundaries of the self. Shadows have countless layers, which extend in all directions; yet they can be reduced to a single image that joins the body and disappears. Shadows *rasuk* ("fit exactly," "enter into," "possess"); they are of the body, yet they are not confined by boundaries.

Meratus sometimes say that the shadow of a deceased person joins the shadows of that person's living kin. A shaman calls upon the shadows of his teachers, his parents, and his grandparents. But these are also with him in his own shadow. Shadows blur the lines between individual identities. With shadows, the shaman expands to embrace a community.

As the shaman opens the boundaries of his own body through the chant, so, too, he must open the boundaries of the patient, in order to bring the patient to a healthy state. The shaman asks for a renewal of the patient's connection to the cosmos. "Don't lock the door of the wind; don't lock the door of the waters," the shaman chants over the patient's body. The cure restores a freer interaction of body and cosmos, allowing replacement of the patient's resources from cosmic sources. "If lacking in water, replace the water; if lacking in wind, replace the wind," the shaman chants.

If the patient had maintained open body boundaries, he or she might never have acquired the suligih splinter. Rather than the weakened boundaries of Banjar theories, it is rigid boundaries that cause illness. The healthy body incorporates others into its own definition. The isolated body sets up boundaries, refuses connection, and becomes vulnerable to the intrusion—or, perhaps, "redefinition"—of alienated foreign bodies such as the suligih. Shamans explained to me that the suligih splinter is a part of the self, a creation of the body. The suligih "does not come from elsewhere," one shaman told me. "How could a foreign body enter? If a foreign body entered us, we might die!" The suligih is a creation of the isolated and alienated self.

Meratus discuss illness as an ordinary human occurrence. Self-isolation and alienation are unavoidable features of daily life. It is the shaman's role, then, to reconnect people to health-maintaining social and cosmic networks.

Womb work

At this point, let me return to the chant which opens this chapter: Awat Kilay's invocation of Putir Galuh, the putir who taps the power of birth. My translations were made from a tape of a curing ceremony in 1981, in which Awat Kilay was curing Ma Luba of stomach pain. The chant begins as Awat Kilay burns incense, thus creating a bridge for spiritual travel. The chant traverses familiar places in the house and swidden before moving toward more distant locations. It then offers a detailed description of the shaman's visit with a putir supernatural. The shaman arrives at the porch and asks if he may enter. The supernatural looks out, sees that he is attired as a shaman and that he is waiting, auspiciously, by the pillar (*tihang turus*, the backbone, the teachings of past shamans, and/ or the pillar that separates earth and sky). The supernatural invites the shaman in and offers him tobacco and betel. The shaman asks for the supernatural's help.

These lines are not spoken in trance. Sometimes shamans are overwhelmed by their talk with spirits. They may even faint; but this is not the condition of spiritual travel. The shaman is not a self-absenting medium. The chant heightens, rather than douses, consciousness. The description of the visit creates a separation between spirit and shaman. Yet the shaman is aware that this separation is a way station as he calls on the resources of his body. His words bring out the potential of the body.

Appropriately, Awat Kilay's first visit with Putir Galuh takes place in the place of speech:

> At the hall in the highest sky,
> At the hall in the farthest sky.

This is a description of the mouth. Through speech, Putir Galuh descends with Awat Kilay and lends him the power to cure.

> Orate tonight, Galuh,
> Orate today,
> Speak, shaman,
> Enter the matrix of the self,
> Enter the matrix of the appearance . . .
> Stand up Putir with the long tongue [to suck out splinters],
> Stand up Galuh with long hands [to remove splinters],
> Stand up Putir with long fingers . . .
> Look in the matrix of the self, Galuh.
> Look in the matrix of the body.
> Where is Galuh with the long tongue?
> Where is Galuh with the long hands?
> Where is Galuh who travels mystically,
> Travels in the matrix of the self?[7]

Talk of "entering the body" blurs the needs of shaman and patient. The power of Putir enters the shaman to conduct the cure. Putir also enters the body of the patient to remove the splinter.

Blurred lines become even more explicit as Awat Kilay works up the energy to suck out the splinter.

> Where is Putir? Where is Galuh?
> We say, Sucking Putir,
> We say, Grabbing Putir,
> Who plays around at the door of the self,
> Who plays around with the disease splinter,
> Hey, speak for us.
> Where is Galuh who travels madly?
> Mad within the waves of the self,
> Mad within the waves of the body . . .
> If there is a disease splinter, Galuh,
> Speak in the matrix of water.
> Speak in the matrix of self.

Putir "plays around" in the doorway ("like a mosquito," Awat Kilay explained) and excites a "mad" passion.[8] In these lines, the body has the fluidity of waves and water. Here, "water" refers to blood as well as to extrasomatic fluids, again offering a conception of the body as unbounded.

Such boundary blurrings are common to all putir curing; curing with Putir Galuh has the special power of a return to origins. With Putir Galuh, the shaman encompasses the origins of perception and knowledge by travelling to his birth, for birth is phenomenologically identical to the beginning of the world, as experienced by an individual. The shaman calls upon the four siblings with which he was born—the amniotic fluid, the fetal membrane, the placenta, and the bloods of birth. In his chant he confuses his identity as parent and as child by moving back and forth across this line. In the following section, Awat Kilay arrives at the "base of the sky's pillar," that is, the base of the backbone—here, the mother's genitals. He calls "Galuh the Black Ruler." "Black" is the color with which the bloods of birth are described. As the birth progresses, he moves from the *base* of the sky's pillar to its *tip*, that is, to the head of the emerging baby. The baby has grown from "a drop of water"—semen. The identity of Putir Galuh (and, thus, of the shaman who invokes Putir) encompasses all these partners in the birth.

Where else shall I arrive?
To the base of the sky's pillar,
To Galuh the Ruler of Familiars,
To Galuh the Black Ruler,
Whose bedrock hall has eight sides,
Whose mattress is clotted blood,
Leaning at the base of the eight-tiered pillar,
On to the tip of the sky's pillar,
To Galuh Ruler of Familiars,
Familiar of a drop of water,
Whose hall rests on the sky's pillar,
Help us speak.

Leaning at the base of the mother's backbone, the shaman finds himself at the tip of the baby's head. Are we back with Kristeva at the boundary between the undifferentiated maternal body and the selfhood of paternal law? Is the shaman a poet who replenishes his selfhood at the abyss of the maternal? These stories take us in the wrong direction. The shaman's chant begins with the mother and moves to the child as the woman/shaman is delivered. The chant moves not into the womb but out of it. The shaman takes on a maternal identity as a speaking subject, not as the hell or haven that resists all speaking. Yet the maternal speaking subject runs up against basic European (and Banjar) assumptions about gender. Is not maternity, by definition, that which marks women as never fully rational and articulate? To avoid imposing this interpretation, other understandings of gender must be considered.[9]

One place to begin is with the name, Putir Galuh. To avoid the confusion of inappropriate gender assumptions, I have not yet mentioned its female connotations. *Galuh* means "girl" in Banjar, although the term is not in ordinary Meratus usage. Furthermore, *putir* itself is probably related to Banjar *putri*, "princess." In shamanism, putir never has this exclusively female implication; but in some Meratus folktales, the word refers (as part of a name) to a young woman. Thus, Putir Galuh is at least as female as is rice, which is ritually addressed as *diang*, another Banjar word for "girl." As with rice, this female identification is far from exclusive. Every shaman I spoke to insisted that the word *putir* does not refer to female spirits or to a particular gender category.[10] Putir Galuh, for example, is also *Pandara Galuh*, the warrior Galuh. In this guise, s/he is associated particularly with male imagery, such as the following (also from Awat Kilay's chant):

Galuh in the middle of the sea,
Who guards the crocodile's penis as big as a drum in the
    middle of the sea [crocodiles' penises are Banjar male
    aphrodisiacs],
In the form of the great teacher,
Walking in leaps across the sea.
Pandara Galuh of the setting sun . . .
Stand like the edge of a kris!
Stand like the edge of a splinter!

If this Galuh is a woman, s/he is a woman with a penis.

The image of the spirit/shaman as a woman with a penis is, in fact, helpful in explaining the contrast between European gender assumptions and those endorsed by putir shamans. In the former, particularly in psychoanalytic theory, a woman is an emasculated man; she is a (hu)man without a penis. Men have generic, unmarked bodies; women's bodies are signs of difference. In contrast, I argue, Meratus speak of women as ordinary, generic humans. The putir shaman invokes the "girl" Galuh as his well-loved, ordinary body; he travels in the maternal body as part of regular human experience. *Female* is not his principle of difference.[11]

The shaman is like other wo/men; but, at the same time, he is different. He is the one who can transcend ordinary experience to make cosmic connections that encourage health and increase. He articulates a powerful self-consciousness about the body that ordinary wo/men do not achieve. Yet the anatomical possession of a penis alone is not enough to mark a man as a shaman or any other kind of leader. He must learn to use it as a tool of power. A shaman is not a representative of men, as a gender, but an individual who has extended himself beyond ordinary limitations. He is a Superwoman—remembering that women are generic humans. He offers leadership because, unlike ordinary wo/men, he can reach out to incorporate the unbounded power of the world.

This brings me back to a more general exploration of the difference between those I call "leaders" and "ordinary people." This is not a distinction defined by gender, yet it is a gendered distinction to the extent that men have advantages in seeking leadership roles. Men—and not women—regularly become shamans because of men's advantages in training, travelling, and performing. Men learn chants in apprenticeships with senior shamans. They form the widespread social and spiritual connections that offer them prestige and authority. They use their "male" reputations for sexual assertion, violence, and public drama to build charismatic performances. Women, like men, can learn chants from spiritual tutoring in dreams. Learning chants is not enough, however. A successful shaman must draw and hold an audience, and this involves leadership travelling, as well as its sweet talk, intimidation, and drama. In this, men are privileged political actors.[12]

Male performance privilege needs to be seen in the context of Meratus–Banjar relations. Meratus understand shamanic power as deriving from the ability to deal with and incorporate the power of outsiders. Women are disadvantaged at this task, not only through their own travel limitations, but also through the unwillingness of Banjar men to deal seriously with women. In this sense, the organization of ethnicity and gender are linked. Thus, the discussion returns to Meratus–Banjar contrast as it has been generated in this debate over bodies. A brief summary seems in order.

First, whereas Banjar travellers shore up their ethnic boundaries against Dayak incursions, Meratus shamans expand their identities without ethnic lines to "borrow" the power of others. In protecting ethnic identity, Banjar adventurers defend their body boundaries; in extending identity, Meratus shamans open themselves up to the world.

Second, Banjar men must protect themselves against the "female" in the same way that they protect themselves against the "Dayak." Both are principles of unreason that threaten the rationality and autonomy of controlled bodies. In contrast, Meratus shamans are basically wo/men (that is, humans) but more. They move beyond the constraining boundaries of individual, gendered identities to incorporate greater forms of power. Whereas Banjar women must negotiate identity as the Other, Meratus women are merely ordinary.

Third, Meratus gender and ethnic practices cannot be predicted from Banjar technologies of selfhood. Banjar assumptions that Meratus elaborate all that Banjar find distasteful are misinterpretations based on separation and unfamiliarity. At the same time, both Banjar and Meratus systems of understanding depend on constant dialogue with the other. Banjar men need Meratus to confirm their notions of rationality through its inverse. Meratus shamans need external authorities that will lend them power.

Indeed, Meratus interpretations of the interethnic dialogue are essential features in shaping gendered relations of power in Meratus communities. This is especially clear in considering Meratus connections among gender, prestigious language, and sexuality. In contrast to the Banjar situation, in which religious and mystical language are defined as male concerns, men and the phallus have no categorical association with prestigious Meratus speech. The most prestigious Meratus speech is not *male* speech per se but, rather, authoritative outsider (that is, Banjar or Indonesian) speech. (Thus, shaman's chants are full of Banjar and Indonesian words not used in ordinary Meratus talk.) Men tend to know more Banjar and Indonesian usages than do women; they also tend to be more comfortable speaking with strangers. Thus, women are more likely than men to be described (or to describe themselves) as *bungul*, "stupid"—that is, shy, inappropriate, or inarticulate. Women, however, are not *defined* as bungul.

Similarly, heterosexuality is not defined by Meratus in relation to female objectification. I heard a good deal of talk about mutually "delicious" pleasure. There is also a genre of sexual boasting—particularly the talk of travellers—in which women rarely take part. (In contrast to Banjar etiquette, the conversation is perfectly appropriate for gender-mixed company, and a few tough women do join in.) As an American, I found this talk both familiar and strange—familiar, in praising male sexual aggression, yet surprising in its utter lack of attention to the female body. The men never described women's body parts or proportions; they portrayed male desire as completely self-generating. This is the kind of self-made desire that allows ambitious men to transcend the local in the prowess of travel. Its Other is not the female-as-object but the foreigner as a model to be emulated. Encounters with Banjar men, rather than Meratus women, provide the proving ground for ambitious Meratus masculinity. To explore this argument further, I turn to the Banjar–Meratus dialogue about bodies, which reinforces common assumptions as well as ethnic contrasts.

Conversations about bodies

Common standards of communication are created in Meratus–Banjar dialogue about sorcery and its cure. Meratus sell spells and sorcery materials not only to adventuresome Banjar but to other Meratus. They accuse each other (but never Banjar) of sorcery. Indeed, Meratus are sufficiently involved that it is impossible to say this is a "Banjar" discourse. Yet its Banjar connections shape its Meratus contours. Western-foothill Meratus (those in the closest contact with Hulu Sungai Banjar) are the most concerned with sorcery, and they monopolize the antisorcery curing practice. With Banjar support, however, they accuse the "less civilized" people of the central mountains of being the worst sorcerers. In the mountains, ambitious young men learn the sorcery discourse in order to show their cosmopolitan knowledge. They learn to accuse their neighbors, but they seek antidotes from the western foothills or even from Banjar. Similarly, when putir shamans are asked to cure sorcery patients, they follow Banjar tenets to the best of their ability. Such efforts necessarily involve awkward fumbling, as well as personal creativity. An anecdote about the shaman Awat Kilay can illustrate.

Awat Kilay and I hiked to a Banjar town, and, with great anxiety, I brought him to visit Banjar friends. I worried that they would insult or ignore him; but, instead, they gathered around and began to beg him for antisorcery spells and cures. He tried to act appropriately, recalling a well-known Banjar folktale for them and even trying to make use of the Islamic idea of the "power of the book"—in this case, one of my notebooks holding his transcribed chants—to cure a case of sorcery-induced acne.[13] The notebook tactic was unconvincing to his audience, but he did better with spells.

For me, the most memorable spell Awat Kilay devised answered a Banjar schoolteacher's request for a way to negate the effects of poison in a cup of food-stall coffee. Most Meratus drink coffee only when at Banjar markets, but Awat Kilay was not fazed by the question and answered confidently: "You touch the glass, and then you say . . ."—here, he paused dramatically as the men huddled expectantly around him— "Believe in God!" (*Yakin Allah!*, Banjar). I tensed to avoid laughing, but everyone else seemed to be taking it in seriously enough. After all, what could be more appropriate?

Awat Kilay's behavior probably was in part self-conscious performance; but he also took home lessons from his dealings with Banjar to use in Meratus settings. The pervasiveness of Islamic-sounding words in Meratus ritual pays witness to continuing influence, as does the spread of Meratus sorcery charges. After all, Banjar authority is part of Meratus theory; shamans owe their power to their foreign experiences.

Awat Kilay takes pride in incorporating into his shamanic practice the knowledge gained in his travels. He had forty-four teachers, he told me. When I asked him about his life, he dictated two pages of place names, as a way of telling me where he had been. He is a great shaman because he has not limited himself. He argues that all spiritual knowledge has the same basis of authority; one can only gather more. Indeed, taking magical, mystical Banjar Islam as a baseline, he claims to beat it at its own game. How many Muslims, he challenged, know that God has a dual nature? There is God that created the world; then there is God that created each of our abilities to know the world—our parents who created us. To really know God, we must accept this duality. From this perspective, shamanic knowledge is Banjar Islam "plus."[14]

This perspective is one that involves turning the experience of submission into the rhetoric of authority. Let me tell a little more about Awat Kilay's visit with me to the Banjar town. Hiking out of the foothills, we stopped at a Banjar village to have tea at a food stall. The Banjar men at the stall lit into Awat Kilay with aggressive joking, calling him a savage bandit who, presumably because of his Dayak nature, had a lifetime habit of plundering and murdering Banjar travellers. Awat Kilay immediately became humble and shy. He seemed to shrivel up before my eyes, transforming himself from a powerful leader into a slight old man. He joined the joke quietly, stressing that he was old and sexually impotent. I'm sure he did not joke about impotence lightly; yet it allowed him to move on. During our entire trip into town, I barely recognized the Awat Kilay I had known; he had made himself into an aged innocent. Yet he returned home again as a confident authority—with even more experience on which to build.

This trick of transforming humiliation into bravery is crucial to the Meratus formulation of selfhood and identity. The Meratus "speaking subject" develops by turning vulnerability into survival at ever-widening boundaries of power. This is how power is "borrowed." In relation to sexuality, Meratus men play into Banjar feminizations, yet turn them into local masculinity. This is accomplished not by inverting Banjar ideals but, rather, by a different process of subject formation.

In this process, Meratus–Banjar relations create the contours of Meratus discourse, although not on Banjar terms. The issue of male sexuality can illustrate. Meratus men, like Banjar, use claims of a bold, aggressive sexuality to establish authoritative reputations. Yet, Meratus men are often humiliated in front of Banjar men. Although such experiences can be personally devastating, their frequency serves to strengthen the shared assumption that sexual assertion is linked to authority. This common understanding makes it possible for the most ambitious Meratus men to transform their discursive "impotence" in interethnic relations to sexual prowess at home. Because it is supported by Banjar authority, sexual assertion has additional political meaning. As long as Meratus submission occurs within a bantering acquaintanceship, it is not merely defeat; joking creates an alliance with the powerful Other, which reaffirms the masculine sexuality of both parties.[15] Similarly, the spiritually charged language that divides Banjar and Meratus men, provoking misinterpretations, connects them in the common assumption of the power of the word. The courage of a Meratus man to brave interethnic relations demonstrates the potency of both his sexual desire and his spiritual knowledge.

Interethnic dialogue thus supports the position of Meratus men as shamans or community leaders by making male sexual negotiation and mystical language essential to communication. Although Meratus do not interpret these issues in the same way as Banjar, they assent to their central importance in constructing power. This assent disadvantages Meratus women in forming the connections so important to local authority. Women cannot convert encounters with Banjar into prestige at home, because neither their sexuality nor their spirituality meets Banjar standards of communication.

In those Meratus areas where both putir curing and sorcery talk are most pervasive, spiritually charged understanding of the body has become a domain of men's expertise—as confirmed in the contradictions of interethnic dialogue. Meratus women can either support or ignore men's expertise, but they have no special knowledge *as women* with which to discuss the body. The links among spirituality, sexuality, and interethnic communication give them no "female" vantage point from which to offer either dominant or subversive speech; for women, knowledge of the body is not a privileged resource. Indeed, European and North American women who assume that female oppositional consciousness stems from women's special understanding of the body would do well to heed the particularity of the cultural histories in which such gendered understandings have arisen.

Gender experiments

This should be the end of the chapter; as a stopping place, however, it is much too final. To stop would be to ignore the fact that Meratus women can, and sometimes do, draw on other conversations to build an oppositional spiritual authority. A postscript is needed to bridge this chapter's argument and the next section. Here, I can begin to break up the ethnic monolith created by the terms of Banjar sorcery confrontation by showing one way some Meratus women renegotiated their position.

One of the more striking "experiments" I witnessed requires a shift in focus—from the western foothills to the central mountains. In the Ayuh area, the topics and tensions discussed in this chapter possess a much less commanding presence. Even putir shamanism is considered foreign knowledge (emanating from the west side). Sorcery is commonly discussed as an incursion of the 1970s and 80s. Those who accuse their neighbors of sorcery usually suggest that the neighbors probably learned it recently from sources in the western foothills. Indeed, from an Ayuh vantage point, just as men's "science" of body control was coming in from the west, a movement of women out-of-control was coming from the east—a movement of women possessed (*kasarungan*) or kidnapped (*dibawa*) by dewa spirits. Starting in the late 1970s, a number of Ayuh women found themselves spiritually inspired to dance and sing dewa chants. Most of these women were inspired in connection with dewa ceremonies; however, some sang and danced in other contexts as well. Respected shamans and community leaders found this development disturbing; the women, they said, were foolish, outrageous—perhaps dangerous to themselves and others.

Ayuh women's possession is a different form of subversion than the sources of alternative meanings I have referred to so far. It borders on defiance. Were the possessed women victims or shamanic consociates of the dewa? They moved in an ambiguous area where their expected vulnerability as timid community members could become confused with spiritual assertion. Here, their transgression is reminiscent of European women's "hysteria." In discussing French feminist theory, philosopher Elizabeth Grosz outlines the hysteric transgression: "The hysteric's defiance through excess, through *overcompliance*, is a parody of the expected" (1989: 135). The hysteric refuses femininity by feminine overacting. Similarly, Ayuh women took their imagined frailty in relation to the far-reaching world of Banjar, soldiers, power mongers, and spirits to a trouble-making extreme. Kidnapped by dewa—the Banjar of the spirit world—they achieved the spiritual travel and knowledge which could perhaps (but who knows?) put them on a par with shamans.

The difference between the dewa adventures of Ayuh women and the model of European hysteria is also telling. "The hysteric 'articulates' a corporeal discourse; her symptoms 'speak' on her behalf" (Grosz 1989: 135). European women have few defining gifts other than the inarticulate knowledge of their bodies. They must make their bodily knowledge speak. In contrast, Meratus bodily knowledge is the domain of male shamans. Women must move beyond their lack of corporeal expertise if they long to gain the spiritual authority of contact with power. Women kidnapped by dewa spirits achieve wider visions without bodily prowess.

Dewa kidnapping is not an unambiguous event. The episodes I saw were rife with contradictory interpretations. I was attending a large Ayuh festival when I first saw a woman possessed. She had been taking a nap with her husband, and she began to rock and moan. He lay on top of her—to hold her down, as it turns out. I was shocked and embarrassed because I thought they were having public sex. (A Banjar traveller at the ceremony shared my misreading.) Soon enough, however, she rose to sing and dance wildly around the festival's dewa decorations. Yet the confusion grew. Some thought she was faking spiritual contact. Those who took her possession seriously were also divided: Some feared for her; some were angry; some were excited.

Once begun, possession assumed momentum. The young woman danced again the next day, whereupon another woman joined her. Before long, half a dozen women were possessed. Yet, each woman's possession was different. A young girl gyrated wordlessly until she collapsed. She was easily interpreted as a *victim* of dewa spirits, for dewa spirits are known to kidnap children, sometimes leading them far into the forest. Soon afterward, a respected matron, who knew much about dewa shamanism, began singing and dancing. She made it clear that she was no child victim as she called out repeatedly in formal Indonesian, *Siapa guru saya*? "Who is *my* teacher?" The woman's question confronted the shamanic apprenticeship system, which teaches only men. Her spiritual challenge was self-made; that is, it was directly inspired. Still, was the woman a patient to be cured, or was she a healer?

The situation was quite disturbing to the senior shamans, who expected that *they* would be the star performers of the festival. One shaman explained to me that the possessed women might hurt themselves by walking aimlessly at night or falling into a ravine. For him, this was an epidemic of craziness. He worried, however, that the woman's behavior did not respond to ordinary shamanic treatment. Besides, possession was spreading from one festival to the next. Indeed, the women's possession created confusion among all the shamans, who were uncertain whether to ignore the women, treat them, or listen to them. Sometimes women who collapsed were left where they lay, unlike shamans and their apprentices who, when they collapsed, received immediate shamanic attention. This eventually led to a situation in which women who had recovered from possession were reviving others. Yet, if both were patients, this would have been inappropriate.

Spirit-kidnapping stretches Ayuh women's spiritual timidity to conjure the possibilities of power. This confusion nags at men's putir leadership even as it plays within another shamanic tradition. It is in the melange of shamanic styles—rather than in any single style considered alone—that Ayuh women and men negotiate their spiritual options.

In Ayuh, both putir and dewa are considered outside styles, with all the authority that that entails. Central-mountain shamans have their own style, *dewata*; most Ayuh shamans, however, practice at least some putir or dewa, and some specialize entirely in one. Just as putir brings the knowledge of the body associated with the western Meratus frontier, dewa carries the courtly memories of the east side. Although the east coast is tied politically and culturally to western Banjar centers, it has its own distinctive history. The Dutch abolished the courts that controlled trade on each of the area's major rivers only in the early years of the twentieth century; a sense that the spirit of these courts is not dead is strong among east-side residents. Court ceremony provides a past-in-the-present idiom of regional integration beyond ethnic division. Under the kingdoms, Muslim and pagan alike understood ceremony. Thus, Uma Adang's east-side movement endorses regionally integrating royal ceremony to advocate ethnic-religious pluralism. Uma Adang also draws out the gender complementarity that can be found within the conventions of courtly ceremony as interpreted within dewa shamanism. She speaks to the balanced possibilities of "male" and "female" spiritual power. The same kinds of attractions Uma Adang found in the dewa tradition are also available to Ayuh women.[16] The dewa-possession movement drew on familiar spiritual themes at the same time that it created new opportunities for women's spiritual expression.

Some women (such as Induan Hiling, whose spirituality I discuss later) went beyond possession and declared themselves shamans. Even those who limited their activities to wildly inspired singing and dancing expanded the possibilities of women's public performance. Yet women's possession did not usurp the space of men's shamanship. Ayuh festivals are often multi-ring performances. Each style has its own ritual format. Even at moments when only one style is being performed, each shaman chants, dances, and cures independently. Women's possession only adds to the cacophony.

The closest I saw to a confrontation between putir shamanism, sorcery curing, and women's possession occurred at a night-long harvest ceremony in a mountain neighborhood between Ayuh and the western foothills. In this area, putir is the dominant style. Awat Kilay had hiked up from the foothills to conduct the ceremony. Two Banjar men were also in attendance—the trader Haji Biguli (who made an appearance in Parma's story) and an adventurer cruising the area for spells. That evening, Induan A'ar, a young woman from the neighborhood, was kidnapped by dewa spirits—quite inappropriately, given that this was a putir affair.

Even without the dewa spirits, different spiritual agendas clashed and competed. Another young woman was ill with a pain in her chest. Haji Biguli wanted to find her an antisorcery treatment. One foothill Meratus suggested a perpetrator and argued that they should call the police—thus reminding everyone of the official status of sorcery in the region. Nevertheless, the woman was suffering from a classic putir problem, sometimes called "shouldering a thread" (*sadang lawai*), a line of pain that runs diagonally from one shoulder to the opposite hip. The cure deployed was putir. Independent of the agricultural ritual, it was conducted by a young man eager to demonsrate his skills.

Meanwhile, Induan A'ar was acting strangely. Sometimes she was aggressive, even threatening to hit people; then, she became sweet and emotional and held hands with her friends. Furthermore, she was communicating only in sign language. Family members guessed that she was with dewa spirits, and they connected this with her recent trip to market, during which she had perhaps made contact with the dewa (as well as the Banjar). This story did not make much of an impression on the Banjar in attendance. Haji Biguli decided to cure Induan A'ar with blessed water, but his cure had no effect. Finally, a dewa shaman began a dewa chant for her.

When Induan A'ar came out of her possession, she seemed fine. She was articulate about her experience and spoke fluently in shamanic imagery. The dewa had taken her on their motorcycles to the top of the region's highest mountains. They offered her sweet drinks and cakes and bore her away dancing. They took her to the Sea of Blood and threatened to lock her in a seven-layered iron chest that shone like gold and like diamonds. Unless the community held a dewa ceremony within two weeks, they would lock her in the chest and throw it into the Sea of Blood.

These diagnoses, cures, explanations, and threats were occurring in a small, one-room house filled with people—while, all through the night, Awat Kilay chanted for the harvest ritual. Shamans often cure during agriculturally oriented rituals, but Awat Kilay was not getting involved. His activities were still the main event of the evening; he could ignore the rest. Every now and again, however, he gave Induan A'ar a glowering look, taking time to mutter one word: "*Bungul*" ("stupid").

In giving Awat Kilay the last word in this story, I stress that women's possession had little effect on the assumptions or activities of putir shamans. Still, I hope the story gives the reader a sense that women have interesting alternatives as they respond to their limitations within powerful discourses on travel and power. Just as the creative energies of putir shamans are not held within the constraints of Banjar stereotypes, Meratus women develop gender alternatives that putir shamans might neither predict nor fully understand.

In the last part of this chapter, I have argued that both contrasts and compromises in a Banjar–Meratus dialogue about the body advantage men as spiritual leaders. Even as Banjar revile Meratus shamanic knowledge, and ridicule or challenge Meratus men's sexuality, they help support a system in which men can make gender-linked contact with what Meratus accept as Banjar authority. Men are confirmed as privileged travellers on both physical and metaphorical landscapes. Yet, women are neither silent nor demure in accepting their lack of ability to "travel" into power. They are not trapped in the ethnic contours created by the discourse on sorcery. I introduced the Ayuh women's possession movement to offer a sense of women's varied possibilities.

The next part of this book explores a few such possibilities in much greater detail. I consider several women's interpretations of the gender, ethnic, and political challenges that Part Two has outlined. The issues of sexuality and spirituality, as they are tied to the possibilities for powerful travel, remain a central concern. Some women have felt challenged to redefine their travelling sexuality, in order to make it, like men's, translatable into authoritative experience. Others struggle to make their spiritual voices heard, despite their disadvantages in travel and performance. It is in the context of both these kinds of challenges that I return to Uma Adang's gendered reinterpretation of Meratus relations to the region and the state.

PART THREE RIDING THE

HORSE OF GAPS

Women possessed by dewa spirits at a ceremony.
People told me the dewa would not allow
their pictures to be taken. They were correct.

This section of the book tells the stories of several women who called my attention to the importance of off-beat commentary and creative transgression. Their stories have helped me think through a set of issues involving the relationship of ethnographic dialogue, cultural critique, and social transformation. In telling these stories, I do not intend to imply that Meratus men—or other women—are not creative individuals. The traditions of shamanism, leadership, livelihood, and storytelling described thus far contain numerous openings for innovation and experimentation. In talking about creative play in shamanism, I could invoke a half-dozen examples of inspired men. Yet, because women shamans challenge gender conventions in order to perform, the nonconformities through which they construct their "voices" can be especially telling of the interconnections among gender, ethnicity, and political marginality.

The title of Part Three is taken from the words of a shamanic song that was sung by one exceptional woman, Induan Hiling. The "horse of gaps" (*kuda sawang*) is the spirit familiar who guides her in the spaces between the mountains and rocks of accumulated knowledge. More of Induan Hiling's story is told in chapter 8; here, I begin with her song.

Induan Hiling's song

Adu hai,
Riding the horse of gaps, babe,
Swept by the wind,
Riding the horse of gaps, friend.

Finished in a day—
Forging spurs, babe,

Finished in a day.
The horse of distances.

What shall be used, babe?
Forging spurs
Finished in a day.

Used to circle and contain, babe—
That striped cup
The gilded one, babe,
That striped cup
The cup that is composed
To circle and contain.

Swept by the wind.
The child of a cobra, babe,
Soaring to the sun.
If it has scales
They cross across each other.
The scales they point, babe,
Where do they point, friend?
They point to its tail,
They point to its head,
Those scales, babe.

Let's plant bamboo.
I'll plant some.
A clump of bamboo,
A stick of bamboo
It may have hollow stems,
It may have nodes,
It may have a growing bud.

Those stems, babe,
Isn't it so?
Half of them are tall,
Half of them are small,
Half of them are high,
The growing buds, babe.

Adu, it's we ourselves,
Our own mountain, babe.
The mountain called Jungku

With two shoulders,
Hanging there
Swinging where
On our own mountain.

On the summit of the mountain
There's a wild fig tree,
A hanging fig tree,
A swaying fig tree,
Hanging where
Swinging there
Our wild fig tree.

Where does it sway?
Where does it hang?
Yes, it's you and I, babe.

There is a planting:
A cut bamboo.
A bamboo that plays the flute,
A bamboo that sings.
We cut it off
Touching the shoulders,
The scissored bamboo,
The cut bamboo,
Where is it planted?
Where does it hang?

Adu hai, let's sing,
Swept by the wind, and
Riding the horse of gaps, singing,
Counting custom and tradition
In forty-one paragraphs.
The constitution of custom
The law of tradition
The prohibitions of the Basic Constitution.
We'll stand on the center of the Five National
    Principles
With our music to the world.

Adu hai,
At the moment

When God stood up,
And first took care of custom:
The constitution of custom
The constitution of law.
At the moment
When God the One
(I mean, not that God,
Not that God—)
Stood up in the wind,
It was divided into two,

It was named
—Even water was not yet named,
Water was still one—
Du dat
Jat sat
Dat jur
Dat say
Dat
Sut tup.

7 ALIEN ROMANCE

The motor launch that went from the east-side district seat of Sungai Kupang to the regency capital was scheduled to leave by 4:00 A.M. I had hiked down from the mountains and was resting in the darkened front room of a Banjar civil servant's house, waiting for the launch. I drifted off to sleep. When I awoke much later, I was surprised to find myself surrounded by the sound of American English. It was a television playing somewhere in the back of the house.

"I am perhaps the first person in the universe to love someone from another planet," she said to him. "Did you see my image on the wall?"

"The triangle with the curly eyes?"

"Yes, and the three mouths."

"Then you are truly beautiful. Do you know what it means to 'kiss'?"

I smiled and sighed with the shock of recognition. I didn't know this movie (and my quotation—from journal notes made the next day—may be inaccurate); yet I did know it. The U.S. American romance of discovery and conquest is a romance reaching across universes: The white male explorer is rewarded with an alien lover. She loves him, so he teaches her how to kiss.

In this script, romance is the same everywhere. It draws even aliens into a common humanity, capable of love; it makes possible communication and the extension of knowledge. The kiss crosses cultures, proving mutual recognition. Yet mutual is not symmetrical. The (kissing) knowledge of the white explorer shapes the love of the alien woman and, indeed, defines her very existence as his mistress. This is a romance that organizes much U.S. American knowledge of other worlds, not just in science fiction, but in international representations of many kinds. For example, in travel literature, in which the prize of conquest is "experience," romance signals the authenticity and depth of the traveller's insight and allows the traveller to learn from local men "as a man." (As ethnographers acknowledge the ties between their fieldwork experience and the knowledge it produces, such travel stories also enter anthropological writings. Paul Rabinow's well-known essay on fieldwork in Morocco [1977], for example, juxtaposes the researcher's wordless sexual pleasure with a woman and the tensions of his talk with other men; these are interrelated aspects of his quest for knowledge of the Other.) Furthermore, the travel tale of white men's romance and experience has its anticolonial converse in the story of women as weak betrayers of Third World communities, seduced by the colonizer into giving up their men's knowledge.

Yet this is a romantic parable whose terms do not go unchallenged. Those alien lovers have their own stories to tell, stories that show women's initiative as well as their deference. Their stories make it a little less possible to assume that powerful tales of conquest through romance, and of resistance through women's confinement and protection, are really "true." This chapter tells stories of three Dayak women I met in South Kalimantan, each of whom briefly had a foreign man as a lover. Their stories formulate an oppositional commentary from the edges of Dayak experience about sexuality, gender, and the construction of knowledge.

After my efforts in the previous chapter to specify the regional and ethnic contours of gender, it may seem confusing to now invoke a discourse which asserts that love knows no borders. Yet I introduce this discourse to show its very specificity, not to universalize from it. Its relevance is threefold. First, I draw attention to South Kalimantan entanglements in internationally ramifying gender discourses. Meratus dilemmas are not contained by their borders with Banjar, nor even by their negotiations with state officials; this chapter spreads a wider net. Second, I come back to the issue of my own research: In negotiating the contradictions of being both woman and traveller, I was continually reminded of the importance of gendered opportunities and constraints on lives other than my own. Finally, the stories of these three women allow me to explore issues of situated social commentary. In their stories, these women disrupt the flow of legitimate knowledge and authority, as they turn around and recast the story of alien romance.

Research connections

Let me begin with Tani. Tani was one of the first Dayak women to be-friend me when I began my South Kalimantan research. She had a small food stall near the Dayak-Banjar border, in the Balanghan River valley. Tani was also a farmer, living with her husband and small son. Unlike many Dayak women I met during this difficult first period, Tani was not chronically shy with me; she was willing to tell me something of farming and ritual and eager to hear about my life. One of the first stories she told me about herself was like a handshake, opening a channel of connection and explaining away the need for shyness. After all, she seemed to imply, we were both women with experience of the pleasures and limitations of other ways of life.

A few years earlier, Tani had been angry with her husband and family. She had left home. She travelled to a city in East Kalimantan, where, for several months, she managed to make a living peddling vegetables. Some-how she was introduced to a Filipino camp boss who worked for a lum-ber company. He took her on as his companion, and she moved into his quarters. There she had little to do all day except take naps and wait for him to come home. It was a time of both great luxury and great limita-tion. She remembered the smoothness of the linoleum-papered floor and the expansiveness of the bed. The man jealously watched her movements; she rarely went out.

He was also, she thought, in love with her. First, he asked Tani to come with him if he were transferred. Then he offered to marry her. It was an enticing—and a frightening—prospect. Tani told the man that she needed to go back to her village for a few days to get her things, that she would be back within a week. She went back to the village. And she never re-turned to the Filipino camp boss. Perhaps, she said with some nostalgia, he might still come to reclaim her some day.

Tani's story is not typical. She is not even a Meratus Dayak; she is a Balanghan Dayak, a subgroup of the cluster known regionally as Dusun. Further, most Dayak women in South Kalimantan, whether Meratus or Balanghan, have never been to the city, much less been companions of Filipino men. Yet, hearing her story helped to move my thinking toward globally ramifying processes that involve not only Meratus women but also my own research and writing about them. Tani's story draws atten-tion to a regional pattern of meaning and power: In South Kalimantan, Dayak women are the preferred lovers and personal servants of sojourning Asian men. The story also framed the possibilities of my research during a period when no one else would say much to me. Indeed, the story brings together Tani's dilemmas and mine as women seeking knowledge in a context where knowledge is a male conquest. These dilemmas involve constraints as well as possibilities. Tani's story allows me to discuss the powerful discourses on male desire that shape both ethnographic research and local knowledge—along with the sites of resistance they create, from which women can offer critical alternative perspectives.

First, I must return to my own project. My interest in exploring the agency of Dayak women developed in a North American context in which Asian women are seen as exemplars of sexy docility. The feminization of Asia and the exoticization of women come together in images of Asian women as willing slaves of tradition and hierarchy, victims who nevertheless love their submission. It is in this context that feminist Asian Americans and Asian studies scholars stress the complexities of cultural differentiations among women in Asia and the subtle, as well as overt, signs of resistance and refusal of dominant meanings and power arrangements.

The politics of conventional Western knowledge about Asian women is starkly revealed in the model of the Asian mail-order bride catalog. I refer to the burgeoning new businesses that connect middle-aged white men with young women from Asia (Wilson 1988; Villapando 1989). In joining one of these services, a man receives a catalog in which photos of nubile Asian women are labelled with the woman's name, her age, and a few of her hobbies. The man may request a woman's address and begin a correspondence. Like scholarship on Asia, mail-order services claim that they facilitate intercultural communication. In fact, the services allow women to present themselves—through pictures and the listing of hobbies as excerpted from the letters they submit. Yet the framework in which these photos are presented is clear: The women are exotic, docile, and poor. As catalog readers are reminded by the accompanying material, the women are sexy, yet selfless—a pleasant alternative to selfish American women. The words excerpted from the women's letters confirm this image: Their hobbies are childish; their English is broken. The catalogs, like so much scholarship, create a gaze in which we victimize and homogenize even as we learn "a woman's story."

Yet there is another way to read these catalogs. They can be seen as mapping contested spaces and encoding gaps in understanding. The photographs and letters that American men interpret as signs of sexy selflessness are, for the women who choose to send them in, features of a search for self-actualization. The women's intentions contradict the catalogs' assumptions, refusing to be totally absorbed. Such rereading does not cancel the power of the dominant gaze; but it does show that the hegemony of this gaze is not claimed without a struggle.

These catalogs are important to my stories, not just as an analytic model, but in their substance. They participate in creating a world in which Westerners are not surprised that Asian women, including Dayaks in Indonesia, might become personal sexual slaves. In South Kalimantan, however, the significance of this international semiotics of gender and desire is mediated by what at first appears to be an inversion of the objectification of Asian women: Pin-up photos of *white* women in negligees and bikinis adorn the bedrooms and kitchens of many Banjar. In fact, the pictures of white women are joined with pin-ups of others identified as urban and non-Muslim, particularly Hong Kong Chinese and belles from Jakarta. I am not digressing: The Dayak women's stories that I heard were responses to both their placement and my own within the regional discourse made evident through these smiling pin-up girls.

Initially, I was surprised to see these posters. Because I wrongly equated Banjar Islam and U.S. American Christianity, I thought it odd that proudly pious Muslims would decorate their houses with pornography. But Banjar do not intend to banish sexuality; rather, they hope to contain it within an appropriate place. No one puts pin-up girls in the front of the house, where male guests are received; the pictures are hung in parts of the house associated with women and bodily desire. As one man put it, the pictures stimulate men's appetites; appetites are appropriate in certain places.

The logic of containment also protects Banjar women's sexuality. Women must know their appropriate spaces to protect themselves from the danger of uncontained men on the streets; maneuvering within this knowledge, Banjar women have considerable mobility. Going to the town market during the day is a routine, friendly outing; at night without a male escort, it is asking for harassment. Is it men's sexuality, or women's, that is most threatening? The contradictions of a female sexuality that is both dangerous and vulnerable are tentatively resolved by the intervention of the pin-up girls. For these girls show the essence of desire embodied in foreign, cosmopolitan, nonreligious women who have the sophisticated skills of allurement. These are also the women whose sexuality is the most difficult to contain. Banjar women thus appear sexually controlled—as their walls remind them of the pleasures and dangers of uncontrollability.

Foreign women are loose women, loose on the streets. This is a region where almost all prostitutes are imported from Java. It is a region where, as a U.S. American woman, I was always fair game to the police and petty officials who sidled up to me to say, "Tell me about free love in America." Dayak women rarely mingle in Banjar towns, yet they also figure in this discourse—present in their absence. Banjar men and women often commented on how badly Dayak women dressed and how poor their etiquette was. As women of the wild, they are not competitors for the attentions of Banjar men. They are invisible; they have neither the skills of allurement nor the safety of containment.

It is precisely the innocence and invisibility of Dayak women that make them attractive mistresses for foreign Asian men working in the region. (Almost all foreign men working in the region are Asians: Koreans, Filipinos, Malaysians, Chinese, Japanese.) Banjar women are difficult to pry from their containment; they are too likely to have relatives to protect them. Bringing in a Javanese woman is possible; but cosmopolitan women chafe at the isolation of a tin-roof barracks in a raw clearing cut from the jungle—the common fate of a timber company employee. According to the regional discourse, only Dayak women are available, innocent, and unprotected. They can be captured into an all-encompassing privacy, in which every whim of a man's love and arrogance can be satisfied.

This set of meanings is one context in which to appreciate Tani's story. Another is the course of events through which Tani and I met, for her story juxtaposed her travels with mine. In refusing to portray herself as either a victim or a slut, she suggested reinterpretations of my own research dilemmas.

I was received with extraordinary warmth and generosity in Banjar areas as long as I was associated with a local family. People allowed me a great deal of flexibility: When I conducted business in offices and banks (where women rarely go), people treated me with the respect accorded foreign men; in social visits I was offered the company and friendship of women. Travelling to a new place was a problem, however. On the one hand, men—especially petty local officials who had some power over my movements—tested me with sexual threats and innuendos. On the other hand, they were prepared to limit my movements to protect me from these same tests. Indeed, these forms of harassment were sometimes combined, as, for example, one day, when some policemen barged into my hotel room unannounced at 6:00 A.M., to ask me to account for where I had been the day before and then to invite me to join them for a cozy picnic.

This kind of combined threat plagued me when I first tried to situate my research in Tani's Balanghan village.

In the northern Meratus Mountains, on both sides of the mountains, Balanghan Dayaks form a buffer between Meratus and Banjar. Unlike Meratus, Balanghan Dayaks speak a central Bornean language and maintain a system of traditional ranking that is tied to forms of ceremony that are otherwise quite similar to Meratus forms. I was excited by the possibility of doing research in this area, because of its rich ceremonial life and fascinating history of ethnic blending, differentiation, and hostility. However, my troubles started on the way there, as I had to fend off the advances of the Banjar district office employee who escorted me to the Balanghan area. My spirits were revived by the warm welcome I received from local Dayak elders, who seemed eager to tell me about everything. But the district office man must have said something to the Banjar local officials, because suddenly my welcome turned cold. The Dayak elders disappeared, and the Banjar local officials became suspiciously solicitous about my welfare. They refused me permission to travel even to neighboring settlements, telling me that wild animals would attack me. (Not realizing that they meant hominids, I naively argued that there were no particularly aggressive animals in the area.) When I finally relocated the Dayak adat head, he wanted me to sit with his shy young wife, who had nothing in particular to say to me. In hindsight, I see that I had been classified as a woman out of place. A travelling woman is a disorderly woman. At the time, however, I felt abashed and confused.

It was at this point that Tani befriended me. She answered the questions I had carefully prepared for the unavailable adat leader. With her story, she established a connection in which she implied that we were both women travellers, unafraid of the dangers of male sexuality. In this context, her story re-signified my position as well as her own; we were women with initiative and experience—not women lacking male protection. This was a position from which both of us could acquire knowledge, as well as the authority to offer that knowledge to others. Tani thus created an ethnographic space in which I could ask my questions, and she could, similarly, both teach and learn. But this was an interpretive move that struggled in opposition to official readings.

I am not arguing here that I had special access to "the women's point of view," as if there were such a unitary thing. As my experience with the adat leader's reticent wife recalls, I had problems speaking to shy women at this time. Throughout my research I spent much of my time talking with men, especially ambitious men who had the greatest interest in spending time with a foreigner. In many ways, I had the prestige usually associated with male regional authorities; yet, my uncomfortable position in relation to regional authorities sometimes surfaced. I could not form male-to-male ties with police, traders, or district officials. In such contexts, my status as a woman emerged as problematic. In this uncomfortable position I was privileged to learn about the perspectives of local women who, in their own way, were critical of women's exclusion from knowledge, authority, and regional travel. Thus my own limitations in relation to state and regional culture drew my attention to Dayak women's limitations, and to the creative alternative perspectives some women offered to meet the challenges of their exclusions. Tani's story of alien romance as the kind of experience that allows a woman to speak was my introduction to such oppositional positionings.

Ethnographic perspectives

For various reasons, I soon relocated my research to work with Meratus Dayaks of the central Meratus Mountains. Here, indeed, I was out of reach of administrators seeking to impose regional standards of travel and sexuality. My Meratus friends appreciated my willingness to travel; to them, travel made me an exceptionally competent woman rather than an antiwoman. For quite some time, I did not think much about Tani's story—not until I heard a few Meratus women's stories that reminded me of that initial encounter. Like Tani's story, these were not stories I elicited; in each case, a woman offered a story to me. The women spoke to me as a woman and an outsider, asking me to verify their understandings and to share our common travelling experience. Like Tani, these women recalled their foreign lovers with amazement, highlighting contrasts between the forms of their experiences and familiar Dayak forms of love and work. As a result, I began to think differently about both my cultural premises and theirs.

In presenting themselves as women of unusual experiences, these women opened up a critical space of commentary and reflection. Indeed, their stories alerted me to the importance of such self-consciously cross-cultural reflections for anthropology's understanding of both gender and women's lives. Yet, the anthropology of gender has made little room for local women travellers who comment from the margins of ordinary experience. Scholars in the field have been preoccupied with establishing the coherence of bounded cultures and the "typical" views of the women within them. This has led to a problematic opposition, however, between the transcultural perspectives of Western feminist researchers, on the one hand, and the cultural containment of the Third World women they study, on the other. Listening to women as cross-cultural commentators offers one alternative, and one kind of commentary is expressed through wonder and amazement.

I turn to Uma Hati's story, which uses wonder to comment on gendered notions of love, work, and self-determination. Uma Hati is Uma Adang's aunt and a close neighbor. At the time, Uma Hati's husband was village head. We had known each other for several months before she told me this story as we were relaxing one day in the hut next to her rice field. As a young woman during World War II, she had been married to a Japanese officer stationed in the nearby district seat. As she remembered her experiences with him ambivalently, with both attraction and repulsion, her story made both of us pause to think about foreign as well as local notions of gender and personhood.

Uma Hati lived with the officer in his barracks for two years. There she learned to serve him. Each day, she sat in the barracks and waited for him to come home. As he approached, she would go out to greet him. She would bring him inside and remove first his hat, then his shoes and socks, and then his other clothes. She would wipe him with cloths; she would bathe him carefully; she would dry him. She even learned to wipe the sweat off his body as he slept.

Before Uma Hati, the officer had had another Dayak wife in another Bornean town. He taught Uma Hati by explaining the previous wife's techniques. She learned, too, from the other officers' women. Each of the half-dozen Japanese officers in the barracks had a Dayak wife. There were also nine Javanese maids in the barracks, who did the cooking and cleaning. Except for occasionally cooking pastries or sewing, the wives did nothing all day but wait for their husbands.

The husbands loved their wives, Uma Hati recalled. One officer loved his Dayak wife so much that he would bathe her, comb her hair, and have her sit on his lap. He took her with him to his next post. Uma Hati's officer loved her, too, and wanted to take her with him when he left. But she decided not to go. If she left, she thought, when would she see her parents again? The officer was sad. On the night before they parted, he filled the room with the light of thirty-one candles, and he cried.

To share the nuances of this story, I must stress that Uma Hati told it with amazement, as if she were describing a visit to another planet. She was not disturbed by the temporary nature of the marriage; indeed, she had been married briefly twice before this marriage. (Many Meratus women go through several short marriages before settling into a longer-term relationship.) And there had been a recognizable, albeit alien, wedding. Uma Hati remembered being clothed in a long white dress with a hood and white shoes. There was even a gift of bridewealth and a Japanese who officiated in an unfamiliar ritual.

But the strangeness accumulated. Uma Hati's parents attended the wedding, but all of her other relatives stayed home. "They were afraid to come," she explained. Thus began a time of intensive isolation from Uma Hati's family and community. Her only companions were the wives of other officers, whom she had never met before. In contrast, Meratus women usually remain closely tied to their natal families and extended kin after they marry. Even the most agreeable marriage is solidified and supported by a wide array of kin and neighbors; it is not just a private affair between spouses. Many young married women continue living and farming with their parents until the birth of two to three children; throughout their married lives, both husband and wife continue close contact with their parents and siblings. Marriage increases the density of a woman's kinship network, rather than providing a secluded space for husband and wife.

To compound her isolation, Uma Hati was confined to the barracks with no activity that seemed to be a form of livelihood. Meratus women organize their daily lives around the concerns of subsistence livelihood, including farming, making such household items as baskets and mats, gathering forest products, raising chickens and the occasional pig, and preparing rattan for marketing. Although Uma Hati was in awe of the luxurious leisure possible, in the end she had trouble imagining her identity outside of livelihood activities. She expressed some of this in justifying why she left: "If you are born a poor farmer, you just have a hard life. There is nothing to be done about it." Hers would be a life of work because that was what she imagined it meant to be a person.

Finally, the aspect of the marriage that most amused and amazed Uma Hati was her husband's expectation of her personal service. Romance is important to Meratus women, but it is a romance of mutual flirtation, not female obedience. Marriage revolves around mutual goals in forming an umbun to raise crops and children. A wife is not a servant, to undress her husband or deal with his clothes. Meratus men and women wash and care for their own clothes. "Do women bathe their husbands in America?" Uma Hati asked me half-mockingly.

Uma Hati's Japanese officer brought his notions about male-female relations to this marriage. But this was not a Japanese marriage; it was his attempt to realize a fantasy appropriate for a Bornean barracks. There, in a private cubicle, he had spoken in his own hybrid language. Uma Hati listed words they were able to exchange: eat, full, defecate, urinate, angry. . . . These are words that speak of bodies removed from work and community. Although Uma Hati listed them as a single unfamiliar language, I heard them as a combination of Indonesian and what I assumed was Japanese. Within the privacy of his barracks room, the officer had the power to set the terms of their communication; but he too was limited by his ability to imagine her, and her regional context, in particular ways.

Uma Hati complied, but she was not overwhelmed by this power. Even telling the story years later, her struggle against his redefinition was clear. Her surprise, for example, had remained. As she spoke of privacy, leisure, and service, she suggested their "unnatural" contrast with locally important Meratus notions of community, work, and personal autonomy. In claiming the difficulty of learning these unnatural skills, Uma Hati challenged me to share her wonder at this conjuncture of power and cultural difference. Moreover, by retaining a tinge of romantic fascination with the experience, she was also able to undermine the certainties of the cultural community to which she returned.

Uma Hati's story influences the kind of story I can tell about Meratus women. It expands the terrain of thought to an international scale and makes it impossible for me to tell a story of women inside a closed system of understandings and practices. Yet, having taken the reader through the gendered terrors of research, I must turn here to the gendered terrors of writing. Uma Hati's story forces me to confront the conventions of writing that have encouraged feminist anthropologists to tell only of "typical" women's experiences as these are shaped by the unchallenged principles of clearly bounded cultures. The cross-cultural study of gender has specialized in culture-to-culture comparisons that, in theorizing separate "cultures," offer no room for the transcultural experiences of local women. Even those authors who present individual narratives are more anxious about whether their informants are representative of a culture than they are about situated positionings (for example, Shostak 1989:231). Indeed, even as distinguished an anthropologist as Barbara Myerhoff is said to have worried that her work was not anthropology because she wove her informants' critical and reflexive narratives into her interpretations (Prell 1989:255). Why do conventional anthropological writing styles have such power?

To establish professional credibility, feminist anthropologists have had to bend over backward to prove both their training and their appropriate good sense. Two ways of being discredited have loomed particularly large: First, these scholars can be classed with the semi-professional wives of male scholars and administrators who write popular accounts of their travels; second, they can be classed as radical "sisters" who ignore the tenets of scholarship in formulating a political creed. One important response has been to avoid these threats by drawing on the most holistic and system-oriented currents in anthropology to establish a feminist writing style for analyzing gender. This style usefully facilitates discussion of questions about the cultural construction of gender. In avoiding any assumptions that women anthropologists have a special rapport with the women of other cultures—since that kind of thinking is the province of the "sisters" and "wives"—this style foregrounds ideas and political relations that *all* men and *all* women share. It avoids unusual stories and personal experience in favor of structure. Indeed, it overstates stability and homogeneity and creates clear boundaries around cultural systems. (Ironically, textual critics seized upon this historically specific style—ignoring the ongoing traditions of the "sisters," the "wives," and other marginals and mavericks—to argue that feminist anthropologists are textual conservatives [Clifford 1986:20–21]).

Other responses have developed as well. Yet their proponents have had difficulty escaping from a fluctuation between accession to the demands of male-dominated scholarship and retreat to a position in which the author's status as a "woman" becomes the basis of her authority to tell a tale. Unlike either a man or a scholar, a woman is not empowered to tell about an entire culture or a political system; she cannot represent (portray or act for) the whole. If she resists assimilation into the male/scholar position, she has but one easily acceptable alternative: She can talk to other women because she *is* a woman. From this position, she is forced to assume an essential woman-to-woman connection; and it becomes difficult to discuss cultural differences or even what it means to be a woman at all. For ethnographic analysis, a woman author must leap back into the bounded cultural worlds of the scholars, despite the fact that this frame may not account for some of her most interesting material. (I think, for example, of the awkwardly alternating sections of authoritative ethnography and woman's story in Marjorie Shostak's *Nisa* [1981].) My point is not to deny the privilege in representing the world shared by women and men in the West. It seems useful, however, to draw attention to the gender-asymmetrical risks that feminist ethnographers incur in writing "experimental" texts. Like women who travel, women who write must juggle contradictions and evade hazardous interpretive barriers. In analyzing the unconventional ethnographic perspectives of Meratus women, I am pressed to resituate my own.

Conventional styles of feminist anthropology are inadequate for discussing such stories as Uma Hati's, because Uma Hati takes cross-cultural storytelling into her own hands and refuses to sit quietly inside the analytic boundaries of a culture. As a tale that cannot be contained within cultural boundaries, her story recalls what feminist theorist Gloria Anzaldua (1987) calls the "borderlands"—the critical spaces created as contrasting discourses of dominance touch and compete in a contested hierarchy. The borderlands have no typical citizens; experiences there undermine the safe ground of cultural certainty and essential identity. Furthermore, the borderlands are an analytic placement, not just a geographical place. All stories told to an anthropologist can be interpreted through the borderlands. It is a zone that challenges Western analysts' privileged claim to critical perspectives.

Uma Hati's story suggests that ethnographic insight emerges, not from culture-to-culture confrontation nor woman-to-woman communication, but, instead, from the stories told by one situated commentator to another. Uma Hati's critical feminist ethnography makes mine possible.

Alien commentary

Women's stories of alien romance are a form of commentary on local and regional gender relations. As introduced in the preceding chapter, male-to-male sexual negotiations are important in the formation of men's regional alliances. Meratus women are endangered by travel because of its association with male sexual aggression; many women spoke of being "not brave enough" to travel. Thus, women are disadvantaged travellers; indeed, they are sometimes characterized as those who are afraid to travel. But because travel and regional experience are important in constituting authoritative Meratus subjects, a Meratus woman must turn gender assumptions about travel around in order to show herself as a subject of knowledge and experience. Women sometimes joked when they travelled, just as men did, about finding themselves a new lover. In their travel between Meratus neighborhoods, this joking gained them a certain amount of credit as "brave." In dealings with men outside the Meratus area, however, such sexual immodesty (unlike Meratus men's deference to Banjar men, which could be reinterpreted as alliance) risked provoking a dangerous fight. With no respectable alternative, most of the Meratus women I knew pretty much avoided personal dealings with non-

Meratus men. Yet, there were important exceptions—women willing to challenge the dangers of negotiations across sexual and ethnic lines. Uma Hati was one such exception; another was Irah, a younger, more alienated woman.

Many of the same elements I heard in Uma Hati's story were present in the story Irah told me about the two foreign lovers she had had—a Korean and a Malaysian Chinese. Superficially her situation was different. Rather than a wife, she was classified as a personal maid, working at timber company base camps during two separate periods in the late 1970s. Yet Irah's duties were not that different from Uma Hati's. Irah took meals to the man she worked for (both camps were supplied with cooks), made him special breakfasts, aired out his sleeping mat, took care of his light laundry, and provided personal services, including sex.

Like Uma Hati, Irah spoke of the relative ease of life, the demands of personal service, and the restriction on mobility and sociality. Being a maid rather than a wife was no protection from absolute confinement. Irah stressed that, because of the jealousy of the bosses, each maid was constrained to stay in the quarters of her own boss. Fights were common, and the threat of physical violence helped ensure her monogamous service.

One important difference was that Irah was paid. The wage relation calls attention to the fact that the "luxury" of these relationships is not merely an illusory ideological effect but a niche in the regional political economy. Irah made Rp 20,000 a month (about U.S. $30),[1] and she was provided with food, cigarettes, and birth-control pills as benefits. To Irah, this seemed a high salary. Ordinary family maids in the provincial capital were paid Rp 7,000 a month (about U.S. $10), for much harder jobs that did not even include food. The only other option she knew for work outside her community was to peddle cigarettes, piece by piece—a very precarious livelihood. Furthermore, as a personal maid, bonuses and salary increases could be negotiated privately with a willing man; Irah said some women she knew were making Rp 70,000 (or more than U.S. $100) a month through private arrangements. By regional standards, this was good money.

Irah was more estranged from any local community than were either of the other women whose stories I have discussed. When she told me her story, she was living on the Banjar side of a Meratus–Banjar border, together with her mother, who had recently married a Banjar trader. (The year before, both had moved with him from the Meratus area where Irah grew up.) Although Irah was farming, she had not really settled down, and I thought she might wander off again, as she had done before. She was more dependent than most Meratus women on the larger regional economy, with its limited options for women. For her, being a mistress and a maid was a job to be compared with other subsistence possibilities.

Yet, echoing the other stories, Irah insisted that both of her bosses were in love with her, that they were ready to marry her and take her anywhere. The Malaysian Chinese dismissed her when his wife was scheduled to visit, but after his wife left, Irah claimed, he came looking for her again, begging her to rejoin him. The Korean, too, wanted her to marry him, but she refused.

This insistence on the strength of the man's unrequited love, found in each of these women's accounts, is key to understanding the challenges of their stories within the local Meratus context. In describing the men's unfailing love, the women turned the focus of the stories from victimization toward alien romance gained through bravery and travel. Meratus women do not often have brave stories of travel. These stories challenge the characterization of women as fearful and shy, and they usurp men's exclusionary rights to a reputation for bravery and attractiveness. In this sense, they stand as both claims to status and critical commentary.

It may be useful here to bring up a more conventional Meratus discourse on romance. One need think only of the love songs described in an earlier chapter. Attractive men are portrayed metaphorically as travellers from far away, who come upon lovely but stationary women, portrayed as trees. Although no Meratus men I knew of had ever been employed by the army or by a timber company, in these songs the romantic male traveller is often called an army officer or a timber company worker to stress his beauty, wealth, and bravery. These qualities allow him to chop down the tree—that is, to win the woman. The women's stories I have told are like these songs, in pointing to the glamour of the powerful stranger; yet the women's stories also invert the conventions of the songs. In them, women go out to find romance in faraway places. In these stories, the courage to travel outside the community implicitly becomes the courage to question local standards of male privilege. The stories dislodge local conventions of women's fear and silence.

Alien romance is not described as natural, easy, fun, or even satisfactory for the woman; yet these women refuse to be victims. I was impressed that each woman stressed that *she* made the decision to leave; the man's love meant that he was almost *her* slave. Given that the men were planning to stay only a short time, and that most of them had other wives and maids elsewhere, it seems likely that they had rather different stories to tell about these relationships. The women's versions, however, claimed control.

The political-economic context of that control is the fact that these women could go home to communities that had plenty of land for them to farm and had eligible and independent men for them to marry.[2] They could go home to tell their stories with pride, not shame. Indeed, like Meratus, Balanghan Dayaks have the economic autonomy that comes with living in out-of-the-way places. They also recognize the power and wealth of regional centers, and the relations of inequality that accompany that power and wealth. Tani's story thus joins the Meratus stories in a related regional commentary.

The stories discussed in this chapter have an almost allegorical quality in describing the Dayak peripheral position from a woman's perspective: As one moves closer to powerful centers, one gains both luxury and servitude; as one moves away, one gains autonomy with hardships. In this sense, they follow conventional local representations of the Other; they are not idiosyncratic. Indeed, these conventions are similar to those invoked in the women's dewa-possession movement described in chapter 6. I think specifically of Induan A'ar's dewa-possession experience. The dewa spirits she encountered were well-dressed men riding motorcycles, the spirit counterparts of regional businessmen, police, and administrators. They took her to spirit cities on top of the tallest mountains and offered her sweet, cold drinks and delicious cakes. At the same time, they threatened to lock her in a casket and throw it into the Sea of Blood. Echoed here with dreamlike overtones is the romance with the opulent and the deadly.

Thus, the stories I have discussed join dewa possession as an ambivalent form of resistance to women's regional exclusions. Neither alien romance nor dewa possession creates leadership roles for women; however, each offers a way for women to claim themselves subjects of knowledgeable experience.

. . . and laughter

This precarious women's knowledge is, in fact, a key feature in my ability to think ethnographically about Dayak women's lives in South Kalimantan. To learn something about gendered inequality, one must figure out what kinds of inequality women care enough about to argue against. Through the particularistic connections I was able to make with Dayak women, I heard about self-assertion, as well as fear and exclusion, and I gained some small sense of the issues that were important enough for them to struggle with. These connections sometimes took our talk outside of daily life in the Meratus Mountains, to muse on the nature of foreign life-styles and their implications for ways of doing things at home. Indeed, ethnography is perhaps often dependent on local discussions of the alien, just as it is dependent on Western notions of the Other. It can only benefit anthropology, feminist or otherwise, to bring a more self-conscious appreciation to this kind of ethnographic interaction.

Dayak stories of wonder and amazement are "ethnographic" stories that can denaturalize both local and regional discourses on gender and power. For me, this was an enlightening process. Let me return for a moment to the pin-up girls. Pin-up posters and calendars are common decorations in Banjar homes; in contrast, I did not see them in the Meratus Mountains. Yet I was present once when a Meratus man of the central mountains brought home a pin-up calendar from a Banjar market. When he arrived, everyone gathered around to gape at the new merchandise. Though fascinated by the photos, they found them incomprehensible. As I argue in discussing Awat Kilay's shamanship, Meratus do not imagine an eroticism that depends on objectification of female body parts. Indeed, no one in the group viewing the pin-up calendar seemed to realize that the photos were intended to be erotic. Even as portraits, they were confusing. Why, one woman asked me, would women who have the resources to dress beautifully and create an imposing impression choose instead to have their pictures taken laughing, and with so few clothes? Think about it again, she challenged. Why?

Amazement denaturalizes; it also provides critical comment. When wonder becomes parody, the elements of commentary and challenge become even clearer. Here, the women who speak from the borderlands are experts; the commentary I offer must sit respectfully beside theirs. In situating myself as co-commentator, I leave this chapter with an image offered me by Uma Hati, the woman once married to a Japanese soldier. Where the pin-up story took place in the central mountains, this one is set on the eastern Meratus border. Similarly, this is a mixed gathering of women and men. In a moment of mutual hilarity, Uma Hati pulled up her skirts to show her aging thighs and ragged undershorts, and she challenged me to take her photograph. In this gesture, she suggested a joint parody—hers and mine—of women's sexual objectification. My commentary can do no better than to present her laughter.

8 RIDING, WRITING

Adu hai,
Riding the horse of gaps, babe,
Swept by the wind.

Thus begins a song composed by a Meratus woman I call Induan Hiling. Induan Hiling has already made a cameo appearance as a neighbor of The Bear who cooked so well for the visiting police sector officer that he lost sight of his complaints about underdevelopment. There I argue that her narrative is not "just" a woman's story, a story from the kitchen. Induan Hiling explained ideas about hospitality and appeasement that are equally important to Meratus men and women. Here, I reverse the direction of my inquiry to ask what difference it makes that her stories—and her songs, esoteric "writings," and commentaries on aesthetics, ethnicity, and politics—are the work of a woman.

Induan Hiling is not a "representative" woman. In a context in which almost all shamans are men, she is a woman who dares to call herself a shaman. At least, some of the time. Sometimes, Induan Hiling calls herself a *pinjulang*, a shaman's accompanist. It is an expression of humility—or, at least, the ambivalence of her ambition—for Induan Hiling to call herself an assistant, an accompanist, a woman who sings to the shaman but never directly to the spirits. But Induan Hiling assists no man; she works directly with spirits, just as any other shaman does. At other times, Induan Hiling calls herself "Irama," after the Indonesian pop star, Rhoma Irama, whose posters and cassette tapes were everywhere in the markets at the time I knew her. Induan Hiling is not just an ordinary shaman; she is an entertainer. She confuses local categories; she stretches them; she even mocks them. In the process, her spiritual expression raises persistent questions about the gendered status of these categories. How can she be both a shaman and a woman?

Many of the preceding chapters have shown that shamanic spirituality is a key site for the negotiation of Meratus politics. Shamanism forms an important marker of authority within Meratus communities. Shamans distinguish themselves as people worth listening to. They understand power—whether the violence of the military, the ritual of administration, or the magic of religion. They combine authoritative knowledge, articulateness, and the ability to draw an audience; they are thus leaders. At the same time, shamanic spirituality is constituted as an aspect of Meratus subordination: In South Kalimantan, shamanism forms the exotic Other of Banjar ethnic and religious discourse. Within the Indonesian nation, shamanism marks the Meratus as outside legitimate religion and thus possibly subversive (amoral) and certainly archaic (uncivilized). These are the terms of regional and national integration. And Meratus accept, manipulate, and argue about their ethnic and political status through shamanic discussion and ceremonial practice.

Shamanic practice is also a site of gender differentiation. As I have discussed, most shamans are men. Women (like men) are assistants, patients, set-up artists, and members of the audience; they are rarely star performers. Women who claim the right to spiritually powerful speech must challenge shamanic conventions. Because shamanism is an important route to political voice, women who take exception are pressed into extraordinary self-consciousness about the gendered conditions of both local and extra-local politics. Induan Hiling is one such woman. This chapter tells of her shamanism—as an unusual, but telling, interpretation of the shamanic tradition; as a struggle within and against conventions of gender, performance, and politics; and as a gender-sensitive recasting of Meratus ethnicity and national status. I begin by discussing the importance of Induan Hiling's story for cultural theory.

Eccentric experiences

Stories of individuals have been very helpful in theoretical projects that point to sites of exclusion, struggle, and creativity beyond the scope of dominant discourses. Thus, for example, in the emergent feminist scholarship of the 1970s, biographies, memoirs, and other kinds of stories of individuals as "women" helped establish the excitement of exploring gender difference.[1] In the 1980s, personal essays by U.S. American women of color challenged the theoretical normalization of white women's experiences in the United States and showed the importance of race in defining "woman."[2]

Individuals' stories are most exciting in cultural analysis to the extent that they open new conversations about agency and difference. As historian Joan Scott (1992) argues, stories of individuals can also be read as if their experiences were transparent concomitants of the social category (gender, race, class, and so on) stressed in the account, thus reconfirming unself-conscious assumptions about those categories instead of leading to a consideration of how those categories were constructed. Furthermore, if personal stories are read as representing the "authentic voice" of a particular category of people, they can become further exclusionary devices that marginalize all those who speak outside of an imagined authenticity (Moraga 1983; Martin and Mohanty 1986).

The challenge, then, is to construct accounts of individual agency and yet attend to the cultural formation of that agency. This point is related to that made by anthropologist Lila Abu-Lughod in her criticism of recent uses of the concept of resistance. Accounts of resistance show the contours of power in which resisting subjects are themselves constituted (1990). Yet, as feminist theorist Judith Butler puts it, "to claim that the subject is constituted is not to claim that it is determined" (1992:12). People play with, pervert, stretch, and oppose the very matrix of power that gives them the ability to act. The excitement of an individual's story lies in the story's ability to expand and unbalance dominant ideas of the contours in which familiar subjects are made.

Teresa de Lauretis's notion of the "eccentric subject" (1990) is useful here in conceptualizing the kinds of individual stories I find most theoretically intriguing.[3] De Lauretis (1987:26) uses a film metaphor of the zone of "space-off" just outside that caught by the film camera's frame. In this zone—outside the main orienting framework of a dominant discourse—eccentric subject positions are constituted. Subjects understood as "eccentric" in this sense are those whose agency demonstrates the limits of dominant categories, both challenging and reaffirming their power. This is a useful way to think about subject positions within the zone of exclusion and creativity that I have been calling "marginality." The agency of eccentric subjects is further complicated and enlivened when this zone is seen as one in which multiple overlapping (and sometimes contradictory) discourses comingle or collide. Eccentric subjects are multiply and complexly constructed according to their relationship to power and difference.

The "eccentricity" of the shaman Induan Hiling begins with her odd relationship to the expected gender division of labor, in which Meratus shamans usually are men. In Induan Hiling's area of the central mountains, there is an important female role in shamanic ceremonies; *pin-*

julang, shaman's accompanists, are generally women. But pinjulang are not independent spiritual experts. They never summon spirits, sponsor ceremonies, or initiate a round of chanting within a ceremony. In contrast, Induan Hiling's claim to personal spiritual insight and ability to lead and cure separates her from pinjulang and puts her in competition with shamans.

Induan Hiling's gender disruption does not place her personal strategies outside Meratus conversations. To show herself a shaman, she crafts a spiritual identity and practice that can be recognized by other people as shamanic, even as she stretches the boundaries of their recognition. Her creative strategies do not escape conventional notions about personal initiative, or those about ethnic vulnerability and state authority. These notions inform the possibilities of creativity in this context. Yet Induan Hiling approaches ordinary expectations with a difference.

Negotiating convention

Induan Hiling traces her sense of difference from her peers to her decision to emulate her father rather than merely admire him. As a child, she told me, she learned to climb trees—a sign of bravery usually reserved for young men. She said she had never been afraid to travel.

Her father was a great shaman; he is remembered as a panggalung— one who coils, loops, ties—that is, a shaman so powerful he could gather people from all around through his spiritual charisma. After his death, several years before I met her, Induan Hiling began to receive teachings from him in her dreams. Soon, she was on her way to becoming a shaman herself.

Induan Hiling thus locates her talent within a tradition of male mentorship; she also, however, tells of her ties with women. Her mother and younger sister are both skilled pinjulang; both have consistently been supportive of Induan Hiling's spiritual explorations. Further, Induan Hiling considers herself an adoptive sister and a disciple of Uma Adang. Induan Hiling draws on the power of Uma Adang's teachings in explaining her innovative shamanship. I, too, was part of this circle of discipleship. Induan Hiling performed for me as a gift from one of Uma Adang's "sisters" to another.

Induan Hiling was first moved toward a shamanic career through the women's dewa-possession movement I described at the end of the last section (Chapter 6). Like several other women in her area, she found herself singing and dancing with dewa spirits. It all seemed rather uncontrollable, and Induan Hiling was about ready to accept the judgment of her husband's relatives that she was crazy. But she consulted with Uma Adang, who told her that she was a shaman-in-training. It was only then that she realized she was receiving teachings from her deceased father. Since then, her dreams have been visited by other spiritual mentors, who come to teach her songs, choreograph dances, and dictate drawings and writings.

When I knew Induan Hiling in the early 1980s, she was in her mid-thirties, the married mother of three sons. Her fields, which formed a common cluster with those of her pinjulang mother and sister, were only a few minutes' walk from the fields of some of her husband's siblings. The entire group assembled for festivals several miles upstream, at The Bear's ritual hall. As the neighborhood's most skillful pinjulang, Induan Hiling's mother often worked closely with The Bear during these festivals. The neighborhood alliance was unstable and uneasy, however; each subgroup took offense at slights, continually threatening to join festivals and work groups somewhere else. In this social context, Induan Hiling's shamanic quest posed a challenge (if, perhaps, a minor one) to The Bear's claims of neighborhood leadership. She had reason to expect a receptive audience among her neighborhood subgroup. None of the men of her cluster were especially ambitious, and none were shamans. Along with her mother and sister, Induan Hiling had the strongest claim to shamanic knowledge in the cluster. This was fertile ground, then, for Induan Hiling's spiritual development.

How is this account relevant to the cultural construction of creative subjects or to the eccentric subject positions from which culture is creatively negotiated? First, Induan Hiling's story reiterates conventional Meratus models of gender and community: Shamans are exceptional people who transcend the gender-unmarked (that is, female) community of their peers. As I have argued, shamans are "superwomen" in a context where women embody the ordinary human condition. By her own account, Induan Hiling is no different. Yet, second, the resources for transcendence are tied to the technologies of gender. Most male shamans, for example, apprentice with senior male shamans; they learn by sitting next to, and dancing behind, an experienced shaman and following the words of his chant. Through these apprenticeships, young men learn the inner workings of shamanic performance and receive the blessings of their elders. Shamans also build reputations that depend on extra-local ties with other Dayak men of note in far-flung locales, as well as with male Banjar traders, police, and civil officials. These gendered resources have not been available to Induan Hiling. She is forced to fall back on learning from a dead man and other spirits who visit in her dreams. (Male shamans also learn from spiritual mentors in their dreams, but this is normally only one of several learning strategies.) And she networks with women, including the one great woman shaman of her acquaintance—Uma Adang. Such means of constructing her "exception" place Induan Hiling in an awkward relationship with dominant Meratus models of shamanship and creativity. Even when she replays a common cultural theme, she does so with unexpected harmonies and dissonance.

Inversions and revisions

Analyzing Induan Hiling's dissonance requires a realignment of much of the anthropological literature on women's creative expression. Anthropological writings have tended to explore stable, segregated female traditions in which women, for all their difference, do not challenge the limits of gender appropriate behavior or the discourses of authority.[4] Unlike the women discussed in this literature, Induan Hiling does not limit herself to a conventionally female domain, but, instead, attempts to insert her work into a tradition in which men predominate. Although her work is not intended as insurrection, it does challenge and rework the tradition to the extent that it evades or reinterprets its gendered features. To ask about this work, I find myself turning to literary approaches: Literary critics have a long tradition of investigating the conditions of creative self-expression.

Induan Hiling has a keen sense of her shamanic improvisation. Her work draws eclectically from familiar metaphors and genre conventions. As she uses pieces from one tradition to revise others, she creates products that—as has been suggested for the writings of Western women novelists and poets—seem open to multiple and sometimes contradictory interpretations.[5] Although Induan Hiling's work builds on the dominant tradition, it also interprets this tradition in ways that are linked to her awkward status as a woman creator.

Induan Hiling inverts and revises both male and female expressive traditions in her repertoire. For example, male shamans use hand-held rattle bracelets to control rhythm and cue the drummer; Induan Hiling puts rattling bells on her ankles, thus setting the rhythm with her steps without appearing to control it. Her dance movements—featuring small, circumscribed steps and graceful body and arm movements—resemble secular dances performed by women at festivals. Male shamans tend to include much more prancing and stomping. But, diverging from the slow, mincing gait of the women parading at festivals, Induan Hiling moves to a lively, energetic rhythm, responding to her own inspired singing. Whereas women at festivals normally dance with their faces away from the audience, Induan Hiling dances with her face to the audience, thus dramatically unmuffling her voice.

Like male shamans, Induan Hiling sings, telling of her spiritual travels. In the song fragment that begins this chapter, she rides a flying horse. Later in the song, she chooses a flying cobra, a more conventional familiar of Meratus shamans. (The complete song is translated in the introduction to Part Three.) The cobra's scales map the route of spiritual flight, as it extends both forward and back:

> Child of a cobra, babe,
> soaring to the sun.
> If it has scales,
> they cross across each other.
> The scales they point, babe,
> Where do they point, friend?
> They point to its tail,
> They point to its head,
> Those scales, babe.

Although this fragment replicates no other shaman's text I heard, it is recognizably shamanic travel. Yet, there are disorienting aspects. For example, the use of "babe" (*ding*; literally, "younger sibling," and, through extension, "romantic partner") as a line marker seems out of place—until it becomes clear that Induan Hiling is using the melodic structure and refrains of love songs (*dunang*), rather than ordinary shamanic melodies. Both women and men sing and compose dunang; it is a comfortable, familiar medium for a woman. Induan Hiling fills her songs with the spiritual imagery of shamanism, concocting a hybrid genre.

Induan Hiling's songs refer to the gendered metaphors of conventional love songs, but they transform the metaphors in gender-free spiritual directions. Like love songs, her songs are filled with references to vegetation. In love songs, shining, golden, healthy yet passive plants represent the beautiful women pursued by male suitors, who are portrayed as birds, wandering soldiers, and treecutters. Induan Hiling transforms the passive vegetation into an extremely active element, singing of "swaying" fig trees and "singing" bamboos. Moving vegetation even further out of the love-song context, she omits the male half of the tree/bird and tree/tree-cutter contrast. Vegetation becomes a metaphor for aspects of human spiritual expression, rather than for women.

The following fragment shows a complex set of associations for bamboo:

There is a planting:
A cut bamboo,
A bamboo that plays the flute,
A bamboo that sings.
We cut it off
Touching the shoulders,
The scissored bamboo,
Touching the waist.
Babe, the scissored bamboo,
The cut bamboo,
Where is it planted?
Where does it hang?

In a number of love songs, bamboo is female. To the extent that the bamboo in Induan Hiling's song carries female resonances, its activity in singing and playing the flute establishes it as a creative subject, not an object of courtship admiration. Induan Hiling's dominant metaphor, however, is not one of bamboo-as-woman but of bamboo-as-hair; this is a common shamanic reference for this gender-neutral spiritual attribute of the body. To make the move to human spirituality clear, Induan Hiling establishes the gender symmetry of her metaphor. As she explained it to me, she simultaneously invokes a male subject, whose hair is "touching the shoulders," and a female subject, whose hair is "touching the waist." She transforms a reference to women into a reference to spiritual experience that applies equally to men and women. She also draws other ungendered metaphors into the portrait. She compares the bamboo to ritual streamers that are intricately "scissored" (actually, cut into designs with a knife) and later "cut" (tied up) to close the performance. As earlier references in the song make clear, the bamboo is also the shamanic route itself, the pathway of spiritual expression. Induan Hiling removes female resonances from the context of an asymmetrical male-female contrast and places them among spiritual references as features of a human spirituality that does not depend on gender difference.

The dualism of love songs is not entirely lost in this transformation. The vegetation enters into a different opposition—with mountains and rocks rather than birds and treecutters. Induan Hiling explained mountains and rocks as representing an internal, inspirational knowledge, the not-yet-articulated wisdom of origins. In contrast, her vegetation represents the ritual apparatus used in shamanic ceremony and the well-worn ritual practices within which shaman's chants emerge. Rocks and mountains contrast with vegetation as inspiration contrasts with tradition. By implication, both elements are needed for ritual efficacy; inspiration is articulated through tradition.

This complementarity is a motif often repeated in Induan Hiling's work. She sings of a fig tree on a mountain, which also refers to the hair growing on our heads:

> On the summit of a mountain
> There's a wild fig tree,
> A hanging fig tree,
> A swaying fig tree,
> Hanging where
> Swaying there
> Our wild fig tree.

Elsewhere, she repeats the vegetation-mountain opposition in singing of bamboos on rocks and, using an image borrowed from "city people," of flowers on a table. This is *not* a gendered opposition. Transcending the gendered duality of love-song imagery with nongendered spiritual text is essential to Induan Hiling's ability to cast her work as shamanism. Yet, her use of the two-element opposition as a motif has its roots in the love song.

Induan Hiling draws the same opposition into the pictures she learns from dreams. Drawing is not a common form of creative expression in the Meratus Mountains. Other than the scribbling of a handful of schoolchildren, almost no one writes or draws. Induan Hiling's dream-inspired drawing and "writing" revise familiar themes in a new medium of spiritual expression. The complementarity of rocks and plants—as text and ritual apparatus or inspiration and tradition—is also key to the pictures' message.

Figure 8.1 is a drawing of a tree next to a rock. As Induan Hiling explained, the tree is a ritual stand complementing the rocks' written text, that is, the scribbled lines that depict the internal knowledge of the shaman to be expressed in the chant. Although Induan Hiling herself could not read the message, she assured me that the scribbled lines in the rocks are "writing." (The English words on the side of the page do not represent "writing" in the same sense; I will come back to them.) Induan Hiling features such dream-dictated "writing" in several of her drawings.

8.1 Bamboo altar and shaman's text

Her explanation of shamanism as inspiration externalized and articulated through traditional form is both an innovative and perceptive interpretation. Conventional shamanic apprenticeship encourages a reading of the chants that stresses the endless elaboration of complexity and diversity rather than oppositions. Mountains and vegetation are common symbolic elements in shamans' chants, but only in Induan Hiling's work did I see the two elements so clearly identified as complementary pairs, with such consistently resonating reference to the possibilities of spiritual expression itself. Her interpretation of the tradition successfully clarifies a number of key elements. Her oppositions speak of the necessity for both shaman's chants and ritual decorations in a performance. They also recall the use within the chants of linked images of primal knowledge and carefully learned tradition, as well as the complementarity of dreams and apprenticeship in learning. Yet, her interpretation is also a challenging one, pointing to the possibilities of simplification and codification of that which shamans say can never be simplified or codified.

Induan Hiling's engagement with the dominant traditions of Meratus shamanism results in a perceptive interpretive framework. As a woman shaman, she has needed to forge original paths to achieve legitimacy.

These paths have led her not only to innovative revisions, but also to imaginative and insightful views on Meratus shamanism.

The conditions of creative production

Humanist literary approaches have guided me to look at Induan Hiling's creative revisions of shamanic conventions. Structuralist approaches can also open new questions. I find structuralism most useful in thinking about Induan Hiling's critical interpretations.[6] Like a structuralist critic, she looks beneath the riotous variety of shamanic poetry to find underlying conceptual oppositions that are productive of this variety. Yet, of course, Induan Hiling is not just a critic of shamanism; she is a shaman. The split between critic and creative artist that pervades—and helps define—Western scholarship in the humanities is irrelevant to her self-definition. Her critical challenge is, at the same time, an aesthetic and political strategy. Her structuralist poetics form one aspect of a move toward a more codified shamanism which sidesteps the male-biased performance requirements of shamanic expression.

One might view this codification project as a "poststructuralist" move in her work, for with it, she deconstructs the taken-for-granted grounds of shamanic representation. Induan Hiling exposes the gender biases of its excesses and its marginalia. She crafts a language of its differences and deferrals. This is a topsy-turvy deconstruction in which the conditions of performance, rather than the logic of texts, have privileged status. In her project, "writing"—even in an extended Derridean sense, which might include ritual structure—does not encode patriarchal law. Instead, her writing becomes the banner of a critical inquisition of the power of performance, as this extends beyond the possibilities of structure. It is precisely those aspects of performance that cannot be formalized—dramatic upsets, lapses, surprises—that she takes on. Certainly, this turnabout from Eurocentric expectations offers a reminder of the cultural and the contextual limits of every theoretical strategy. It also suggests how theories (or bits of theories) can be retooled so as to be sensitive to locally significant challenges.

Induan Hiling intends her drawings as encapsulations of, or substitutes for, performance. The drawings, especially the more complex ones, are themselves shamanic ceremonies. Indeed, in the contrast between picture or script as ceremony, and the more conventional shamanic performance, Induan Hiling draws attention to the gendered grounds of Meratus ritual representation.

8.2   Flying over mountains, rocks, grass, and trees

In the complex drawing reproduced as Figure 8.2, Induan Hiling presents a complete ritual performance—a curing ceremony. She has drawn not only the mountain-vegetation opposition described above, but also the shaman who brings together tradition and inspiration. On each side of the drawing are rocks; the triangles dominating the landscape are mountains. On the rocks and mountains grow vegetation: At the peak of the darkest mountain is a wild fig tree; a wild palm grows on the mountain to its left, and herbs and grasses, including the plant that appears to have drifted off the top, are found near that mountain's summit. At the left of the picture, Induan Hiling has drawn the dreamer in the form of an airplane. The airplane-dreamer energizes and experiences the dream landscape. Meratus commonly describe airplanes as vehicles of spiritual travel. Here, the representation of spiritual travel empowers the drawing as a shamanic ritual. Induan Hiling's sister, who was suffering from leprosy, kept this picture as an aspect of her cure. The drawing is not meant as a reminder of a shamanic performance; it is itself a curing ritual.

The picture—particularly with its addition of the spiritual travel of the shaman—incorporates a number of key elements of more conventional performances. Yet, there are significant differences between this picture and a conventional performance. Most important, perhaps, the picture produces no dramatic action; it flattens the performance, abolishing performance time.

The time of the performance involves not just duration but the capture of attention. A successful ceremony establishes the centrality of the shaman within the attention of the audience. Indeed, the listeners often sleep; if they did nothing but sleep, however, the ceremony would be less effective. The listeners might just sleep—despite the beauty of the dance, the decorations, and the poetry—except for unpredictable elements in the performance and the possibility for dramatic upsets or excess. If the ritual preparations are badly done, for example, the spirit may be angry or even dangerous. Perhaps the shaman will be overwhelmed within his chant and fall into a faint, and it may be difficult to revive him. Unlike the decorations and chants, these elements are never described as being necessary to a ceremony. In fact, they involve messing up the rules, rather than following them. Still, they are key elements of performance time.

Dramatic upsets and excesses are the performance elements most clearly associated with male experience and male political advantage. Outside the context of shamanism, men, much more than women, use the threats and surprises of impressive speeches and angry outbursts to position themselves focally within social gatherings. When shamans improvise with their knowledge and ferocity, they call upon these dramatic talents to sustain the drawing power of the performance. This is not so much a matter of local gender rules as it is of men's ability to go beyond them, and thus lead the communities the rules circumscribe.[7]

Most performances require an entire night. That performance time is significant for gender privilege is suggested by the comment of one male shaman, that women tend not to become shamans because they do not want to stay up all night. He was ignoring the fact that pinjulang do stay up to accompany the shaman. But there is a difference in the wakefulness of the shaman and the wakefulness of his woman accompanist. The attention of the former is also attention-drawing—wakeful for the audience—while the latter is awake merely for herself and for the shaman. The ability to wake up the audience, at least sporadically, is a crucial skill of the shaman.

Sometimes women can seize the dramatic center. The possessed women with whom Induan Hiling began her spiritual career manipulated the attention of the audience with their wild dancing and bursts of spirit-inspired song. Without these excesses, Induan Hiling might not have had a platform from which to rise. Yet, most of the women, by representing themselves as inarticulate victims of spiritual power, were willing to lend credence to shamans' views of them as patients rather than as healers. Furthermore, the most ritually knowledgeable women, the pinjulang, avoided possession, thus reinforcing the idea that women could be either knowledgeable (and shy) or dramatic (and inarticulate), but not both knowledgeable and dramatic. Without gender-appropriate ways of bringing together dramatic self-presentation and claims to traditional knowledge, women have difficulty breaking into the mainstream of male-dominated spiritual expression.

Induan Hiling's work succeeds by sidestepping performance requirements that advantage men. Thus, even in its omissions, the work exposes gender asymmetries in the conditions of spiritual expression. In this regard, we see some of the advantages Induan Hiling gains by using the love-song format instead of the chant. If she feels more comfortable calling her chants dunang, "love songs," perhaps it is because the performance requirements of the two forms differ significantly—rather than because she cannot put together a conventional chant. Whereas shamans must convene a formal ceremony to perform chants, love songs are sung while caring for children, resting, and socializing with friends. Although both forms use an improvisational style that responds to context and audience, as well as the intentions of the singer, the kind of attention sought by shamanic chants and love songs is different. Love songs tease, flatter, soothe, and flirt, thus drawing attention to the subtle attractions of daily interaction. Shamanic chants alternately amaze, wheedle, praise, pontificate, or startle—all in an attempt to convene a spiritual community around the performance of the shaman. Induan Hiling's innovation has been to use informal daily contacts, the audience of love songs, as a community base for spiritual leadership. Because public ritual performance grants a privileged role to male expressive leadership, Induan Hiling, ingeniously, avoids it.

Her pictures bypass performance requirements even more clearly. They do away entirely with performance in favor of the codification of spiritual knowledge and authority. This codification has a number of significant features. First, Induan Hiling's drawings, unlike shamans' performances, are easily reproducible. She was happy to allow me to copy the drawings; in two cases, she requested my copy and gave me the original, because my copy was on cleaner paper and seemed likely to last longer. Second, her drawings work toward an impersonal visual author-

ity rather than the contextually grounded authority of shamanic dialogue. Although shamans may claim to chant time-honored traditional
poetry that cannot be altered, the performance, in fact, changes with the
purposes of the ceremony and the moods and motivations of both shaman and audience. In contrast, the drawings cannot change their shape as
they are called into different contexts of healing. (Interpretations, of
course, may change.) Third, Induan Hiling's drawings claim the authority of script. "Writing" gives her message the permanence of an artifact
and, at the same time, disengages it from performance politics.

In all these aspects of codification, writing becomes a woman's project
through which male privilege can be countered, evaded, and exposed. In
avoiding the shaman's task of drawing an audience through unpredictability and drama, the "writings" show these performance elements as
gender-asymmetrical conditions of expression. Induan Hiling's writing
encodes a form of resistance to male performance privilege.

Writing the horse of gaps

Induan Hiling's difficulty in breaking into the male-dominated domain of
ritual performance has encouraged her to develop new forms of ritual—
spiritual songs with love-song melodies, as well as pictures and texts that
invoke the authority of codification rather than performance. Her empowering spirit familiar, "the horse of gaps," is her ability to weave her
creativity in and out of the empty spaces of male-dominated modes of
expression.

My attention to Induan Hiling's use of such empty spaces was inspired
by the provocative work of Hélène Cixous, a feminist theorist who has
looked for female expression in the gaps and margins of male-dominated
signification. Induan Hiling's "writing," however, does not tempt me to
construct a theory of "female" expression similar to the pre-Oedipal *ecri-
ture feminine* of Cixous (1980). Instead, it points me away from an analysis limited to gender to attend to the ways that the gender-specific features of any cultural project are structured within a particular class and
ethnic situation. Induan Hiling's dreamwriting draws from a source of
authority which, while not extensively exploited by male Meratus shamans, is male-dominated. Her writing invokes the authority of the written word as used by government officials, traders, and settlers, all of
whom increasingly draw the parameters of Meratus possibilities.

Here, I return to the disturbing label "Made in China" in the margin of
Figure 8.1. No one in the Meratus Mountains besides me could read that

phrase; I imagine Induan Hiling copied it off of an item bought at market, perhaps a tin plate. Yet she knew it was foreign writing—the powerful foreign writing, in any language, with any message, that motivated her commitment to codification of Meratus tradition. Her dream of textualization grew within the challenge of competing foreign scripts. Indeed, just as dramatic excesses in performance reveal something of the conditions of shamanic expression, Induan Hiling's marginal notes reveal something of the conditions of representation for her own project.

The very unreadability of the rest of her written text (note that she could have formed letters) follows from its opposition to the foreign letters, also unreadable but in a different sense. Meratus say that when God handed out the Holy Books, the Meratus ancestor ate his and thus ensured both internal inspiration and its essentially unarticulated script. Induan Hiling's unreadable writing proposes an ethnic agenda in which Meratus Dayaks challenge and are challenged by powerful, literate foreigners.

This is an *ethnic* agenda, because it recomposes the Meratus as a distinctive group, aligned beside other groups as separate but equal under the nation-state's protection of ethnic pluralism. "Writing" is an important part of this agenda, since it constitutes Meratus with the same prerogatives as literate groups. The patronage of the state depends on the assumption that literacy is a precondition of appropriate citizenship. Induan Hiling's "writing" is an uppity, separate-but-equal literacy that could be seen as making fun of this requirement of cultural citizenship. As with her mentor, Uma Adang, however, play is a tool for serious business. This is even more evident in Induan Hiling's playful identification with the popular music star, Rhoma Irama.

To contextualize Induan Hiling's moves here, I must mention two kinds of popular music in Indonesia. One is commercially recorded popular music that is played on the radio and sold, even in backwoods weekly markets, on tape cassettes. Rhoma Irama was a big name in this field at this time.[8] The other kind of popular music is that identified with ethnic diversity in Indonesia. Along with architectural styles and costumes, state models of diversity legitimate an elaboration of music styles, as an appropriate expression of ethnic difference. At the time, it seemed possible to turn on the television on any day and find songs and dances of yet another ethnic group, each choreographed into bland similarities with only a shade of difference to remind the viewer of pluralism. Many an official reception is graced by a performance of "local culture" to honor the highest official present. Communities strain to turn local music, dance, and religion into something that can be performed for officials. To be a legitimate expression of ethnic identity, local culture must become harmless, officially sanctioned "entertainment."

Meratus have been spectators at the fringe of both cultural developments. There are radios and tape decks in the mountains. As of the early 1980s, there were no televisions and no official receptions; but mountain Meratus knew something of both cultural forms. Induan Hiling works from this vantage point. Her insight has been, first, to recognize that, to be officially recognized as local culture, shamanic performance must be a form of "entertainment," and, second, to bring the glittering attraction of commercial music[9] into the legitimating realm of ethnic "folk" performance.

"Irama," Induan Hiling said, is the name she was given in a series of dreams. The connection to Rhoma Irama seems to have been self-evident to her.[10] She spells the name out in Figure 8.2, where it takes the written form ASTARAMA (pronounced, she said, "Irama"), for this drawing was generated by herself as Irama. In some ways, this is an unsettling identification for a woman who has worked so hard to enter a male field. At that time, those aspects of Rhoma Irama's persona readily available in South Kalimantan suggested anything but a feminist consciousness. The posters I saw displayed in Banjar shops, for example, highlighted Irama's masculinity. In one, he is shown wearing a battle-stained headrag while fighting at the barricades. In another, he stands before a prayer rug with a woman kneeling at his feet. These gendered features were not relevant to Induan Hiling's incorporation of his identity; however, she was interested only in his charisma as an entertainer.

It is illuminating that Induan Hiling portrays herself as combining the inspiration of a shaman with the attraction of a rock star. The charismatic image of Rhoma Irama further explains Induan Hiling's use of love songs as shamanic text. Here, too, is a domain of power—nationally, if not locally. Induan Hiling's identification ties her singing performances to her project of shamanic codification. Love songs are more reproducible than shaman's chants, for they are not as shrouded in secrecy and pass easily from one singer to another. In calling herself Irama, Induan Hiling also draws attention to the mechanical reproducibility of recorded popular music, to which love songs can be compared. However, the "commodification" in which this codification takes part refers more to the political production of ethnicity than to the market economy. Her shamanism cum entertainment participates in an imagined state capitalism whose product is ethnicity.

Induan Hiling's attempts to connect ethnicity and entertainment are clearer in the comments with which she surrounded her songs than in the songs themselves. This was especially striking as we recorded some of the songs; she introduced herself and her songs on the tape with the formality of a cultural ambassador. She was sending these songs to America with me, she said, as part of her official duty and mine. She was explaining custom. She had been "ordered" to perform. The Indonesian term she used—*perintah*—is associated with government orders and not with the requests of parents, neighbors, and the like.

Once, we had a funny exchange in which she stopped singing and refused to go on until I had agreed formally with her that I had "ordered" her to continue. I felt uncomfortable ordering her; so we went back and forth until I finally figured out what I was supposed to say. Then she sang, "I've been ordered to perform custom," turning the phrase into a refrain. These performances, she stressed, were not for pleasure, but duty.

The word I translate as "perform" is the Indonesian *main*. I heard no other Meratus shaman use this term to describe shamanic performance. With this term, Induan Hiling brings together spirituality and entertainment. When she extends herself spiritually to Java through song—a conventional shamanic move—she sings that she is "performing Java." Thus, too, she "performs custom."

Some of her official-sounding talk about "custom" (*adat istiadat*) comes from Uma Adang, although Uma Adang's ethnic-codification project extends far beyond Induan Hiling's, with much more careful attention to a codified customary law and a religion that can talk back to Islam. Induan Hiling is a big fan of Uma Adang's and explicitly tries to reproduce her rhetoric. For example, in the song I have been quoting through much of this chapter, Uma Adang's rhetoric stands out in the last two verses. This section begins:

> Adu hai, let's sing,
> Swept by the wind, and
> Riding the horse of gaps, singing,
> Counting custom and tradition
> In forty-one paragraphs.
> The constitution of custom
> The law of tradition
> The prohibitions of the Basic Constitution.
> We'll stand on the center of the Five National Principles
> With our music to the world.

One can almost hear Uma Adang coming up with all the pompous-sounding words she has heard in government speeches: the Basic Constitution, the Five National Principles, even *custom* and *tradition*. The next part of the song continues Uma Adang's voice, with its talk of mysticism, theology, and, finally, esoteric syllables with no clear meaning. Induan Hiling is doing her best to "perform" Uma Adang. Only the last line of the section quoted above reminds me that this is Induan Hiling's song. She is still mimicking official talk; but she has returned the subject to entertainment. The presentation and preservation of local custom must take place, she implies, through the arts.[11]

"We are the same," Induan Hiling said, explaining her contrast with Uma Adang. "Only, I can 'play.' Uma Adang can do 'history.'" Like Uma Adang's "history," Induan Hiling's "play" is designed for an imagined state patronage. She conflates Rhoma Irama's electric music with ethnic folksongs and dances that take the form of state-designed people's culture. Why shouldn't she take Irama's successful image to present her ethnic music to the world?

Induan Hiling is not being childish. She came closer than any other Meratus I knew to appreciating an official model of ethnicity as entertainment and incorporating it into her own self-presentation. Ethnic groups *are* defined by music and dance styles; that is how they can present their distinctiveness appropriately. Induan Hiling's vision of ethnicity as entertainment is unusual in the Meratus context; yet it is close to an important official strand of thought about ethnicity in Indonesia.

Undomesticated ethnicity

Induan Hiling's shamanism promotes new understandings about Meratus relationships to literacy, ethnic performance, and the state. Is this a "female" ethnic agenda? This is a question one must approach with caution. It is particularly important to avoid overgeneralizing assumptions that women are somehow always disposed for or against a particular model of society. For example, a classic article by Edwin Ardener, from West African materials, suggests that models of society which stress rules and boundaries are men's models that ignore women's commitments to more fluid conceptions. "All [classificatory] ways of bounding society against society," he says, "may have an inherent maleness" (1975:6). Yet, sometimes women may be more articulate than men about social group boundaries. In her book about the *zar* possession cult of the northern Sudan, Janice Boddy (1989) argues that women who become possessed by alien spirits enact an allegory of local identity. The spirits define the integrity of local womanhood, as a symbol of the local group, by dramatizing all that is "Other." Women better express local identity than men, she says, because womanhood represents purity and enclosed spaces. Besides, unlike their men, who are involved in migrant labor and other travelling identities, women are more stable members of the local community. In this setting, women express their womanhood through concern about social boundaries.

At first glance, Induan Hiling's concern with shamanic codification seems to fit the latter model of gender difference. I have already established that male shamans and leaders shy away from models of ethnic boundedness so as to emphasize their connections with regional power. Male leaders do not position themselves within communities through contrast to outsiders; to do so would undercut their claims as leaders who continually expand their communities beyond all presupposed bounds. The commitment to expansion, rather than boundary maintenance, is part of how I understand the fact that I encountered no male attempts to codify Meratus shamanism as "difference." Given the regional and national pressures on Meratus to formulate ethnic identities, it makes sense that women like Induan Hiling and Uma Adang might become influential in reformulating Meratus shamanism as a reactive alternative to authoritative, outside models of civilization and ethnic identity. As women, they have far fewer opportunities to form ties with market traders, army officers, and bureaucrats—and thus less ability to cast themselves as brokers for these agents of power. Instead, they take advantage of a gap in male attention to draw from other regionally powerful models.

It is important to note that, unlike the Sudanese women described by Boddy, Induan Hiling does not represent Meratus womanhood in her spiritual expression. Although there are many ways that her shamanism is shaped by her status as a woman, she does not perform womanhood; she performs transcendence. She constitutes herself as an extraordinary person—that is, a shaman. Induan Hiling does not fight for the voices of ordinary women to be heard; she does not speak for women. Like male Meratus shamans, she is a shaman because she moves beyond ordinary limitations. She mediates between the vulnerability of the community and the power which she has the special talent to understand.

It is from this vantage point that one can see how Induan Hiling's notions of ethnic expression differ from what the state has in mind in promoting music-and-dance models of ethnic diversity. In the state model, ethnic expression should be the authentic, traditional music and dance of the people. When the people's traditional culture is placed under the sponsorship of the nation, the identities of communities are drawn into an appropriately disciplined national citizenship. Yet, contradicting this ideal, Induan Hiling offers inspired verse—music which, by definition, ordinary people do not know. Like male shamans, she mediates between the community and greater powers; she is not an exemplification of the community. Like male shamans, she composes her performances to tap locally unavailable sources of power. Like them, she emulates state models to help create her shamanic position; only, she has chosen a different set of state models. And—just as male shamans do—in her very attempts to tap outsiders' models of power and order, she makes these models unrecognizable to those same outsiders. Her codification of shamanism is not the version of ethnicity demanded by the state, with its assumptions of nationally disciplined identities for entire communities. Like her neighbor, The Bear, Induan Hiling imagines state administrative demands as a sporadic ritual best managed by a talented leader. That in her case the ritual can be read as a text does not change the shaman's self-positioning.

This is, perhaps, an undomesticated model of ethnicity. It cannot stand up to national ethnic standards, in part because it does not "domesticate" gender difference. The national model of gender requires a domestic complementarity between men and women: Men are heads of families, while women are wives and mothers. This model facilitates the use of domestic family households as a unit of administration, while also assuring the participation of both women and men (though in different ways) in projects of ethnic and national identity.

In contrast, Induan Hiling does not imagine a world of household heads and their wives. She works hard to show the irrelevance of gender difference as she proves herself a shaman. In claiming her father as a mentor, in reworking both standard shamanic chants and love songs, in creating drawings that substitute for performances—in all the strategies discussed, her goal is to erase gender privilege, not to reinstate gender difference. Her project in making it as a shaman has been to make gender less relevant to spiritual expression. The superficiality of her rapprochement with state ethnic models is due, in part, to her unwillingness to embrace deeper lines of gender identity.

Induan Hiling's is a "female" project; but it is not the only one around. The women with whom Induan Hiling was first possessed, but who never aspired to be shamans, also had "female" projects. Uma Adang has another, different, "female" project, one that attempts to come closer to national models of gender difference. In concert with this division, In-

8.3   *Spirit as soldier, shaman as star*

duan Hiling and Uma Adang construct their shamanism differently; Uma Adang's new gender lines depend on a transformation of shamanism even further away from its conventional performance features, toward a shamanism of etiquette, theological speeches, and law.

Before turning to Uma Adang, I can bring Induan Hiling's gender and ethnic challenges into clearer focus through a final image from one of her dream-inspired drawings. The drawing is presented in Figure 8.3.[12] This time, I begin my explication of the drawing's elements from the frame and work inward. At the bottom of the drawing, letters spell out "ruMAh bARu," literally, "new house" in Indonesian. I was unable to get Induan Hiling to help me understand just what meaning these letters had to her. (In answer to my questions, she said in various ways, "The spirits are guarding this mountain.") One way for me to think about them is as words that evoke the context of government development efforts that frame Induan Hiling's concerns with ethnic representation. She may have found the words in a schoolbook; perhaps she saw them on a project building somewhere en route to the coast.

Induan Hiling explained the numbers on the right, "100/30," as marking the 130 spirits she met in her dream; these numbers also show the framing context of literate, official forms of knowledge. Inside these contextualizing formalities, one sees the mountains and vegetation I have pointed out as key elements in all of Induan Hiling's drawing. Above the mountains and vegetation are three figures. Leading the way through the air is a fierce spirit, a soldier, an agent of state and spiritual power in the guise by which he is best known in the mountains. He carries weapons and wears what appears to be the flat velvet cap that Meratus interpret as marking national loyalty. Following the spirit is the shaman, the dreamer, in the shape of a multicolored star. Last in line is a chickenlike bird.

"The birds in flight are left behind," sing shamans in their chants, telling of the speed of spiritual flight. Induan Hiling reminded me of this line as we studied the picture; the bird cannot catch up with the spirit and the shaman. However, I think it also relevant that the bird is "like a chicken," as Induan Hiling described it. As The Bear explained, chickens are political dependents. In this sense, it seems reasonable to argue that the chicken represents the community. Induan Hiling, as the star-shaman, stands between the chicken-community and the soldier-spirit. She mediates between the community and power. She speaks for the community by not confining herself to it. It is important that, unlike male shamans, she makes no attempt to cast herself in the image of the soldier or to blur their distinctions. Male shamans tend to describe spirits, shamans, and chickens as all of a piece; the dramatic force of shamanic oratory pulls the shaman from one pole to another. Induan Hiling has separated discrete elements. As the star, she is altogether different from the soldier-spirit as well as from the chicken-community. Unlike male shamans, she attempts a more codified, "textual" knowledge. For this kind of knowledge to be simultaneously local and powerful depends on her mediating-yet-distinct positioning. Indeed, Induan Hiling's inspiration takes her riding into and above a gap—here, shown as the gap (*sawang*) between two mountains. In this gap, she can move beyond the ordinary constraints of gender. From this self-positioning, she surveys traditional knowledge—confirming, challenging, and transforming it with her creative skill.

9 THE HISTORY OF THE WORLD

Dayaks of the Meratus Mountains have no choice about dealing with issues of marginality. They are defined by their marginal status in nationally and regionally dominant ways of thinking. Articulate, ambitious Meratus women and men I met made the terms of marginality particularly explicit as they attempted alternative interpretations and forged creative self-positionings that could turn disadvantage into community leadership. No one I knew, however, went as far as Uma Adang in forcing self-consciousness about the conditions of marginality. All Meratus leaders copy foreign models of power to establish their own knowledge; but only Uma Adang goes so far as to copy them verbatim, taking the words out of foreigners' mouths and juxtaposing them wildly. The effect is disconcerting; it is a wall of broken mirrors fastened at odd angles, overlapping and askew. What visitor would not wince at her own stylized, distorted reflection?

Certainly, I felt self-conscious imagining myself collecting traditional knowledge from so strange an interlocutor. Yet Uma Adang was insistent in pushing me into my most ardent "anthropologist" guise, demanding interviews, with the formality of notes and tape recordings and careful repetitions of items not to be forgotten. She reminded me of the necessity and the power of the guise. Besides, she implied, there is a secret every cultural traveller should know. We won't talk of secrets, she whispered conspiratorially—not now, not here. Someone might be listening. To learn the power of the imagination is, perhaps, always a dangerous game, full of secrets. Indeed, she told me that rumors flew from disgruntled neighboring villages that she and I, working together, were communist spies or religious fanatics. Yet these rumors misinterpreted our work entirely. What I learned from Uma Adang's mentoring could be called oppositional or even protest, but it was not devotion to an underground cause. The committed alienation I saw in her is much closer to the sharp edge of parody. The secret of the guise is that there is a secret.

It might be useful to think of Uma Adang as crafting a "postmodern" eclecticism. Uma Adang flirts with those powerful "modern" discourses that are available in South Kalimantan—discourses that would have one embrace national, ethnic, or religious identities as badges of commitment to progress and reason—but she stacks together all these discourses, and much more, like items at a rummage sale. Most other Meratus leaders I knew worked somewhat harder for coherence in the self-identities they forged as they transformed the self-consciously foreign knowledge from which they drew; Uma Adang, instead, reveled in an identity of mimicking fragments. This "postmodernism" does not rest easily with the work of theorists who think in terms of evolutionary cultural steps. It is not an effect of electronic mass media, urban cosmopolitanism, refugee displacements, or late-capitalist consumption patterns. It does not follow on the heels of a hegemonic modernism; nor is it the signal for a new era of thought in South Kalimantan. If it is a postmodernism, it is one that nips at the pretensions of cultural periodizations and refuses their hegemony. Perhaps this kind of mocking, and self-mocking, style has long existed in the cracks and accommodations of colonizing modes of knowledge.

The postmodernism of marginality does not displace the coherence of modern dominance and exclusion; rather, it refracts modern dominance from other angles. Where artists and architects of the center might devote their attention to the *form* of fragmentation, from a position at the periphery too much is at stake in particular compositions and decompositions. The eclectic fragments of marginality argue for survival. Even their deconstructions press for a space to stand on the (already undermined) platform of power. If this is parody, it is no joke but a gesture of respect toward how much imagination it takes to stay alive.

Such fragmented refractions from the margins mark a meeting place for two key agendas in recent social theory. One agenda ("social history") attends to the agency of ordinary people, arguing that they are not mere puppets of great leaders or great structural forces.[1] This work explores everyday strategies and subcultural styles of resistance; it asks about the roles of such strategies and styles in reconstructing hegemonies and transforming structures of domination. The other agenda ("post-

structuralism") pursues the construction of this agency through subject-
producing discursive practices; agency can exist only within the fields of
power and knowledge that make it imaginable and effective.[2] In recent
years, advocates of each approach have criticized the other.[3] Together,
they have set the challenge of retaining a focus on political transformation at the same time as refusing to treat the interests and identities of
oppressed groups as self-evident.

Uma Adang's "postmodern marginality" requires an analysis that
looks both ways. She claims an agency crafted from the fragments of
dominant discourse. Her marginal discourse is less coherent and less autonomous than is the political consciousness imagined by much resistance
theory. At the same time, the discourse is more serious, more engaged,
than the ironic (self-)mocking sometimes associated with poststructuralism. The political subjects Uma Adang constructs—the neighborhood
community, the village, the ethnic group—demand protection from the
state, from religion, from hallowed local custom. Their demands simultaneously reproduce, ridicule, and refuse the constraints and categories of
everyday domination. They are completely committed at the same time as
they draw attention to their own constructedness.

What is needed here is an analysis that can look back and forth between parody and passion.

The history of the world

> Welcome . . . including "To the honorable" speaking in the history
> of the world. (*Wassalam bermasuk kepada yang terhormat menga-
> takan dalam sajarah dunia.*)

The commitments of Uma Adang's provocations, both bizarre and serious, are forged in the way she uses words to create new forms of attention and, thus, new strategic forms of community. Her words conjure up
audiences who are awkwardly, tentatively repositioned in relation to regional and national discourses which require certain kinds of communities. In this conjuring act, it is not her words themselves that design new
identities, but, rather, the acts of remembering and forgetting—other
words, genres, stories, memories, or current events—involved in listening
to them.

Uma Adang's innovations are both ordinary and eccentric. All Meratus shamans experiment as they manipulate and borrow powerful knowl-

edge. Uma Adang, however, goes farther than most in creating new forms of speech, new regional positionings, new local and global "histories." Unlike other shamans, she participates little in public performances of shamanic chants. She "directs" large festivals, telling everyone what to do and adding her speeches and prayers; she chants in small ceremonies held by close kin and allies. Like Induan Hiling, though, Uma Adang avoids conventional public shamanship. Her leadership depends on public oral presentations: speech-prayer chants in a genre of her own making. These speeches are formal and carefully formed; some are also nearly incoherent. Because they deploy regionally known genres of political and religious talk, they sound familiar. Yet, it is often hard to tell what they are about, since they combine genres in an incongruous, disorienting way.

This doubled sense of familiarity and disorientation is key to audience interest in her speeches. Everyone knows that something important is happening, but no one knows exactly what. The incomprehensible chanting of Arabic-sounding words ("*al ai se na el ha*") must be "religion." The mind-teasing abbreviation of ordinary words (*satu* ["one"] is *sat*; *tutup* ["close"] becomes *tup*) must be "magic." The invocation of dates, titles, and formal-sounding words must be national "politics." In the awkward, strained use of Indonesian official language, one catches the pedantic coughs of the politician somehow caught in the midst of a stilted official letter:

> To the honorable ["Dear Sir"],
> everyone [?],
> from the Gentlemen, the Citizens, the Ladies,
> the Younger Brothers and Sisters who are Attending,
> above the sentence . . .
> (*Kepada yang terhormat untuk so-isi dari bapak-bapak dan saudara-saudara ibu-ibu adik yang menghadiri diatas kalimat . . .*)

Or the accelerating exaggerations of the preacher:

> The history . . . has been enacted, or spread, through the state, or the country, above the great cities, to give announcement, or to let it be known, so that the prophet Lahat of God will be worshipped every day and every night. (*Sajarah . . . sudah berlaku dilabarkan antiru negara ataupun negeri di atas kota-kota besar untuk diberikan siaran atau diberitahu supaya nabi lahat dar alah untuk disembah setiap hari dan malam.*)

Or the mystery of the melodiously sung Koran, but with Indonesian magical words peeping through:

> *Walnabi ma la wasi diri kun ta allah assei di wal diri asal di untuh puhun dari kurat kun. Wala allah walah kun ta'allah. Wasei di lakun sidir kun tum alamun. Wallahsei dat alam sei dat gumi sekidat air kuntar dit dat.*

This verse, sung with a plausibly "Koranic" melody, is untranslatable; yet, it is laced with familiar Indonesian words, such as *alam* ("world") and *air* ("water"), and with such Islamic terms as *Allah* ("God") and *kun* ("Come into being!"). This is not Meratus.[4] Neither are the other quotations above; they are intended to be Indonesian—foreign, formal, powerful. Further, in trying to stress the nonlocal features of the national language, Uma Adang invents unique pronunciations, prepositions, and verb forms. I have included the original language so that conversant readers can get a sense of her strange usages; neither my transcription nor my translation, however, captures all of this awkward play with language.[5]

These playful, disorienting genre-twisters are aimed at creating a savvy, knowing audience at the edge of cosmopolitan power. A number of elements recur in shaping this effect. *Mimicry* is Uma Adang's tool for constructing new relations of intertextuality; it acknowledges the power of varied genres. In contrast, *secrecy* obscures and mystifies her genre repositionings, as it only half-reveals her commitments to any position. What ties these two together is the nonsense aspect of her talk—its awkwardness, grandiosity, and sporadic incomprehensibility. This aspect reminds a listener that this talk is about social and textual positioning, not explication. Listening to Uma Adang, one begins to think that all talk is positioning: over-told mimicry and half-told secrets.

These experiments in form require new talents from Uma Adang's audiences. Like the speeches of other Meratus leaders, they show power as external to the familiar and the local. Yet, here, the familiar, local community of listeners is not portrayed as awed potential victims of external power. Instead, Uma Adang's speeches call for a community of listeners who are full participants in national and regional genres. The "community" thus conjured moves closer to the inspiring Other. It is as close as a mimic's speech is to its original.

Uma Adang advocates new forms of sociality which have a chance under the government's ever-widening gaze. Her programs sponsor "community" institutions, such as a rice swidden (the "Unity Field") shared collectively by each neighborhood. Here, she blesses the Unity Harvest:

> Asking for peace and perfection
> to fall on the Unity Adat,
> For the harvest to be even across the entire village,
> so that we can become a village [*berkampung*].

Creating unified, level communities requires further experiments in forging ethnicity and gender as forms of solidarity. Uma Adang works hard to conjure an ethic of pluralism to create complementary niches: male and female, Banjar and Meratus. Yet, she knows, as do those around her, that the forms she advocates—however powerful their national backers—are not locally internalized "identities." At most, they are forms of proper etiquette to be guarded carefully on the occasion of public ceremonies. As people preen and squabble over the correct rules of propriety, their inventedness becomes obvious. For cultural analysts immersed in presumptions about the solidity of gender, ethnic, and community identities, such mocking yet serious etiquettes can be a sobering denaturalization of familiar categories.

This is accommodation; this is resistance. Many social movements borrow their terms of community-building from dominant discourses but use such discourses to serve partially subversive ends. This is passion; this is parody. Where the idea of the unified "community" is absurd (in the Meratus Mountains, where are such "communities"?) serious "community" organizing runs easily into parody. Incongruity does not translate well, however. Parody is interesting only within the constraints and contradictions of a local setting. Socially engaged parody is a constant reminder of the "local" through which global histories emerge.

The purposeful incongruities and disorientations of Uma Adang's speeches are difficult to analyze from a perspective within the speeches. The kinds of speeches I am talking about are not "poetry," in the Bakhtinian (1981) sense of a genre aimed at achieving a unified voice from which to make its statements.[6] These fragment-filled speeches resemble a string of graffiti more than they do a continuous narrative; each segment hints at wider stories but offers only their sign. To follow them, the listener must shuttle between the words themselves and what they evoke or erase: other stories, prayers, memories, social programs, arrangements. Neither a poetics of Uma Adang's words nor a social analysis that explains them away can follow this shuttling. Instead, my inquiry blurs distinctions between text and context to travel in "the alien words, value judgments and accents" which Bakhtin eloquently describes as the "dialogically agitated and tension-filled environment" the word encounters "in its path toward its object" (1981:276).

The history of the world

The most important source of insight and spiritual power for Uma Adang is what she calls *sajarah*, "history." Sajarah is what she learns from the voices of Majapahit and the various prophets who speak to her in their divergent languages and genres. From these sources she has reconstructed the "history of the world" (*sajarah dunia*). It was this history that she offered me to complete my task as a student searcher on a mission backed by generals and presidents.

When Uma Adang first dictated the history of the world to me, I did not realize that she intended it as a text; it seemed improvised and choppy. Only after she had repeated it on several occasions—with considerable consistency among versions—did I learn to view her history as a single unit of composition. Even then, I underestimated its importance. Perhaps I still hoped to find something archaic or locally unique. After all, how could an obscure woman from the Meratus Mountains have anything useful to teach about the history of the world?

Uma Adang's history of the world is easy to ignore, not only because she is obscure and unimportant, but also because the text is a miscellany of fragments. It is easy to ignore because this miscellany threatens to expose the embarrassing quirkiness of internationally accepted stories of world history. It is easy to ignore, too, because, although it creates niches of autonomy from global hegemonies, the niches created are not the solutions to the world's ills of which romantics dream, but, rather, are specific to the current needs of an obscure place. It creates no heroes but instead comments on continual processes of displacement. Yet, for all these reasons, Uma Adang was correct, that what I needed to learn was her history of the world. The story teaches an extraordinary mode of creating commentary.

History everywhere is a political matter. Benedict Anderson (following Walter Benjamin) draws attention to secular conceptions of "homogeneous, empty" time associated with the rise of modern nationalism; he contrasts these conceptions with cosmologically structured temporal notions associated with empires (1983:28–40). Each conception creates a separate story of history. Thus, too, Nick Dirks (1990) argues that secular, linear chronologies as "history" are "a sign of the modern." Yet, in any political situation, however closely associated it is with modern nations, historical logic may be complex and contested. Certainly, in many contexts in Indonesia, the logic of empires vies and blends with nationalist logic. The prominence of a national-development framework provokes a vocabulary of progress in which history moves up a straight path, leaving the archaic and the backward behind. At the same time, citizens are invited to participate in the state's legacy of once and future kingdoms. An army-sponsored volume on South Kalimantan, for example, begins with the founding of the Banjar kingdom and its principles, still alive today. The opening poem asks each soldier to see himself as the reincarnation of an officer of the ancient court (Manihuruk et al. 1962:8). Uma Adang's confusing historical logics join an already established fray. The voices of Majapahit, which instruct her in reclaiming the empire's time for her own benefit, may also have instructed a considerable number of generals and presidents.

Uma Adang, however, throws together too many kinds of time for most generals to understand. She includes folktales, genealogies, and religious tracts, along with imperial and secular chronologies. They fit together awkwardly, challenging one another's assumptions. In many ways, she remains a shaman travelling through her chant; instead of travelling across the space of a spiritual landscape, however, Uma Adang travels in time. Just as more conventional Meratus shamans refuse the boundaries separating the body, the local, the regional, and the foreign, Uma Adang confuses chronology and structure. Her history moves, but it does not go in only one direction. She plays with metaphors of descent and ascent, so that one is never sure whether either metaphor takes one closer to the present. She takes on the spiritual power of different kinds of time, just as more conventional shamans "borrow" the power of different kinds of space. Nevertheless, Uma Adang's history is deliberately less coherent than the chant of an ordinary shaman. Her history borrows the forms, as well as the places and peoples, of regional and national power.[7]

I turn to the history of the world, then, as a way of exploring the self-conscious construction of a margin through the recalling of multiple, intertwined, but never fully articulated "histories." The version I use is a short one which Uma Adang asked me to record; thus I can give the entire text as I transcribed and translated it. The speech was spoken gravely and very slowly. It may be useful to the reader to speak Uma Adang's sections word by word. This is not a narrative but a proclamation, a list, a holy book, a petition. It demands a wandering, yet awestruck, attention. Between segments, I move back and forth among the stories the speech cues, other stories they cue, stories they do not cue, and the social programs with which all this cueing and noncueing intersects. Each section of the speech is a starting point for my exploration of Uma Adang's repositionings.

The history of the world

> Now the history of the world will be opened
> beginning with Adam and Hawa.
> In the beginning were Adam and Tikhawa
> who had children, the forty-one *nabi*.
> Forty-one nabi, altogether the nabi were forty-one.

In a complexly interconnected world, the vegetation of creation is not the forest primeval but an overgrown garden of weeds, an abandoned lot. Who can be surprised that the origin of the world is most majestically revealed in a weedy, abandoned heap of stories? Where stories are corrupted and corroded, debased and degraded, a coarse yet ingenious alchemy of illegitimate concoctions is formed. In Uma Adang's weedy heap, origin stories give birth to each other, while refusing the possibility of a prehistory that predates their own skirmishes.

Even Meratus ought to know that God created the world, and the Word, from nothingness. Here is how The Bear begins it: "The heavens did not exist yet. There was only God. And the world was emptiness going above and going below. 'Hai,' said God, 'I want to make the world.' And then God said, 'What shall I use as my place to stand?' God looked down three times and looked up three times. And then God said, 'I wish a place to stand.' God said, *'Nur Jaya Alah,'* and there was wind. That was the name of the wind. And there was a shelf of wind for God to stand upon, and only then did God stand. . . ." God's word is the oneness that precedes all difference and deference. Uma Adang cuts off this tip and begins in the middle with the two.

Adam and Hawa are the Muslim world's first couple. Meratus call the woman "Tihawa"; except for the first occurrence here, I heard Uma Adang name her "Tikhawa." For those who have read the scriptures, Tihawa's name is an ethnic blunder, a joke. I was alerted to this by Banjar anthropologist H. Nor'ied Radam, who pointed out that Banjar speak of "Siti Hawa" to offer Hawa a female honorific title. Meratus hear the name as "Si Tihawa," in which *Si* signals the name of a person—particularly, an "ordinary Joe." By mishearing and misinterpreting the respectful title, Meratus rename the lady a peasant. In the weedy heap of stories, she rises again, stinking of butchered boars.

Christian scripture, too, spreads widely and unevenly. Many Meratus have heard that Tihawa was created from Adam's rib. Not so Uma Adang, who found this story a foolish debasement of the woman. Removal of a rib was just the opening for the operation, she explained. God was looking for Adam's heart, which was split down the middle like an areca nut. Certainly, the first woman would have a full complement of internal organs.

Who knows all the sources of Meratus tales of Adam and Eve—Muslim, Christian, local, idiosyncratic? Though unfamiliar to me, some were regionally widespread and crossed ethnic lines. Such, for example, was the popular story of Adam's iron penis: When Adam first tried to have intercourse with Tihawa, she refused him because of his iron penis. She ran off, and he chased her. In their running, they spread out the dot of earth at the base of the pillar separating earth and sky which had been their home. They stomped out mountains and valleys and widened the earth to its present size. Only when God exchanged Adam's iron penis for a fleshy one did Tihawa agree to stay with him. One Balanghan Dusun version I heard was more gender-balanced: Tihawa had an iron vulva to match Adam's iron penis. Neither was satisfied with the other until their parts were exchanged for flesh. Even idiosyncratic stories such as Uma Adang's account of Adam's heart are crafted from regionally familiar materials.

Adam and Tihawa had forty-one children, the *nabi*. Nabi is a common term from the regional warehouse of stories: At least three kinds of nabi form a frame for endless bricoleur-like combinations. The government tells of the "prophets" (nabi) that legitimate each official religion. The Christian nabi is Jesus; the Muslim nabi is Muhammad. One can hardly have a "religion" without one. Uma Adang has invented her own Meratus nabi of this sort—Nabi Lahat. He is flanked by two associate nabi with more scriptural names: Daud ("David") and Dar Alah. But the last two draw on a second meaning of nabi, which contradicts the first. Muslims in South Kalimantan do not consider Muhammad a nabi; he is the *Rasul Allah*, the messenger of God. Nabi instead refers to Adam and his notable descendants, including Abraham and Jesus, who, genealogically, lead to Muhammad; all told, there are twenty-five nabi. Yet, in the Meratus Mountains, a third kind of nabi is better known; every kind of plant and animal has its nabi, or guardian spirit. The proliferation of different species, each according to its kind, is in the hands of these nabi.

The identity of the forty-one nabi children flickers through the garbled, inauthentic territory around these nabi types. Like Muslim nabi, the children—or, at least, the first forty—are descendants of Adam. They appear, however, in one generation and become the guardians, if not the prophets, of human diversity. Their story is a common one told throughout the Meratus area:

Of the forty children, twenty were boys and twenty were girls. Some were beautiful, some were ugly. Adam and Tihawa planned to marry off the pretty ones to the ugly ones, to even out the children's inheritance. But the two most beautiful eloped; then the next most beautiful eloped, and so forth, until only the two ugliest were left at the base of the pillar between the earth and the sky. The descendants of those who eloped are the other peoples of the earth, including the Javanese, Banjar, Dutch, Chinese, and Americans. Those who stayed are the ancestors of the Meratus.

This self-deprecating story brings ethnic asymmetry back to the beginning of the world. Yet, too, there is a measure of equality among the sons and daughters of Adam and Tihawa. There is material here for a subversively pluralist vision which challenges the discriminatory policies of God's better-known peoples and prophets.

Moreover, sometimes the underrated have a special magic. Thus it seems for the not-yet-mentioned forty-first child, whose story brings the discussion back to the imaginative construction of the world. A Meratus favorite, it is told in countless versions ranging from the flash of recognition in the knowing exchange of the nabi's secret name to the wanderings of an evening's shamanic journey. The magic of the forty-first nabi presages Uma Adang's own magic in inventing new conceptions of power and community.

After the forty brothers and sisters were married and grown, Tihawa had another child, Nabi Bungkun. This child had neither arms nor legs but was round like a watermelon. (I call the child "it" to mark the fact that it was neither male nor female; no such pronoun-awkwardness is necessary in Meratus.) When Nabi Bungkun was grown, it began to ask about its inheritance. But Adam and Tihawa had already given all the inheritance to the forty brothers and sisters. Nabi Bungkun called them together to ask for a share of the inheritance, only to learn that the brothers and sisters had spent their shares. There had been gold, silver, and diamonds, they admitted; but these things were gone. The youngest child thought about this. Finally, Nabi Bungkun asked the brothers and sisters if they would agree to a plan. If it could think of anything that had not already been divided, would not this belong to the youngest child? The brothers and sisters agreed. Then the forty-first child said, "Who owns the heavens and the earth?" These had not been divided, for no one had ever thought of owning them. So Nabi Bungkun became the owner of the heavens and the earth. Whoever wants wealth from the heavens and the earth must seek permission from this nabi.

The moral is simple, yet elegant: Effectively reconceptualize wealth and power, and they are yours.

Yet, there is also a secret. Perhaps it is well known, but it was always told to me in great privacy and with awe. The secret is that Nabi Bungkun is not hard to find; it is right in our midst. Nabi Bungkun is the iron rice pot that always hangs at the hearth; it provides the strength to search the heavens or the earth for our daily luck and livelihood.

◆

> And our nabi is Nabi Lahat.
> Nabi Lahat is the one to whom we bow,
> To Nabi Lahat Dar Alah.
> Nabi Lahat descended to Nabi Daud.
> Then Nabi Daud originated women's shamanism.
> That is the name of this voice;
> Nabi Lahat has come down to our shamanism,
> Nabi Daud is our voice. And our words of adat.

Here, Uma Adang is speaking a defensive theology bred at the borders of Banjar Islam and missionary Christianity. The history of the world has moved into the history of religious prophets, and Uma Adang wants her share. This is how, in one of her explanatory moods, she put it: "The Christian nabi are Jesus, Moses, and Jacob [Isa, Musa, Yakub]. The Muslim nabi are Muhammad, Yosuf, and Darun. The *Kaharingan* [Dayak religion] nabi are Lahat, Daud, and Dar Alah." As far as I know, Lahat, the primary prophet of Meratus religion, is Uma Adang's idiosyncratic discovery. Nabi Daud resonates with the scriptural King David. Sometimes, "Dar Alah," as in the version above, is a part of Lahat's name and sometimes it is a separate "voice" coming out of history.

This is a strange history which moves in many directions, refusing linear chronology. Lahat "descends" to Daud, Uma Adang said. In at least one version, Daud then "rises" to Dar Alah, who then "descends" to the shaman Mambur, whose genealogy brings her story to the time of male shamans. "This history," she explained, "rises and descends, rises and descends. From the top, it descends to the bottom. Then from the bottom, it rises to the top. Then three times, it descends again."

This is a history that rides uneasily on another set of tales, which, to Uma Adang, do not count as "history"—the stories people tell about their lives and about the lives of their immediate forebears. "History" does not acknowledge these tales, but it depends on them. Although we spoke little of this time, Uma Adang must have been a young teenager when her eastern Meratus area was overrun by Ibnu Hajar's Muslim rebels (*Gurumbulan*) in the late 1950s. Meratus neighborhoods just upstream dispersed; many lived hidden in the forest for several years. The regional government—fractured by tactics of undercover support for the rebels amid its open deterence—lost direct control of the area as the Jakarta-directed army moved in. In counterpoint, the rebels drew from and augmented a regional Islamic pride, as well as dissatisfaction with secular, centralizing trends in the building of the nation. (To the rebels, the nation, all too often, seemed to reproduce the colonial authority the nationalist fighters had just overthrown.) This was a time of Islamic prophecy and magic. Combatants and noncombatants alike relied on religious amulets and charms to protect themselves from the uncertainties of gunfire. Meratus learned to respect the power and terror of Islamic resurgence. Years after armed rebellion was stifled, the lessons about the power of religion remain clear.

More recent events serve to underline the political necessity for religious dialogue with Banjar to defend Meratus rights and resources. In the late 1970s, Banjar from the crowded west-side plains immigrated in increasing numbers to the eastern Meratus forests. Timber roads allowed immigrants motor-vehicle access deeper into the forest. The administrative realignment of the early 1980s created more district seats in the area, with their promise of offices and markets. Besides the future hope of government services, administrative centers offered immigrants the more immediate promise of state protection against Meratus land and resource claims: As far as the regional government was concerned, the land was open and free. The 1980s was a time, then, of growing ethnic tensions in the eastern Meratus area. Meratus leaders throughout the area were worried about rights to land and resources. These leaders knew no one would listen to their demands as long as they were devalued as primitive pagans, outside the cosmopolitan world of knowledge and religion. This is the context in which it seemed so important to Uma Adang to establish a religious pluralism in which Meratus have their own prophets.

Yet, religious discussion was not as transparent a political instrument as this might sound; religious talk overflowed political categories and redefined them. Religion refused politics while reshaping it through secret revelations. The countryside was rife with what Uma Adang and her neighbors called *politik*—"secrets," "codes," "hidden agendas." Politik refers to "politics" in the national language, but these rural secrets were not at all "political" in the cosmopolitan sense of the term. This was not the straightforward talk of elections, of the police, or policies on family planning to which a political scientist or a student activist might be drawn. Instead, secrets took the form of inspired religious revelation, hidden names, and magic numbers. The form cross-cut religious and ethnic lines, forging possibilities for dialogue as well as disparagement. In some ways, they formed a regional "antipolitics" of silences and whispers that seemed at once so irrelevant to political concerns and yet so central. Power, it was whispered, is that which cannot be spoken about aloud.

Two contexts are particularly relevant to understanding the "antipolitics" of politik secrets. One is the mystic Islamic tradition that is widespread in the Malay–Indonesian countryside—and that was regionally used and developed by Ibnu Hadjar's rebels. This tradition has long both obscured and cultivated its political possibilities. Here, power is, by definition, a secret. The other context is the political silences which, throughout the country, followed the mass killings of 1965–66, in which the nation rid itself of communists and potential communists. Here, to speak of power is a dangerous crime. Within these contexts, the evasions of Uma Adang's pronouncements seem ordinary. That she invokes a religiously potent past which might shape an empowered future seems politically inspired.

Yet there is something more. The space of secrets is a fertile place for creating grand-sounding nonsense. The scope of Uma Adang's claims call attention to the frailty of the institutions available to her for developing these claims. Great visions offered by small shamans are, perhaps by definition, nonsense. It is here that the revelation of secrets turns to religious and political parody.

◆

Here is women's shamanism, which may be revealed or broadcast. Anyone who wants to hear, please go ahead:

> The incense is not casually burnt,
> The incense is not casually turned to smoke.

Burning smoke to make a bridge,
Burning incense to make a porch,
Let it fall circling the house,
Let it fall circling the hall,
Let it fall becoming a bridge.
Counting out the porches,
Counting out the bridges,
Where is the first spirit?
Stand up to become a porch, the spirit.
Counting out the bridges of the shaman.
I'm inviting the girl who orders the hall,
I'm inviting the one who orders the house,
Who orders the protected world.
Going out [unintelligible] along the porch,
Heading for the flowers of the great hall,
Crossing the bridge of the great wind.
Its porch is beautiful.
Asking for clean water,
Borrowing cleansing water,
Clean water to cleanse and purify,
To purify the protected world,
To purify the fenced-in world, seven villages,
    seven countries.
Appealing to you every night,
Appealing to you every day,
Excuse me, spirit.

That was the shaman praising Nabi Lahat or Nabi Daud for the original women's *dukun* shamanism from the era of the year seventy million seventy million that includes seventy million seven million years of women's shamanism.

Nonsense continues in a new genre. Uma Adang has switched from a chantlike speech to a chant within a speech. Sandwiched between the pompous proclamations of the opening and closing lines, the shamanic chant sounds about as conventional—even "traditional"—as anything I heard from Uma Adang. Yet this is "women's shamanism," one of Uma Adang's uniquely inspired creations. No one else living practices this "women's shamanism."

I could have been disappointed. For days I had been begging Uma Adang to teach me a little of this "women's shamanism"—her special talent, the secret of her difference. But a secret revealed is always disappointingly familiar; secrets describe the power we already know. Uma Adang's obliging response to my request was to offer the history of the world, which I had already heard several times; this time, though, the lines of shamanic chant were inserted. They were familiar lines. Earlier I had played a tape for her of The Bear chanting dewa shamanism. In this instance, Uma Adang's "women's shamanism" sounds very much like The Bear's dewa.[8] She had a fine ear for detail, as well as a strong competitive streak. On another occasion, Uma Adang did "women's shamanism" in the form of Koran chanting, and then what sounded like Bible reading in a foreign language. By then it made little sense for me to be surprised that the unique, the mysterious, the original and the originary would turn out to be a mimic's careful reproduction. In my own mimicry, I might note that it is authoritatively said that Derrida said it: "Everything begins with reproduction" (1978, quoted in Smith 1988, quoted in Strathern 1991:1).

Mimicry can create authority; it can also turn into play and even mockery. The distinctions are subtle. We listen for exaggeration, for unexpected mixing of genres, for fragments taken out of context. Uma Adang uses all these techniques but without falling into slapstick or other publicly self-conscious humor. She is completely serious and expects her listeners to be, too. Yet, she carefully overdoes her improvisation to highlight the importance of form in the modes of authority she both draws upon and exposes. Why set the stage seventy million seventy million years ago? We had been having a conversation about birds in which I introduced the idea that life on earth could be measured in millions of years. Earlier, Uma Adang had told the history of 777 years, sometimes even 7,777 years. Here, though, she adopted and stretched my historical knowledge until it was recognizable only as an artificial form—one more alien, yet local, guise.

By surrounding the shaman's chant with a speech, Uma Adang dislocates that text as well. A chant lays a shaman's path with words. But Uma Adang's chant leads only to itself; it is an example of a chant, an artifact of shamanic knowledge, a sign only of its cultural specificity. It is not fortuitous that Uma Adang's agenda in this recalls Induan Hiling's experiments, which I called shamanic "codification," or even "commodification." As Induan Hiling's mentor, Uma Adang takes the codification project further, turning shamanic travel into a semiotic object for examination or display.

The difference between the projects of the two women is also striking. Induan Hiling's shamanism is not "women's shamanism"; her endeavor is to ungender the shamanic enterprise and develop the spiritual power that men have monopolized. In contrast, Uma Adang professes to perform a distinctly gendered shamanic style, claiming it as separate but certainly no less than equal.

To even imagine "women's shamanism" requires that Uma Adang dispose of many of the ordinary ideas and practices of Meratus shamanship. For example, she acknowledges women's ambivalent relationship to knowledge-creating travel by avoiding shamanic travel chants in favor of proclamations and prayers, spells and speeches. Yet she cannot merely reposition herself in relation to established conventions; she is forced to reinvent gender in order to make sense of a system in which women's spiritual accomplishments are parallel to men's.

She builds from available materials. Gender complementarity is a principle of adat and the division of labor throughout the Meratus area. Uma Adang enlarges the scope and significance of gender complementarity by encouraging new forms of propriety that might become avenues of gender-segregated creative agency. She insists, for example, on gender-segregated seating. Even in informal gatherings in her house, women sit against one wall, and men sit against another; she sits in the middle. (At Uma Adang's bidding, I sat next to her.) Clearly, she is not all-powerful. Her success in this arrangement draws on the existence of other gender-segregated socializing in the east-side Meratus–Banjar border area, an area influenced by Banjar and east-side Dusun. Nor is she always successful. For example, at ceremonies I attended, she pronounced that people should eat in four groups: male adults, female adults, male children, and female children. Adult men and women did, in fact, eat separately—much to my surprise, since I associated this arrangement only with Banjar. However, children of both genders ate with the women, as is customary among Banjar.

Uma Adang invented "women's shamanism" within the dewa tradition, which features the gendered counterpoint of male shamans and female pinjulang accompanists and sometimes inspires women's as well as men's efforts to contact spirits. Yet despite its precedence, this discursive shift toward gender complementarity is an effort that can be measured as much by its failures as by its successes. For example, on several occasions I was present when Uma Adang tried to coax other women into becoming apprentices in "women's shamanism." She was met by shy silences and awkward stutterings even from devoted friends. No other local woman had seriously taken up the calling. The women were willing to follow Uma Adang's rules of propriety, but they had not begun to think of themselves as "female" creative subjects, that is, as potential women shamans.

Equally problematic for Uma Adang's plan was the fact that, in numerous gatherings I attended—as in Meratus assemblies elsewhere—women sat around the outside of the group making jokes or otherwise ignoring the central proceedings. Men's talk remained the focal point of community affairs, which forced Uma Adang to join that talk in order to show herself a community leader, thus reproducing the asymmetry. (On several occasions, she pulled me away from a group of women to go with her to join the men.) Ideals of gender complementarity had not reorganized community politics.

In practice, gender symmetry may be shaky; but Uma Adang insists on the principle. For her, symmetry is not an invention but a revelation, a discovery. Beneath the ebb and flow of social life, there is a code, a secret. It is the key to one's personal magical science (*ilmu*), as well as to understanding the world. It is the underlying mechanical model that, even half-revealed, empowers the knower. This is the secret of Dualities (*dua-dua*). Since Adam and Tihawa, the first man and woman, the world has been organized by the symmetrical duality of gender. All other dualities follow: maturity and youth, sun and rain, day and night, life and death.

Twice, I watched Uma Adang teach the Dualities as a core secret, the deep structure of the world. Each time, she listed a number of oppositions, including gender and some of the others above, leaving her audience to chime in as they got the idea with oppositions of their own. "Good and bad," said one man, "big and little; vulva and penis." "Humans and rice," added another.[9] "Rich and poor," suggested a third, and mining this rich vein of thought, he continued: "Gold and diamonds . . . silver and iron . . . silver and lead." The listeners were excited, jumping in with the enthusiasm of university students learning about structuralism for the first time. At each suggestion, Uma Adang nodded approvingly, with the wisdom of a professor who embraces all interpretations. It could have been a send-up of my own training, in which, according to many hoary authorities, dualities really do structure the experience of the native but at such a deep, all-pervasive level that the native cannot explain them, much less invent them as a speculative science.

"Structuralism is the thought guaranteed by the state," wrote philosopher Guy deBord from the heartland of French civilization (1970:202). Indeed, Uma Adang's dualities anxiously anticipate state guarantees.

♦

> Then there came to be adat from Majapahit,
> including in Majapahit:
> number one, iron statues,
> second, iron ladles,
> third, dragon daggers,
> fourth, china plates,
> fifth, pomegranate rings,
> sixth, carved scrapers,
> seventh, several kinds of iron goods made
>   by Majapahit,
> altogether 141 kinds.

Through Majapahit, Uma Adang enters the national discourse on history and the state. In Indonesia, Majapahit is virtually a code word for the beginning of civilization. The contemporary state continues to identify just enough with this Javanese kingdom of the twelfth to fourteenth centuries to make the resonances of the name worth contemplating for citizens. Majapahit *is* empire—once, now, and forever. Majapahit extended its reach to southeastern Kalimantan in the fourteenth century. In the Banjar chronicles, the story is told that a group from the land of Kaling (variously interpreted in the twentieth century as India or Java) settled in southeast Kalimantan and imported a king from Majapahit. As in other Indo-Malay royal-origin tales, the imported king marries the local water nymph and establishes a prosperous realm. The king sires a royal line, which goes on to rule the Banjar kingdoms, as well as smaller kingdoms of the south and east coast.[10] Every regional history begins with this tale.[11] Majapahit authorizes the beginning of civilized history and state rule in Kalimantan: so, too, in Uma Adang's account.

Before Majapahit, Uma Adang told me, was the Stone Age, when people worshipped stones and made fire from friction stones and palm-hair tinder. Iron was unknown. Everyone followed the same *Hindu* religion. Then everything changed. This was the secret of Majapahit: "Water becomes stone. Stone becomes iron." We see its beginnings in stalactites dripping from limestone caves: "Water becomes stone." This, I thought, is the secret of change beyond what was previously imaginable; it is the secret of transmogrification. With Majapahit, the old economy of goods and meanings was swept away as transmogrified objects commanded the scene—goods of iron, porcelain, and brass, and silver money. Uma

Adang listed more of these royal goods: the seven knives, the seven gongs, the seven nesting plates, the seven trays, the seven metallophones, the seven omen stones that cry. . . . She showed me a silver piece, a strange uneven oval with faint tracings. This, she said, is money from Majapahit. All these were goods of a new kind of power.

While not everyone imagines Majapahit in the same way, many in South Kalimantan focus on the importance of Majapahit *things* in creating state power. Banjar as well as Meratus told me that Majapahit was an ancient ruler known because his son-in-law, Supa, was the first ironworker. Majapahit's objects are not just utilitarian. There are miraculous daggers pinched into shape when red hot by the fingers of ancient blacksmiths. There are china plates of intricate design. Antique collectors still scour the Meratus Mountains looking for goods such as these, ready to trade them for newer objects—costume jewelry, used radios, watches. Are these objects sacred regalia or ordinary items of trade? The power of the things of empire extends from the center along lines of delegated authority, tribute, and trade; even the humblest iron daggers and china plates thus carry imperial magic. Such objects promote royal power precisely because they are dispersed. From the perspective of capitalism, empires are stereotyped as monopolizing all the goods for court elites. The diffusion of things with power, however, has been key to imperial administration—just as it has been, more recently, to development schemes with their model housing or cuisine. Meratus continue to know the state through its aesthetics of powerful material and material power. In Uma Adang's history, the magic of things creates a stable fund of state power stretched between the past and the future.

◆

> Then women's shamanism fell to men's shamanism.
> Then it included adat,
> several elements of adat,
> beginning from women's *dukun* shamanism,
> coming down to Majapahit's seven Garagu styles.
> Then there were all the elements of adat
> of the Kaharingan religion, or Buddhism.

Majapahit is the imagined state that protects all its subjects through religious and ethnic pluralism. "Garagu 7" is a term used primarily by Dusun when referring to various shamanic styles of southeastern Kalimantan. According to Uma Adang, the legitimate religious diversity of the Garagu 7 is Majapahit's project.

This idea of plurality is not far removed from attempts by the contemporary state to orchestrate religious and ethnic diversity. Yet, the terms of diversity have always been a site of contestation. The regional government has not always been as benevolent to religious diversity as Uma Adang wants to imagine it. Officially, the Department of Religion reigns over a pluralism of six legitimate religions; but, in South Kalimantan, officials conventionally see themselves as spokespersons for Islam. Meratus "religion" never had a chance with them. To regional officials, Meratus ceremony represents backwardness, not belief. Propelled by the dream of development, east-coast Religious Department officials have proclaimed, nagged, and patiently explained to visiting anthropologists that pagan ceremonies waste community resources which could be used to develop a dynamic, entrepreneurial economy. Meratus in Uma Adang's area told me that they had been offered housing and cash subsidies if they would convert to Islam. Children must convert in order to attend school; a student has the choice between Christianity in missionary schools and Islam in government schools.

One Meratus response has been to argue for recognition of shamanic practices as an official religion. In the western foothills in the 1970s, a group of shamans tried to persuade officials to register *Balian* (literally, "shaman") as a religion. Meanwhile, on the east side, groups were arguing that shamanism was a form of Buddhism, which had already been recognized as a state-approved religion. In the 1980s, Meratus began to endorse the term *Kaharingan*, a Central Kalimantan term for Dayak religion.[12]

The stakes are high for religious recognition, because religion is key to Indonesian politics and ethnic status vis-à-vis the state. The importance of Islam in the nationalist revolution has given Islam, as well as some of its recognized religious counterparts (including Christianity and Hindu-Bali), a continuing political role.[13] Further, since 1965, lack of an official religion risks being interpreted as affiliation with communism and, thus, subversion.[14] Religion is required on the identification cards citizens must carry when they travel, even locally. In this context, Uma Adang's reference to local Meratus custom as Kaharingan and/or Buddhism proclaims an imaginary state protection for local rights.

Uma Adang's Majapahit is the protector of adat. She may be right in pointing to a connection between Indic kingdoms and adat—the unity of

law, ritual, and cosmology. It is Dutch colonialism, however, that codified adat as a system of local administration, thus making adat a symbol
of pluralism and community autonomy.[15] Of course, it is Majapahit, and
not the Dutch, that makes the contemporary claim for state protection.
Majapahit makes it possible to imagine local rights held in respect. Thus,
Uma Adang proclaims that in ancient times community boundaries were
drawn sharply and clearly through the forest. No one was permitted to
hunt or gather fruit—much less farm—on another community's forest
land without explicit permission. This is the adat of Majapahit, she says.
The implication is clear: If only the state recognizes this adat—rather than
encouraging Banjar immigration, Javanese transmigration, and transnational timber-cutting—things would be as they should be.

Uma Adang has a special responsibility for teaching adat because the
voices she hears from Majapahit tell her its proper but long-forgotten
forms. Of all the Meratus I met, it was Uma Adang who was most willing
to dictate rules for social life, fines for every possible transgression, and
models for the spectrum of ceremonial occasions. Her adat was not out of
line with regionally available assumptions, including those of other Meratus. Her recitations are reminiscent of the presentations I was offered in
Dusun villages. Dusun have a long colonial and postcolonial history of
claiming local village rights through adat; Meratus neighborhoods are
not as disciplined. Thus, I could not help but be impressed that Uma
Adang actually got Meratus to participate in her obsession with form and
formality. I sat through meetings in which people discussed etiquette and
paid fines for uncourteous behavior. People *did* ask permission to move
in and out of local neighborhoods. The planning of ceremonies was formalized, with lists of each person's contribution. In reviving Majapahit
adat, Uma Adang works hard to form a community of rules. For the
imagined state that lavishes adat protection, this passion for form is a
bureaucrat's dream. (Real bureaucrats surely would be suspicious of such
community organizing.

In discussing Induan Hiling's work, I mentioned some reasons why an
ambitious Meratus woman might turn to rules and codification of authority. By focusing on the formal knowledge and power of adat, Uma
Adang can evade the show of prowess men use to claim leadership. Uma
Adang argues for a formal gender symmetry in which women and men
have parallel and complementary contributions to community leadership. Uma Adang's Dualities support her adat codes, as well as her claims
to power as a female leader. All of this is upheld by the imagined state rule
of Majapahit.

The contradiction here involves the fact that Uma Adang is well aware that the state endorses male leadership of communities. She can never even be the official adat head of her neighborhood, although she takes solace in the fact that she has placed her right-hand man in the position and that she had herself informally titled *Panatik Adat* ("Adat Enthusiast").[16] She fantasized that perhaps she could become the local representative to the Family Bureau (PKK), which does, indeed, use prominent village women to spread the word that loyal female citizenship is best cultivated through the domestic arts. Uma Adang's idea was that, by travelling around teaching others to cook, she would also be teaching adat. But when she dressed up in the masculine clothes she thought proper for the post, including khaki green army pants to show her authority, there seemed little chance that the refined, domestic ladies in Javanese sarongs would even talk to her. The government offers few positions for insubordinate women.

Even Majapahit, in Uma Adang's history, associated itself with "men's shamanism." Women's shamanism "fell" to the men. Women have the power of priority, but they are relegated to a mystical prehistory. Yet, too, this historical account denaturalizes men's privilege in becoming shamans; there have been gender-varied ways, the account implies, to achieve shamanic prowess.

Other stories intrude, emphasizing Uma Adang's choices of what to omit and what to tell as "history." The most common Meratus tale about the origin of shamanism tells of Mambur, the first shaman.[17] Mambur had a shamanic prowess that no longer exists: He could chant over a corpse and make it live again. As I understand the story, this prowess was incompatible with the world of women—that is, with the world of ordinary people.

Mambur travelled everywhere, curing. He never came home. His wife finally became so mad at him that she killed his favorite child, their youngest. Mambur sensed the death and came home. He brought the child back to life. But he went away again. Again, his wife became angry. Again, she killed the child. Mambur returned and revived the child. This happened seven times. Each time, the wife disposed of the child's corpse more efficiently, so that it became more and more difficult for Mambur to bring the child back to life. The last time she disposed of the corpse so well that not even a hair remained, and Mambur could do nothing. Whereupon, he disappeared. No one has had Mambur's prowess again.

Male shamans tell this story as a charter for the limited but still potent skills they possess as they attempt to transcend the constraints of ordinary fe/male social life. I think of Adam with his iron penis; he, too, could not live in the world of women with so much male prowess. It makes sense that what power there is goes to men, with their heritage of transcendence once much greater. In contrast, in Uma Adang's history, men's shamanism does not arise from the nature of gender asymmetry, but from a particular historical moment of state support.

◆

> Now, more than that,
> after we had the adat of the Majapahit era and men's
>   shamanism,
> along with Majapahit was Gambar Kamanikan.
> Gambar Kamanikan stood along with the youth Jiwara.
> The youth Jiwara stood along with Bambang Siwara,
> and along with Sandayuhan.
> And along with them, below that, was Samali'ing,
> including all the events of our adat tradition.

From Majapahit, Uma Adang moves to folktales, offering them the same recognition she gives national histories. The tales bring history closer to home by establishing custom and ethnicity on the regional landscape. Uma Adang's Sandayuhan and Bambang Siwara are the two brothers more commonly known as Si Ayuh and Bambang Basiwara. They are the heroes who allow Meratus to laugh about ethnic difference and asymmetry. Si Ayuh is the bumbling older brother, ancestor of the Meratus, who can never quite replicate the feats of his clever younger brother, ancestor of the Banjar.[18] Si Ayuh, however, is also known for some prodigious feats. One of his best-known feats is his defeat of the seven-headed monster, Samali'ing, whose name is listed above. Samali'ing had the power to turn people and their possessions into stone merely by fixing the gaze from one of his heads on them. The Meratus landscape is littered with stone remnants of Samali'ing's victims. Si Ayuh tricked Samali'ing with a spell that turned the giant's gaze back upon himself, thus transforming Samali'ing into the stone cliffs called Gunung Kapala Pitu ("the Seven-Headed Mountain").

One person who told me this story figured that this was Si Ayuh's last feat, after which he disappeared to become a spiritual presence at Mecca—a rather open-minded location for Si Ayuh to choose, considering the ethnic and religious boundaries he had to cross to join that place of power. In other tellings, Si Ayuh has a more oppositional role to play at Mecca. In one of them, he kills the Sky Pig (whose jawbone is preserved as the V-shaped group of stars in the head of Taurus) with a spring trap made from the constellation we call Orion. With wicked ethnic cheek, the dying pig falls to earth and becomes the Great Mosque at Mecca. As Uma Adang continually suggests, local tales are not merely about the local; they remap the relation of near and far, unsettling their hierarchies.

♦

> Then our shamanism descended down and down,
> and then arrived at the kingdom.
> The kingdom descended down and down,
> and then our shamanism was to purify the kingdom.
> These were ancient times,
> these times of old;
> many things were truly great, or the highest.
> That was our shamanism descending down.

Travelling in time, Uma Adang has come to a minor kingdom of the southeastern coast of Kalimantan. Its center was a court at the mouth of the S—— River, in a Banjar area only a few hours downstream from the Meratus–Banjar border. This court, she said, brought Dayak and Muslim together in common devotion to royal ritual. Just as the global rule of Majapahit emerges fortuitously to solve the problem of global ethnic differentiation in the era of Nabi, the centripetal pull of the local court absorbs Meratus–Banjar ethnic tensions raised in the Si Ayuh stories. Subjects are not divided by the ritual of the kingdoms; its endorsements are equalized, and, thus, plurality is preserved.

Uma Adang's story of the founding of the kingdom recapitulates the Banjar story of the founding of the greater Barito delta kingdom, with its imported king from Majapahit, but down a notch in rank and with a gender reversal. Once, she tells, the rain would not stop, and there was no rice. Carrying a bottle of gold dust and a diamond, Datu Limbur was sent by the people to obtain a king from Banjarmasin. He floated all the way, along the east coast, on a raft of nine dammar logs, following the same route back with the king he had obtained. But the king died en route. The rain would not stop. Datu Limbur set out again, this time with two bottles of gold dust, two diamonds, and a great gold belt buckle. This time, he got Ratu Intan, the Diamond Queen, who hiked over the mountains from the west side to her new seat at the mouth of the S—— River. She instituted the dewa rituals performed today, bringing adat, ceremony, and well-being to the local area.

The imagined imperial center—here, Banjarmasin, but from there, removed to central Java—empowers the local kingdom. But, by its very remoteness, the local kingdom can also disturb the plan of empire. The chosen prince dies on his way there, despite the fact that he takes the sensible, easy route along the east coast. Only the princess survives, and she has walked the rugged trails across the mountains. She rules the kingdom with a daughter's voice, that voice which cracks at the moment of enunciation to reveal the split between the questionable power of the speaker and the unquestionable firmness of the father's law. The princess is a woman who never seems to have had children (at least, no one could tell me of any). She is neither a maternal figure nor an ancestor in anyone's direct line. It is unclear whether she ever married. She began everything that can be called "local"—not only ritual and custom, but also that knowledge of connection to a wider historical scene from which "local" predicaments spring. Perhaps the contradiction of daughterly rule is one way of thinking about why everything "local" here is always slightly askew.[19]

The Diamond Queen of the title of this book has finally made her quiet appearance. Certainly, she is a role model for Uma Adang, as well as a stimulus for Uma Adang's connection to me. Uma Adang had been married but had confidently left her husband to give birth to her son alone and to live as an unmarried woman and the eccentric center of a social network. Her husband did not understand her voices, she said; besides, he refused to divorce his first wife as he had promised before their marriage. At any rate, Uma Adang was too headstrong and charismatic for a conventional marriage. Like the Diamond Queen, she preferred a kingdom. Uma Adang stressed that femaleness is no impediment to leadership: Even the Netherlands have a queen. Then I had come along to confirm the possibility of irregular authority.

The Diamond Queen rules over wobbly reproductions. She ushers in structure and history repeating themselves inaccurately. She is the queen of utopian commitments to unpredictable, newly inflected repetitions. She is also the queen that makes it possible for history to be told at all. Through the Diamond Queen, local places become historic; rites become venerable, ancestors are made imaginable. Even in hiking over the mountains, the Diamond Queen offered her storytellers the chance to list all the places she passed. She created a path that is remembered in litanies of the landscape. The rites and ceremonies she instituted are told in detail; they are a litany of ritual forms. Another list begins with the local captains that gathered around her and spread her influence. It is a list of names with a hesitant, yet deeply valued connection to the present; for, although the Diamond Queen herself had no children, her followers did. According to her own account, Uma Adang is descended from a local captain of the queen. So is everyone else in the area who wants to be so considered.

◆

> It was continued by the era of the events of our ancestors,
>   our great-great-great-grandparents.
> It was continued to our great-great-grandparents,
>   descending to our great-great-grandparents.
> And it was completed by our great-grandparents,
>   descending down to our great-grandparents.
> Continuing, it happened down to reach our grandparents,
>   or our grandfathers.
> After grandfathers, it descended to our fathers.
> Our fathers continued it to the children.
> Children to grandchildren.
> Grandchildren continue to great-grandchildren, or
>   descendants.
> All of us spreading our history.
> Or all of us announcing history, already so many
>   generations, that is truly our adat.

Can an anonymous genealogy linking the past and the future be history? Not to classical anthropologists, who made kinship terms and descent lines represent the social continuities that stand outside history. This is a bizarre historical terrain.

It is also an odd genealogical terrain. Although I have translated Uma Adang's terms with genealogical regularity, the text actually is more confusing. What are these kinship terms? Generally, Meratus keep track only of relatives they have actually known. The proper terms for more distant ascending and descending generations are considered a form of esoteric knowledge, and there is wide disagreement about them. In this text, Uma Adang adds to the confusion by introducing terms that might also refer to officials from the time of kingdoms. For example, I translated the term *datung* as "great-grandparent" simply because of its order in the sequence. In another version, Uma Adang put this term in the context of a

list of obsolete officials—*datung, mangku, mantir, tumanggung, singa*—
which she inserted in the genealogy. Further, the list is muddied by the
inclusion of too many of the kinds of Indonesian phrases that Uma Adang
likes best—empty, formal, foreign-sounding connector words. (For example, she begins the fourth line above with *Terus diadakan kepada sampaikan ataspun*, which is barely translatable, if at all.) Yet there is a point,
I believe: The categories of history that lead up through the kingdoms
also lead to the present and the future. In a dewa chant, listeners know the
shaman is coming home to the ritual hall when they hear him travel upstream on a sequence of rivers. Uma Adang returns through time. The
bumps and confusions of the journey are part of what makes it possible
to tie a great past to a small present and to unknown futures.

Like the landscape of the conventional Meratus shaman, this landscape of time is impersonal, larger than local. This is not Uma Adang's
genealogy. (The ego generation is entirely absent; the history goes straight
from ascending to descending relatives.) Just as other shamans do,
Uma Adang travels in a landscape of power, in which she is a seeker who
is granted no automatic authority. Uma Adang is a marginal element.
This self-positioning points to her social similarities with more conventional shamans. Like The Bear or Awat Kilay or the other Meratus shamans I knew, she gathers a small community around her. Those who
attend Uma Adang's ceremonies praise her insight. Somewhat removed
are her detractors, who criticize Uma Adang's leadership and scoff at her
knowledge.

At the same time, Uma Adang is different. She sees as the distinguishing
mark the fact that she does not eat rice. Symbolically and practically, rice
is central to Meratus livelihood. Uma Adang positions herself outside the
world rice consumption creates, to see beyond it.[20] And, indeed, because
she does not eat rice, she also does not plant, weed, harvest, thresh,
pound, sun-dry, cook, or serve rice. These are time-consuming, identity-
creating activities for almost all Meratus women. Uma Adang grows
beans and peanuts as cash crops, along with some other vegetables for
home use; she takes care of her own needs (although frequent visitors
often bring food, cooking and serving it). Her voices do not allow her to
remarry; when I knew them, her teenage son mainly took care of himself.
Thus, more than any other Meratus woman I knew, Uma Adang has time
in which to convene meetings, make speeches, offer ritual advice, and
whisper political secrets. She is more independent of the rice-farming
cycle than either men or women in the area. In her view, it is this freedom

from the dailiness of concerns with rice that allows her to expand her imaginative frameworks. She sees beyond diversifying social networks, imagining more unified, bounded, and respected communities.

Several of Uma Adang's innovations in Kalawan and its abutting neighborhood Risi have been attempts to build such communities at the local level. Her most distinctive project is a system of rotating responsibility for a community rice swidden. Harvest from this field is used for community ceremonies, visiting dignitaries, and as a pool for families in need. Each neighborhood has one. Most Meratus harvest-festivals honor the sum of the harvests of that year's host umbun. In contrast, in Kalawan and Risi, the rice from the Unity Field is honored.

Thus, Uma Adang superimposes a common, shared resource on the flexible networking of neighborhood life. She and her followers convinced members of these neighborhoods to donate cash with which to buy plates and kitchen equipment for ceremonies. Community property is supplemented by adat fines from neighborhood members. As is true in several Meratus neighborhoods, a government development subsidy has been obtained for upgrading the ritual hall. Unlike many neighborhoods—in which cooperation was so strained that building materials sat neglected in the forest or newly built halls deteriorated—in Kalawan, Uma Adang organized people into work groups to build and carefully maintain the hall. I have already mentioned the importance of adat and the fact that people in Kalawan (as well as Risi) ask permission to move in and out of the neighborhood. This attention to adat and local authority is stimulated in part by the ethnic tensions and administrative visibility of the Meratus–Banjar border area. At the same time, they are signs of her hoped-for revision of local community.

Moreover, Uma Adang's notion of adat includes all Meratus as an ethnic-religious group. Unlike most Meratus leaders I knew, who claim real or imaginary alliances that cut across ethnic boundaries and political status to include, for example, the police, Uma Adang sees herself as a spokesperson for all Meratus. She knows that Banjar officials have little interest in dealing with her. As a Meratus woman, she can hardly expect to have a serious conversation with a regional official, and that makes it much more difficult for her to claim regional ties. Instead, she conceptually formalizes the separation as an ethnic-religious one. She imagines her travel agendas, too, more on a model of a queenly procession through a unified Meratus kingdom than as a shamanic networking into terrain that is always alien. About once a year, she goes into the mountains to see her fans there and dispense advice about adat and other matters. Although she travels as lightly as any other Meratus, she expects to be treated like a queen; people are supposed to come to her with their disputes, questions, and praise. In her telling, at least, they *do* come, allowing her to spread word of a unified adat that cuts across strategies of competitive leadership. She has a good number of devoted disciples in the mountains.

Perhaps I found Uma Adang's movement intriguing because, in contrast to other Meratus strategies, I saw in her movement many of the moves of the identity politics I knew in the United States. I could follow her desire to build ethnic pride, unity, and the right to speak. In contrast to Uma Adang, the rhetoric of social movements in the United States brazenly defies the state, although, here too, minorities have worked hard to conjure up an ethic of pluralism that is not everywhere self-evident. In this imagined pluralism, a group's right to cultural autonomy is respected if it can establish that it carries a separate identity. The utopian improvisation of Uma Adang's vision reminded me of various U.S. radical feminisms and cultural nationalisms as these movements have had to manufacture authentic and hallowed cultural identities by inverting and displacing the stereotypes of others. Uma Adang's work raises the question of whether even some of the most reductive and essentialist visions of identity politics—glorifying female biology, for example, or the spiritual essence of Asia or Africa—might not have gained political effectiveness through the parody effect of mimicking dominant categories in inappropriate contexts. Of course, when the stakes are high, even liberated zones must be based on known logics of safety—that is, on dominant assumptions. Yet, the cutting edge of political organizing often is the simultaneously dissociating and validating effect of parroting dominant discourse out of context.

It is in this spirit, I believe, that Uma Adang leaves this version of the history with an announcement to the world that she has no secrets at all. After she has worked hard to establish that she *does* know a secret, she turns around and proclaims that there is nothing to be alarmed about, she is merely promoting loyal subjection to religion and state. This passage is one of her most convincing reproductions of formal government and Islamic rhetoric. She appeals to the Supreme God (*Tuhan Yang Maha Esa*) who tops the state's Five Principles of Loyalty. All Indonesians, as a condition of citizenship, are required to acknowledge Tuhan Yang Maha Esa. She invokes the Muslim–Christian Heaven (*Surga*), offering pious-sounding prayers. It all sounds very respectable, despite her turn to the idiosyncratic Nabi Lahat. Yet, her own untranslatable words still jump out at the end, disturbing the listener's ability to fully enter the appropriate proprieties. Is Uma Adang revealing a secret or just clearing her throat? Here is her envoi:

Truly adat requires no surmises. Our adat from Nabi Lahat. The contents are nothing [alarming] at all. We hope, we believe; our belief is in Heaven and the Supreme God. Truly we praise the prophets, pray to Heaven, and ask that everything exist in peace and perfection. To Heaven, God, *Yek Hak* [?] The Most Powerful—Wassalam.[21]

REPRISE

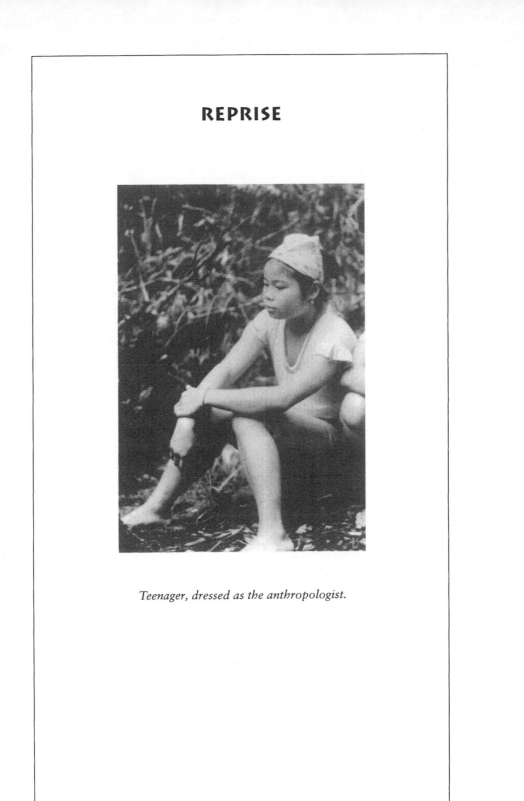

Teenager, dressed as the anthropologist.

Maps of South Kalimantan drawn since the 1970s tend to include a dotted line marked "proposed highway" leading from the Hulu Sungai Banjar plains, crossing the Meratus Mountains near its highest peak, and heading to the east coast. To the best of my knowledge, this road has not yet been built, although timber-extraction roads—following the short-cut logic of competitive concessions rather than the planned lines of national development—have cut deeply into the mountains from both sides. (Road-building is a major cause of erosion in hilly rainforest terrain.) The dotted line signals more than an imagined road, however; it marks out an entire dream of development in which the untidy forests and backward peoples of the Meratus Mountains are tamed and transformed. Not totally surprisingly, the line follows the ancient track of the Golden Bridge, the spiritual route which, according to east-side Banjar, once connected the Banjar royal palaces with sacred places on the east coast and offshore Laut Island.

Meanwhile, in boardrooms and offices around the world, there is a popular notion that roadbuilders, development planners, and timber merchants have no cultural commitments. They just follow the obvious natural dictates of efficiency and progress. According to this view, they erase local cultures in their path, for better or worse, but they have none of their own. Against such notions, I would argue that efficiency and progress always are projects of the imagination. The connections formed between remote rural areas and cosmopolitan centers involve impositions of meaning, as well as political and economic expansions. In this spirit, I have tried to show the imaginative features of nation-building, ethnic formation, and state rule as experienced from the margin. Regional, na-

tional, and international imaginings form frameworks for cultural negotiations in the Meratus Mountains, in which power relations and religious, ethnic, and gender identities are formulated. Conversely, marginal
perspectives can illuminate both the potency and the limitations of more
central visions. State power is both enacted and challenged through reinterpretations and misinterpretations from the provinces.

In describing out-of-the-way places, the more common strategy has
been to cordon off local perspectives from those of the writer and his or
her readers, who are, thus, to represent a unified, cosmopolitan modern
world. In this strategy, marginal groups speak to the modern imagination
only from the outside—as the wise, innocent, savage, or exotic Other. As
experts on the "primitive," anthropologists have often deployed this
strategy; but it extends far beyond the discipline in the international
imagination. Indeed, the strategy is elegantly illustrated in a recent novel
by Mario Vargas Llosa, *The Storyteller* (1989), in which anthropology is
located as a modern fragment encompassed by the great contrast between
primitive and modern cultures. The novel counterposes European and
Amazonian storytellings across an unbridgable cultural abyss. The first
narrator is a Peruvian travelling in Europe who remembers a college
friend who studied anthropology. Dissatisfied by the limitations of anthropology as a modern science, the friend goes native, or so the Peruvian
believes, in order to become the Indians' greatest storyteller. The second
narrator is the friend—now a white native who tells haunting traditional
tales among his chosen people. The stories of the first narrator are filled
with names, places, and dates that constitute the modern sense of history.
The second narrator tells mythical stories in which all men have a single
name (women have no names) and there is no distinction between natural
and supernatural. These stories cannot touch, except in their contrasts.
To build these contrasts, the first narrator must tell his story from Europe, despite the fact that he is a Peruvian. Only Europe provides the
distance from which to block out all consciousness of the Latin American
national context in which Amazonian Indians and urban Peruvians might
tell intertwined stories of neocolonialism, development, and the exclusion
of Indians from cultural citizenship. Across the abyss, Amazonian stories
are beautiful and timeless; their incipient death appears an inevitable consequence of their own insistent difference.

To tell cultural difference in another way requires rethinking the shape
of the world. The alternative possibility I favor is elegantly set forth in
another novel. In *The Shadow Lines* (1988), Amitav Ghosh tells of an
interconnected world always lived imaginatively but from different

standpoints. The narrator is a citizen of India who longs to and eventually does travel to Britain. His is a trip through an inventory of postcolonial imagined geographies: the Britain he conjured from descriptions in his childhood; the India envisaged by his British friends; the more transitory geography of a cousin, who travelled so much that she remembers cities by the location of the ladies' rooms in airport transit lounges. The narrator also tells of imagined geographies that do not take Europe as a reference point, such as those that mobilize Muslims across national boundaries and those that fuel Indian ethnic violence. This is a world in which everyone must take responsibility for a positioned imagination. Here, too, there is a role for anthropology: The narrator's uncle is an archaeology student who teaches the narrator to appreciate the pattern of other places, that is, to use his imagination carefully, with detail and precision.

This is an understanding of the world that opens up possibilities for an anthropology of intersecting global imaginations. The present book contributes to such an anthropology by showing its importance in even the most out-of-the-way places. I have shown how the Meratus have become a meaningful, coherent social unit through the powerfully institutionalized discursive spaces created by development plans and dreams, religious boundary-marking, and administrative conceptions of order. Meratus both bend to state power and evade it as they point to the violence of administration and the ritual order of development. Meratus men search out the opportunities within state rule and ethnic asymmetry to create charismatic leadership and enhanced mobility; they thus confound order and its subversion. And their gendered accommodations and protests inspire further creative manipulations and reversals as ambitious women both copy and criticize the men's stances. These are some of the issues through which I have explored the particularities of Meratus positionings within the region and the nation.

Critics of a focus on global interconnections worry that the beauty and originality of diverse cultural communities will be lost in such an approach. In part, this worry is due to the fact that an earlier scholarship downplayed symbolic aspects of political and economic history, for example, exploring colonialism without attending to its cultural dynamics. During one period in the history of U.S. anthropology, a division grew up between symbolic analysts who wrote about the imaginative vitality of disconnected local cultures, and political economists who examined global interconnections but who cared little about creative expression.[1] The possibilities for imagining the world were strangely narrowed by the conceptual categories of this division. Thus, in the anthropology of gender, scholars seemed to suggest that there is a conceptual choice between imagining gender alternatives—in independent local cultures—and recognizing a familiar patriarchal system—in colonial and neocolonial connections.[2] What happened to the possibility that alternatives could arise within connections? In this book I have paid special attention to reinterpretations from different positions, to unexpected challenges, and to creative developments. These are important features of every system of domination and exclusion, even the most widespread economies and most hierarchical political regimes.

Despite the problematic heritage of ethnographic writing, ethnographies—with their focus on the specificity of social arrangements and points of view—are a possible site for drawing attention to both local creativity and regional-to-global interconnections. In part, this is because ethnographies are messy; like novels, they tend to include an overabundance of detail, much of it extraneous to the main argument. Rather than condemn this messiness as boring (Pratt 1986:33) or outdated (Fox 1991), I prefer to build from it as a source of analytic heterogeneity and promise. In this messiness, for example, there is room for elements that simultaneously draw readers into projects of cultural comparison, regional cultural history, and local/global positionings.

To reemphasize the possibilities for combining such projects, I turn to one more Meratus story. Again, this is Uma Adang's telling; but it is a very different piece than the one analyzed in the last chapter. Unlike the "history," this piece is not particularly fragmented or graffiti-like; rather it creates a coherent set of imagery. Its careful aestheticism makes it possible to call it a "poem." It is a poem about fetal development and birth; it tells of individual autonomy amid power and inequality. It is a piece I love because of its elegance. It would be easy to use the poem to tell of local wisdom. Unlike stories of police or rock stars, it is challenging to place this poem within national and global cultural politics. By taking up this challenge, I can illustrate multiple layers of ethnographic possibility.

Here is the immediate social context in which I heard the poem. A man who lived in the mountains came to Uma Adang's house for advice. He was in love with a woman and had decided to divorce his wife and marry the other woman. Community elders disapproved of this decision and were pressuring the man to change his mind. Uma Adang counseled him to listen carefully to the elders and to use mature good sense. At the same time, he should also follow his heart. She spoke of the individual, unpredictable nature of love relationships (*juduh*): "There are juduh that last as long as a touch; there are juduh that last through fondling breasts; there are juduh that last through becoming lovers; there are juduh that last two or three months. Even if you already have children, if your juduh is over, then nothing can keep you together." The statement sounds surprisingly disruptive when one considers the context of the national language, where the term *jodoh* refers to an appropriate match, marriage partner, or mate. It holds some sense of a preordained, and thus durable, couple. In contrast, Uma Adang was making room for more tentative, shifting arrangements.

As one aspect of her advice, Uma Adang began telling the story of the fetus's development in the womb. Fetal development is a familiar Meratus framework for understanding personal agency: Fetal autonomy signals individual autonomy in a world of social demands. Meratus say that the fetus "meditates" (*batapa*) for nine months and nine days in the womb to find its *rajaki*, its future livelihood, luck, health, and wisdom. Because each fetus finds its own rajaki, each individual at some level goes his or her own way in life. Uma Adang's telling also emphasizes the relationship of the fetus with God (*Tuhan*). Indeed, there was considerable talk of God that night. Perhaps it was important that the man had an ambiguous ethnic identity: He was born Banjar but brought up by a Meratus family and currently living in a Meratus community. Uma Adang did not talk to him of her theories of Meratus religion or of adat. Instead, she stressed the regionally transethnic discourse of a mystical God. This was a discourse in which, as Uma Adang and her close friends stressed, God is an aspect of the self "closer than our fingernails."

That night, Uma Adang wove an exceptionally beautiful and haunting version of the story of the fetus. I was so moved that I asked her to repeat the story the next day so that I could record it. She did, in a somewhat abbreviated, but equally poetic fashion. The version I have translated below is the taped version, with a few minor additions from my notes on the earlier telling. The written format is my attempt to give the piece a slower, more formal, oral rhythm.[3]

Beginning with origins.

Water is placed by the father,
   it is entered inside the mother,
   it is enclosed in the mother,
   the water of nine months and nine days.

The water becomes blood,
   the blood becomes eyes,
   the eyes becomes fibered extensions,
   and are filled out into a head.
The fibers are enlivened
   becoming arms
   or becoming legs.
They harden to become bones
   and are blanketed by ligaments,
   wrapped in muscular flesh.
The flesh fills out
   and is covered by skin.
Thus one month, or two months.

At three months we enter into questions.
"What is your desire to eat or drink?"
Everything will be given, every food or drink.
   The mother eats sour fruits and all kinds of sour things
   [for those are the desire of the child].
Our every intention and desire is satisfied.
Thus six months.
We reach our strength and begin to move.
Our food requests follow each other,
   our many desires,
   and all are eaten, whatever is requested.
The vitality of the child in its mother's belly accompanies the
mother's breath.
   For in the belly one cannot breathe, but only go along
   with the mother's breath.
And then it is completed.
All the foods are sufficient in the womb, and at last the child
is ready to be birthed by the mother,
completing nine months and nine days.
Then it is God the Powerful that asks the human being in its
mother's belly,
   "What is your strength?
   "Where is your power?"
And we answer,
   "I am yet water and blood."

This we answer three times.
And then God asks,
    "What are your desires in life?
    "What will be your strength?
    "How will you form your desires, you
       there in the womb of your mother?
    "How is it that you choose to die?
    "Will you die falling, or seized by a crocodile,
       or will you die an ordinary death of illness
       and pain?
    "Will you be killed by another, what is your
       choice?"
These are God's questions that create our vitality in the womb.

And we say,
    "Akrana, akrana, I would have my breath."
And God says we must decide what it is we want, coming out
into this world. Only then can we be born, we who were held
by our mother for nine months and nine days. But we first
must acknowledge these questions. And to this humble
subject in the mother's womb, God asks again,
    "What will be your death?
    "What are your desires in this world, so broad
      and so wide?"
And perhaps we say,
    "I will die like this."
Perhaps we say,
    "I will live ninety-nine years."
And we ask for our rajaki in this world, as great as it may be.
We ask for peace and perfection in the world. And the whole
world in a tiny drop of water is realized, and we acknowledge
God and we acknowledge the questions.
    "Truly," we say, "I ask for the vital essence of God."
And only then are we given vitality.
We are given our rajaki, our life's wisdom, and we hold this
balled up in the palms of our hands.

    And only then do we emerge from the womb,
      birthed by the mother.
    At the moment of birth, we at last receive our breath.

In surprise we cry out,
  "A! Owa!"
and we open our fists and our rajaki is scattered. It falls to the
ground with the blood of birth and is scattered across the
earth. And the rest of our lives we must follow that rajaki; we
must work to follow it wherever it takes us. For it may take us
to many villages, and we must always follow to gather it up.

When it is gone, our years are over.

The fetus about to be born chooses its own future life. It chooses its lovers, however few or many; it chooses its travels; it chooses its time and
manner of death. Surprised by our passage into the world and the power
of our own breath, each of us, as a newborn, lets go of all that wisdom
and spends the rest of life working to regain it.

Here, Uma Adang draws from familiar local and regional ideas about
fetal development.[4] Her story aims to create a local political effect. Most
specifically, it gave a friend permission to follow his own path in choosing
a wife. It also aims farther as a statement about personal autonomy; it is
an interpretation, a positioning within regional political culture.

Uma Adang's wider ambition was evident in her willingness to record
the story for me; she urged me to take her story to the United States. In
accepting her challenge and incorporating the poem in my ethnography,
I take on the responsibility of explaining her themes. How might these
enter an English-oriented conversation?

As a U.S. American, it is difficult for me to consider Uma Adang's story
without thinking about United States issues concerning women's reproductive rights, for fetal narratives have been a central element in recent
U.S. debates. Since the 1970s, feminists in the United States have worked
to make more reproductive options, including abortion, available to
women. In the 1980s, an equally passionate movement seeking to crimi-
nalize abortion gained increasing institutional support. The antiabortion
movement depends heavily on creating verbal and visual imagery with
which to show the fetus as separate from the mother. Appreciation of the
fetus as a separate entity, a child who happens to be in a womb, is used to
activate assumptions that the fetus, like a child, is innocent, vulnerable,
and in need of the state's protection. Thus, antiabortonists pass out plastic fetus dolls and show and reshow photographs of sleeping fetuses floating in watery space. One antiabortion film, *The Silent Scream*, has been
described as particularly successful because of the way in which it uses

ultrasound and fiber optics to create the sense of an independent (yet vulnerable) and responsive (yet threatened) child in the womb (Petchesky 1987; Ginsburg 1990).

The success of antiabortion fetal imagery can be measured in part by the inability of feminist critics to respond. Even critics dare not contest assumptions of the transcendent innocence of the fetus-as-child; further assumptions about the necessity for maternal sacrifice and paternal state protection follow easily. Pro-choice activists tend either to ignore fetal imagery or, if they respond to it, to find themselves in the weak position of characterizing abortion as an unfortunate cruelty to innocents in a flawed world. The entrenched interpretation of fetal imagery overwhelms and stifles feminist creativity.

How different a fetus Uma Adang's poem conjures! Her fetus is wise, not innocent; it demands respect, not sacrifice or protection. No dependent being living at the command of paternal law or dying from unregulated, selfish female neglect, this is a fetus who determines its own birth and death. The gaze is shifted from that of a potential parent contemplating an unself-conscious but valued object to that of a once-wise fetus now grown, remembering his or her own origins. Uma Adang's narrative of fetal development stretches the imagination of North Americans, whether feminist or antifeminist. If we could visualize a *wise* fetus, we might not assume that the "rights" of the fetus demand the sacrifice of the mother.

Of course, this use of Uma Adang's poem takes it entirely out of context. Yet, it can be a radically illuminating experience to extend one's imagination with fragments taken out of context from someone else's stories. This is the "cultural critique" of a strong thread of U.S. anthropology, from the works of Ruth Benedict (1959) and Margaret Mead (1928) to the more recent arguments of Marcus and Fischer (1986). For these authors, ethnography serves to argue against false universalizations (spread, so often, by taking privilege for granted) and to remind U.S. Americans of their own unnatural foibles. It would be a mistake to describe the shape of power and meaning in the world *only* with an us-versus-them, comparative message; at the same time, it is an approach that deserves credit for its insights. The power of Uma Adang's poem to disturb U.S. perceptions of fetal development is worth appreciating.

There are other U.S. resonances of Uma Adang's imagery—some that begin to push the issues back toward the Meratus. As in South Kalimantan, fetal imagery in the United States is both infused with and generative of images of political action in general. In the United States, the move-

ment to protect fetuses reverberates self-consciously with other movements to protect the innocent, including children, wildlife, and people
(like the Meratus) who live in tropical rainforests. With the U.S. with-
drawal from Vietnam, with its sense of the failure of aggressive patriotism, both conservatives and progressives began to portray the protection
of innocents as the remaining justifiable rationale for political action. In
this climate, "protective" causes proliferated, with a diverse array of activists and bureaucrats working to save whales, battered women, abused
children, rainforests, and medical students in Grenada, as well as fetuses.
These are not politically homogeneous causes. (I support some and not
others.) I group them only to point out the rhetoric of protecting fragile
and dependent victims, with which advocates of each tried to make their
cause attractive to the public. This rhetoric has also colored attempts at
advocacy for so-called "tribal" peoples whose ways of life are threatened
by the spreading reach of capitalist resource-extraction. Many advocate
groups have worked closely and carefully with activists from the groups
they aim to help. However, the prevailing assumption, that the protection
of innocents is the proper inducement for political action, has encouraged
advocates to highlight such themes in popularizing their cases. Rain-
forest-dwellers, to the extent that they are worth supporting, become
guileless primitives.

Meratus are easily placed in this framework of endangerment; certainly, they are threatened by ecosystem destruction and military rule.
Yet, reading Uma Adang's poem alone is enough to warn against political
models that turn marginal peoples into needy dependents. The Meratus
who grow from Uma Adang's fetuses are autonomous individuals able to
assess their own political situations. They are ready to form alliances but
not to beg for protection. In refusing to portray her people as victims
awaiting help, Uma Adang presents a way of thinking about political
action that can jolt U.S. Americans away from prevailing stereotypes.

Presented in such a way, this reading of Uma Adang's poem is just as
out of context as the first one offered. Uma Adang was not in dialogue
with a U.S. model of politics when she spoke of the meditation of the
fetus. The ideas about conserving nature held by the international environmental movement remain relatively irrelevant to Meratus; no one has
ever offered to protect and conserve their culture or environment. Nature
lovers—both Indonesian and foreign—have hiked through; but, in the
main, they have not conveyed to local people the discourse that has produced the endangered "nature" they see.[5] When I brought up with Ma
Salam the option of fighting for a Meratus nature preserve that might be

promoted for its protection of endangered wildlife, he remained skeptical about the concept and puzzled about what people were supposed to do with all those rare animals.

Cultural comparisons have been criticized as rendering essential and exotic Others (see, for example, Abu-Lughod 1991). Comparison, however, can also stimulate culturally sensitive global histories in which cultural critics are forced to position their own analytic vantage points. Because the world is politically interconnected, there *are* links between the ideas of political agency Uma Adang presents and those I am familiar with from the United States. Comparisons can be a beginning point for what Kamala Visweswaran (1992) calls "homework"—a situating of analysis in the joined, divergent, and asymmetrical personal and institutional histories of both anthropologist and informant. But such homework requires more than an us-versus-them contrast; it involves a journey through shifting, intertwined histories which many scholars, including myself, feel unprepared to take on all at once. It is impossible to expect that justice will be done to both local detail and larger histories in every book. Yet, I have depended on a general awareness of the wider terrain every time I allude to the power of the discourses and institutions that shape Meratus lives and make cultural negotiations in the Meratus Mountains unequal. In this final section, I suggest interconnections between the political commentary of Uma Adang's poem and that of other Indonesians, as well as people in the United States and elsewhere.

Sometimes the most relevant connections are tangential and out of synchrony. They may work despite, or against, the stream of progress-oriented expectations that picture the Third World as constantly moving toward the West. For example, one might note Indonesia's influence on the politicization of fetuses in the United States. What? Indonesia's first president, Sukarno, was an architect of anticolonial rhetoric for what we have come to know as the Third World. The ideas, rhetoric, and optimism of anticolonial politics helped inspire U.S. second-wave feminism during its formative period in the late 1960s. Anticolonialism shaped notions of "liberation"; "women's liberation" was parallel to, or part of, anticolonial liberation (see, for example, Morgan 1970; Burris 1971). Many activists in the abortion campaign of the early 1970s were heavily influenced by anticolonial ideas of political agency.

The pro-life response of the 1980s turned the discourse on abortion toward the moral authority of the political center, the ethical state that protects fetal life. This recentering in political discourse could be said to have found its strongest statement in U.S. attempts to consolidate a "New

World Order." (After the collapse of the Soviet Union, U.S. political leaders began to imagine a New World Order in which linked nation-states would develop their economies without wasting their attentions on "political" concerns about social justice. In this vision, every country would be ruled by the kind of regime Indonesia's President Suharto has imagined: a regime in which internationally enforced "order" replaces political debate.) From here, it is hard not to return, if only by the agency of a pun, to the U.S. entanglement in Indonesia's own New Order. The neocolonial network in which Suharto created the New Order is the same network which, somewhat later, fostered the U.S. political agenda of protecting innocents. The chain connecting the United States and Indonesia does not lead to parallel developments, however. Uma Adang's fetus works in a politically opposite way from the U.S. pro-life fetus; it is not dependent on the state, but, rather, is autonomous. The personal spirituality of the fetus frees it from authority. It is this personal spirituality that provides the next link for investigation.

The U.S. government was an important part of the international economic and political support that ushered Suharto into power. For example, CIA officials recently admitted to providing the Indonesian army with death lists for communists in 1965, in self-conscious practice of tactics that would be used soon again in Vietnam (Kadane 1990). The political culture of Indonesia's New Order, with its focus on stability and economic growth, has grown up within the framework of an expansionist international capitalism in which the U.S. government continues to play an important role.

The politics of the New Order fostered a turn to personal spirituality and mysticism in both national and regional cultural expression. In renouncing the raucous politics of the Sukarno era, Suharto created a regime ostensibly "without ideology." Political parties were quieted, banned, or merged; student demonstrations were outlawed. Newspapers that wished to continue publishing learned to exercise self-censorship. A political silence descended; mysticism thrived. The spiritual forms that have developed possess deep roots in regional cultures across Indonesia; yet their contemporary importance shows not their timeless authenticity but, rather, their current centrality in national projects and their local renegotiations (cf. Pemberton 1989; Mulder 1978).

The shift to spirituality has been particularly clear in national literary production. Whereas the literature of the Sukarno era tended to be concerned with issues of social injustice, in the New Order, literature turned to personal and mystical themes. Some critics see this as social commitment with a new face. In a recent conference on the arts in Indonesia, the playwright and director Ikranagara argued that theater in the New Order turned away from Western and nationalist models in a search for traditional Asian forms of expression (1992). Yet other participants spoke of censorship and self-censorship as major factors contributing to the new theatrical themes. From their discussion, I gathered that the turn toward spiritual approaches encompasses a refusal of politics as well as political criticism. The critic and translator Harry Aveling describes a similar shift in the writing of poetry and prose from Sukarno-era politics to New-Order spirituality. Aveling argues that mystical writing is continuous in many ways with the sentiments of earlier, more explicitly political writing, but without its Westernized shell (Aveling 1986a). Yet he too sees equivocal possibilities in New-Order writing that could turn toward self-absorption or open new horizons of commitment (Haridas 1986.)

In some ways, it may be useful to say that Uma Adang speaks as a poet within a growing Indonesian tradition that addresses political action through the personal spiritual quest. Her poem may be read together with nationally known writers such as Danarto, who explore spiritual expression and a mystical knowledge of God (Aveling 1986). Yet, Uma Adang lacks the status and resources that national literary figures have. She cannot reach for the patronage of national elites nor call upon the resources of an international literary network. From this perspective, her poetry departs from the national literary scene to share the separate forms of bravery and accommodation of popular expression in rural areas. Uma Adang's poetry accepts the prevailing framework of political culture; its bravery lies within this framework. To depict autonomy as a basic feature of human nature is to set a small challenge for the prerogatives of hierarchical authority.

Uma Adang's poem is self-consciously transethnic; it appeals to widespread Indonesian understandings. Within the transethnic context of rural popular culture, Uma Adang is not idiosyncratic in using notions of a personal search for spiritual efficacy for an oppositional political discourse. Indeed, her poem resonates with the statements about personal spiritual responsibility I heard Banjar make in the mid-1980s, during a period in which Islam had become an oppositional discourse within the nation. During this period, the Banjar I knew were much more ready to criticize government policy than they had been a few years earlier; but criticism always took the form of statements about personal spiritual responsibility. Banjar spoke against corruption and the misuse of state power in a discourse that stressed the importance of individuals—both bureaucrats and those outside the bureaucracy—upholding personal religious standards even if it meant opposition to superiors. Uma Adang, too, uses spiritual notions as a counterdiscourse against the demands of authority. Meratus–Banjar divergences dissolve in her appeal to personal autonomy.

Meanwhile, such rural protests are interpreted by national elites and foreign travellers as timeless spirituality. International agencies have revived interest in disappearing spiritual cultures. Tourism flourishes as North Americans, Europeans, and Australians flock to see such cultures. Tourism forces rural religious practices into national consciousness, thus completing the circle of unpredictable influences. The consequences are contradictory. Tourism not only increases state revenues, but also, on occasion, creates new arenas for the extension of state authority. For example, Toby Volkman (1990) has shown how Toraja ritual has been adapted to a role as a national showcase sporadically monitored by central government officials. At the same time, national and international figures draw on notions of authentic rural spirituality to fuel criticisms of state policy. In this vein, Rendra's banned play, *The Struggle of the Naga Tribe* (1979), shows the imaginary Naga tribe fighting off the materialistic greed of state officials and their multinational allies through calls to spiritual harmony. Such groups as the Meratus find themselves in the middle of these overlapping and conflicting agendas. As one guide to Indonesian travel states: "To see Dayak tribes, most tourists head off to [Central Kalimantan], where people no different from those of the Banjar area live. For the real thing, go to the Loksado or Batu Benawa areas" in the Meratus Mountains (Dalton 1991:805). Looking for an archaic authenticity in the tribal countryside, tourists and writers, like anthropologists, come back to re-present garbled and reconstituted Meratus visions and to offer new challenges to such spokespersons as Uma Adang, who have been working hard to create a space to speak within the powers of the present. I do not exclude my own practice.

Global interconnections do not necessarily mean a spreading homogeneity. Rural leaders, such as Uma Adang, do not have the same agendas as nationally known poets, tourist agents, or U.S. and European activists and travellers—all of whom, ironically, care a great deal about the fate of isolated cultural minorities like the Meratus. Their divergent agendas, however, are tied by complex, indirect, tentative links to form part of a common world. It is by acknowledging these links that one can appreciate Uma Adang's poem, not just as a mirror of cultural difference, but as a creative cultural intervention in a world we share.

Writing this in the 1990s, I am uncertain about whether to discuss these political agendas as existing in the present or the past. Everything I have described seems to be changing dramatically. A report from the Meratus Mountains suggests that, in some areas, timber-company-managed forest destruction, Banjar immigration, and government-sponsored resettlement may have changed the possible meanings of "personal autonomy" beyond superficially obvious recognition (Rifai 1991). The United States political climate is changing—with the aggressive patriotism of U.S. involvement in the 1991 Gulf War, with the recognition of the sinking status of the U.S. in the world economy, as well as with rising new hopes for domestic social justice. Protecting innocents may not be a central agenda much longer. Meanwhile, urban Indonesians seeing President Suharto age contemplate the current mixture of authoritarian rule, development rhetoric, and commitment to an idealized Javanese culture, and wonder how long it will hold. In the process, they may be bringing about a political revival. At a recent conference in the United States, Indonesian activist scholars read explicit protest poetry as they discussed the breaking of political silence. Uma Adang's poem speaks to both Indonesians and foreigners within shifting and limited frames of meaning. This—not timeless truth—is the power of all creative work. We reread and write today to draw from this heritage and move beyond it.

NOTES

Preface

1 A pretty good sense of the Tasaday controversy can be gleaned by consulting the following references: Balien (1986); Berreman (1991); Dumont (1988); Molony (1988); Nance (1975).

2 The two feature-length films are *Blowpipes and Bulldozers: A Story of the Penan Tribe and Bruno Mansur* (1988, Gaia Films) and *Tong Tana: A Journey into the Heart of Borneo* (1990, First Run/Icarus). Brosius (1989) comments on the first of these as an anthropologist who has conducted field research with Penan. Other representations of the Penan struggle against the timber companies (and here I include a mix of popular educational materials, news, critical analyses, and scholarly reports) are Davis and Henley (1990); Hong (1987); Sesser (1991); Western Canada Wilderness Committee (1989); and World Rainforest Movement, Sahabat Alam Malaysia (1989).

3 Linguistic references for Meratus and Banjar of South Kalimantan include Artha (1974); Durasid (1977); Hapip (1976, 1977); and Ismail et al. (1979).

Opening

1 Of the many vocabularies for understanding culture and power currently circulating, I have already introduced two in the last two paragraphs: the first ("discourse") associated with Foucault and the second ("hegemony") with Gramsci. The former vocabulary is particularly useful for bringing together issues of meaning and practice in examining the construction of power; the latter calls attention to divergent political stakes in processes of social transformation. Used together eclectically, they make it possible to ask how people reshape the very ideas and institutions that make it possible for them to act as subjects.

2 See, for example, Boserup (1970); Etienne and Leacock (1980); and, for Southeast Asia, Chandler, Sullivan, and Branson (1988).

3 See, for example, Appadurai (1990); Dominguez (1989); Ferguson and Gupta (1992).

4   The speech from which this fragment is taken is discussed in more detail in Tsing (1987). The article discusses Uma Adang's movement in the context of regional political and cultural history.

5   Clifford and Marcus (1986); Fabian (1983); and Geertz (1988) have been influential in urging anthropological self-consciousness about textual construction. Reflexive anthropological work on European and U.S. cultures has been influenced by scholars such as Schneider (1980); Myerhoff (1978); and Bourdieu (1984).

6   Spivak carefully marks the contradictions of her own postcoloniality, writing, for example, of the need for "a persistent unlearning of the privilege of the postcolonial elite in a neocolonial world" (1989:289). Since all intellectual positions involve complicity with power, she argues, every scholar must engage in such "persistent critique" (1989a: 126).

7   In her interview with Afsaneh Najmabadi, Spivak is adamant: "I'm not an essentialist" (1991:128). Yet Spivak (1989a) warns against "anti-essentialist" ire as well as against essentialism. Essentialism is a tool, she suggests, that we may not be able to do without, even as we know its limitations. Nevertheless, her caution here is in striking contrast to Barbara Christian's concerns: Spivak's "persistent critique" brings her political concerns into dialogue with discussions of difference in Western philosophy; Christian stretches academic conceptions of philosophy to forge a dialogue about difference with a nonacademic community.

8   See, for example, Cixous (1980); Irigiray (1985); Grosz (1989).

9   French feminist theorist Hélène Cixous writes explicitly about how her understanding of women's disadvantages draws from a *parallel* with the disadvantages of the colonized. She writes of her girlhood as a Jew in Algeria: "I learned everything from this first spectacle: I saw how the white (French), superior, plutocractic, civilized world founded its power on the repression of populations who had suddenly become 'invisible', like proletarians, immigrant workers, minorities who are not the right 'colour'. Women. Invisible as humans. . . . [T]here have to be *two* races—the masters and the slaves" (Cixous and Clement 1986:70, cited in Young 1990:1).

10 Woodward (1990) argues that Javanese models of hierarchy and state rule are not Indic models at all, but rather are Islamic models. This is a fascinating and nicely supported proposal. For my purposes here, however, the important point is that state power depends on cultural understandings, whatever their histories.

11 The exceptions I know of are special administrative areas such as Yogyakarta, in which the national government continues to recognize nonappointed political agents above the village level.

12 I do not pay much attention to the national contestations that make up "the state" at any given time. Yet the state is never a monolithic entity. Various political tendencies vie for state legitimacy. (President Sukarno's attempts in the early 1960s to balance the power of the anticommunist army and the Communist Party are a striking example.) Two bureaucrats with no political disagreements may still have no idea what the other's agency is up to. (In South Kalimantan, forest territories may be simultaneously committed to conservation, timber concession, and transmigration without common knowledge among bureaucrats.) From the perspective of a politician, these internal differences define the stakes that make debate and action worthwhile. This book is not a study of national state-making, however. My goal is to explore the relationship between local political dynamics, on the one hand, and regional and national politics, on

the other. In this task, I emphasize the coherence of state power as it both shapes and threatens Meratus community formation.

13 See Colchester (1986) for a review of the nationwide goals of this program.

14 *Pembinaan* has been translated into English with terms as politically varied as "guidance" and "indoctrination." An army-sponsored volume on South Kalimantan tellingly links the term to military control; the army's "maintenance" of the territory (*pembinaan wilayah*), with its "ideological, economic, social, and military aspects," is explained as a prerequisite of national defense (Manihuruk et al. 1962:186–7).

15 Some, such as Trinh (1989) and Sandoval (1991), argue that it is this search for a totalizing coherence that has supported notions of an autonomous, universally powerful European or Euroamerican perspective.

Part One

1 A comparison of key works on Indonesian kingdoms, colonialism, and nationalism highlights contrasts among these kinds of "state power." Clifford Geertz's *Negara* (1980) stresses the importance of court ceremony in the political architecture of precolonial kingdoms. Ann Stoler's *Capitalism and Confrontation in Sumatra's Plantation Belt* (1985) shows the importance of coordination between state and estate plans for labor and territorial control in the colonial era. Benedict Anderson's *Language and Power* (1990) illuminates the process of building national consciousness and administration in postcolonial Indonesia.

2 Anthony Reid's *Southeast Asia in the Age of Commerce* (1988) offers a rich portrait of the cultural fluidity of precolonial Southeast Asia. Benedict Anderson (1987) discusses the colonial invention of ethnicity.

3 Mallinckrodt (1928) is the standard reference for Kalimantan.

4 Benedict Anderson's *Imagined Communities* (1983) stimulated scholarly appreciation of the specificity of national political consciousness.

5 J. J. Ras (1968) analyzes two versions of the Hikayat Banjar, the chronicle of the Banjar delta kingdoms.

6 Schwaner (1853:368) describes Meratus as shy, fearful people who run away from visitors. Mallinckrodt (1927) and Tichelman (1931) also mention Meratus in passing, noting Banjar influence and suggesting little need for administrative attention. Other early European sources concur about the marginal status of Meratus: Grabowsky (1885) pioneered the theory that Meratus have forgotten their original language due to Banjar influence. Lumholtz, travelling during World War I, spoke to Meratus shamans, "who knew nothing worth mentioning." "Almost everything had been forgotten," he continues, "even the language" (1921:302).

7 See, for example, Proyek Pembinaan Perguruan Tinggi Agama (1978) and Djajamadi Babas (1978).

8 Chronologies of the Banjar kingdoms are gathered from Banjar chronicles (Ras 1968) and from Majapahit records. The Banjar chronicles begin with settlers from the land of Keling, interpreted variously as India or Java (see, for example, Ras 1968:183), who created the court of Negara Dipa in southeast Kalimantan. Saleh (1975:14) sets this settlement in the twelfth century. Hudson (1967:57) suggests "sometime before the mid-fourteenth century" because Tanjung Nagara is mentioned as a tributary of Majapahit in the *Nagarakrtagama* of 1365 (1967:61).

9   Ras (1968:196) argues that the Banjarmasin court was founded "slightly before the middle of the sixteenth century." Hudson (1967:61) adds that the Islamization of southeast Kalimantan must have begun before 1588, when Demak fell to Mataram. Saleh (1975:26–28) discusses various dates for the founding of the port of "Banjarmasih," later to become Banjarmasin, and decides on 1526.

10 Hudson (1967:65–68) and Saleh (1976) describe this Banjar pepper expansion.

11 Beeckman, an English captain who traded at Banjarmasin in 1713, describes his inability to bypass the Banjar to trade directly with Dayaks (1973 [1718]).

12 Posewitz (1892:319–330) describes the gold-prospecting technology of nineteenth-century southeast Kalimantan.

13 Dutch and British politico-economic adventures in the area during this period are described in Irwin (1955); Hudson (1967:68–75); and Propinsi Kalimantan (1953: 360–88).

14 All the sources listed in the proceeding footnote tell this story, including the final Kalimantan source. This source, however, gives a good deal of detail on the continuing resistance to the Dutch takeover (Propinsi Kalimantan 1953: 380–88).

15 Hanafiah (1977:43–45) does not mention the 1787 treaty and dates the war "1859–1905." Manihuruk et al. (1962:558–61, 452–55) neglect the 1787 treaty and date the war "1859–61" in a list but "1859–1905" in a more extended account.

16 The kingdoms of Cengal Manunggul and Bankala'an, Cantung and Sampanahan, Batulicin, Pulau Laut, and Sebamban were abolished in 1905 (Syachril 1975:2–3).

17 Lindblad (1988:58–78) offers a detailed review of rubber cultivation in southeast Kalimantan. He mentions that during the boom of the 1920s, southeast Kalimantan "counted the highest proportion of hadjis in the entire Islamic world" (1988:70).

18 The pictures of Kalua market in Vortsman (1931) are particularly striking.

19 See Lindblad (1988:74). In 1937, a system of individual quotas was adopted; these may be the "coupons" Meratus described.

20 Lindblad (1988:137–50) discusses taxation policies in southeast Kalimantan in the colonial period. Nothing in his account, however, helps me understand Meratus reports that they suddenly were assessed per capita cash taxes in the 1930s. One would need further information on the application of tax policies in peripheral rural areas.

21 Mayur (1979) describes many occasions in which Banjar nobles took refuge in Meratus locations. For example, he suggests that in 1861, Pangeran Hidayat, a major leader, joined family members who had retreated to Ulu Lok Basar (1979:84). The presence of Banjar nobles in the mountains during this war is also described in Meratus oral tradition.

22 Schwaner (1853:369) describes nineteenth-century east-side Meratus as being on the defensive against raids by Pari Dayaks. Meratus stories describe raids from various directions.

23 Colonel Hassan Basry, commander of the nationalists' regional forces, describes the Kalimantan guerilla struggle in *Kisah Gerila Kalimantan* (1961).

24 Manihuruk et al. (1962:160–81) describe the rebellion led by Ibnu Hajar from the army's point of view. Other rebellions of the same period are also mentioned (1962:431–35).

25 See Robison (1986:186).

26 See Anderson (1987a).

27 See Suhud Pribadi (1979). This document is discussed further in chapter 2.

28 A publication in 1980 lists eight completed resettlement villages, two being built, and more in the planning stage (Team Survey 1980:9–11).

29 One largely Christian Meratus village is found at the west-side base of the Meratus Mountains.

30 Meratus in the various zones are on a more equal footing in relation to other state services, demands, and communications. Some services are evenly *un*available: Government-sponsored health care is found in district seats, but is inaccessible to basically all Meratus because of distance and unfamiliarity. Some requirements are evenly spread: Everyone who travels must have a government identification card; and, in order to get this card, he or she must have a religion. State communication transcends distance: Even in the central mountains, many young men have radios; Banjar and government broadcasts theoretically are available to many, but tastes and poor batteries limit listening time. In the early 1980s I did not know any Meratus with access to television, although the regional government had promised (and reneged on) gifts of generator-driven televisions to rural communities in the area. Despite such bad promises, the format of state bureaucracy knows no exceptions here: Government titles and community classifications are distributed in a regular fashion across the Meratus Mountains.

Chapter One

1 H. Noer'ied H. Radam (1982:19) argues that the term *Bukit* means "origin" or "base," for example, the base of a tree. Radam, who has done extensive ethnographic research in the area, feels that the term Bukit is appropriate for Meratus Dayaks. Other scholars who have done recent Meratus research using the term Bukit are Dove (1981) and Ismail et al. (1979). Reports on Meratus culture in the 1970s and 80s used the term *suku terasing*, for example, IAIN Antasari (1973). Another choice is to use specific geographical or administrative-area terms; one report, for example, refers to *Suku Dayak Pembakulan dan Hinas Kiri*, "Dayaks of Pembakulan and Hinas Kiri" (Team Research 1969). Tjilik Riwut (1958) lists the following Dayak groups of the Meratus Mountains as separate *suku* ("ethnic groups"): Dayak, Tapin, Labuan Amas, Amandit, Alai, Bukit, and Pitap. Still others come close to the usage I have chosen, referring to "the people of the Meratus Mountains," for example, Proyek Pembinaan Perguruan Tinggi Agama (1978).

2 The most extensive study of Meratus language of which I am aware is Ismail et al. (1979).

3 Mulder (1978:4–6) describes the formation of the six official religions. Kipp and Rodgers (1987) offer a number of articles that explore the consequences of state policies for minority groups; Atkinson's essay on the Wana of Sulawesi is particularly useful in showing how religious discourse in minority areas is formed (1987).

4 An introduction to the cultural and economic successes and predicaments of South Kalimantan Banjar can also be found in Artha (1974); Vondal (1984); and Departemen Pendidikan dan Kebudayaan (1982).

5 My discussion here builds on a rich literature on Borneo social organization. Most striking to anthropologists has been the absence of unilineal descent groups. Linked

analyses of kinship and social organization in Borneo have challenged the assumptions of earlier kinship theories by showing the possibilities for social systems that do not depend on lineage organization or even, in some cases, on perpetual corporate groupings of any sort (Appell 1976a). J. D. Freeman's pioneering work on Iban kindreds (1961) and *bilek* families (1958, 1970) opened this discussion and stimulated comparative scholarship on related social systems (for example, Appell 1976b; King 1978; Hudson 1967; Whittier 1973). Flexible systems of social networking—comparable in many ways to the Meratus situation I describe—are common in the area (see especially Miles 1976).

Chapter Two

1 In my use of "stories," I do not intend to cordon off Meratus culture as primitive or childlike. The construction of narratives is an aspect of politics in general. In an article on legal cases in the United States, I show one way that "stories" are key to U.S. politics (1990a).

2 Most Meratus leaders are not unaware of the historical framework in which administrative eras succeed each other. In South Kalimantan, this history begins with the Banjar kingdom sponsored by the Majapahit empire and proceeds through the Dutch colonial era, the Japanese occupation during World War II, and the competing revolutionary and Netherland Indies Civil Administration eras (1945–49), into the Indonesian national era (sometimes split into the Old Order, 1949–65, and the New Order, 1966 to the present). In foothill and border Meratus areas, these eras (*jaman*) are frequently referred to in talking about political memories; in the central mountains, other ways of talking about the past predominate. Even in border zones, eras can be pushed aside when referring to the structural continuities of state rule.

3 One way to think about Meratus revisions of official agendas is to see both within an ongoing tension between nation-state and imperial models of power. Indonesian politicians at national and regional levels claim indigenous empires as a heritage for their power. The appropriation of empire—with its regalia, sacred places, cosmic harmonies, and mystical knowledges—is central to their understanding of "national" rule. Just as these politicians turn empire into nation-state, however, central-mountain Meratus leaders turn nation-state into empire. Rejecting a narrative of development, they conjure up an imperial state that thrives on spectacle and requires no legitimization of its violence. The imperial state facilitates the kind of communities these Meratus leaders can coordinate. At the edge of empire, Meratus communities gain both from protection and from neglect; their leaders are shamanic messengers. In contrast, the nation-state rejects its marginals, making them objects of derision and forced reconditioning. Leaders must learn to be ethnic representatives or else mainstream. Meratus leaders take advantage of the unstable flux between imperial and nation-state agendas to press for their own survival and that of the communities they know how to lead.

4 From the central mountains, the horizon would not appear as low as from these karst cliffs overlooking coastal plains. *Tuan Maskapi* could be a Meratus variation on *Tuan Maatschappij*, "Mr. Company"; I owe Mary Steedley this insight. This passage and the Meratus quotations that follow in this chapter (with the exception of the spell and the shamanic chant) are translated somewhat loosely from my written notes.

5 *Lastar* was also given to me as *Laskar*, which means "soldier" in other Malayic dialects. The Bear may have been referring to older versions of "government headhunting." Most of the other names are ethnic or geographic names found in the northeast and west. Rousseau (1990) describes headhunting in nineteenth-century central Borneo; his descriptions are useful as context for The Bear's account of the southeast corner of the island.

6 The king disappeared in a spiritual way, creating an enduring presence.

7 Meratus sometimes speak as if the *sound* of guns and bombs creates their harmful effect: To silence a weapon is to escape harm. I believe this is why The Bear described a *deaf* man as able to pick up a bomb.

8 See, for example, Coppel (1983:145–49) and Jenkins (1978).

9 See, for example, Wallerstein (1974) and Wolf (1982).

10 From the 1950s until the 1980s, questions about cognatic social structure dominated the anthropological literature on Bornean social groups; these questions stimulated synchronic and comparative analyses. See, for example, Freeman (1970); Appell (1976); King (1978). Several authors used these frameworks to ask specifically about "social change," for example, Sutlive (1978); Deegan (1973).

11 Dove (1988) offers a thoughtful set of critical articles that show various ways to move away from the pitfalls of contrasting the backward "tradition" of rural peoples with the progressive "modernity" of development programs in Indonesia.

12 See, for example, Foucault (1977, 1978).

13 Paul Rabinow (1988) offers a collection of anthropological analyses that show the globally spreading effects of a uniformly conceived modernity. In contrast, Lisa Rofel (1992) insightfully argues against analyses that posit the global uniformity of modernity.

14 Other criticisms of Scott's influential work can be found in Hart (n.d.); Kondo (1990: 219–21); and Mitchell (1990).

15 Drake reviews literature that shows the widespread nature of construction-sacrifice rumors in Borneo. See Hansen (1988:187) for an account from a Euro-American traveler who identified with the headhunters. Erb (1991:118–19), asking about related rumors of headhunting in Eastern Indonesia, brings up the possibility that European construction practices in which blood is used to strengthen mortar have been a source of these rumors.

16 Mulder (1978:91) describes "development" building projects in central Java in the early 1970s. The projects he mentions renewed already servicable roads and buildings in an effort to raise the ceremonial stature of government-sponsored development. Shelly Errington (n.d.) similarly describes the construction of underused but status-raising government buildings in Sulawesi in the 1980s.

17 The most respectable schedule in southern Kalimantan for both bathing and drinking would be twice a day. In the areas I knew best, Banjar expected people to bathe once in the morning and once in the late afternoon. Meals with rice were served for lunch and dinner; breakfast generally did not include rice and so was not considered a true meal.

18 I never saw a python inside a house. The only other Meratus story I heard was similar to the one I am retelling. Two English tourists, people said, had hiked to a resettlement village; as they slept on a mat in a Meratus family's house, a python crawled over them. Pythons seem to go for important guests.

19 The word I translate as "sour spices" is *asam*. In other areas of South Kalimantan, *asam* is "tamarind." I never saw central-mountain Meratus with tamarind; central-mountain people sometimes cook with various sour leaves, which they call *asam* (cf. *masam*, "sour"). It is also possible that Induan Curing had tamarind and served it to the police officer, which would certainly have been appropriate.

20 My analysis of the "learner's text" is made possible by the fact that I participated in many dewa ceremonies, often recording (and later transcribing) the shaman's chant, as well as attending to the activities of assistants and audience. I also spoke at length to a number of dewa shamans other than The Bear. The analysis here asks about the political "worlding" of the chant, that is, about what Sweeny (1987:1) calls the "author and audience" that it attempts to create. Dewa chants are part of shamanic efforts to create political communities. Particular basanggar banua ceremonies may be more or less successful in these efforts. (In chapter 4, I discuss political negotiation over the attendance at two of The Bear's ceremonies.) The chant itself is relatively stable from ceremony to ceremony. Despite this stability, in particular ceremonies, it would be possible to do a rich reading of the social dynamics between audience and shaman. Yet that is another task; I refer readers to the exciting analyses of shamanship in other Southeast Asian areas: Atkinson (1989); Freeman (1967); Laderman (1991); Miles (1966); Roseman (1991).

21 The word I translate as both "sacred kingdom" and "aura" is *karamat*. The word translated as "hero" or "fighting magic" is *pahalawan*. The range of meaning of the words is difficult to convey in a single English word; thus I alternate translations.

22 This is the mountain known on national and international maps as Mt. Besar.

23 Meratus do not use highly stylized political oratory, although one might want to consider the mimicry of national political oratory, such as that of Uma Adang, an emergent high style.

Chapter Three

1 See, for example, the work of Ginsburg (1989); Haraway (1989); Martin (1987); Ong (1990a); and many of the articles in Ginsburg and Tsing (1990) and Morgen (1989).

2 Chernichovsky and Meesook (1981) describe the history and organization of Indonesia's family-planning program. The authors (World Bank consultants) quote an earlier World Bank report in explaining the success of family planning: "To sum, the success of the FP program 'rests fundamentally on a political commitment to use an established administrative system which is capable of reaching from the center through successively smaller administrative units to the village itself. This involves authority, power and respect relations resting on traditional forms of relationships, but strengthened as the fundamental framework for order and policy implementation by the present government' (Freedman 1978:5)" (1981:24).

3 Hartmann writes: "The top-down approach toward birth control means it is not popularly perceived as a tool of reproductive choice, but as a means of social control" (1987:83).

4 One can certainly add a touch of irony to statements such as the following, quoted by Hartmann (1987:80) from an AID report: "The most ready explanation given for the success of the Indonesian family planning program is the strong hierarchical power

structure, by which central commands produce compliant behavior all down the administrative line to the individual peasant."

5 See, for example, Sacks (1979) and Gailey (1987).

6 This is a common claim in Southeast Asia; see Laderman (1983:78). I do not know exactly what Pa'an Tini's aunt did or whether it was ever successful.

7 One Banjar social scientist I knew cited the Meratus as a model of family planning using traditional methods. He told me that the central government, following up on a United Nations mandate to codify and revitalize traditional medical practices, had sent a commission to learn traditional contraception from the Meratus. I can only imagine strange meetings, rife with misunderstandings, between project officials and Meratus border-area women. Yet such meetings offer a model of how derogatory Banjar stereotypes can incongruously lead to new opportunities for Meratus women to acquire regional authority.

8 I have written about some of these legal cases in "Monster Stories: Women Charged with Perinatal Endangerment" (Tsing 1990a).

9 The classic anthologies on the cross-cultural construction of gender stress the differences among cultures: Rosaldo and Lamphere (1975); Reiter (1975); MacCormack and Strathern (1980); Ortner and Whitehead (1981); Collier and Yanagisako (1987). However, exciting work has also been done on the "hybrid" formation of gender in intergroup dialogues. See, for example, Yanagisako (1985); Stoler (1989); and Kondo (1990a).

10 Again, my generalization misses important exceptions. See, for example, Sacks (1979) and Comaroff (1985). Gough (1971) is an important early exemplar of attention to the linked formation of gender and community organization.

Chapter Four

1 I translate the term *pangulu* alternately as "marriage official" or "wedding sponsor." This is a title usually held by a neighborhood's senior shaman, who conducts the ceremony of local weddings.

2 My discussion of gender asymmetry in this chapter builds on recent writings about gender in Southeast Asia (for example, Atkinson and Errington 1990). Note 9 in chapter 6 lists some of the work most relevant to my discussion of Meratus male-leadership strategies.

3 These are the same disputes referred to in chapter 2.

4 This was the same trip to Rajang that I referred to in describing the Rajang *basambu*, the details of which I did not learn until this time.

5 I am referring to nomadism as discussed in anthropology and Western popular culture, not to a Deleuzian "nomadology." My interest in showing the difference between Meratus travel agendas and nomadism should become clearer in the next chapter, where I discuss government attempts to resettle "nomads."

6 The fight for land and resource rights for minority groups in Indonesia increasingly depends on arguing for the validity of adat. I do not intend to work at cross-purposes to efforts at building the national and international legitimacy of adat; I hope, rather, that my analysis of adat negotiation will complement such attempts. For an introduction to the contemporary status of adat law, see Koesnoe (1971); for adat rights in forested areas, see Zerner (1990); and, for Kalimantan, see Vargas (1985).

Chapter Five

1   Harold Conklin (1957:3) divides shifting cultivation systems into "integral" and "partial"; the former he further divides into "pioneer" and "established." Administrators and conservationists have often based their derogatory stereotypes of shifting cultivation on partial and pioneer types, in which forest may be destroyed with little attention given its regeneration. The established, integral systems of relatively sparse populations of hill peoples are more likely to maintain a long-term balance between forest and swidden. Conklin's study of the Hanunoo of the Philippines (1957; see also 1963) offers a model of detailed attention to the technology and ecology of the agricultural practices of particular groups. Similarly, careful exploration of the relationship of integral shifting cultivation and forest use for Dayak groups in Borneo can be found in the work of Chin (1985); Dove (1985); Jessup (1981); and Peluso (1992). The work of such scholars as these is beginning to change assumptions held by current agricultural administrators. As Dove (1989) points out, however, there is still a long way to go.

2   Meratus shifting cultivation is discussed in more detail in Tsing (1984).

3   Whether this kind of mapping endangers or protects Meratus livelihoods depends on shifting forestry policies. In the 1980s, the "unbroken-forest" look made the area an inviting spot for new timber exploitation. In the 1990s, policy may be turning toward the rapid conversion of areas classified as "degraded forest," in which case, Meratus may be at a slight advantage due to the government's mapping.

4   To help protect the privacy of the people with whom I worked, I do not identify the precise area or the directional orientation of either map.

5   The study of Dayak forest-resource use, and its relation to that of other forest users, has grown tremendously in the last decade. My work on this topic draws from and contributes to this developing literature in Kalimantan cultural ecology. See, for example, Peluso (1983); Kartawinata and Vayda (1984); Jessup and Peluso (1986).

6   See, for example, Radam (1982); Babas (1978); Ismail et al. (1979); Aziddin et al. (1980–81); Team Survey (1980); and Proyek Pembinaan Perguruan Tinggi Agama (1978).

Chapter Six

Some of the material in this chapter was published in "Healing Boundaries in South Kalimantan," *Social Science and Medicine* 27(8):829–39, 1988.

1   All references to Kristeva's work in this chapter are from *Powers of Horror* (1982). I give only the page numbers in the text.

2   Kristeva argues that, in the development of the subject, abjection is analytically separate from, and chronologically prior to, objectification and Othering. Abjection results from the processes in which the infant first becomes capable of signification; objectification is a feature of later symbolic processes, which assume an already constituted subject within signification. Abjection involves separation from the maternal body, whereas objectification is the working out of paternal law. This distinction is key to Kristeva's project of inserting her concerns within psychoanalytic theory. In contrast, my project is not dependent on this developmental frame. I see the embodied reactions of "abjection" as one possible element of Othering, rather than as a separate mode.

3   In a related vein, feminist critics of Kristeva have argued that her fear of feminist

"essentialism" leads her to ignore differences between men's and women's subjectivities. Kristeva's speaking subject is singular, male, universal. Grosz (1989:92–104) offers her own criticisms and summarizes those of Luce Irigaray. To ask about the contradictory and unpredictable effects on "women" of woman-making technologies is not a naive identity politics. In the next two chapter, I explore gender divergent kinds of subjectivity and consciousness among Meratus Dayaks.

4   My comments below refer to Hulu Sungai Banjar of the towns and villages I knew best, which lie due west of the Meratus Mountains. For the purposes of this analysis, I ignore major differences among Banjar. Wealthy traders, civil servants, and poor farmers differ markedly in their "strategies of identity." Microregional differences are also relevant. In this chapter, however, I piece together common assumptions of Othering.

5   See Siegel (1969) and Ong (1990) for a more detailed exploration of this framework.

6   Kristeva and Irigaray disagree about numerous issues. Both, however, use the ideas of Lacan and Derrida in asking questions about the relationship of subjectivity, language, and gender. Since the major reason I use the work of either theorist in this chapter is to draw attention to the existence of such questions, it seems fair to move from one to the other.

7   The term I translate as "matrix" was explained to me as referring to densely interconnected webs. I am tempted to speak of "fabric," but no cloth metaphor is implied. In agricultural ritual, the term refers to the webs of the earth. Here, structural similarities are drawn between the body and the earth.

8   The term I translate as "mad" is gila. Gila can refer to aggressive, overexcited, chaotic, or weird behavior. A rabid dog is gila. Men in fights are gila. But there is no sense of "irrational" here; this is not a madness contrasted to civilization.

9   My analysis of gender builds on the path-breaking work of Michelle Rosaldo (1980) and Jane Atkinson (1989). Rosaldo began with the observation that the domestic and public domains she expected to find were little in evidence among the Ilongot of the northern Philippines (1974). She argues that, in part, this was related to the absence of a defining focus on women as mothers. Instead, the Ilongot she knew saw women and men as basically the same. Yet men could aspire to something more; men, they said, had "higher hearts" (1980). Atkinson uses this framework to study related gender constructs among the Wana of Sulawesi. The Wana whom Atkinson studied spoke of women as "Everyman" (1990). They played down the specificity of women's roles in procreation by arguing for the unseen participation of men in pregnancy. They stressed male-female similarities and complementarities at the same time that they allowed men the most prestigious roles as shamans and community leaders. My Meratus analysis draws on these insights and on the generous advice of both these authors.

10   Balanghan Dusun, to the north of the Meratus Dayaks, work with supernatural putir who are specifically female. Putir, they say, is like a female child who must be cared for. Putir is also the spirit of the rice. Laderman (1991:7) discusses various connotations for the related Malay term main puteri, which refers to shamanic performance in which princesses (puteri) may or may not have a role.

11   Difference, as I have been arguing, does not rest on the alterity of the maternal. Furthermore, in the Meratus Mountains, female and maternal are not synonymous. Women are not defined as potential, actual, or failed mothers. It seems interesting in this regard that menstruation is not particularly marked. Similarly, Laura Appell (1988) describes the lack of marking of menstruation among the Rungus Dusun of northern Borneo.

Rosaldo and Atkinson (1975) use a structuralist analysis to discuss the absence of maternal symbolism among the Ilongot of the Philippines.

12 I elaborate on the importance of gender in the dynamics of Meratus community leadership in Tsing (1990).

13 Indonesian Muslims distinguish the legitimacy of "religion" from the illegitimacy of "traditional beliefs," such as those of the Meratus, by reference to the scriptural power of the Koran. Awat Kilay was attempting to enter this religious discourse on more equal terms.

14 Many Banjar, in fact, would agree with Awat Kilay's formulation of the phenomenological/cosmological duality of God as our creator. Rural Banjar Islam and Meratus cosmology overlap and converge at many points. Of course, the specification of overlap and divergence is always open to debate on both sides of the ethnic border.

15 Just as Meratus men appear impotent in Meratus–Banjar relations, Meratus women appear disorderly; yet, disorderly sexuality cannot be a form of submission to, or alliance with, Banjar. I never saw Meratus women use talk of sexuality as a way of gaining power across the Meratus–Banjar line. I did see accusations that seemed about to turn into fights. For a discussion of women's use of sexuality in constructing regional ties that bypass Banjar for a wider reach, see chapter 7.

16 Uma Adang is well known in Ayuh; so perhaps it is not surprising that the Ayuh women's dewa possession movement was blamed on her, particularly by detractors. Uma Adang did, in fact, offer encouragement to at least one Ayuh woman whose spiritual career began with possession (see chapter 8). However, Ayuh women are perfectly capable of contact with dewa spirits without Uma Adang's tutoring.

Chapter Seven

1 These equivalents are based on the then current exchange rates, which fluctuated between Rp 600 and Rp 700 per U.S. dollar.

2 What if the women had had children with their alien lovers? None of the women I spoke with about these relationships did have children with the foreign men. For at least one (Irah), I know this was deliberately managed; I did not discuss birth control with the others. My guess is that the women would have felt equally free to come home if they had had children. Having children would not have affected their welcome, their marriageability, or their ability to imagine romance. The irrelevance of motherhood here is in sharp contrast to national discourses, in which motherhood stands for domestic and therefore social responsibility. In the Meratus Mountains, social is not synonymous with domestic; childless women and mothers alike participate in building dense social networks. Motherhood is not a privileged symbol of female status or responsibility.

Chapter Eight

Parts of this chapter were published as "The Vision of a Woman Shaman," in Joyce Nielsen, ed., *Feminist Research Methods*, (Boulder: Westview Press, 1990), 147–71. Reprinted by permission of Westview Press.

1 The special "Women's Oral History" issue of *Frontiers* (2[2], Summer 1977) gives the flavor of the 1970s rediscovery of women as social agents.

2 See, for example, Cole (1986); Anzaldua (1990).

3 As should be clear from the ensuing discussion, I am dealing with a very different set of "technologies of gender" than those analyzed by de Lauretis. In particular, the centrality of sexuality and sexual representations in constituting gendered subjects, which is key to de Lauretis's recent work, is not a useful starting place for my Meratus analysis.

4 See, for example, Bell (1983); Messick (1987); Weiner (1976).

5 See, for example, Gilbert and Gubar (1979).

6 The conventional use of structuralism in anthropology would be to turn to the structure of the chants and performances themselves. Without denying the usefulness of this, I am stressing the power of an analysis which, instead, looks at Induan Hiling's innovations and interpretations.

7 See Tsing (1990).

8 Frederick (1982) offers a fascinating introduction to Rhoma Irama and his music. Irama's national significance, however, is not exactly the same as his meaning to people in South Kalimantan. The Meratus I knew in the early 1980s were unaware, for example, of Irama's religious and political stances, as well as the complex meanings of his stylistic innovations for "national culture."

9 On the national music scene, Rhoma Irama is associated with the promotion of a lowbrow Indonesian genre called *dangdut* or (more commonly in South Kalimantan) *orkes melayu*; see Siegel (1986:215–18). In Jakarta, orkes melayu is a "village" form. In contrast, from the vantage of the Meratus Mountains, it is an accessible representative of urban cosmopolitan styles, perhaps because more "sophisticated" urban music is less available at rural markets. Rhoma Irama is also associated with politically oppositional Islamic militancy. Again, this national sense of his "difference" from other pop singers was hardly noticeable in the 1980s in the Meratus Mountains, where he was seen as a representative of emergent national standards.

10 *Irama* means "rhythm" in Indonesian, but I never heard the term in ordinary Meratus speech. Although we spoke only of the Rhoma Irama connection, Induan Hiling may have also intended the further reverberation.

11 The word I translate as "music," *kesenian*, is an Indonesian term for all the arts. Only Meratus music and dance, however, have a chance of counting nationally.

12 Figures 8.2 and 8.3 are reproduced from tracings of Induan Hiling's original drawings in red and blue pencil. Scott Morgensen traced Fig. 8.3; I traced Fig. 8.2.

Chapter Nine

1 The writings of E. P. Thompson (1963); Raymond Williams (1977); and James Scott (1985) have been especially influential in formulating ideas about agency and resistance.

2 The work of Michel Foucault (1978) and, to a lesser extent, Jacques Derrida (1976) have been crucial in rethinking the construction of "subjects." Joan Scott (1988); Judith Butler (1990); and Gayatri Spivak (1987) have been influential in bringing poststructuralist agendas into feminist theory. Lila Abu-Lughod's (1990) self-criticism and Timothy Mitchell's criticism of James Scott (1990) stage the Foucaultian confrontation with what I called the "social history" agenda. These writers examine the exclusionary operations through which all political programs, including those of resistance and struggle, are formed.

3 The exchange between Linda Gordon and Joan Scott in *Signs* (Summer 1990: 848–60) shows some of the stakes raised as debates on this topic have become polarized. Poststructuralists criticize the essentialist moves involved in establishing oppressed groups as the "subjects" of history. Scholars of social movements and political change worry that poststructuralism leads to an untheorized—and, ultimately, conservative—removal of the scholar from the political arena being studied. The essays edited by Butler and Scott (1992) address the challenges raised in this confrontation. While some statements in the collection seem to imply that poststructuralism positions other people's politics without having any of its own (for example, 1992:xiv), many of the essays are concerned to show self-consciously political uses of the analysis of political discourse. This move requires of analysts that they recognize their own stakes as well as the stakes of the people about whom they write. Donna Haraway (1988) writes eloquently about this issue.

4 There are a few non-national-language Banjar/Meratus words in the verse quoted, for example, *wasi*, "iron," "knife," and *gumi*, "earth." Yet, Uma Adang was doing her best to speak a nonlocal language.

5 Uma Adang also spoke to me in her nicely simulated but incomprehensible versions of "English" and "Chinese."

6 I analyze one of Uma Adang's more "poetic" (in this sense) pieces in the next chapter.

7 The hybrid cultural referents of Uma Adang's history may not seem unusual to connoisseurs of Southeast Asian folk arts. (The literature on Malay folk arts is especially rich in discussions of cultural mixing; see, for example, Laderman [1991:6–10], who reviews literature on Malay shamanic performance.) Syncretism has even been seen as the defining trait of Southeast Asian culture: "The history of the region has been largely interpreted in terms of the importation and adaptation of ideas and institutions from India, China, the Islamic world, and the West" (Williams 1976:24). Scholars acknowledge the creative role of Southeast Asians by stressing their ability to give these foreign mixes local coherence; thus the historian continues, "It has been precisely [the] power [of Southeast Asians] to absorb without being absorbed that has bound the various peoples together historically" (Williams 1976:24). Uma Adang fits neatly into this tradition of local appropriation. She can also teach area scholars more than most accounts of syncretism acknowledge. Her active pursuit of foreign knowledge is a cultural politics, not just a cultural flexibility. "Civilization" presses its terms on those at its margins; it defines the superior unity of customs, religions, laws, and norms, yet offers these to the unwashed only in fragments. To pick up those fragments and create one's history with them is a repositioning in relation to this "civilization." The more she relies on what Homi Bhabha has called "the artifice of the archaic" (1988:19)—a past that must fight for its inclusion among other available histories—the more committed and utopian her gesture. Its promise is the continued possibility of the communities she leads.

8 It is not an exact replication. Uma Adang uses a different melody and includes some of her own emphasis. Yet, her version is close enough to make it difficult to ignore The Bear's influence in stimulating this version.

9 Rice is an important cosmic entity in Kalimantan; human life depends on it. Humans-rice is, thus, a reasonable entry in the list of oppositions.

10 Ras (1968) presents and discusses the Banjar chronicles. He also describes the evidence for early connections with Majapahit.

11 See, for example, Manihuruk et al. (1962); Saleh (1975); Hudson (1967).

12 In 1980, Central Kalimantan Dayaks were successful in getting the Department of Religion to recognize Kaharingan as a form of Hindu-Bali, an officially endorsed religion (Weinstock 1981). However, when I was in Uma Adang's area, neither regional officials nor local people knew about the Department of Religion's decision.

13 Boland (1971) offers an historical account of the political importance of Islam in Indonesia. The politics of Islam during the New Order have been contradictory. On the one hand, the government has enthusiastically sponsored the forced Islamization of non-Islamic areas. On the other hand, particularly in the 1980s, Islam became a rallying point for government critics, and a number of important Muslim leaders were harassed or prosecuted.

14 Whittier (1973:146) describes East Kalimantan Dayak conversion to Christianity that responded to fear of being harassed for not having an official religion. The political frame of minority religious responses in Indonesia is nicely discussed by Atkinson (1987).

15 Whittier (1978) offers insightful analysis of the changing meaning of adat among East Kalimantan Kenyah in response to colonial codifications.

16 Rita Kipp (personal communication) reminds me that the term *panatik*, or "fanatic," has a derogatory feel in some parts of Indonesia. In South Kalimantan in the early 1980s, I heard it used only positively. Banjar boasted, without irony, of being *panatik agama*—not "fanatics" but "pious believers" or "religious enthusiasts."

17 Mambur is not mentioned in this version of the history of the world; in other versions, Uma Adang offered his name beside the Garagu 7. In this way, his story is framed as one voice among many in her imagined, state-sponsored pluralism.

18 I told one of their stories in chapter 1.

19 The importance of theorizing "the moment of enunciation" was brought to my attention by the work of Homi Bhabha (1988).

20 My occasional metaphors of "vision" in this chapter are intended as a shorthand for movement-building that English speakers can understand. Yet, let me add for the record that they are entirely wrong. Uma Adang's movement is all about *hearing*, not seeing beyond. Yet to speak in English of hearing voices implies craziness, while "vision" implies dedication to a goal. Indeed, it is possible to argue that this disjunction between vision and voice is key to Uma Adang's "wobbly reproduction" of national and international disciplinary regimes.

21 What follows is my transcription of Uma Adang's *Sajarah dunia*. Uma Adang attempts Indonesian in this text, but it is not standard Indonesian. Through my spelling, I have tried to give the flavor of her idiosyncratic pronunciation. She fluctuates between "Banjarized" and exaggerated non-Banjar Indonesian. In contrast, the indented chant ("women's shamanism") is not Indonesian, but rather Meratus. Its language use is reasonably standard and comprehensible.

> Sekarang untuk mambuka sajarah dunia
> atas terisi dari Adam dan Hawa.
> Asal Adam dan Tikhawa
> Adalah ba'anak ampat puluh satu nabi.
> Ampat puluh satu nabi, samua nabi ampat puluh satu.

Salalu nabi kami adalah Nabi Lahat
Nabi Lahat sambahan kami,
kepada Nabi Lahat dar Alah.
Nabi Lahat turun kepada Nabi Daud.
Salalu Nabi Daud mangadakan balian bini-bini.
Yahlah ini nama siwara,
dan kata-kata adat kami.

Inilah balian bini-bini
untuk dibuka ataupun di siarkan.
Barangsiapa yang mau dangar,
Samua parsilahkan:
   Kada sibarang dirabun,
   Kada sibarang dipuyuh,
   Puyuh dahupa oli titian.
   Rabun manyan oli tumpakan.
   Rabahnya mamusing sungkul,
   Tumbangnya mamusing balai,
   Rabah ma'ulah jadi titian,
   Bajutata bahitung-hitungan di tumpakan ai.
   Kah mahitung di titian, ai.
   Kamana dayang sa'ulun kun?
   Mancagat jadi tumpakan, diyang sa'imang.
   Mahitung titian balanut.
   Maka ku janang panata balai.
   Maka ku janang panata sungkul,
   Manata alam payungan.
   Bajutata [unintelligible] di tumpakan.
   Tujuh ka bunga balai basar,
   Batitian di angin basar.
   Batumpakan yang indah nasun.
   Maminta air barasih,
   Maka manyambah air cuci.
   Air barasih panudusan palangsiran
   Maka malangsir alam payungan,
   Ku malangsir alam kandangan, tujuh banua, pitung nagari.
   Mayambah setiap malam,
   Mayambah setiap hari,
   Tabi-tabi aku hiyang.

Itulah balian manadar kepada Nabi Lahat ataupun Nabi Daud untuk
balian bini-bini asal dukun jaman di tahun tujuh puluh juta tujuh puluh
juta yang terisi tujuh puluh juta tujuh juta tahun balian bini-bini.

Salalu terada adat dari Majapahit.
Ma'isikan Majapahit
   nomor satu, basi patung
   kedua, ilat patung

ketiga, naga runting
keampat, malawin
kelima, dulema
keanam, ukuran senyawa
ketujuh, ketujuh ada beberapapun besi bikinan Majapahit
Semua adalah saratus ampat puluh satu.
Salalu balian bini-bini jatuh kepada balian laki-laki.
Lalu berisi adat
Adat beberapa adat
Mulai di balian bini-bini dukun
Dijatuhkan kepada Majapahit Garagu Tujuh.
Adat lalu semua ada adat agama kaharingan
Ataupun agama Buda.

Sekarang selebih daripada itu
Sudah kami ada adat jaman Majapahit dan balian laki-laki,
Semping Majapahit dengan Gambar Kemanikan,
Gambar Kemanikan semping dengan bujang Jiwara,
Bujang Jiwara semping dengan Bambang Siwara,
Salalu semping dengan Sandayuhan,
Salalu semping dibawa adalah Samali'ing,
Derisi dengan keada'an adat-adat.
Salalu balian kami turun manurun.
Lalu sampai dari karaja'an,
Turun manurun karaja'an,
Lalu balian kami adalah mandudus dengan atas karaja'an,
Jaman akan untuk parubahkala yang jaman dulu
Babarapa sungguh besar ataupun tertinggi.
Itulah balian kami turun manurun.

Diteruskan kepada jaman keada'an muyang dan anggas.
Diteruskan kepada datu turun manurun datu.
Dan derisikan kepada datung turun manurun datung.
Terus dikadakan kepada sampaikan ataspun ya ninik
    ataupun awat.
Sudah awat itu diturunkan kepada bapak kami.
Bapak kami itu diturunkan kepada anak.
Anak kepada cucu.
Cucu diteruskan kepada iyut ataupun piyut.
Semua kami ini yang malebarkan sajarah,
Ataupun semua kami yang manyiarkan sajarah,
Sudah beberapa turun adahlah seadat-adat nya.

Memang adat ti'ada terkap. Adat yang terkena dari Nabi Lahat. Isi
bukan apa, tidak. Harap yakin ataupun keyakinan kami kepada Surga,
Tuhan Yang Maha Esa. Memang kami menadar kepada Nabi, bardoa
kepada Surga, minta semua akan selamat dan sempurna, kepada Surga
Tuhan Yek Hak Yang Maha Kuasa—Wassalam.

Reprise

1   The 1960s and 70s saw calls for research in each direction (for example, Hymes 1972; Schneider 1980 [1968]). By the 1980s, many anthropologists were reflecting on the separate directions taken. See, for example, Ortner (1984); and Marcus and Fischer (1986). In the 1980s, the approaches of Raymond Williams (for example, 1977) and Michel Foucault (for example, 1978) were influential in pushing symbolic analysis in a more political direction. Similarly, new concerns with transnational cultural processes have pushed political economy toward issues of meaning, style, and cultural identity (see, for example, Appadurai 1990; Taussig 1987).

2   In the late 1970s and early 1980s, anthologies in feminist anthropology were neatly divided along these lines. For the first alternative, see Ortner and Whitehead (1981); and MacCormack and Strathern (1980). For the second alternative, see Etienne and Leacock (1980); and Nash and Fernandez-Kelly (1983). More recent works have proposed agendas that cross and confuse these lines, creating new analytic possibilities; see, for example, Ong (1987); Martin (1987); and Ginsburg and Tsing (1990).

3   The translation and transcription attempt to render Uma Adang's original faithfully. Yet, in the conversion of a contextually specific oral presentation to a written text in another language and tradition, there is much that shifts. I have taken certain liberties with the tape transcript, in order to preserve the spirit of what I heard. I have omitted sections from the last third of the tape transcript in which Uma Adang repeated lines and inserted impenetrable mystical phrases. *Akrana, akrana* remains as the only indication of these mystical phrases. I have added minor details from her rendition the evening before and have placed the text on the page in a way that refers to the oral spacing as it also makes it more possible, I hope, to read the piece with pleasure. My point here is to offer the reader something of the sense of Uma Adang's story, and I have made my editorial choices in line with this goal.

4   Many Southeast Asians tell related stories about fetal development (for example, Laderman 1983:85, 142). Jane Atkinson (personal communication) usefully comments: "The notion that the child learns its fate in utero is a theme in the wider region. The fact that Uma Adang is elaborating a regional theme does not undercut the creativity of her 'cultural intervention,' but it does recall that bricolage draws on cultural stockpiles which may even exhibit certain structural properties!"

5   The phenomenal growth of the Indonesian environmental movement in the late 1980s and early 90s may be changing this situation. For an introduction to this movement, see Elderidge (1989) and the journals *Environesia* and *Setiakawan*.

REFERENCES CITED

Abu-Lughod, Lila. 1986. *Veiled Sentiments: Honor and Poetry in Bedouin Society*. Berkeley: University of California Press.

———. 1990. "The Romance of Resistance: Tracing Transformations of Power through Bedouin Women." *American Ethnologist* 17 (1): 41–55.

———. 1991. "Writing against Culture." In *Recapturing Anthropology: Working in the Present*, edited by Richard J. Fox, 137–62. Santa Fe, N.Mex.: School of American Research Press.

Anderson, Benedict. 1972. "The Idea of Power in Javanese Culture." In *Culture and Politics in Indonesia*, edited by C. Holt, 1–69. Ithaca, N.Y.: Cornell University Press.

———. 1983. *Imagined Communities: Reflections on the Origin and Spread of Nationalism*. London: Verso.

———. 1987. "Introduction." In *Southeast Asian Tribal Groups and Ethnic Minorities*, 1–15. Cultural Survival Report no. 22. Cambridge, Mass.: Cultural Survival.

———. 1987a. "The State and Minorities in Indonesia." In *Southeast Asian Tribal Groups and Ethnic minorities*, 73–81. Cultural Survival Report no. 22. Cambridge, Mass.: Cultural Survival.

———, ed. 1990. *Language and Power: Exploring Cultures in Indonesia*. Ithaca, N.Y.: Cornell University Press.

Anzaldua, Gloria. 1987. *Borderlands/La Frontera: The New Mestiza*. San Francisco: Spinsters/Aunt Lute.

———, ed. 1990. *Making Face, Making Soul/Haciendo Caras: Creative and Critical Perspectives by Women of Color*. San Francisco: Aunt Lute.

Appardurai, Arjun. 1990. "Disjuncture and Difference in the Global Cultural Economy." *Public Culture* 2 (2): 1–24.

Appell, George, ed. 1976. *The Societies of Borneo*. American Anthropological Association Special Publication no. 6. Washington, D.C.

———. 1976a. "Introduction." In *The Societies of Borneo*, edited by George Appell, 1–15. American Anthropological Association Special Publication no. 6. Washington, D.C.

———. 1976b. "The Rungus: Social Structure in a Cognatic Society and Its Ritual Symbolization." In *The Societies of Borneo*, edited by George Appell, 66–86. American Anthropological Association Special Publication no. 6. Washington, D.C.

Appell, Laura W. R. 1988. "Menstruation among the Rungus of Borneo: An Unmarked Category." In *Blood Magic: The Anthropology of Menstruation*, edited by T. Buckley and A. Gottlieb, 94–112. Berkeley: University of California Press.

Ardener, Edwin. 1975. "Belief and the Problem of Women." In *Perceiving Women*, edited by Shirley Ardener, 1–27. New York: Wiley and Sons.

Artha, Artum. 1974. *Beberapa Masalah Kebudayaan Banjar*. Surabaya, Indonesia: PT Bina Ilmu.

Atkinson, Jane Monnig. 1987. "Religions in Dialogue: The Construction of an Indonesian Minority Religion." In *Indonesian Religions in Transition*, edited by Rita Smith Kipp and Susan Rodgers, 171–86. Tucson: University of Arizona Press.

———. 1989. *The Art and Politics of Wana Shamanship*. Berkeley: University of California Press.

———. 1990. "How Gender Makes a Difference in Wana Society." In *Power and Difference: Gender in Island Southeast Asia*, edited by Jane Monnig Atkinson and Shelly Errington, 59–93. Stanford: Stanford University Press.

Atkinson, Jane Monnig, and Shelly Errington, eds. 1990. *Power and Difference: Gender in Island Southeast Asia*. Stanford: Stanford University Press.

Aveling, Harry. 1986. "Introduction." In *Crossing the Border: Five Indonesian Short Stories*, edited by Harry Aveling, 1–9. Clayton, Australia: Monash University Centre of Southeast Asian Studies.

———, ed. 1986a. *Crossing the Border: Five Indonesian Short Stories*. Clayton, Australia: Monash University Centre of Southeast Asian Studies.

———. *See* Haridas, Swami Anand.

Aziddin, Yustan and Sjarifuddun, M. Idwar Saleh, and M. Nasai. 1980–81. *Sistem Kesatuan Hidup Setempat Daerah Kalimantan Selatan*. Proyek Inventarisasi Dokumentasi dan Kebudayaan Daerah, Departemen Pendidikan dan Kebudayaan, Republik Indonesia.

Babas, Djajamadi. 1978. *Pembinaan Pendidikan Agama di Masyarakat Terasing Cantung, Kota Baru, Pulau Laut*. Banjarmasin, Indonesia: Institut Agama Islam Negeri, Antasari.

Bailen, Jerome B. 1986. *A Tasaday Folio*. Quezon City, Philippines: University of Philippines, Department of Anthropology.

Bakhtin, M. M. 1981. *The Dialogic Imagination*. Austin: University of Texas Press.

Basry, Hassan. 1961. *Kisah Gerila Kalimantan*. Banjarmasin, Indonesia: Lambung Mangkurat.

Beeckman, Daniel. 1973 [1718]. *A Voyage to and from the Island of Borneo*. Folkestone, England: Dawsons of Pall Mall.

Bell, Diane. 1983. *Daughters of the Dreaming*. Melbourne, Australia: McPhee Gribble.

Benedict, Ruth. 1959. *Patterns of Culture*. Boston: Houghton Mifflin.

Berreman, Gerald D. 1991. "The Incredible 'Tasaday': Deconstructing the Myth of a Stone Age People." *Cultural Survival* 15 (1): 3–45.

Bhabha, Homi K. 1988. "The Commitment to Theory." *New Formations* 2: 5–23.

———. 1989. "Remembering Fanon: Self, Psyche, and the Colonial Condition." In *Remaking History*, edited by B. Kriger and P. Mariani, 131–48. Seattle: Bay Press.

———. 1990. "The Other Question: Difference, Discrimination and the Discourse of Colonialism." In *Out There: Marginalization and Contemporary Cultures*, edited by R. Ferguson, M. Gever, Trinh T. Minh-ha, and Cornel West, 71–81. Cambridge: MIT Press.

Boddy, Janice P. 1989. *Wombs and Alien Spirits: Women, Men and the Zar Cult in Northern Sudan*. Madison: University of Wisconsin Press.

Boland, B. J. 1982. *The Struggle of Islam in Modern Indonesia*. The Hague: Nijoff.

Bookman, Ann, and Sandra Morgen. 1988. *Women and the Politics of Empowerment*. Philadelphia: Temple University Press.

Boserup, Ester. 1970. *Woman's Role in Economic Development*. London: Allen and Unwin.

Bourdieu, Pierre. 1977. *Outline of a Theory of Practice*. Translated by Richard Nice. Cambridge: Cambridge University Press.

———. 1984. *Distinction: A Social Critique of the Judgement of Taste*. Translated by Richard Nice. Cambridge: Harvard University Press.

———. 1990. *The Logic of Practice*. Translated by Richard Nice. Stanford: Stanford University Press.

Brosius, Peter. 1989. "The Penan Encounter with Development in Sarawak, East Malaysia." Paper presented at Midwest Conference on Asian Affairs.

Burris, Barbara. 1973. "The Fourth World Manifesto." In *Radical Feminism*, edited by A. Koedt, E. Levine, and A. Rapone. New York: Quadrangle.

Butler, Judith. 1990. *Gender Trouble: Feminism and the Subversion of Identity*. New York: Routledge.

———. 1992. "Contingent Foundations: Feminism and the Question of 'Postmodernism.'" In *Feminists Theorize the Political*, edited by Judith Butler and Joan Scott, 3–21. New York: Routledge.

Butler, Judith, and Joan Scott, eds. 1992. *Feminists Theorize the Political*. New York: Routledge.

Chandler, Glen, Norma Sullivan, and Jan Branson, eds. 1988. *Development and Displacement: Women in Southeast Asia*. Monash Papers on Southeast Asia, no. 18. Clayton, Australia: Monash University Centre of Southeast Asian Studies.

Chernichovsky, Dov, and Oey Astra Meesook. 1981. "Regional Aspects of Family Planning and Fertility Behavior in Indonesia." World Bank Staff Working Paper no. 462.

Chin, S. C. 1985. *Agriculture and Resource Utilization in a Lowland Rainforest Kenyah Community*. In *Sarawak Museum Journal* (Kuching, Sarawak) n.s. 35.

Christian, Barbara. 1988. "The Race for Theory." *Feminist Studies* 14 (Spring): 13.

Cixous, Hélène. 1980. "The Laugh of the Medusa." In *New French Feminisms: An Anthology*, edited by Elaine Marks and Isabelle de Courtivron, 245–64. Amherst: University of Massachusetts Press.

Cixous, Hélène, and Catherine Clement. 1986. *The Newly Born Woman*. Translated by Betsey Wing. Manchester, England: Manchester University Press.

Clifford, James. 1986. "Introduction: Partial Truths." In *Writing Culture: The Poetics and Politics of Ethnography*, edited by James Clifford and George Marcus, 1–26. Berkeley: University of California Press.

———. 1988. "On Ethnographic Authority." In *The Predicament of Culture: Twentieth-Century Ethnography, Literature and Art*, 21–54. Cambridge: Harvard University Press.

———. 1992. "Traveling Cultures." In *Cultural Studies*, edited by Lawrence Grossberg, Cary Nelson, and Paula Treichler, 96–112. New York: Routledge.

Clifford, James, and George Marcus, eds. 1986. *Writing Culture: The Poetics and Politics of Ethnography.* Berkeley: University of California Press.

Colchester, Marcus. 1986. "Unity and Diversity: Indonesian Policy Towards Tribal People." *The Ecologist* 16 (2/3): 89–98.

Cole, Johnetta, ed. 1986. *All American Women: Lines That Divide, Ties That Bind.* New York: Free Press.

Collier, Jane, and Sylvia Junko Yanagisako, eds. 1974. *Gender and Kinship: Essays Toward a Unified Analysis.* Stanford: Stanford University Press.

Comaroff, Jean. 1985. *Body of Power, Spirit of Resistance: The Culture and History of a South African People.* Chicago: University of Chicago Press.

Conklin, Harold. 1957. *Hanunoo Agriculture: A Report on an Integral System of Shifting Cultivation in the Philippines.* Rome: Food and Agriculture Organization of the United Nations.

———. 1963. *The Study of Shifting Cultivation.* Washington, D.C.: Unión Panamericana, Secretaria General, Organización de los Estados Americanos.

Coppel, Charles A. 1983. *Indonesian Chinese in Crisis.* Kuala Lumpur: Oxford University Press.

Dalton, Bill. 1991. *Indonesia Handbook.* 5th ed. Chico, Calif.: Moon Publications.

Davis, Wade, and Thom Henley. 1990. *Penan: Voice of the Borneo Rainforest.* Vancouver: WILD.

deBord, Guy. 1970. *Society of the Spectacle.* Translated by Black and Red. Detroit: Black and Red.

Deegan, James. 1973. "Change among the Lun Bawang, a Borneo People." Ph.D. diss., University of Washington.

de Lauretis, Teresa. 1987. *Technologies of Gender: Essays on Theory, Film, and Fiction.* Bloomington: Indiana University Press.

———. 1990. "Eccentric Subjects: Feminist Theory and Historical Consciousness." *Feminist Studies* 16 (1): 115–50.

Departemen Pendidikan dan Kebudayaan. 1982. *Adat Istiadat Daerah Kalimantan Selatan.* Jakarta: Departemen Pendidikan dan Kebudayaan, Proyek Inventarisasi dan Dokumentasi Kebudayaan Daerah.

Derrida, Jacques. 1976. *Of Grammatology.* Translated by Gayatri Spivak. Baltimore: Johns Hopkins University Press.

———. 1978. *Writing and Difference.* Translated by Alan Bass. Chicago: University of Chicago Press.

Dirks, Nick. 1990. "History as a Sign of the Modern." *Public Culture* 2 (2): 25–32.

Dominguez, Virginia. 1989. *People as Subject, People as Object: Selfhood and Peoplehood in Contemporary Israel.* Madison: University of Wisconsin Press.

Dove, Michael. 1981. "Masalah Ekologi-Mikro dan Pembangunan-Makro: Suata Kasus Di Kalimantan Selatan." *Agro Ekonomika* 12 (14).

———. 1985. *Swidden Agriculture in Indonesia: The Subsistence Strategies of the Kalimantan Kantu.* Berlin: Mouton.

———. 1985a. "The Agroecological Mythology of the Javanese and the Political Economy of Indonesia." *Indonesia* 39 (April): 1–36.

———, ed. 1988. *The Real and Imagined Role of Culture in Development: Case Studies in Indonesia.* Honolulu: University of Hawaii Press.

———. 1989. "Interpretations of Peasant Resistance on State Plantations in Indonesia:

Beyond the Anthropology of Peasants, beyond the Anthropology of Anthropologists." Paper presented at Cornell University, Southeast Asia Program and Department of Rural Sociology.

Drake, Richard A. 1989. "Construction-Sacrifice and Kidnapping-Rumor Panics in Borneo." *Oceania* 59:269–79.

Dumont, Jean Paul. 1988. "The Tasaday, Which and Whose? Toward the Political Economy of an Ethnographic Sign." *Cultural Anthropology* 3 (3): 261–75.

Durasid, Durdje. 1977. *Struktur Bahasa Banjar Hulu*. Banjarmasin, Indonesia: Departemen Pendidikan dan Kebudayaan.

Ebron, Paulla. 1991. "Rapping between Men: Performing Gender." *Radical America* 23 (4): 23–27.

Elderidge, Philip. 1989. "NGOs in Indonesia: Popular Movement or Arm of Government?" Working Paper no. 55. Clayton, Australia: Monash University Centre of Southeast Asian Studies.

Erb, Maribeth. 1991. "Construction-Sacrifice Rumors and Kidnapping Scares in Manggari: Further Comparative Notes from Flores." *Oceania* 62 (2): 114–26.

Errington, Shelly. 1989. *Meaning and Power in a Southeast Asian Realm*. Princeton: Princeton University Press.

———. 1992. "Making Progress on Borobudur: An Old Monument in New Order." Paper presented at the Conference on Ruins, University of California, Santa Cruz.

———. N.d. "The Cosmic Airport of the Javanese." Typescript.

Etienne, Mona, and Eleanor Leacock. 1980. *Women and Colonization: Anthropological Perspectives*. New York: Praeger.

Fabian, Johannes. 1983. *Time and the Other: How Anthropology Makes Its Object*. New York: Columbia University Press.

Ferguson, James, and Akhil Gupta, eds. 1992. "Space, Identity, and the Politics of Difference." *Cultural Anthropology*, theme issue, 7 (1).

Foucault, Michel. 1977. *Discipline and Punish: The Birth of the Prison*. Translated by Alan Sheridan. New York: Pantheon Books.

———. 1978. *The History of Sexuality*. Vol 1: *An Introduction*. Translated by Robert Hurley. New York: Pantheon Books.

Fox, Richard J. 1991. "For a Nearly New Culture History." In *Recapturing Anthropology: Working in the Present*, edited by Richard J. Fox, 93–113. Santa Fe, N.Mex.: School of American Research Press.

Frederick, William. 1982. "Rhoma Irama and Dangdut Style." *Indonesia*. 34:103–30.

Freedman, Ronald. 1978. "Evaluation and Research on Family Planning, Fertility, and Population in Indonesia." World Bank. Mimeo.

Freeman, J. Derek. 1958. "The Family System of the Iban of Borneo." In *The Development Cycle in Domestic Groups*, edited by Jack Goody, 15–52. Cambridge: Cambridge University Press.

———. 1961. "On the Concept of the Kindred." *Journal of the Royal Anthropological Institute* 91:192–220.

———. 1967. "Shaman and Incubus." *The Psychoanalytic Study of Society*. 4:314–43.

———. 1970. *Report on the Iban*. New York: Humanities Press.

———. 1981. "Some Reflections on the Nature of Iban Society." Occasional Paper of the Department of Anthropology, Research School of Pacific Studies, Australian National University, Canberra.

Gailey, Christine Ward. 1987. *Kinship and Kingship: Gender Hierarchy and State Formation in the Tongan Islands.* Austin: University of Texas Press.

Gates, Henry Louis. 1991. "Critical Fanonism." *Critical Inquiry* 17 (3): 457–71.

Geertz, Clifford. 1980. *Negara: The Theatre State in Nineteenth-Century Bali.* Princeton: Princeton University Press.

———. 1988. *Works and Lives: The Anthropologist as Author.* Stanford: Stanford University Press.

Ghosh, Amitav. 1988. *The Shadow Lines.* New York: Viking.

Gilbert, Sandra, and Susan Gubar. 1979. *The Madwoman in the Attic.* New Haven: Yale University Press.

Ginsburg, Faye D. 1989. *Contested Lives: The Abortion Debate in an American Community.* Berkeley: University of California Press.

———. 1990. "The 'Word-Made' Flesh: The Disembodiment of Gender in the Abortion Debate." In *Uncertain Terms: Negotiating Gender in American Culture,* edited by Faye D. Ginsburg and Anna Tsing, 59–75. Boston: Beacon Press.

Ginsburg, Faye D., and Anna Tsing, eds. 1990. *Uncertain Terms: Negotiating Gender in American Culture.* Boston: Beacon Press.

Gough, Kathleen. 1971. "Nuer Kinship: A Re-examination." In *The Translation of Culture: Essays to E. E. Evans-Pritchard,* edited by T. O. Beidelman, 79–121. London: Tavistock.

Grabowsky, Fritz. 1885. "Die 'Orang Bukit' Oder Bergmenshen von Mindai in Sodost-Borneo." *Das Ausland* 58:782–86.

Grosz, Elizabeth A. 1989. *Sexual Subversions: Three French Feminists.* Winchester, Mass.: Allen and Unwin.

Hall, Stuart. 1990. "Cultural Identity and Diaspora." In *Identity: Community, Culture, Difference,* edited by J. Rutherford, 222–37. London: Lawrence and Wishart.

Hamda, M. J. 1979. "Pembangunan Masarakat Pedesaan Melalui Proyek Pengembangan Kesejahteraan Masarakat Terasing." Paper distributed at the Seminar Pembinaan Masarakat Pegunungan Meratus di Kalimantan Selatan, IAIN Antasari, Banjarmasin, Indonesia.

Hanafiah, A. Gaffar. 1977. *South Kalimantan in Brief.* Banjarmasin, Indonesia: Banjarmasin.

Hansen, Eric. 1988. *Stranger in the Forest: On Foot across Borneo.* Boston: Houghton Mifflin.

Hapip, Abdul Djebar. 1976. *Kamus Banjar–Indonesia.* Jakarta: Pusat Pembinaan dan Pemgembangan Bahasa, Departemen Pendidikan dan Kebudayaan.

———. 1977. "Bahasa Banjar dan Tipologi Dialek Banjar Hulu dan Banjar Kuala." *Vidya Karya,* Special Edition no. 1.

Haraway, Donna. 1988. "Situated Knowledges: The Science Question in Feminism and the Privilege of Partial Perspective." *Feminist Studies* 14 (3): 575–99.

———. 1989. *Primate Visions: Gender, Race and Nature in the World of Modern Science.* New York: Routledge.

Haridas, Swami Anand [Harry Aveling]. 1985. *Sastra Indonesia: Terlibat atau Tidak?* Yogyakarta, Indonesia: Kanisius.

Hart, Gillian. N.d. "Engendering Everyday Resistance: Production, Patronage, and Gender Politics in Rural Malaysia." Typescript.

Hartmann, Betsy. 1987. *Reproductive Rights and Wrongs: The Global Politics of Population Control and Contraceptive Choice.* New York: Harper and Row.

Hastrup, Kirsten. 1990. "The Ethnographic Present: A Reinvention." *Cultural Anthropology* 5 (1): 45–61.

Hefner, Robert W. 1990. *The Political Economy of Mountain Java: An Interpretive History.* Berkeley: University of California Press.

Hepell, M. 1975. "Iban Social Control: The Infant and the Adult." Ph.D. diss., Australian National University, Canberra

Hong, Evelyn. 1987. *Natives of Sarawak: Survival in Borneo's Vanishing Forests.* Pulau Pinang, Malaysia: Institut Masyarakat.

hooks, bell. 1989. *Talking Back: Thinking Feminist, Thinking Black.* Boston: South End Press.

————. 1990. *Yearning: Race, Gender, and Cultural Politics.* Boston: South End Press.

Hudson, Alfred B. 1967. "Padju Epat: The Ethnography and Social Structure of a Ma'anjan Dajak Group in Southeastern Borneo." Ph.D. diss., Cornell University.

Hymes, Dell H., ed. 1972. *Reinventing Anthropology,* New York: Pantheon.

IAIN Antasari. 1973. *Pembinaan Kehidupan Beragama Masyarakat Suku Terasing Dayak Labuhan Atas, Kabupaten Hulu Sungai Tengah, Kalimantan Selatan.* Banjarmasin, Indonesia: Institut Agama Islam Negeri Al-Jamia Antasari.

Ikranagara. 1992. Presentation at the Conference on Art, Media, and Censorship in Indonesia, University of California, Santa Cruz.

Irigaray, Luce. 1985. *Speculum of the Other Woman.* Translated by Gillian C. Gill. Ithaca, N.Y.: Cornell University Press.

Irwin, Graham. 1955. *Nineteenth-Century Borneo.* Singapore: Donald Moore Books.

Ismail, Aburachman, A. K. Ismail, A. Aini, M. Yusni, and N. Nasusfi. 1979. *Bahasa Bukit.* Jakarta: Pusat Pembinaan dan Pengembangan Bahasa, Departemen Pendidikan dan Kebudayaan.

Jameson, Frederic. 1991. *Postmodernism, or the Cultural Logic of Late Capitalism.* Durham, N.C.: Duke University Press.

Jenkins, David. 1978. "The Last Headhunt." *Far Eastern Economic Review,* 30 June, 25.

Jessup, Timothy. 1981. "Why Do Apo Kayan Shifting Cultivators Move?" *Borneo Research Bulletin* 13 (1): 16–32.

Jessup, Timothy, and Nancy Peluso. 1986. "Minor Forest Products as Common Property Resources in East Kalimantan, Indonesia." In *Proceedings of the Conference on Common Property Resources,* 515–39. Washington, D.C.: National Academy of Sciences.

Kadane, Kathy. 1990. "CIA Role in 1965 Bloodbath: Agents Recall Death Lists in Indonesia." *San Francisco Examiner,* 20 May.

Kartawinata, K., and A. P. Vayda. 1984. "Forest Conversion in East Kalimantan, Indonesia: The Activities and Impact of Timber Companies, Shifting Cultivators, Migrant Pepper-Farmers, and Others." In *Ecology and Practice: Establishing a Scientific Basis for Land Management,* vol. 2, edited by F. Dicastri, F. W. G. Baker, and M. Hadley. Paris: UNESCO.

King, Victor, ed. 1978. *Essays on Borneo Societies.* Oxford: University of Hull.

Kipp, Rita Smith, and Susan Rodgers, eds. 1987. *Indonesian Religions in Transition.* Tucson: University of Arizona Press.

Koesnoe, Mohammad. 1971. *Introduction into Indonesian Adat Law.* Publicaties over Adatrecht van de Katholieke Universitat te Nijmegen, no. 3. Nijmegen, Netherlands.

Kondo, Dorrine. 1990. *Crafting Selves: Power, Gender, and Discourses of Identity in a Japanese Workplace.* Chicago: University of Chicago Press.

Kondo, Dorrine. 1990a. " 'M. Butterfly,' Tony Award-winning Play by David Hwang: Orientalism, Gender, and a Critique of Essentialist Identity." *Cultural Critique* 16: 5–29.

Kristeva, Julia. 1982. *Powers of Horror: An Essay on Abjection.* Translated by Leon S. Roudiez. New York: Columbia University Press.

Laderman, Carol. 1983. *Wives and Midwives: Childbirth and Nutrition in Rural Malaysia.* Berkeley: University of California Press.

———. 1991. *Taming the Winds of Desire: Psychology, Medicine, and Aesthetics in Malay Shamanship Performance.* Berkeley: University of California Press.

Lewis, Diane. 1973. "Anthropology and Colonialism." *Current Anthropology* 14:581–602.

Lindblad, J. Thomas. 1988. *Between Dutch and Dayak: The Economic History of Southeast Kalimantan, 1880–1942.* Dordrect, Netherlands: Foris.

Lorde, Audre. 1984. "The Master's Tools Will Never Dismantle the Master's House." In *Sister Outsider: Essays and Speeches*, 110–13. Trumansburg, N.Y.: Crossing Press.

Lumholtz, Carl. 1921. *Through Central Borneo.* London: T. Fisher Unwin.

MacCormack, Carol, and Marilyn Strathern. 1980. *Nature, Culture and Gender.* Cambridge: Cambridge University Press.

McVey, Ruth. 1982. "The Beamtenstaat in Indonesia." In *Interpreting Indonesian Politics: Thirteen Contributions to the Debate*, edited by Benedict Anderson and A. Kahin, 84–91. Ithaca, N.Y.: Cornell University Press.

Mallinckrodt, J. 1927. "De Stamindeeling van de Maanjan-Sioeng-Dajaks, der Zuider- en Ooster-Afdeeling van Borneo." *Bijdragen tot de Taal-, Land-, en Volkenkunde* 83:552–92.

———. 1928. *Het Adatrecht van Borneo.* Leiden, Netherlands: Dubbleman.

Mani, Lata. 1987. "Contentious Traditions: The Debate on SATI in Colonial India." *Cultural Critique* 7 (Fall): 119–56.

Manihuruk, A. E., and editorial team. 1962. *Kodam X/LM Membangun.* Banjarmasin, Indonesia: Kodam X/LM.

March, Kathryn. 1983. "Weaving, Writing, and Gender." *Man*, n.s. 18:729–44.

Marcus, George, and Michael M. J. Fischer. 1986. *Anthropology as Cultural Critique: An Experimental Moment in the Human Sciences.* Chicago: University of Chicago Press.

Martin, Biddy, and Chandra Mohanty. 1986. "Feminist Politics: What's Home Got to Do with It?" In *Feminist Studies/Critical Studies*, edited by Teresa de Lauretis, 191–212. Bloomington: University of Indiana Press.

Martin, Emily. 1987. *The Woman in the Body: A Cultural Analysis of Reproduction.* Boston: Beacon Press.

Mayur, S. H. 1979. *Perang Banjar.* Banjarmasin, Indonesia: C. V. Rapi.

Mead, Margaret. 1928. *Coming of Age in Samoa.* New York: W. Morrow.

Messick, Brinckley. 1987. "Subordinate Discourses: Women, Weaving, and Gender Relations in North Africa." *American Ethnologist* 14 (2): 210–25.

Miles, Douglas. 1966. "Shamanism and the Conversion of the Ngaju Dayaks." *Oceania* 37 (1): 1–12.

———. 1976. *Cutlass and Crescent Moon.* Sydney: Centre for Asian Studies, University of Sydney.

Mitchell, Timothy. 1990. "Everyday Metaphors of Power." *Theory and Society* 19:545–77.

Moehji. 1983. *Perkembangan Industri Perkayuan di Kalimantan Selatan.* DP/BPPI/BBS/17/

83. Bandung, Indonesia: Departemen Perindustrian, R. I., Badan Penelitian Pengembangan Industri, Balai Besar Penelitian dan Pengembangan Industri Selulosa Bandung.

Moertono, S. 1968. *State and State Craft in Old Java*. Monograph Series, Southeast Asia Program, Cornell University. Ithaca, N.Y.

Mohanty, Chandra, Ann Russo, and Lourdes Torres. 1991. *Third World Women and the Politics of Feminism*. Bloomington: Indiana University Press.

Molony, Carol H. 1988. "The Truth about the Tasaday." *The Sciences* (Sept./Oct.): 12–20.

Moraga, Cherrie. 1983. "A Long Line of Vendidas." In *Loving in the War Years: lo que nunca pasó por sus labios*, 90–144. Boston: South End Press,

Morgan, Robin. 1970. *Sisterhood Is Powerful: An Anthology of Writings from the Women's Liberation Movement*. New York: Random House.

Morgen, Sandra, ed. 1989. *Gender and Anthropology: Critical Reviews for Research and Teaching*. Washington, D.C.: American Anthropological Association.

Mulder, Niels. 1978. *Mysticism and Everyday Life in Contemporary Java: Cultural Persistence and Change*. Singapore: Singapore University Press.

Myerhoff, Barbara. 1978. *Number Our Days*. New York: Simon and Schuster.

Najmabadi, Afsaneh. 1991. "Interview with Gayatri Spivak." *Social Text* 28:122–34.

Nance, John. 1975. *The Gentle Tasaday: A Stone Age People in the Philippine Rainforest*. New York: Harcourt Brace Jovanovich.

Nash, June, and Maria Patricia Fernandez Kelly. 1983. *Women, Men and the International Division of Labor*. Albany: State University of New York Press.

Ong, Aihwa. 1987. *Spirits of Resistance and Capitalist Discipline: Factory Women in Malaysia*. Albany: State University of New York Press.

———. 1990. "Japanese Factories, Malay Workers: Class and Sexual Metaphors in West Malaysia." In *Power and Difference: Gender in Island Southeast Asia*, edited by Jane Monnig Atkinson and Shelly Errington, 385–422. Stanford: Stanford University Press.

———. 1990a. "State versus Islam: Malay Families, Women's Bodies, and the Body Politic in Malaysia." *American Ethnologist* 17 (2): 258–76.

Ortner, Sherry. 1984. "Theory in Anthropology since the Sixties." *Comparative Studies in Society and History* 26 (1): 126–66.

Ortner, Sherry, and Harriet Whitehead, eds. 1981. *Sexual Meanings: The Cultural Construction of Gender and Sexuality*. Cambridge: Cambridge University Press.

Peluso, Nancy. 1983. "Markets and Merchants: The Forest Products Trade of East Kalimantan in Historical Perspective." Master's thesis, Cornell University.

———. 1992. "Beyond the Slash and Burn." Invited paper, University of California, Santa Cruz.

Pemberton, John. 1989. The Appearance of Order: A Politics of Culture in Colonial and Postcolonial Java. Ph.D. diss., Cornell University.

Petchesky, Rosalind. 1987. "Fetal Images: The Power of Visual Culture in the Politics of Reproduction." *Feminist Studies* 13 (2): 263–99.

Posewitz, Theodor. 1892. *Borneo: Its Geology and Mineral Resources*. Translated by Frederick Hatch. London: Edward Stanford.

Potter, Leslie. 1992. "Impacts of Government Policy on Rural Areas of Outer Indonesia." Invited paper, University of California, Berkeley.

Pratt, Mary. 1986. "Fieldwork in Common Places." In *Writing Culture: The Poetics and Politics of Ethnography*, edited by James Clifford and George Marcus, 27–50. Berkeley: University of California Press.

Prell, Riv-Ellen. 1989. "The Double Frame of Life History in the Work of Barbara Myer-hoff." In *Interpreting Women's Lives: Feminist Theory and Personal Narratives*, edited by Personal Narratives Group, 241–58. Bloomington: University of Indiana Press.

Propinsi Kalimantan. 1953. *Republik Indonesia: Propinsi Kalimantan*. Kalimantan, Indonesia: Propinsi Kalimantan.

Proyek Pembinaan Perguruan Tinggi Agama. 1978. *Upacara Religi dan Beberapa Adat Istiadat Masyarakat Pegunungan Meratus di Kalimantan Selatan*. Banjarmasin, Indonesia: Institut Agama Islam Negeri, Antasari.

Rabinow, Paul. 1977. *Reflections on Fieldwork in Morocco*. Berkeley: University of California Press.

———, ed. 1988. "Anthropology and the Analysis of Modernity." *Cultural Anthropology*, theme issue, 3 (4).

Radam, H. Noer'ied. 1982. *Budaya Orang Bukit di Alai dan Hamandit*. Banjarmasin, Indonesia: Universitas Lambung Mangkurat.

Ras, J. J. 1968. *Hikajat Banjar: A Study in Malay Historiography*. The Hague: Martinus Nijoff.

Reid, Anthony. 1988. *Southeast Asia in the Age of Commerce, 1450–1680*. New Haven: Yale University Press.

Reiter, Rayna Rapp, ed. 1975. *Toward an Anthropology of Women*. New York: Monthly Review Press.

Rendra, W. S. 1979. *The Struggle of the Naga Tribe*. Translated by Max Lane. New York: St. Martin's.

Rifai, Mien A. 1991. "That Was a Dayak Dusun Day That Was." Paper presented at the Conference on Interactions of People and Forests in Kalimantan. New York Botanical Gardens, New York.

Robison, Richard. 1986. *Indonesia: The Rise of Capital*. North Sydney: Allen and Unwin.

Rofel, Lisa. 1992. "Rethinking Modernity: Space and Factory Discipline in China." *Cultural Anthropology* 7 (1): 93–114.

Rosaldo, Michelle Zimbalist. 1974. "Woman, Culture, and Society: A Theoretical Overview." In *Woman, Culture, and Society*, edited by Michelle Zimbalist Rosaldo and Louise Lamphere, 17–42. Stanford: Stanford University Press.

———. 1980. *Knowledge and Passion: Ilongot Notions of Self and Social Life*. Cambridge: Cambridge University Press.

Rosaldo, Michelle Zimbalist, and Louise Lamphere, eds. 1974. *Woman, Culture, and Society*. Stanford: Stanford University Press.

Rosaldo, Michelle Zimbalist, and Jane Monnig Atkinson. 1975. "Man the Hunter and Woman: Metaphors for the Sexes in Ilongot Magic Spells." In *The Interpretation of Symbolism*, edited by R. Willis, 43–75. London: Malaby Press.

Rosaldo, Renato. 1989. *Culture and Truth: The Remaking of Social Analysis*. Boston: Beacon Press.

Roseman, Marina. 1991. *Healing Sounds from the Malaysian Rainforest: Temiar Music and Medicine*. Berkeley: University of California Press.

Rousseau, Jerome. 1990. *Central Borneo: Ethnic Identity and Social Life in a Stratified Society*. Oxford: Clarendon Press.

Sacks, Karen. 1979. *Sisters and Wives: The Past and Future of Sexual Equality*. Westport, Conn.: Greenwood Press.

Said, Edward. 1978. *Orientalism*. New York: Pantheon Books.

Saif, Muhammad Rusjdie. 1978. "Menegenal Kehidupan Suku Dayak Haruyan Dayak di Proyek PKMT Biang I." Proyek PKMT Biang, South Kalimantan, Indonesia. Typescript report.

Saleh, Mohamad Idwar. 1975. *Banjarmasih*. Banjarmasin, Indonesia: Almamater.

———. 1976. "Pepper Trade and the Banjarese Ruling Class of Banjarmasih in the Seventeenth Century." *Vidya Karya* 5 (34): 56–72; 6 (35): 2–22.

Sandoval, Chela. 1991. "U.S. Third World Feminism: The Theory and Method of Oppositional Consciousness in the Postmodern World," *Genders* 10:1–24.

Schneider, David M. 1980 [1968]. *American Kinship: A Cultural Account*. 2d ed. Chicago: University of Chicago Press.

Schwaner, C. M. 1853. "Historische, Geographische, en Statistieke Aanteekeningen Betreffende Tanah Boemboe." *Tijdschrift voor Indische Taal-, Land-, en Volkenkunde* 1:335–71.

Scott, James C. 1985. *Weapons of the Weak: Everyday Forms of Peasant Resistance*. New Haven: Yale University Press.

Scott, Joan Wallach. 1988. *Gender and the Politics of History*. New York: Columbia University Press.

———. 1992. "Experience." In *Feminists Theorize the Political*, edited by Judith Butler and Joan Scott, 22–40. New York: Routledge.

Sesser, Stan. 1991. "A Reporter At Large: Logging in the Rain Forest." *New Yorker*, 27 May, 42–67.

Shostak, Marjorie. 1981. *Nisa: The Life and Words of a !Kung Woman*. Cambridge: Harvard University Press.

———. 1989. "What the Wind Won't Take Away: The Genesis of Nisa—The Life and Words of a !Kung Woman." In *Interpreting Women's Lives: Feminist Theory and Personal Narratives*, edited by Personal Narratives Group, 228–40. Bloomington: Indiana University Press.

Siegel, James. 1969. *The Rope of God*. Berkeley: University of California Press.

———. 1986. *Solo in the New Order: Language and Hierarchy in an Indonesian City*. Princeton: Princeton University Press.

Smith, Paul. 1988. *Discerning the Subject*. Minneapolis: University of Minnesota Press.

Soetanto Saleh and team. 1978. *Proyek Pengembangan Kesejahteraan Masyarakat Terasing (PKMT Atiran) Kabupaten Hulu Sungai Tengah*. Banjarmasin, Indonesia: Kantor Wilayah Departemen Sosial.

Spillers, Hortense. 1987. "Mama's Baby, Papa's Maybe: An African American Grammar Book." *Diacritics* 17 (2): 65–81.

Spivak, Gayatri Chakravorty. 1987. "Subaltern Studies: Deconstructing Historiography." In *In Other Worlds: Essays in Cultural Politics*, 197–221. New York: Routledge.

———. 1987a. "Draupadi." In *In Other Worlds: Essays in Cultural Politics*, 179–96. New York: Routledge.

———. 1989. "Who Claims Alterity?" In *Remaking History*, edited by B. Kruger and P. Mariani, 269–92. Seattle: Bay Press.

———. 1989a. "In a Word." Interview with Ellen Rooney. *differences* 2:124–54.

Stoler, Ann. 1985. *Capitalism and Confrontation in Sumatra's Plantation Belt: 1870–1979*. New Haven: Yale University Press.

———. 1989. "Making Empire Respectable: The Politics of Race and Sexual Morality in Twentieth-Century Colonial Cultures." *American Ethnologist* 16 (4): 634–60.

Strathern, Marilyn. 1987. "An Awkward Relationship: The Case of Feminism and Anthropology." *Signs* 12 (2): 275–92.

———. 1988. *The Gender of the Gift.* Berkeley: University of California Press.

———. 1990. "Out of Context: The Persuasive Fictions of Anthropology." In *Modernist Anthropology: From Fieldwork to Text,* edited by M. Manganaro, 80–122. Princeton: Princeton University Press. 80–122.

———. 1991. "What Is a Parent?" Paper presented at the Melanesian Colloquium on Embodiment and Sexuality, Manchester, England.

Suhud Pribadi. 1979. "Fungsi Pembinaan Masyarakat Terasing Dalam Rangka Membina Kelestarian Tanah dan Hutan." *Penyuluh Sosial* 43:37–41.

Sunardi Setyodarmodjo. 1975. "Pengetrapan T.P.I. (Tebang Pilih Indonesia) di Hutan Kalimantan Selatan." *Proceedings Seminar tentang Reforestation dan Afforestation di Indonesia,* 127–31. Yogyakarta, Indonesia: Fakultas Kehutanan Universitas Gadjah Mada.

Sutlive, Vinson. 1978. *The Iban of Sarawak.* Arlington Heights, Ill.: AHM Publishing.

Sweeny, Amin. 1987. *A Full Hearing: Orality and Literacy in the Malay World.* Berkeley: University of California Press.

Syachril, M. 1975. *Seperempat Abad DATI II Kota Baru.* Kota Baru, Indonesia: Pemerintah Kabupaten Dati II, Kota Baru.

Taussig, Michael. 1987. *Shamanism, Colonialism and the Wild Man: A Study in Terror and Healing.* Chicago: University of Chicago Press.

Team Research Mahasiswa Fakultas Sjariah. 1969. *Adat Istiadat dan Kepertjajaan Suku Dayak Pembakulan dan Hinas Kiri Hulu Sungai Tengah.* Banjarmasin, Indonesia: Institut Agama Islam Negeri Al-Jami'ah Antasari.

Team Survey. 1980. *Laporan Survey Masyarakat Terasing dan Kemungkinannya Dipindahkan dalam Pemukiman Baru di Matanggapi Rahmat, Desa Panggungan, Kecamatan Padang Batung, Hulu Sungai Selatan.* Banjarmasin, Indonesia: Kantor Wilayah Departemen Sosial, Propinsi Kalimantan Selatan.

Thompson, E. P. 1963. *The Making of the English Working Class.* New York: Vintage.

Tichelman, G. L. 1931. "De Onderafdeeling Barabai (Zuider en Osterafdeeling van Borneo)." *Tijdscrift van het Koninklijk Nederlandsch Aardrijkskundig Genootschap* 48:461–86, 682–711.

Tjilik Riwut. 1958. *Kalimantan Memanggil.* Jakarta, Indonesia: Endang.

Trinh T. Minh-ha. 1989. *Woman, Native, Other: Writing Postcoloniality and Feminism.* Bloomington: Indiana University Press.

Tsing, Anna. 1984. "Politics and Culture in the Meratus Mountains." Ph.D. diss., Stanford University.

———. 1987. "A Rhetoric of Centers in a Religion of the Periphery." In *Indonesian Religions in Transition,* edited by Rita Smith Kipp and Susan Rodgers, 187–210. Tucson: University of Arizona Press.

———. 1990. "Gender and Performance in Meratus Dispute Settlement." In *Power and Difference: Gender in Island Southeast Asia,* edited by Jane Monnig Atkinson and Shelly Errington, 95–125. Stanford: Stanford University Press.

———. 1990a. "Monster Stories: Women Charged with Perinatal Endangerment." In *Uncertain Terms: Negotiating Gender in American Culture,* edited by Faye D. Ginsburg and Anna Tsing, 282–99. Boston: Beacon Press.

Vargas, Donna. 1985. "The Interface of Customary and National Land Law in East Kalimantan, Indonesia." Ph.D. diss., Yale University.

Vargas Llosa, Mario. 1989. *The Storyteller*. Translated by Helen Lane. New York: Farrar, Straus and Giroux.

Villapando, Venny. 1989. "The Business of Selling Mail-Order Brides." In *Making Waves: An Anthology of Writings by and about Asian-American Women*, edited by Asian Women United of California, 318–26. Boston: Beacon Press.

Visweswaran, Kamala. 1992. "Feminist Ethnography as Failure." Paper presented at the Conference on Feminist Dilemmas in Fieldwork, University of California, Davis.

Volkman, Toby. 1990. "Visions and Revisions: Toraja Culture and the Tourist Gaze." *American Ethnologist* 17 (1): 91–110.

Vondal, Patricia. 1984. "Entrepreneurship in an Indonesian Duck Egg Industry: A Case of Successful Rural Development." Ph.D. diss., Rutgers University.

Vorstman, J. A. 1931. "Maleiers In Zuidoost-Borneo." *Tropisch Nederland* 4 (7, 8): 99–103; 115–19.

Wallerstein, Immanuel. 1974. *The Modern World System*, vol. 1. New York: Academic Press.

Weiner, Annette B. 1976. *Women of Value, Men of Renown: New Perspectives in Trobriand Exchange*. Austin: University of Texas Press.

Weinstock, Joseph A. 1981. "Kaharingan: Borneo's 'Oldest Religion' Becomes Indonesia's Newest Religion." *Borneo Research Bulletin* 13 (1): 47–48.

West, Cornel. 1990. "The New Cultural Politics of Difference." In *Out There: Marginalization and Contemporary Cultures*, edited by R. Ferguson, M. Gever, Trinh T. Minh-ha, and Cornel West, 19–36. Cambridge: MIT Press.

Western Canada Wilderness Committee. 1989. *Western Canada Wilderness Committee Educational Report*. NTIS 8 (6).

White, E. Frances. 1990. "Africa on My Mind: Gender, Counter-Discourse and African-American Nationalism." *Journal of Women's History* 2 (1): 73–97.

Whittier, Herbert L. 1973. "Social Organization and Symbols of Social Differentiation: An Ethnographic Study of the Kenyah Dayak of East Kalimantan." Ph.D. diss., Michigan State University.

———. 1978. "Concepts of Adat and Cosmology among the Kenyah Dayak of Borneo: Coping with the Changing Social Cultural Milieu." *Sarawak Museum Journal* 26 (47): 103–13.

Williams, Lea E. 1976. *Southeast Asia: A History*. New York: Oxford University Press.

Williams, Raymond. 1977. *Marxism and Literature*. Oxford: Oxford University Press.

Wilson, Ara. 1988. "American Catalogues for Asian Brides." In *Anthropology for the Nineties*, edited by Johnetta Cole, 114–25. New York: Free Press.

Wolf, Eric. 1982. *Europe and the People without History*. Berkeley: University of California Press.

Woodward, Mark. 1990. *Islam in Java: Normative Piety and Mysticism in the Sultanate of Yogyakarta*. Tucson: University of Arizona Press.

World Rainforest Movement, Sahabat Alam Malaysia. 1989. *The Battle for Sarawak's Forests*. Penang, Malaysia: World Rainforest Movement and SAM.

Yanagisako, Sylvia Junko. 1985. *Transforming the Past: Tradition and Kinship among Japanese Americans*. Stanford: Stanford University Press.

Young, Robert. 1990. *White Mythologies: Writing History and the West*. New York: Routledge.

Zerner, Charles. 1990. *Legal Options for the Indonesian Forestry Sector*. Report UTF/INS/065/INS: Forest Studies Field Document 6-4. Jakarta: Food and Agriculture Organization of the United Nations.

INDEX

abjection, 186, 187, 312n.2
abortion controversies, Uma Adang's imagery applied to, 294–295
Abu-Lughod, Lila, 232, 297, 315n.2
adat, 29–31; activation required for, 138; codified by Dutch, 42, 274, 317n.15; community and, 274, 281; gender and, 34; instability and, 152; of Majapahit, 29–30, 273–274; negotiation of, 128–129, 152, 311n.6; in Parma's story, 135–136, 137, 138, 139, 140, 145; sources of, 29–30; of Uma Adang, 29–30, 35, 274, 281–282, 283; in women's shamanism, 272
administrative boundaries, 60; adat and, 274; Dutch as stabilizers of, 42; neighborhoods and, 64–65
age, *umbun* affiliations and, 63, 64
agriculture. *See* farming practices; shifting cultivation
"alien romance," 214–229
Anderson, Benedict, 88–89, 124, 259, 305nn.1 and 4
animal protection, Uma Adang's imagery and, 296–297
anthropological focus: adat and, 152; criticisms of, 15–17; economic development and, 289; ethnographic interaction in, 228–229; gender differences and, 186–187, 220–221, 223–225, 290; "homework," 297; imagination and, 288–290, 295; marginality and, 14–15, 17, 36, 51–52, 90–91; mobility and, 51–52, 65–66, 123–125; modernization and, 87–91; postcolonial changes in, 13–14; power

and, 14, 88–89; separation of Other and, 288, 296; social identity studies and, 8, 9; travel and, 123–125, 139; women researchers and, 216, 223–224. *See also* cultural theory
antibiotics, use of, 109
Anzaldua, Gloria, 21, 225
Appell, George, 308n.5
Appell, Laura, 314n.11
Ardener, Edwin, 248
army posts, 89. *See also* military
Artocarpus species, 168, 169
asam (sour spices), 95, 96, 310n.19
asbah, 128, 129
Asian women, North American view of, 216–217
asymmetry: feminist writing and, 224–225; gender, 70–71, 128, 186, 244. *See* marginality; regional asymmetry
Atkinson, Jane Monnig, 307n.3, 313n.9, 314n.11, 317n.14, 320n.4
authority: leadership and, 150–152; ritual, 173–175; spiritual opposition to, 299–300
autonomy: economic, women and, 227, 228; fetal development story and, 294–295, 298, 299; land-use patterns and, 62–63; local leadership and, 65; mobility as source of, 53, 61; social groups and, 63–65; as source of authority, 300; of *umbun*, 64
Aveling, Harry, 299
Awat Kilay, 37; Banjar visit by, 198, 199; cosmology of, 198–199, 314n.14; curing

chant by, 178–179, 191–195; Induan
A'ar and, 204; pin-up photos and, 229;
rice chant by, 157–159
Awat Lumuh, in Parma's story, 129, 133,
135, 138, 139, 143, 144, 145, 148, 149,
151
Awat Pasta, in Parma's story, 133, 142–
143, 144
Ayuh region, women's dewa adventures in,
200–205
back talk: adat negotiations and, 152; by Induan Bilai, 135, 152
Bakhtin, M. M., 258, 259
balai (ritual hall), 64
Balanghan Dusun, 219; creation story from,
262; economic autonomy and, 228; putir
and, 313n.10; Tani as, 215
Bali, family planning in, 107
Balian (shamanic practice), as religion, 273
balukaran (year-old field), 163, 164
Bambang Basiwara/Si Ayuh stories, 56–60,
69, 71, 276–277
bamboo: in songs, 237; uses for, 170
bancir (male transvestites), 185
Banjar: adat of, 30; Awat Kilay's visit to,
198, 199; Bambang Basiwara and: *See*
Bambang Basiwara/Si Ayuh stories; body
boundary protection by, 186, 188, 196;
chronicles of, 305n.8; cosmology and,
198–199, 314n.14; dewa shamanism
and, 77; Dutch rule and, 43, 44, 306n.21;
economic status of, 55–56; family planning and, 107, 113; gender and status in,
35; immigration to Meratus from, 45;
Islam and, 28–29, 42–43, 54–55, 181–
182; language differences with, 53–54;
Majapahit story and, 271; Meratus and,
29, 42, 43, 53, 85, 179–180; Meratus as
refuge for, 79, 99, 130, 306n.21; Meratus
studied by, 172–173; military presence
in, 44; pepper plantations and, 43,
306n.10; political role of, 56, 299–300;
regional dominance of, 28–29, 42–43,
55; resistance and rebellion by, 43, 44,
78–83, 265, 306n.14–306n.15; settlement in Meratus by, 48; sexuality in,
217–218; trade role of, 42, 43, 55–56,
306n.11; travel practices of, 125, 181.
See also Hulu Sungai Banjar
Banjarmasin: founding of, 306n.9; local
kingdom empowered by, 277, 278

Barito River delta kingdoms: trade regulation by, 42; Uma Adang story and,
277
basambu ritual, in Parma's story, 141–142,
143
basanggar banua (fencing the village), 96–
102, 310n.20; in Parma's story, 144
basket weaving, 69
Basry, Hassan, 80, 306n.23
bathing, 92, 309n.17; Japanese vs. Meratus
customs, 221, 222; ritual protection by,
184
bawanang festival, 147; in Parma's story,
147, 148
"Bear, The," 73–74; creation story of, 261;
hospitality of, 83, 84; Induan Hiling and,
95, 234; leadership problems of, 140–
141; mediation by, 84; in Parma's story,
129, 133, 140–141, 143–145; resettlement role of, 176; Ukut dispute mediated
by, 132; Uma Adang and, 268, 316n.8;
village fence ritual by, 96–102, 144; on
village settlements, 102–103; war stories
told by, 76–85
Beeckman, Daniel, 306n.11
Benedict, Ruth, 295
Benjamin, Walter, 259
Besar, Mount (Halao-halao Mountain), 99–
100, 310n.22
betel, given to guests, 67, 147
Bhabha, Homi, 14, 16, 17, 316n.7, 317n.19
Biguli, Haji: in dewa kidnap story, 203,
204; in Parma's story, 133, 144, 146,
147, 148
Bingan Sabda, 52
binjai trees, 168
binturung trees, 169
birth control. *See* family planning
"black magic," 182. *See also* sorcery
blood: of childbirth, 185, 186; menstrual,
184
blood-sucking monsters (*kuyang*), 184,
185–186
Boddy, Janice P., 248–249
body boundaries: cultural theory and, 180–
181; gender and, 184–187, 200; language
and, 179; opening up, 188, 189–191,
196; protecting, 183, 186, 188, 196; rationality and, 183–184; sorcery/healing
and, 187; travel through, 190–191
Boland, B. J., 317n.13

borders/border crossings: critical perspective and, 225; imagery of, 21; language and, 54; leadership role at, 73

Borneo: classical anthropology and, 87–88, 309n.10; headhunting in, 309n.5; shifting cultivation in, 312n.1; social organization in, 307n.5–308n.5. *See also specific regions*

"borrowing" power, 128, 196, 199

boundaries, administrative. *See* administrative boundaries

boundaries, body. *See* body boundaries

boundaries, social, women and, 248–249

Bourdieu, Pierre, 10, 123

bridewealth, in Parma's story, 134, 149

bridge building, headhunting and, 86, 90–91

brothers. *See* "two brothers" stories

Buddhism: shamanism and, 273; as state-recognized religion, 54

Bugis, east-side region, 48

building: as community activity, 281; as development activity, 90–91

Bukit, 52, 54, 307n.1

Bungsukaling epics, 59–60

Butler, Judith, 232, 316n.3

cannibalism, in war stories, 77, 78

Catholicism, as state-recognized religion, 54

censuses, Dutch and, 42

ceremonies. *See* ritual

change, classical anthropological view of, 87–88, 309n.10, 309n.11

chants: curing, 178–179, 189, 190, 191–195; political power and, 96–102; rice-planting, 157–158, 173–174; symbolism in, 238, 239; village fence, 96–102

Chernichovsky, Dov, 107, 310n.2

"chickens of the government," 102–103; Induan Hiling drawing and, 252

childbearing, gender responsibilities in, 117, 118–119

child protection, Uma Adang's imagery and, 295–296

children: attitudes toward, 113; female status and, 314n.2; as requirement for leadership, 114; *umbun* groupings and, 63–64

Christian, Barbara, 16, 304n.7

Christianity: Dayak conversions to, 317n.14; nabi and, 264; as state-recognized religion, 54, 273

Christian village, 307n.29

Cixous, Hélène, 244, 304n.9

Clifford, James, 124, 224, 304n.5

clothing, Japanese vs. Meratus customs, 221, 222

codification, shamanic: by Induan Hiling, 243–244, 246, 247, 249; by Uma Adang, 268

colonial discourse: anticolonial movement's influence, 297; postcolonial criticism of, 15–17; traditional anthropology as, 13; travel patterns and, 124

colonial rule. *See* Dutch colonial rule

communism: lack of religion seen as, 273; U.S. Indonesia role and, 298

community: adat as basis of, 274, 281; creation of, 258, 281; isolated vs. marginal, 7–8, 9–10; leadership role in, 74–75; shaman as mediator for, 249, 250, 252, 257; state and, 8, 17, 25–27, 74, 304n.12; Uma Adang and, 280, 281; use of term, 65

Confucianism, as state-recognized religion, 54

Conklin, Harold, 312n.1

contraception. *See* family planning

cooking, appeasement through, 95–96

cosmology, Meratus vs. Banjar, 198–199, 314n.14

craft work, 69

creation, stories of, 261–262

creativity: of female shamans, 235–236; of Induan Hiling, 235–236, 244; in marginality, 8–9, 31, 244; openings for, 209; of Uma Adang, 255–256

criticism: of ethnographic writing, 32; postcolonial, 15–17

cultivation. *See* farming practices; shifting cultivation

cultural anthropology. *See* anthropological focus; cultural theory

cultural gaps: border crossings vs., 21; political culture and, 25–26

cultural heterogeneity. *See* heterogeneity

cultural history, subjectivity and, 186–187

cultural identity: administrative decentralization and, 60–61; language and, 53–54, 58–59; place and, 123–124; religion and, 54–55, 307n.3; terminology and, 52–53, 307n.1. *See also* ethnic identity; ethnicity

cultural negotiations, frameworks for, 287–288

cultural theory: border crossings and, 22; challenge for, 31; eclecticism in, 32; ethnographic writing and, 32–33; fixed cases and, 123, 124; global interconnections and, 289–290; individuals' stories and, 231–232; local engagement and, 31–32, 240; marginality and, 13–15. *See also* anthropological focus

"culture," New Order view of, 24

curing: Banjar folk remedies, 187; chants, 178–179, 189, 190, 191–195; drawing of, 241–242; performance time in, 242–243; by shamans, 187, 188–195

"custom" (*adat istiadat*), performing, 247

Dalton, Bill, 300

damar trees, 169

dam building, headhunting and, 86–87, 90–91

dancing, by male shamans vs. Induan Hiling, 235–236

Datu Limbur, 277

Dayaks: "alien romance" stories of, 214–229; Banjar view of, 181–182; in eastside region, 48; forest products traded by, 42–43; as headhunters, 85, 86, 87; historical role of, 42–43; *kuyang* among, 185–186; marginal status of, 42; Meratus, origin of term, 52–53, 307n.1; Muslims vs., 43, 181–182; nabi of, 264; raids by, 44, 306n.22; religion of, 273, 317n.12. *See also* Meratus Dayaks

death, of neonate, 117

deBord, Guy, 270

decentralization: political culture and, 60–61; regional asymmetries and, 53

de Lauretis, Teresa, 232, 315n.3

dependents, *umbun* groupings and, 63–64

Derrida, Jacques, 268, 313n.6, 315n.2

desire, reason vs., 183–184

development: anthropological focus and, 289; building as focus of, 90–91, 309n.16; ceremonial aspects of, 91, 309n.16; enthusiasm for, 45; government headhunter stories and, 85–87, 90–91, 309n.15; imagination and, 287–288; official vs. Meratus views and, 154–155; political culture and, 24; stories arising from, 85–96. *See also* resettlement programs

dewa spirits, 41, 77; chants to, 96–102; food offerings to, 94; Induan Hiling and,

233–234; "kidnapping" by, 201–202, 203–204, 242–243; shamanistic style and, 189; women and, 200–205, 208, 228

dialects, 53–54

Diamond Queen, 6, 7, 36, 277–279; as conceptual space, 22

Dirks, Nick, 259–260

disabilities, *umbun* affiliations and, 63, 64

disagreements: adat and, 152; marginality and, 151–152

discourse: feminist perspective on, 33; power issues and, 8, 303n.1. *See also* colonial discourse

disease splinter (*suligih*), 189, 190, 191

displacement, marginal culture as, 7–8

disputes, adat and, 152

diversity: among Meratus, 60–61; mobility and, 51–52, 61, 62; shifting cultivation and, 62–63; state views of, 24. *See also* pluralism

division of labor, female shamans and, 232–233

divorce: in Parma's story, 134, 138–144, 146, 147; requirements for, 139

Dove, Michael, 307n.1, 309n.11, 312n.1

Drake, Richard A., 90, 309n.15

drawings: as curing rituals, 241; by Induan Hiling, 238, 239, 240–242, 243–244, 251–252

dreams, shamanic learning in, 238, 239

duality, gender and, 270

durian tree: dispute about, 132, 148, 151; fruit of, 168

Dusun Dayaks: adat of, 274; in east-side region, 48. *See also* Balanghan Dusun; Rungus Dusun

Dutch colonial rule: adat codified by, 42, 274, 317n.15; Banjar and, 43; beginnings of, 43; influence of, 42; in Kalimantan, 41–42, 43; rebellion stories, 78–81; war stories about, 77

Dutch East India Company, territories ceded to, 43

East Timur, armed resistance in, 45

eating patterns, 92, 93, 309n.17

"eccentric subject," concept of, 232

economic autonomy, women and, 227, 228

economic development. *See* development

economic status, regional asymmetries and, 55–56

Elderidge, Philip, 320n.5
elderly, *umbun* affiliations and, 63, 64
empire, nation-state vs., 308n.3
entertainment: "local culture" and, 245–
    246; popular music, 245, 246; shaman-
    ism as, 246–247
enunciation, moment of, 278, 317n.19
environmental movement, Uma Adang's
    imagery and, 295–297
Errington, Shelly, 23, 309n.16
essentialism, 16, 304n.7
ethnic identity: colonial emphasis on, 42,
    305n.2; economic status and, 55–56; In-
    donesian view of, 28, 245; labeling and,
    52–53; language and, 53–54, 58–59;
    "local culture" and, 245–246; negotia-
    tions with state on, 287–288; political
    status and, 56; religion and, 54–55; "two
    brothers" story and, 56–60; "writing" by
    Induan Hiling and, 245. *See also* cultural
    identity; ethnicity
ethnicity: body boundaries and, 179, 180;
    in cultural analysis, 7, 8, 9, 33–34, 51–
    52; entertainment as expression of, 245–
    246, 248, 249–250; gender and politics
    and, 33–34, 196, 250; Majapahit and,
    277; sexuality and, 199, 314n.15; state
    view of, 24, 42, 305n.2. *See also* cultural
    identity; ethnic identity
ethnographic interaction, advantages of,
    228–229
ethnographic writing: border crossing im-
    agery and, 22; cultural theory and, 32–
    33; gender differences and, 32, 33–34,
    223–225; interconnections found in, 290
Eurocentric approach: local engagement
    vs., 31–32; search for coherence and,
    305n.15
exceptional women, 8–9; creativity by, 209;
    shamans as, 234, 249; as source of
    knowledge, 36
"exemplary centers," political culture and,
    22, 23
export, rubber production for, 43

factory workers, women, 90
family planning, 104–120; Banjar and, 107,
    113; kinship rhetoric and, 110–111;
    knowledge about, 112–113; oral contra-
    ceptive use, 109, 111, 119–120; Pa'an
    Tini's list and, 108–109; state power and,
    109–110, 310nn.2 and 4; traditional

methods of, 112, 113, 311n.7; *umbun*
    and, 110; women's attitudes toward, 112
Fanon, Frantz, 14, 16
farming practices: "disorderly," 45; rice
    harvest, 68; social groupings and, 63–65;
    state control and, 45; weeding, 68. *See
    also* shifting cultivation
female shamanism, 35, 194–196, 202, 203–
    204, 230–231; codification of, 243–244,
    246, 247, 268; creativity in, 235–236; In-
    duan Hiling, 230, 231, 233, 234–252;
    learning resources closed to, 234–235;
    Uma Adang on, 266–268, 269–270, 275
feminism: ethnographic writing and, 32,
    33–34, 223–225; marginality and, 17–
    18; of Uma Adang, 34–35
"fencing the village," 96–102, 310n.20
fertility practices, marginality and, 105–
    114, 118–120
fetal development story, 291–294, 320n.4;
    antiabortion movement and, 294–295;
    political action focus and, 295–296
fieldwork, mobility and, 65–66
films, villains in, 87
Fischer, Michael M. J., 295
flooding, causes of, 19, 20
food: eating patterns, 92, 93, 309n.17; for-
    est fruits, 168; refusing, 189; spiritual use
    of, 94
food-oriented hospitality, religion and, 55
food poisoning, 183; spell to prevent, 198
foothills, resettlement in, 45, 92–93,
    307n.28
force, state power and, 91
foreigners, romance with, 214–229
foreign workers, Dayak women and, 216–
    217, 218
forest areas, 160–170; claims in, 170; log-
    ging of, 166–167; primary vs. secondary,
    160–164; resources in, 167–170, 312n.5;
    swidden sites in, 160, 163, 164–166;
    umbun cooperation in, 175
forest-products trade, Banjar role in, 42, 43
Foucault, Michel, 88, 303n.1, 315n.2,
    320n.1
founding of the kingdom, 277–279
Fox, Richard J., 290
Frederick, William, 315n.8
Freedman, Ronald, 310n.2
Freeman, J. Derek, 152, 308n.5
fruit trees, in forest, 168–169, 170
funeral, of neonate, 117

Galuh (spirit agent), 178–179
"Garagu 7," 272–273
Gasai, Parma and, 129, 135–141, 143, 144, 145, 147, 149, 150
Gates, Henry Louis, 16–17
Geertz, Clifford, 88, 304n.5, 305n.1
gender: anthropological focus and, 186–187, 220–221, 223–225, 290; asymmetries of, 70–71, 128, 186, 244; body boundaries and, 184–187, 200; childbearing responsibilities and, 117, 118–119; in cultural analysis, 8–9; dualities and, 270; ethnicity and, 34, 196, 250; ethnographic writing and, 32, 33–34, 223–225; healing and, 189; interethnic communication and, 200; leadership and, 106, 114, 195–196, 274–276, 278, 281–282; love songs and, 71; marginality and, 17–18, 71, 119; maternity and, 194, 313n.9; in Meratus society, 34–35; performance privilege and, 196; political status and, 8, 34, 59, 108, 112; putir shamans and, 194–195, 204–205, 313n.10; religion and, 184; reproduction and, 105–107; segregation by, 269; shamanism and, 194–196, 231, 243, 275–276. See also female shamanism; storytelling and, 59–60; subjectivity and, 186, 313nn. 3 and 6; travel and, 68–69, 127, 128, 196, 227, 229; umbun groupings and, 63–64, 110; work and, 68. See also sexuality; women
geneology, history and, 279
Ghosh, Amitav, 288–289
gila (mad), 193, 313n.8
global interconnections: anthropology based on, 289–290; outsiders' agendas and, 300
gold, 43, 306n.12
Gordon, Linda, 316n.3
gossiping, 69
Gough, Kathleen, 311n.10
government, community and, 8, 25–26. See also state
government headhunters, 85–87, 90–91, 309n.15; in Parma's story, 148
Grabowsky, Fritz, 305n.6
Gramsci, Antonio, 303n.1
Grosz, Elizabeth A., 201, 312n.3
guerilla bases, 44, 306n.23
Gurumbulan (Banjar rebels), 82, 265

Hajar, Ibnu, stories about, 82–83, 265, 266
Haji Biguli. See Biguli, Haji
Halao-halao Mountain (Mount Besar), 99–100, 310n.22
hambawang trees, 168
Hamda, M. J., 92
Hanafiah, A. Gaffar, 306n.15
Hanunoo (Philippines), shifting cultivation by, 312n.1
Haraway, Donna, 316n.3
Haridas, Swami Anand, 299
Hartmann, Betsy, 310nn. 3 and 4
headhunters, 77, 309n.5; conflicting views of, 85; government, 85–87, 90–91, 309n.15
head-taking, 44
head tax, 44, 306n.29
healers: gender of, 189; males as, 200; shamans as, 187–188
health: body boundaries and, 183–184, 188, 189, 190; causes of illness, 189, 191; rajaki and, 190; of women vs. men, 184. See also public health issues
Hefner, Robert W., 25
hegemony: of colonial discourse, 16; local responses and, 8, 303n.1
Hepell, M., 152
herbal medicine, for contraception, 112, 113, 311n.7
heterogeneity: anthropological focus and, 14; marginal communities as part of, 9–10
heterosexuality, Banjar vs. Meratus, 197
Hindu-Bali: Kaharingan and, 317n.12; as state-recognized religion, 54, 273
historical setting, 41–49, 74, 75, 308n.2
history: geneology and, 279; kinship and, 279, 280; local, 265; politics and, 259–260; shifting cultivation and, 164–165; of the world, by Uma Adang, 259–265, 316n.7
home life, 222; in the evenings, 69; with Ma Salam umbun, 67–69. See also livelihood
"homework" (anthropological), 297
homosexuality, 185
honeybees, damar trees and, 169
honey hunt, in Parma's story, 135, 136, 137
honey trees, claiming of, 169
"horse of gaps" song, 209–212, 244
hospitality: protection through, 83; religious differences and, 55; ritual, 94–96
household, gender segregation in, 269

housing: in central mountains, described, 67; collective halls, 46, 48; government aesthetics and, 93; in resettlement villages, 46, 48, 62, 93

Hudson, Alfred B., 305n.8, 306n.9

Hulu Sungai Banjar, 313n.4; body boundaries and, 186; religion and, 181–182; sorcery/healing and, 187, 188–189, 197–198

humanist approaches, limitations of, 14

hunting: forest trees used in, 169; movement required for, 159

hutan belukar (secondary regrowth), 160, 161, 162

hutan lebat (primary forest), 160, 161, 162

hydroelectric dams, headhunting and, 86–87, 90–91

Hymes, Dell H., 320n.1

"hysteria," dewa possession and, 201

IAIN Antasari, 307n.1

Ibnu Hajar, story about, 82–83, 265, 266

illness, causes of, 189, 191

ilmu (esoteric science), 128; gender symmetry and, 270

ilmu hirang (black sciences), 182

Ilongot, gender assumptions of, 313n.9, 314n.11

imagination: in anthropological focus, 288–290, 295; development and, 287–288; of power, 72–73, 91

imperial rule, national rule vs., 308n.3

incense burning, with curing chant, 192

Indonesia: adat community seen in, 152–153; current changes in, 301; marginality of Meratus vs., 17, 22; marginality of in world, 22, 23; political culture in, 22–26; postcolonial relations with Meratus, 44–46, 82; religious policy of, 54, 273; state power changes in, 41–42, 44, 305n.1. *See also* Jakarta; Java; state

Indonesian Selective Felling System, 167

Induan A'ar, kidnapped by dewa, 203–204, 228

Induan Amar, childbirth story of, 114–118

Induan Bilai, in Parma story, 129, 133, 134, 135, 146

Induan Hiling: background of, 233–234; The Bear and, 95, 234; drawings by, 238, 239, 240–242, 243–244, 251–252; as "eccentric subject," 232–233; gender ir-

relevance and, 250; hospitality by, 94–96; as "Irama," 230, 246; on Parma's story, 151; recording by, 247; on resettlement, 93; as self-declared shaman, 203, 230, 231, 233; shamanic codification by, 243–244, 246, 247, 249; songs of, 209–212, 230, 236–238, 243, 247–248; Uma Adang and, 95, 233, 234, 235, 268, 269; "writing" by, 238, 239, 240, 244–245

Induan Kilay, 62; contraceptive pills and, 104, 119–120

indu wanyi (wild honeybees), damar trees and, 169

instability, adat and, 152

interethnic relations: sexuality and, 199; as source of power, 199–200

Irah, story of, 226–227, 314n.2

"Irama" (Induan Hiling), 230, 246, 248, 315n.10

Irama, Rhoma, 245, 246, 315n.8, 315n.9

Irian Jaya, armed resistance in, 45

Irigaray, Luce, 186, 312n.3, 313n.6

ironwood, 48

Islam: Banjar and, 28–29, 42–43, 54–55, 181–182; beginnings of in Kalimantan, 306n.9; family planning and, 107; Meratus cosmology and, 198–199, 314n.14; nabi and, 264; New Order politics and, 317n.13; political opposition and, 299; rebels inspired by, 44, 82, 265; as state-recognized religion, 54, 273, 317n.13

Ismail, Aburachman et al, 307n.1, 307n.2

"Isolated Populations": defined by mobility, 155–160; resettlement program for, 45, 92–93. *See also* resettlement programs

IUDs (intrauterine devices), 107

Jakarta: rebellion against, 44, 45, 82–83. *See also* Indonesia; Java; state

Jameson, Frederic, 10

Japanese: as invaders, 44; Meratus view of, 44; as pepper plantation owners, 44; Uma Hati and, 221; war stories about, 78

Java: Banjar rebellion against, 82–83; family planning in, 107; "Outer Islands" vs., 23, 25; political dominance of, 24, 56; prostitutes from, 218; studies of Meratus by, 171–173. *See also* Indonesia; Jakarta; state

jobs, for women outside Meratus, 226

Kaharingan (Dayak religion), 273, 317n.12
Kalawan: first meeting with Uma Adang in, 5–7; floods in, 19–20; second visit to, 10; third visit to, 18–20; as transmigration site, 19; Uma Adang's innovations in, 281
Kalawan, Mount, in dewa chant, 98
Kalimantan: Banjar dominance in, 28–29, 42–43; Dutch takeover of, 43; state rule changes in, 41–42
kapuhun, illness caused by, 189
kariwaya, birds lured with, 169
kasai (Pometia pinnata), fish lured with, 169
KB (Family Planning Program), 108
Ke'e, 69, 70
keluarga berencana (family planning), 108
kidnapping, by dewa spirits, 201–202, 203–204
Kilay, Induan, 62
kinship: activation required for, 138; history and, 279, 280; marriage and, 222; political leadership and, 110–111
Kipp, Rita Smith, 307n.3, 317n.16
Koran, Uma Adang melody based on, 257
Kristeva, Julia, 179, 180–181, 182, 186, 187, 194, 312n.1–313nn.3 and 6
kuda sawang (horse of gaps), song about, 209–212
kulidang trees, 169
kuyang (blood-sucking monsters), 184, 185–186, 197
kwini trees, 168

Laderman, Carol, 313n.10, 316n.7
lahung burung trees, 168
lahung trees, 168
lamah bulu (weakened body boundaries), 183; gender and, 184
land-use patterns, 62–63
language: cultural identity and, 53–54, 58–59; Uma Adang's use of, 256–257
leadership: characteristics of, 72; children required for, 114; community survival and, 74–75; emphasis on order by, 95; empire vs. nation-state and, 308n.3; gender and, 106, 114, 195–196, 274–276, 278, 281–282; government view of, 172–173; imagination of power and, 72–73; importance and weakness of, 129; internal marginality and, 119; local requirements for, 65; marriage as means to, 132;

regional authority and, 150–152; resettlement programs and, 176; by shamans, 72, 73, 75, 85, 100–102, 231, 310n.20. *See also* political leadership
Lindblad, J. Thomas, 306nn. 17, 19, and 20
lingut (singing worms), 57
literacy, ethnicity and, 245
literature, Sukarno era vs. New Order, 298–299
livelihood: daily activity and, 222; mobility required for, 154, 156–160; travel-knowledge and, 175, 176. *See also rajaki*
Llosa, Mario Vargas, 288
logging: debris left by, 167; development and, 48; as flooding cause, 20; forest composition and, 166–167; mapping and, 312n.3; by Meratus, 48; resettlement and, 45. *See also* timber industry
love songs, 69–71, 227, 236; Induan Hiling's chants as, 237–238, 243, 246; vegetation in, 236, 237–238
luak trees, 169
Lumholtz, Carl, 305n.6

Ma Amar, Induan Amar and, 115, 118
Ma Buluh, 69
"madness," in curing chant, 193, 313n.8
magic. *See* sorcery
mail-order bride catalogs, 216–217
Majapahit: adat of, 29–30, 273–274; ethnic tensions resolved by, 277; regional history's beginnings in, 271–272; trade regulated by, 42, 305n.8; Uma Adang and, 259, 260, 272–275
Majapahit, Queen, 99
Ma Jawa: Parma's story and, 133, 136–137, 144–145, 146; story of death of, 78–80, 136
Ma Kapal, Parma and, 129, 133–146, 148, 149, 150
Malayic dialects, Banjar and Meratus, 53–54
Malaysia, women factory workers in, 90
males. *See* gender; masculinity; men
Ma Linggu, in Parma's story, 129, 133, 142, 144, 145
Mallinckrodt, J., 305n.3, 305n.6
Ma Luba, curing of, 191–192
Mambur, story of, 275–276, 317n.17
"management" (*pembinaan*), 28, 305n.14
Management of Isolated Populations, resettlement program, 45, 92–93

mangapuhun, 189
mangos, 168
Manihuruk, A. E., 306n.15, 306n.24
Ma Pasta, in Parma's story, 129, 133, 137, 144
maps: Dutch and, 42; political use of, 160
Ma Rani, 58, 60
Marcus, George, 295, 304n.5
marginality, 5; anthropological focus and, 14–15, 17, 36, 51–52, 90–91; border crossings and, 21–22, 54, 73, 225; of community vs. state, 17, 25–27, 304n.12; creativity in, 8–9, 31, 244; cultural gaps and, 25–26; cultural negotiations and, 287–288; cultural theory and, 13; in Dutch colonial era, 42; eccentric subjects and, 232; in empire vs. nation-state, 308n.3; fertility practices and, 105–114, 118–120; gender and, 17–18, 71, 119; global interconnections and, 289–290; in Indonesia, 23; interacting vantage points in, 22, 288–289; internal, 119; local disagreements and, 151–152; political culture and, 22; political decentralization and, 53, 60–61; political isolation and, 8; postcolonial criticism and, 16; postmodernism of, 254–255; power and, 89–90; "primitive" culture vs., 7–8, 9–10; regional, 29, 53; regional asymmetry and, 53–56; storytelling and, 59–60; theoretic eclecticism and, 32; travel and, 36, 37, 46; Uma Adang's consciousness of, 253; in unstated choices and attitudes, 115, 119; urban focus and, 17
markets, weekly: armed forces posts and, 44, 48; in Meratus foothills, 48; movement and, 159–160; products traded at, 55–56. *See also* trade
marriage: adat and, 128–129, 135–136, 137, 138, 139, 140; Japanese vs. Meratus customs, 221–223; official role in, 128, 311n.1; short-term, 221–222; *umbun* groupings and, 64
marriage payment, in Parma's story, 134, 149
Martin, Biddy, 232
Marxist approaches, limitations of, 14
Ma Salam, 58–60; home life with, 67–69; map drawing by, 160, 163, 164; on nature preserve, 296–297; in Parma's story, 131–132, 133, 135–137, 141, 142, 144–150; travels with, 66–67, 68

masculinity: love songs and, 71; spells and, 76–77. *See also* gender; men
maternity. *See* motherhood
Ma Tupai: in *bawanang* festival, 147; in Parma's story, 129, 133, 137, 141, 142, 145–150
Ma Ulin, in Parma's story, 129, 133, 134, 136, 138, 144–147
Mayur, S. H., 306n.21
Mead, Margaret, 295
mealtimes, 92, 93, 309n.17
Mecca, Si Ayuh at, 276–277
media, penetration of, 246
Meesook, Oey Astra, 107, 310n.2
men: magic practiced by, 183, 187; as midwives, 114, 116. *See also* gender; masculinity
menstruation, 184, 314n.11
Meratus: adat in, 29–31; anti-Jakarta rebellion in, 44; Banjar and, 29, 42, 43, 53, 85, 179–180; as Banjar refuge, 79, 99, 130, 306n.21; diversity among, 60–61; as ethnic-religious group, 281; gap between government and, 26, 42; gender, ethnic, and political interrelationships in, 33–34; gender and status in, 34–35; historical status of, 41–49; nature preserve proposal for, 296–297; official views of, 41, 42, 61; raids on, 44, 306n.22; recent changes in, 301; relations with state in, 26–27, 28, 30–31, 44–46, 96; resettlement of. *See* resettlement programs; Si Ayuh and. *See* "two brothers" stories. *See also* Meratus Dayaks
Meratus Dayaks: farming by: *See* shifting cultivation; forest products used by, 167–170; as headhunters, 85; language of, 53–54; marginality of, and Indonesian marginality, 17, 22; powerlessness of, 45; religious identity of, 54–55; research advantages among, 220; terminology for, 52–53, 307n.1; tourism and, 300; trade difficulties of, 55–56; travel by, 46, 124–125. *See also* Meratus
Meratus Mountains: administrative penetration in, 46, 48; autonomy in, 61, 62–63; dewa chant places in, 99–100; forest areas in, 160–170; forest mix in, 166–167; logging in, 45: *See also* logging; as Parma's story setting, 130; recent changes in, 301; resettlement villages in, 45, 46, 48, 307n.28, 307n.29; road building in,

Meratus Mountains, *continued*
  42, 61, 265, 287; settlement patterns in,
  46, 48, 62–63; shifting cultivation in, 48,
  62–63: *See also* shifting cultivation; Ukut
  River valley in, 130–131
midwives, males as, 114, 116
military: attitudes toward Meratus of, 89;
  as contact with state, 42; as power, 75–
  76; presence of, in Banjar, 44; presence
  of, in Meratus, 44, 45, 89; relationships
  with, 76; romanticization of, 51, 69–70;
  stories based on, 75–85
mimicry: political success through, 282;
  Uma Adang's use of, 257, 268
minority scholars: political issues and, 15–
  16; theoretical focus of, 13–14
Mitchell, Timothy, 315n.2
mobility: anthropological focus and, 51–
  52, 65–66, 123–125; in categorization by
  state, 155–160; cultural differentiation
  and, 51–52, 61; fieldwork and, 65–66;
  land-use patterns and, 62–63; leadership
  and, 65; official vs. Meratus view of, 41,
  154, 155–160, 177; shifting cultivation
  and, 62–63; as source of autonomy, 53,
  61. *See also* travel
modernity: government headhunter stories
  and, 87–88, 90–91; "traditional" vs., 88
Mohanty, Chandra, 232
"moment of enunciation," 278, 317n.19
Moraga, Cherrie, 232
motherhood: foreign lovers and, 314n.2;
  gender assumptions and, 194, 313n.9;
  marginality and, 118–119
mountains. *See* Meratus Mountains
movement. *See* mobility; travel
Mulder, Niels, 89, 298, 307n.3, 309n.16
music: ethnic and popular, 245–246. *See
  also* songs
Muslims. *See* Islam
Myerhoff, Barbara, 223
mysticism: government use of, 89; New
  Order emphasis on, 298–299
myths, of savage, 87

nabi, 261, 262–264
Nabi Bungkun, 263–264
Nabi Lahat, 262, 264, 282, 283
names for Meratus, 52–53, 307n.1
nangka trees, 169
nationalist rebellion: stories about, 78–81.
  See also rebellion

nation-state, empire vs., 308n.3
"natives," criticism of concept, 124
nature preserve, skepticism about, 296–297
negara, state power and, 88
Negara Dipa, 305n.8
neighborhood groups, 64–65; cooperation
  in, 281
neonatal death, story about, 114–118
Netherlands Indies Civil Administration
  (NICA), nationalist Banjar vs., 44
"New Order," 23–24, 28; Islam and,
  317n.13; spirituality in, 298–299
New World Order, independent fetus imagery vs., 298
Nisa (Shostak), 224
nomadism: official view of, 155; as stereotype, 46; travel vs., 150, 311n.5
nutrition, government standards and, 92,
  93

objects, as source of power, 272
observer, interrelationships with, 21–22
oil wells, headhunting and, 85–86
Old Village Head, in Parma's story, 133,
  138–139, 141, 142, 144, 145
Ong, Aihwa, 90
oratory, 102, 310n.23
order: contraception and, 104; imposition
  of, 91, 92–96; ritual hospitality, 94–96;
  tradition and, 172
Other: Banjar/Meratus interaction and,
  188, 196, 199; creating alliance with,
  199–200; Meratus view of, 51–52, 69;
  psychoanalytic theory and, 180, 312n.2;
  romantic image of, 213–214, 228; separation of, 288, 296; shamanic power and,
  196, 231
"Outer Islands," Java vs., 23, 25

Pa'an Tini, 84–85, 107–108; family planning program and, 107–111, 112; marginality of Induan Amar vs., 119
Pa Bundi, 11
pagar banua (village fence), 101
Pa Hati, 11
pakaian lalaki (men's magic), 183
palm syrup, given to guests, 67
pampakin trees, 168
Panatik Adat (Adat Enthusiast), Uma
  Adang as, 275, 317n.16
pangulu (wedding sponsor), 128; in
  Parma's story, 132, 137

parenting: gender and, 117, 118–119; as source of leadership, 114

Pari Dayaks, raids by, 44, 306n.22

Parma, story of, 128–153; criticisms about, 140–141; denouement, 149–150, 153; first wedding, 132, 133, 134; negotiations, 134–139, 141–147; participants in, 129, 133; second wedding, 139–140; setting for, 130–132; travel as part of, 136, 137–139, 142, 144, 145, 147, 148, 150

parody: as marginality response, 10–12, 19, 27; as political tool, 282; by Uma Adang, 11, 19, 27, 36, 254

Pemberton, John, 23, 24, 298

pembinaan (management), 28, 305n.14

pepper plantations: expansion of, 43, 306n.10; work for Japanese in, 44

performance privilege: gender and, 196, 240, 242; Induan Hiling's drawings and, 240–242, 243–244

Philippines: Ilongot gender assumptions in, 313n.9, 314n.11; shifting cultivation in, 312n.1

pinjulang (shaman's accompanist), 230, 232–233, 242, 243; Uma Adang's call for, 269–270

pin-up photos, of white women, 217, 229

"Planning Flats," 176

pluralism: community building through, 258, 277. See also diversity

poisoning: spell to prevent, 198; weakened body boundaries and, 183

police: attitudes toward, 75; attitudes of, toward Meratus, 89; local leaders' use of, 150; in Parma's story, 133, 145, 146, 147

political decentralization, 53

political isolation: community vs. state view of, 8; internal leadership and, 132; travel and, 150

political issues: anthropological focus and, 289–290, 320n.1; cultural differences and, 15–16, 60–61; current changes in, 301; gender and, 34–35, 290; imagination of power and, 72–73; interrelationships of, 33–34; official view of Meratus, 41, 61; spiritual expression of, 298–300; Uma Adang's imagery applied to, 295–296

political leadership: gender and, 106, 108, 112, 114; kinship and, 110–111; oratorical styles in, 102, 310n.23; resettlement programs and, 106; shamans and, 72, 73, 75, 85, 100–102, 310n.20

politics: historical framework for, 74, 75, 308n.2; history and, 259–260; New Order view of, 24; parody as tool of, 282; performance privilege and, 196; spirituality vs., 298–299; storytelling and, 73, 308n.1; travel and, 128, 130, 150; Uma Adang and, 265–266, 282; women's participation in, 108. See also terms beginning with political

pork eating, 55

Posewitz, Theodor, 306n.12

possession, by dewa spirits, 201–202, 203–204, 242–243

postcolonial scholars: criticisms of, 16–17; focus of, 13–14; marginality and, 16; political issues and, 15–16

postmodernity, 9–10; of Uma Adang, 254, 255

poststructuralist criticism, 254–255, 316n.3

Potter, Leslie, 55

power: anthropological focus and, 14, 88–89; armies and, 75–76; body boundaries and, 179; "borrowing," 128, 196, 199; chants as source of, 96–102; imagination of, 72–73, 91; imperial vs. national, 308n.3; interethnic relations and, 199–200; objects as source of, 272; ongoing relationship with, 90; outsiders as source of, 196; reconceptualization of, 264; resettlement programs and, 92–93; resistance to, 89–90; sexuality and, 184–185, 186, 196–197, 199, 205; of state, 88–89, 90; storytelling as source of, 76, 77; travel and, 125, 128–129, 150, 198, 225–226, 227; violence and, 9, 75, 76, 80, 91; of women, 129–130

Powers of Horror (Kristeva), 179, 180

Pratt, Mary, 290

Prell, Riv-Ellen, 223

premature birth, Induan Amar's baby, 114–118

"primitive culture," marginality theory vs., 7–8, 9–10

pro-life movement, Uma Adang's imagery applied to, 294–295, 297, 298

prophecy, by Uma Adang, 6, 10, 19

Propinsi Kalimantan, 306n.13, 306n.14

Protestantism, as state-recognized religion, 54

Proyek Pembinaan Perguruan Tinggi
Agama, 307n.1
public health issues, in resettlement villages,
45, 92, 307n.30
public works, headhunting and, 86, 90–91
putir: curing with, 188, 190–195, 203, 204;
gender assumptions and, 194–195, 204–
205, 313n.10; shamanistic style and, 189,
202–203
Putir Galuh, 178–179, 191–195
pythons, in houses, 95, 309n.18

rabak (newly cleared field), 163, 164
Rabinow, Paul, 214, 309n.13
Radam, H. Nor'ied, 177, 261
radios, 246
rainforest cultivation. *See* shifting cultivation
rainforest protection, Uma Adang's imagery
and, 295–296
rainforest timbering. *See* logging; timber industry
rajaki (livelihood): fetal development and,
291, 293, 294; health and, 190; movement required for, 159–160; rice-planting
and, 174–175
Rajang: *basambu* ritual in, 141–142, 143;
Parma's story in, 131–132, 135, 136,
137, 141–149; swidden sites in, 164–165
Ras, J. J., 305n.5, 305n.8, 306n.9, 316n.10
rationality, body and, 183–184
rattan, trade sucess with, 114, 130
Ratu Intan. *See* Diamond Queen
rawa-rawa trees, 168
reason, body and, 183–184
rebellion: anti-Dutch, 78–81; anti-Jakarta,
44, 45, 82–83, 265; state control and, 44,
45, 306nn. 21, 23, and 24
regional asymmetry, 53–56; among Meratus, 60–61; language and, 53–54; local
leadership and, 150–152; politico-economic status and, 55–56; religion and,
54–55
regional marginality, 29
Reid, Anthony, 305n.2
religion, 54; bodily desire regulated by,
183–184; Christian village, 307n.29;
communism vs., 273; cultural identity
and, 54–55, 307n.3; gender and, 184;
government requirement for, 54, 273,
307n.30; Meratus, government attitude

toward, 273; Muslim/Dayak cooperation, 277; as political instrument, 265–
266 273; schooling and, 54, 273; shamanism and, 231, 273; Uma Adang and,
265–266, 282, 283, 291. *See also* shamanism; shamans; spirituality
Rendra, W. S., 300
reproductive practices, marginality and,
105–120
research issues: as female researcher, 223–
225; as foreign woman, 215–216, 218–
220
resettlement programs, 45, 307n.28; administrative travel and, 46, 48; cooperation with, 176; "going home" vs., 176–
177; Meratus leadership and, 106; official view of Meratus and, 154; political
advantages of, 45; social identity and, 62;
state power and, 92–93; threat of, 148;
"zoned" social geography and, 46
resources, in forest areas, 167–170, 312n.5
rice consumption, Uma Adang and, 280–
281
rice farming: mobility and, 156–159, 160;
Unity Field, 258, 281
rice harvest, 68; Uma Adang's blessing for,
258; Unity Field, 281
rice-planting ritual, 157–159; official view
of, 171–172; ritual authority in, 173–174
rice storage, 67
Rifai, Mien A., 301
Risi, Uma Adang's innovations in, 281
ritual: authority and, 173–174; healing,
178–179, 189; hospitality, 94–96; maintenance of order through, 24, 27; state
rule and, 26–27
ritual halls, community and, 281
road building, 287; Dutch and, 42; effect of,
61; Meratus reaction to, 265
Robison, Richard, 55
Rodgers, Susan, 307n.3
Rofel, Lisa, 309n.13
Rosaldo, Michelle Zimbalist, 313n.9,
314n.11
Rosaldo, Renato, 21, 123
Rousseau, Jerome, 309n.5
rubber, 43–44, 306n.17
rukun tetangga (RT), 65
rumors, survival role of, 91
Rungus Dusun, menstruation among,
314n.11

sacrifices, 44
Said, Edward, 16
sajarah (history), Uma Adang on, 259–265
Saleh, Mohamad Idwar, 305n.8, 306n.9
Sandayuhan, 276. *See also* Si Ayuh
Sandoval, Chela, 305n.15
Schneider, David M., 320n.1
schooling: in central mountain region, 48; Christian schools, 48; government schools, 48; religion and, 54, 273; in resettlement villages, 45, 48
Schwaner, C. M., 305n.6, 306n.22
"science": "black," 182; of travel, 128–129
Scott, James C., 89, 315n.2
Scott, Joan Wallach, 232, 315n.2, 316n.3
secrecy, Uma Adang's use of, 257
semi-nomads, official view of, 155, 156
"semio-technology," travel and, 46
settlements. *See* resettlement programs; village
sexuality: Banjar view of, 217–218; interethnic relations and, 199, 314n.15; power and, 184–185, 186, 196–197, 199, 205. *See also* gender
The Shadow Lines (Ghosh), 288–289
shadows, in curing ritual, 190–191
shamanic chants. *See* chants
shamanic codification: by Induan Hiling, 243–244, 246, 247, 249; by Uma Adang, 268
shamanism, 54; dewa, 77, 94, 189. *See also* dewa spirits; entertainment and, 246–247; female: *See* female shamanism; food and, 94; gender and, 194–196, 231, 243, 275–276; gender irrelevance of, 250; performance in, 196; putir, 189, 202–203; as religion, 273; storytelling and, 76, 77; styles of, 189, 202–204, 272–273
shamans: Awat Kilay, 37; "The Bear," 73–74; competition among, 173; context for authority of, 173–175; curing by, 188–195; gender assumptions and, 194–196, 275–276; government view of, 172–173; Induan Hiling, 230, 231, 233, 234–252; leadership by, 72, 73, 75, 85, 100–102, 231, 310n.20; learning resources of, 234–235; as mediators for community, 249, 250, 252; as sorcerer/healers, 187; travel by, 100, 252, 280; Uma Adang, 253–282. *See also specific names*

shifting cultivation: attachment to place through, 154–155; ecological advantages of, 156, 312n.1; evidence of, 66; government resettlement vs., 45, 154; history told through, 164–165; in mountain regions, 48, 62–63; official view of, 154, 155, 156; pattern of, 63; *rajaki* and, 160; social context of, 62–63, 64, 66–67
Shostak, Marjorie, 223, 224
Si Ayuh stories, 56–60, 69, 71, 276–277
Siegel, James, 315n.9
singing worms, 57
sinsilin oaks, wild pigs and, 169
Smith, Paul, 268
snakes in houses, 95, 309n.18
social change, classical anthropological view of, 87–88, 309n.10, 309n.11
social geography: resettlement and, 46, 48; shifting cultivation and, 62–63
social groups: administrative groups and, 64–65; autonomy and, 63–65; Borneo social organization and, 307n.5–308n.5; women's awareness of, 248–249. *See also umbun*
social identity studies, cultural anthropology and, 8, 9
social theory, marginality and, 254–255
Soetanto Saleh et al., 92
soldiers. *See* military
songs: of Induan Hiling, 209–212, 230, 236–238, 243, 247–248; of love. *See* love songs
sorcery: Banjar view of, 179, 182, 197–198; healing and, 187–188; *kuyang* monsters, 184, 185–186, 187; menstruation and, 184; practiced by men, 183, 187
"sour spices," 95, 96, 310n.19
Southeast Asia, syncretism in, 316n.7
South Kalimantan: economic differences in, 55–56; ethnographic writing issues and, 32–33; family planning in, 107; Javanese resettlement in, 45; language differences in, 53–54; "management" (*pembinaan*) in, 28, 305n.14; political history in, 308n.2; religion and schools and, 54; religious differences in, 54–55; war stories from, 75–86
space, as ethnographic concept, 22
spells: for healing, 198; power of, 76–77; protection from bullets, 76–77. *See also* chants

spirituality: New Order emphasis on, 298–299; nongendered imagery in, 237–238; political issues and, 298–300; tourism and, 300; of women, 200–205. *See also* religion; shamanism; shamans

spiritual travel: airplane as symbol of, 241; by shamans, 100, 252, 280

Spivak, Gayatri, 15, 16, 17, 304n.6, 304n.7, 315n.2

splinter, disease (*suligih*), 189, 190, 191

state: administrative boundaries by, 60; community and, 8, 17, 25–27, 74, 304n.12; in cultural analysis, 8–9; cultural negotiations with, 287–288; ethnic cultural expression and, 245–246, 249–250; ethnic diversity and, 24; family planning program of, 104, 108, 109–110, 310n.2–310n.4; historical relationship with, 41–49, 305n.1; imagination of power and, 72–73; interrelationships of, 33–34; isolated populations policies of, 155–160; leaders' relationships with, 72; Majapahit and, 271–272, 273, 274; neighborhoods vs. villages and, 64–65; order imposed by, 91, 92–96; power of, 88–89, 90; religion and, 54; timelessness of, 74; tourism and, 300; travel by officials of, 46, 95–96, 100, 124–125. *See also* Dutch colonial rule; Indonesia; Jakarta; Java; Meratus, relations with state in

status, political dichotomies and, 25–26

Steedly, Mary, 308n.4

Stoler, Ann, 305n.1

Storyteller, The (Llosa), 288

storytelling: Bunguskaling epics, 59–60; development and, 85–96; fetal development, 291–294; founding of the kingdom, 277–279; gender and, 59–60; government headhunters, 85–87, 90–91; history of the world, 259–265; as leadership skill, 73; local history, 265; Mambur, 275–276, 317n.17; marginality and, 59–60; neonatal death, 114–118; politics and, 73, 308n.1; on ritual hospitality, 95–96; shamanism and, 76, 77; social science role of, 125–126; as source of power, 76, 77; "two brothers" tales, 56–60, 69, 71, 276–277; war stories, 75–85

Strathern, Marilyn, 33, 124, 268

structuralism: in conventional anthropology, 315n.6; dualities and, 270; Induan

Hiling's shamanism and, 240, 243–244; poststructuralist criticism, 254–255, 316n.3; resistance through, 254–255

Struggle of the Naga Tribe, The (Rendra), 300

subjectivity: cultural history and, 186–187; gender and, 186, 313nn.3 and 6

"subjects" of history, poststructuralist view of, 316n.3

Sudanese women, spirit possession and, 248, 249

Suharto, President, 23, 45, 298, 301

Suhud Pribadi, 93, 155–156

Sukarno, President, 28, 89, 297, 298, 299, 304n.12

suku terasing, 52, 307n.1

Sulawesi, Wana gender assumptions, 313n.9

suligih (disease splinter), 189, 190, 191

Sweeny, Amin, 310n.20

swidden/forest regrowth cycling, 63, 66; bamboo and, 170; forest degradation and, 45; forest regrowth and, 167–168; social context of, 62–63

swiddens/swidden clusters: in central mountains, 48; fruit trees saved or planted in, 168–169; honey trees saved in, 169; shown on map, 163, 164–166; social groups and, 63–65; Unity Fields, 281

tamarind, 310n.19

Tani, story of, 215–216, 218, 219, 220, 228

Tanjung Nagara, 305n.8

tape decks, 246

tarap, 168

tawadak trees, 168–169

Team Research mahasiswa Fakultas Sjariah, 307n.1

television, 246

terminology, for Meratus Dayaks, 52–53, 307n.1

territoriality, culture and, 123–124

theoretical framework. *See* cultural theory

Thompson, E. P., 314n.1

Tichelman, G. L., 305n.6

Tidung: government standards and, 148; in hospitality story, 95–96; Parma's story in, 129, 133–137, 139–148, 151

Tidung festival, Ma Jawa at, 79

timber industry: compensation offered by, 170; road building for, 287; state control and, 45. *See also* logging

Timur, East, armed resistance in, 45

Tjilik Riwut, 307n.1
tobacco, given to guests, 67, 147
tourism, 300
trade: Banjar role in, 42, 43, 55–56,
    306n.11; in herbal contraception, 113;
    historical continuities in, 42; products,
    55–56; regional asymmetry and, 55–56;
    as source of power, 272. See also mar-
    kets, weekly
tradition, official studies of, 171–173
"traditional," modernity vs., 88
trails, roads vs., 61
transmigration, Kalawan and, 19
transvestites, 185
travel: anthropological focus and, 123–125,
    139; attachment to place through, 154–
    155; attitudes toward, 51, 68–69; Banjar
    and, 181; in body, 190–191; in central
    mountains, 48–49; colonial practices in,
    124; by Diamond Queen, 277–278; gen-
    der and, 68–69, 127, 128, 196, 225, 227;
    healing and, 189; identification card re-
    quired for, 307n.30; by leaders, 72; liveli-
    hood and, 181; marginality and, 36, 37,
    46; with Ma Salam, 66–67; by Meratus,
    46, 124–125; nomadism vs., 150,
    311n.5; in Parma's story, 136, 137–139,
    142, 144, 145, 147, 148, 150; politics
    and, 128, 130, 150; resource use and,
    170; road-building route, 287; "science"
    of, 128–129; by shamans, 100, 252, 280;
    as source of glamour, 51; as source of
    power, 125, 128–129, 150, 198, 225–
    226, 227; spiritual, 100, 241, 252, 280;
    spiritual route of, 287; by state officials,
    46, 95–96, 100, 124–125; by Uma
    Adang, 281–282; of woman as re-
    searcher, 218–219. See also mobility
trees, cut for plywood, 169
tribute, to Banjar kingdom, 43
Trinh T. Minh-ha, 18, 305n.15
Tuhan Yang Maha Esa, 54
"two brothers" stories, 56–60, 69, 71, 276–
    277

Ukut: The Bear and, 268; in hospitality
    story, 95–96, 102; Parma's story in, 129,
    130, 137, 138, 141, 145–149
Uma Adang, 253–282; adat of, 29–30, 35,
    274, 281–282; apprentices called for by,
    269–270; The Bear and, 268, 316n.8;
    border crossing built with, 21–22; Bung-

sukaling epics and, 60; community build-
    ing by, 280, 281; current political climate
    and, 301; dewa possession movement and,
    203, 314n.16; Diamond Queen and, 278,
    279; ethnic pride and, 53; "female" proj-
    ect of, 250, 251; fetal development story
    by, 291–294; first meeting with, 5–7; his-
    tory of the world by, 259–265, 316n.7;
    Induan Hiling and, 95, 233, 234, 235,
    247–248, 268, 269; innovation by, 255–
    259, 281; language play by, 256–257;
    leadership concept of, 35, 95; leadership
    role of, 256, 281–282; magic of things
    seen by, 271–272; Majapahit and, 259,
    260, 272–275; Ma Pasta and, 137; mar-
    ginality consciousness of, 253, 254, 255;
    marriage and family of, 278, 280; media-
    tion by, 84; as mentor, 253–254; mim-
    icry used by, 257, 268; movement led by,
    281–283; official status of, 275; parody
    by, 11, 19, 27, 36, 254; perspective of,
    20; politics and, 265–266, 282, 299;
    "postmodern eclecticism" of, 254; proph-
    ecy by, 6, 10, 19; regional differences
    and, 49; religion and, 265–266, 282,
    283, 291; respect of people for, 20; rice
    consumption and, 280–281; second visit
    with, 10–13; secrecy used by, 257, 282;
    sources of power of, 203; speech style of,
    254–257, 258–259; state/community re-
    lationship and, 26–27, 30, 31, 274, 275,
    282; third visit with, 18–20; tourism and,
    300; travel by, 281–282; Ukut dispute
    mediated by, 132; unique status of, 34–
    35; on "women's shamanism," 266–268
Uma Hati, 11–12; laughter by, 229; story
    of, 221–223, 225, 226
Uma Uman, 11
umbun, 63–65; family planning and, 110;
    in rice-planting parties, 174–175; sharing
    by, 175; swidden areas shown on map,
    163, 164–166
"Unity Field" of Uma Adang, 258, 281
upacara (rituals), 24
urban focus, marginality theory and, 17

Vargas Llosa, Mario, 288
village: anthropological focus and, 66;
    neighborhood vs., 64–65; as protective
    space, 101–102; state vs., 24–25. See also
    community
village fence rite, 96–102, 310n.20

Villapando, Venny, 216
violence, power and, 9, 75, 76, 80, 91
vision, metaphors of, 280, 282, 317n.20
Visweswaran, Kamala, 297
Volkman, Toby, 300
Vortsman, J. A., 306n.18

Wana of Sulawesi, gender assumptions by, 313n.9
war stories, 75–85
watershed-protection area, logging in, 45
wealth, reconceptualization of, 264
Weapons of the Weak (Scott), 89
weddings, Parma's story, 128–153
wedding sponsor (*pangulu*), 128, 132
weeding, 68
Weinstock, Joseph A., 317n.12
West, Cornel, 15
Whittier, Herbert L., 317n.14, 317n.15
widowhood, *umbun* affiliations and, 63, 64
wildlife protection, Uma Adang's imagery and, 296–297
wild pigs, 169
Williams, Lea E., 316n.7
Williams, Raymond, 314n.1, 320n.1
Wilson, Ara, 216
Wolf, Eric, 123
women: "alien romance" stories of, 214–229; Asian, North American view of, 216–217; Banjar vs. Meratus views of, 196, 197; childbearing roles of, 113–114;
as cross-cultural commentators, 220, 221; dewa spirits and, 200–205, 208, 228, 242–243; exceptional, 8–9, 36, 209, 234, 249; exercise of power by, 129–130; family planning and, 109, 111, 112–113, 311n.7; identification with outsiders by, 70–71; individual stories of, 231–232; *kuyang* monsters, 184, 185–186; in Malaysian factories, 90; marginal status of, 27; political participation by, 106, 108, 112, 114; possessed by dewa, 200–205, 208; power of, 129–130; research problems of, 215–216, 218–220, 223–224; social boundaries and, 248–249. See also gender
"women's liberation," anticolonial movement and, 297
"women's shamanism." See female shamanism
Woodward, Mark, 304n.10
work, attitudes toward, 68
work groups, for community maintenance, 281
work parties: rice planting by, 174–175; social groups and, 64
writing: cultural theory and, 32–33; in Induan Hiling's drawings, 238, 239, 240, 244–245. See also ethnographic writing

zar possession cult, 248–249
"zoned" social geography, 46, 48